Praise for Michael Daly and

NEW YORK'S FINEST

"NEW YORK'S FINEST is so gripping, it made my heart race. I was only able to read a few chapters a night or I couldn't sleep. The way it penetrates to the heart of these NYPD families, this calling (there is no other word) is so moving and vivid it has changed forever my perception of the police. It manages all at once to be thrilling, heartbreaking, inspiring, and exhilarating. It is Michael Daly's tour de force."

—Tina Brown, *New York Times* bestselling author of *The Vanity Fair Diaries*

"Michael Daly is one of the finest street reporters New York has ever known. The power of his writing derives in part from both his instinctual humanism and his ability to capture the nuances of his people with novelistic aplomb. And when, as in NEW YORK'S FINEST, he writes about those he has deeply admired (if not downright loved), such as Jack Maple and Father Mychal Judge, Michael Daly is at his shining best."

—Richard Price, *New York Times* bestselling author of *The Whites*

"Michael Daly's NEW YORK'S FINEST is the story of the policemen and policewomen who transformed New York from 'Fear City' into the safest big city in America. There have been plenty of books and articles that missed this story. Michael Daly did not."

—Nicholas Pileggi, author, producer, and screenwriter

NEW YORK'S
FINEST

Also by Michael Daly

Under Ground: A Novel
The Book of Mychal
Topsy

NEW YORK'S FINEST

STORIES OF THE NYPD AND THE HERO COPS WHO SAVED THE CITY

MICHAEL DALY

TWELVE

NEW YORK BOSTON

Twelve
Hachette Book Group
1290 Avenue of the Americas, New York, NY 10104

twelvebooks.com

twitter.com/twelvebooks

First published in hardcover and ebook in December 2021
First Trade Paperback Edition: December 2022

Twelve is an imprint of Grand Central Publishing. The Twelve name and logo are trademarks of Hachette Book Group, Inc.

The publisher is not responsible for websites (or their content) that are not owned by the publisher.

The Hachette Speakers Bureau provides a wide range of authors for speaking events. To find out more, go to www.hachettespeakersbureau.com or call (866) 376-6591.

Library of Congress Cataloging-in-Publication Data has been applied for.

ISBNs: 978-1-5387-6434-3 (trade paperback), 978-1-5387-6435-0 (ebook)

Printed in the United States of America

LSC-C

Printing 1, 2022

To Dinah Prince Daly, the one and only.

I owe you my life.

AUTHOR'S NOTE

The year was 1976. I was starting out as a writer at *Flatbush Life* in Brooklyn, and a prosecutor suggested I inspect a bullet hole in a subway sign to further an education left incomplete by Yale. The prosecutor had himself discovered it while investigating the account by a transit cop who said he had nearly been killed with his own gun. It was exactly where it should have been and thereby dispelled the prosecutor's initial doubts.

I sought out the rookie cop whose proximity to violent death was recorded in a .357-inch circle punched in an overhead sign that thousands bustled obliviously past each day. His name was Jack Maple, and he was a perpetual learning experience as we became best friends. We spent many hours riding the trains and walking West 42nd Street, aka the Deuce, when the city was at its wildest.

I went with Jack to the hospital when his daughter, Jacqueline, was born. He drove my wife, Dinah, and me to NYU Hospital when she was about to give birth to our first child. He was trying to avoid potholes, and that prompted an accusation from the back seat.

"I know why you're driving so slow!" my wife cried out. "You want to deliver the baby so you can get in the newspaper!"

Sinead Daly was born soon after at NYU. Jack became godfather to her and to our second girl, Bronagh, to whom he would give his deputy commissioner's shield when he was dying. I repeatedly put him in the newspapers and magazines for many reasons over the years.

I also wrote about Detective Steven McDonald, whom I met through FDNY Chaplain Mychal Judge. Mychal always said that just as the devil is to be found in evil, God is to be found in good. I have never known anybody as godly as Steven. He is who we all should be.

After decades of writing about Jack and Steven and other cops for the

New York Daily News, *New York* magazine, and the *Daily Beast*, I wanted to collect those tales into a book along with stories I had not previously told. Cops in New York have been called the Finest since the aftermath of the Civil War, when the city's writers were seeking heroes to match those of the Union Army. This book is about modern day heroes who have lived up to this name. My focus is on Jack and Steven while including other cops whose lives occasionally intersected with theirs as New York was transformed from Fear City into the safest big city in America. For added source material I drew upon *The Steven McDonald Story*, the 1989 book by Steven McDonald and Patti Ann McDonald with E. J. Kahn III. I also used audio recordings of Jack made by Chris Mitchell, who wrote *The Crime Fighter* with Jack Maple.

Mostly, I was guided by my love for Jack and Steven, along with the other cops who actually are the finest of the Finest. They are well worth remembering—and honoring—at a time when actions of the Lousiest in New York and elsewhere are feeding into an unfortunate tendency to judge the many by the few and giving all cops a bad name. I was with Jack when he died, and I saw Steven in his final hours. I have the privilege of living in the city their sons now serve.

The last I saw, the bullet hole was still there.

Introduction

Winter 1986

Registered Nurse Nina Justiniano placed a stool beside the hospital bed where twenty-eight-year-old Police Officer Steven McDonald lay paralyzed below the joining of his neck and head. He had been shot three times by a fifteen-year-old suspected bicycle thief who had suddenly pulled a gun on an overcast summer afternoon in Central Park five months before. The last bullet had been fired directly into his face, nicking his right eye as he was sprawled on his back. Bullet fragments and bits of bone still impinged on his spine at C2, the second of the seven cervical vertebrae. That is the connection a hangman seeks to break.

Steven remained unable to speak or even breathe on his own and the *whoosh…whoosh…whoosh* of a Bennett 5200 ventilator filled this room on the tenth floor of Bellevue Hospital. The facility's chief doctor had decided that he would be better off dead.

Steven had been offering the same conclusion, repeatedly mouthing four words that Nina had lip-read when she first began caring for him.

"I want to die."

"No, that's not happening today," Nina had told him. "Because I don't make money with dead bodies. You die, and my check is cut off."

Steven had done something he would not have expected to do even if he were able. He laughed.

"Today is not the day, Steven," Nina had continued. "You're not going anywhere. You're going to stay right here with us."

But Steven had soon fallen back into hopelessness. Nina had feared she was going to lose him despite her best efforts.

"People die because they lose the will to live," she would later say. "Steven was at that crossroads."

The *whoosh...whoosh...whoosh* was now joined by the sound of Nina pulling the privacy curtain closed after setting down the stool. She summoned Steven's wife, Patti Ann McDonald, who was twenty-three and had gone from three to seven months pregnant since the shooting. Nina was thirty-four and figured from her own experience as an expectant mother that the baby's movements would have become pronounced enough for her plan to rescue Steven from despair.

"Lift your blouse and put your belly to Steven's face," Nina would remember telling her.

Patti Ann got on the stool and leaned over. Her face appeared above Steven, just as in a vision that had come to him moments after the shooting, when he was bleeding and losing consciousness, silently pleading to God not to let him die.

Only now her face was eclipsed by the swell of her tummy. It was warm, tautly soft against his cheek. And then...

Yes.

He could feel it. All the more vivid in the absence of any other sensations.

"That's your baby," Nina told him.

Steven mouthed a reply.

"My baby."

He kissed Patti Ann's tummy.

"Look what you do!" Nina teased.

The eclipsing tummy pulled away, but the feel of the movement against his face stayed with Steven as Patti Ann stepped off the stool.

"Steven needed to know that was a life that grew in his wife's womb," Nina would recall. "That was God's will that we give life, and he needed to *feel* that life. That's what gave Steven hope."

She would conclude, "That baby saved his life before that baby was even born."

Had Steven died, he would have added one more to the 1,598 total of murders in New York that year. That was up from 1,392 the year before and on the way past 2,000 in New York's seemingly inexorable unraveling into Fear City.

But a cop who had been gunned down by a teen who embodied patholo-gies generated by social inequities in Harlem survived with the help of this nurse who embodied the same neighborhood's great strengths. And the stir-ring against his cheek set in motion thoughts and emotions that churned in him along with Nina's wisdom and Patti Ann's love and a magical priest's prayer as well as his own essential decency distilled from family tradition. The startling result would become known to the whole city at the baby's christening.

At that hospital chapel baptism eight months after the shooting and before he had fully regained the ability to speak, Steven would make a remarkable declaration that reminded New York how good the city could be even when things seemed to be at their worst. He would remain a reminder to his fellow cops of what was best in them even as some of their number became dispirited, a few also turning brutal or corrupt.

At the time of Steven's declaration, a young Transit Police sergeant named Jack Maple was riding through New York's underground in pink high-top sneakers with a squad of decoy cops, developing strategies that would eventually transform the city. The underlying principle arose in part from the officially unsolved murder of Jack's deaf-mute grandmother and the subsequent demise of his deaf-mute grandfather in the decade before he was born. What he viewed as the NYPD's failure to aggressively investigate the deaths added to his determination from his first days as a "cave cop" to treat every crime as if the victim were a member of his family.

The result was a subterranean success so remarkable that when former chief of the Transit Police William Bratton became head of the NYPD in 1994, he elevated Jack in one unprecedented jump to deputy police commis-sioner. Jack would compare it to a Coast Guard ensign suddenly becoming a Navy admiral.

Jack traded in his pink high-tops and emerged from the subway to become an instantly recognizable NYPD icon in two-tone spectator shoes, bow tie, and homburg hat. He wore a straight tie only one day a year.

"You're dressing normal today," a chief at headquarters remarked.

"It's Halloween," Jack replied.

Steven McDonald also became an NYPD icon, a noble figure in a mech-anized wheelchair outfitted with a ventilator. He'd served the public as a reminder of the risks cops take every day. The cops already knew that all too well. His power for them was as a reminder that they really could be the Finest, no matter how bad it got.

"He was a shining example of what every police officer should be," his driver, dear friend, and fellow cop Jon Williams noted. "He did more in that chair than able-bodied police officers could do for the police department."

As Steven sat in dress blues at department dedications and funerals, he was unable to raise his hand to salute. But his very presence *was* a salute to everything worth honoring.

Inspired by the spirit of one icon and guided by the smarts of another, the cops of the NYPD who truly deserved to be called the Finest brought the annual murder count down to 290 in 2017, the lowest per-capita rate in more than seventy years.

That was twenty-five fewer homicides than in 1948, the year the movie *The Naked City* was released. The documentary-style film depicted a fictional investigation into the killing of a young model. It is best known for its final line: "There are eight million stories in the naked city. This has been one of them."

In fact, the actual story count far exceeds the number of New Yorkers, which is now up to 8.4 million. There are hundreds of tales involving just Steven and Jack.

And many thousands more about the finest of the Finest.

These are just a few of them.

PART
I

CHAPTER 1

Steven liked nothing more than to go dancing with his younger sister Clare. They would proceed from club to club until the four a.m. closing time. Or, they would just go to Butters Bar near their home in the suburban Long Island town of Rockville Centre. They had stocked the jukebox with their favorite 45s, and he would seem to become the music itself as he danced, danced, danced.

Any number of young women had been in a tizzy over six-foot-two, gleamingly handsome Steven McDonald. But his interest had immediately narrowed to exactly one when he met Patti Ann Norris at Butters in the spring of 1983. She was pretty and fun and entirely genuine.

Patti Ann was the second of six kids in an Irish Catholic family in the nearby town of Malverne. Her father was an English teacher at the local high school, her mother a homemaker from Boston. Patti Ann worked at Macy's and studied at the Fashion Institute of Technology in Manhattan. Meeting Steven seemed like another step in living life as it should be lived.

Steven was also from an Irish Catholic family, the third of eight kids, and the first boy. He had served as a Navy corpsman and had returned to civilian life to become the supervisor of housekeeping at a Philadelphia hospital, commuting home on weekends. He took a similar job at Mount Sinai Hospital in New York as he and Patti Ann began dating. They had been seeing each other for a year and she had already decided he was "the one" when he first mentioned that he was thinking of becoming a cop.

"By the way, I got a phone call today," he told her. "I'm going to be starting the police academy in a month."

Patti Ann would have been happy if Steven had just pursued a career in hospital housekeeping while she worked in the art department at *Parents* magazine. But Steven was the son and grandson of cops. The tradition stirred him as if it were a kind of melody that carried you from what had been to what should be, making fate more than just happenstance, turning an occupation into a calling.

Steven had grown up hearing tales of his maternal grandfather, James "Smiling Jim" Conway, who had been gassed as a teenage soldier with the Fighting 69th in World War I and then served five years with the Navy before joining the NYPD. Smiling Jim was ninety minutes into a midnight tour in the Bronx on November 12, 1936, when he came upon two gunmen who had just robbed Galvin's Beer Garden on Beach Avenue.

Steven listened to how Smiling Jim had been shot in the chest and then lay sprawled on his back as one of the gunmen stood over him to finish him off. The bullet had struck the pavement beside Smiling Jim's head, and he managed to get up on one knee and fire after the fleeing thieves. He had been reloading and spitting blood when a fellow cop arrived on the scene in a patrol car.

"You do the driving, I'll do the shooting," Smiling Jim had famously said.

Smiling Jim had kept firing as they gave chase, causing the getaway vehicle to crash. Only after the gunmen were in custody had Smiling Jim consented to being taken to Fordham Hospital. He had managed to offer a smile in keeping with his nickname when his wife arrived by subway along with their two young daughters, Anita and Catherine. He recovered and went on to be promoted to first-grade detective after capturing the murderer of an eight-year-old boy who was found sexually assaulted and strangled in an abandoned amusement park in the Bronx.

Smiling Jim's younger daughter, Anita, had been just six when her father was shot and had never forgotten that early lesson in the dangers a cop faces. She had nonetheless married Police Officer David McDonald, the son of a Sanitation Department hostler whose wagon was drawn by a horse named after Tony the Wonder Horse ridden by cowboy movie star Tom Mix. Anita had repeated the same bedtime prayer each time her husband returned safe from another tour: "Thank you, God, for keeping us together another day."

By chance, David McDonald had been standing by the entrance to Manhattan criminal court June 8, 1957, when gunfire erupted inside. A homicide suspect was attempting to flee, and detectives shot him seven times as he reached the bottom of the steps from the second floor to the lobby. David learned that the would-be escapee was Fred Hartjen, one of the two gunmen who had shot Smiling Jim. Hartjen had served twenty years and been freed only to be arrested soon after for murder.

David McDonald had subsequently made sergeant, but he had eight kids at home, and even with the accompanying salary boost he had to work a second job as a manager at Leonard's of Great Neck, a Long Island catering hall. He was too seldom home, and that intensified Steven's memories of such rare moments as standing with his father at the Macy's Thanksgiving Day Parade when he was a youngster. Steven would remember literally looking up to the figure in the uniform with sergeant's stripes and a gold shield on the chest, by every important gauge bigger in his eyes than the outsized balloons that passed.

Steven's father had retired in February 1975, still certain that becoming a cop was the best possible thing he could have done in life.

"Was it a good job?" a police academy classmate who had also retired asked David.

"It was the *only* job," David replied.

But some of the younger cops still on the *only* job in 1975 were about to learn that it could be taken away like any other.

The banks had long been encouraging and assisting the city's borrowing of billions as it struggled with the burden of more than 1 million people on welfare and the exodus of more than five hundred thousand manufacturing jobs. The banks now decided that the city was a bad credit risk. Bankruptcy threatened and mass layoffs were looming in June of that year, when the police union, the Patrolmen's Benevolent Association (PBA), sought to emphasize the need for cops by distributing a pamphlet at the airports.

"Welcome to Fear City: A Survival Guide for Visitors to the City of New York" read the words below a drawing of a black-hooded skull on the cover.

The city had never before laid off cops, and it seemed generally inconceivable to the NYPD rank and file that it would actually happen. Then came the morning of July 1, when the teletypes in all the precincts began chattering on and on and on with the five thousand names of cops who had as of that moment suddenly ceased to be cops.

Those who were laid off had particular trouble getting new jobs because employers knew they would rush back to the NYPD if they were rehired.

White House chief of staff Donald Rumsfeld, in the meantime, urged President Gerald Ford to deny New York emergency assistance.

FORD TO CITY: DROP DEAD read the October 29, 1975, headline in the *New York Daily News*.

The Emergency Financial Control Board of bankers, business leaders, and local officials managed to avert bankruptcy, and the cops were gradually hired back over the next three years. But many were soured with a sense of betrayal. How could you be expected to lay your life on the line at one moment and be laid off at another?

But tradition retained its pull on Steven. His mother's nightly prayer had seemed to be answered when his father safely retired, and now she would be repeating it for her oldest son.

On July 20, 1984, Steven became the latest of his clan to take the oath as an officer of the NYPD. He was one of 1,856 recruits in his academy class, and they had to attend in two shifts, as the facility on East 21st Street could only handle a maximum of one thousand at a time. All recruits were required to fill out registration cards asking questions designed to give the instructors a quick profile of them. Steven reported that his favorite book was *Trinity* by Leon Uris, his favorite play was *Philadelphia, Here I Come!*, and his favorite movies were *The Quiet Man* and *A Christmas Carol*. He was little different from many if not most of his fellow recruits when he wrote that he had joined the NYPD because "Traditionally, policemen have been in a position to help people in many ways, for many reasons, which has led to a high profile. It is a job where I can make a mark and a difference in society. A job I will be proud to be connected with."

While he was in the academy, Steven went out to the movies with Patti Ann and saw *The Razor's Edge*, a 1984 adaptation of a W. Somerset Maugham novel in which a man who has suffered the traumas of war embarks along "the razor's edge" to transcendental meaning. He finds himself, but loses his great love.

The Bill Murray character on screen had just called off his wedding when Steven turned to Patti Ann.

"You know what? Let's get married," he said.

He subsequently went to Patti Ann's mother and father to ask for their blessing and then presented her with a ring. Her parents attended the police academy graduation the following month and met Steven's family for the first time.

During the five and a half months in the academy 101 recruits had either been asked to leave or had simply dropped out. The remaining 1,755 graduated at Madison Square Garden on December 19, 1984. Police Commissioner Benjamin Ward told the graduates that he hoped they had broken in their new shoes, because most of them would be going on foot patrol. Mayor Ed Koch also spoke.

"We see the best in ourselves when we see you," he said.

When cops are either promoted or leave the department, they turn in their shield at headquarters, where it remains until it passes on to somebody else. Steven had requested the one his father wore before making sergeant, and it had been available. Shield number 15231 was shining on his chest as he joined the other graduates in the traditional conclusion of the ceremony. They threw their white gloves ceilingward, looking to him like a huge flock of white doves that then fluttered down as he began his chosen life as a cop.

The rookies started out in Neighborhood Stabilization Units (NSUs), which were fielded as an added, high-visibility police presence. Each rookie was assigned an experienced training officer. Steven had the good fortune not to get one of the cops who remained bitter over the layoffs of nine years before. Detective Bobby Reid was uncommonly smart and had proven as a Marine in Vietnam that he could stay unwaveringly true to his immediate mission even in a monumentally discouraging situation. He took as much pride in wearing the uniform of the NYPD as he had that of the USMC.

Under Reid's tutelage, Steven hit the streets with an NSU that ranged through several precincts in Lower Manhattan and saw a bit of everything. Steven's first arrest was a young man who had been caught using a forged credit card by the private security at a discount electronics store. Steven was processing his seemingly contrite and cooperative prisoner at the Sixth Precinct station house when he discovered that the evidence had disappeared from the table where he had left it. Reid noted that Steven had handcuffed the prisoner to a nearby chair. Reid had a word with the prisoner, who owned up to having stashed the card under a tear in the cover of one of the chair's arms. Reid explained that the lesson for Steven was to never trust anybody.

For a time, his NSU was detailed to the area surrounding Union Square

Park. They were told to pay particular attention to the vicinity of the various dance clubs. And while in earlier days Steven had danced with Clare and her friends at Butters, he was now posted alone at the upper edge of Union Square, across Broadway from the Underground, a disco that occupied a full block. The entrance would be the scene of at least seven murders in the years to come.

On this night, partiers were going in and out of the Underground when suddenly Steven heard a call over his radio of a fellow cop in need of assistance.

"Ten-thirteen! Ten-thirteen!"

The cop was pursuing a suspect across a series of rooftops in Steven's direction. Steven radioed that he was joining the chase, but a squad car pulled up and an NSU sergeant in the passenger seat ordered him to remain where he was in case the suspect came that way. The squad car continued down the street, where other cops were hurrying into buildings and on up to the roofs.

Steven stayed put as ordered and saw a man saunter from a doorway and light a cigarette. The man was a close enough match to the description on the radio that Steven went over to question him. The man immediately protested that he was being singled out because he was Black.

Steven politely asked the man to hold on for a moment and radioed for a repeat of the description. The response generally fit the man before him, but did not include one detail. Steven asked the dispatcher what kind of shoes the suspect was wearing.

"White sneakers" came as a response as audible to the man as to Steven.

Steven grabbed the man by the arm just as he sought to dash away in his white sneakers. Steven held on and he was now the one radioing "Ten-thirteen! Ten-thirteen!" Steven ended up down on the sidewalk with the man, who then tried to grab his gun. Steven would later say that he felt as if he were in some kind of slow-motion dream that ended when his fellow cops arrived.

On learning that the man had just stolen $8,000 in jewelry, Steven was thrilled to have made his first big-time collar. Reid then tutored him on another nuance of being a cop: You give the collar to the guy who was first in pursuit.

The excitement left Steven wanting to work where there was the most action. He sought to be posted to the busier parts of Brooklyn or the Bronx, where he could become a cop in the way of Smiling Jim. He was instead sent to a low-crime command where rookies were not normally assigned.

For all its fame, Central Park was a dumping ground for a particular kind of troublesome cop in the NYPD. Cops who were boss fighters or rule breakers were liable to be punished by being consigned to the very sort of high-crime commands where Steven had hoped to go. Cops in Manhattan who simply had difficulty getting along with the citizenry were liable to be sent to Central Park, where there was less interaction with people than in the surrounding densely populated areas. The idea was they would cause less trouble patrolling among the squirrels, estimated to number more than two thousand.

Then, during the same summer Steven graduated from the academy, a drug dealer at the edge of the park approached a uniformed figure whose hat visor had leaf-shaped gold embellishments. The dealer, who may have been sampling his own merchandise, apparently mistook the man for an airplane pilot and offered to sell him an illegal substance to really fly. The man proved to be Chief Robert Johnston, the highest-ranking uniformed member of the NYPD.

Johnston took this as a personal affront and ordered an immediate boost in the number of cops in the park. That included rookies who had been assigned to deter the drug dealers in much smaller Union Square Park. Steven now began doing much the same in Central Park even as he delighted in watching people jog and cycle and play softball and just stroll.

"The oasis in the city," he called Central Park.

The best dancing of Steven's life was at his wedding on November 9, 1985. He and Patti Ann posed for a photo in a tableau as if in a scene from *The Quiet Man*. He hung a framed poster from *The Razor's Edge* on the wall of their apartment in Malverne, the Long Island town where Patti had been raised. They both loved the city and joined the waiting list for an apartment in Stuyvesant Town, one of the few remaining places in Manhattan below Harlem where a cop could afford to live. Their shared fantasy was to spend their days off wandering the streets and enjoying everything the city had to offer before they were ready to have kids. He wanted eight. She thought maybe four.

On Thanksgiving, Steven was on foot patrol in the park, wearing his father's shield along with a uniform just like the one his father had worn so grandly amid the crowds and the giant balloons of the parade. Now, as when Steven was a youngster, the arrival of Santa Claus marked the culmination of the procession, and the paradegoers scattered, heading off for turkey dinners. Steven remained on duty and walked in solitude, save for figures who slept on the benches. He would remember saying a prayer for those with no home. He went off duty in time for the first Thanksgiving dinner with his wife.

Along with the rookies, the Central Park Precinct had a new Street Narcotics Enforcement Unit (SNEU). The sergeant in charge was Jimmy Secreto, who had lived on his own since he was sixteen, after the premature death of his mother was followed by the premature death of his father.

Secreto would recall having numerous positive as well as negative experiences with the police while growing up in a Brooklyn housing project. The cops would take him and other kids bowling regularly and sometimes to play pool and to go fishing. But there was also a day when Secreto came out of a barbershop to see a group of other kids forcibly take a bicycle from a boy. Secreto chased after them and came upon a radio car parked outside a McDonald's. A cop was sitting in the passenger seat, reading a newspaper.

"Officer, those guys right there just took that bike!" Secreto would recall saying.

"They just left my jurisdiction," the cop said. "There's nothing I can do."

This encounter with a lousy cop roused in Secreto an ambition to become a good one. He also possessed an unwavering moral compass that guided him as he essentially raised himself amid the chaos of the Albany Houses.

"I'm going to become a cop and do the right thing," he would recall telling himself.

But the city had not yet begun hiring new cops following the layoffs. Secreto worked for a time as a conductor in the subway.

"It wasn't bad, but it was not a job you could be proud of," he would recall, then adding: "I always wanted to be a cop and make a difference."

The city finally gave a police test in June 1979. Secreto took it and did so well that he was sworn in five months later as a member of the first academy class in four years. His training officer was one of the cops who had been rehired after being laid off.

"Even though they were experienced, they were very bitter," Secreto later said.

Secreto was nonetheless able to pursue his goal of making a difference when he heard a gunshot and moments later saw a man climb into a double-parked car. Secreto stopped the car just as a report of a person shot came over the radio. Secreto recovered the gun and arrested the man.

"If you lock up somebody who shot somebody, you're helping people, and you're helping the guy he would shoot tomorrow if you didn't catch him," Secreto later reasoned.

As he was subsequently assigned to a series of precincts in upper Manhattan, Secreto encountered many cops who likely had started out just like him but had since become too much like that one who had sat in a radio car, reading a newspaper.

"I think when you come on, you're excited, you're ready to go," Secreto would later say. "And then when you get to the precinct, cops say, 'This is the real world. That academy is bullshit. This is the real thing here. You get involved, you get in trouble.'"

Secreto would sum it up as "Kind of like just do enough to get by. That was the attitude."

Secreto saw that one cop who split his pants had repaired them with a stapler. Another cop had used electrical tape to hold his shoes together when they began to fall apart.

"Apathy," Secreto later said. "An attitude I guess there was back then."

In the 34th Precinct in Washington Heights, Secreto encountered what he remembers as "Guys, they didn't want to be there, had no compassion or empathy for the people."

He went to the 25th Precinct in East Harlem. He recalls, "You had a lot of lazy guys. They didn't want to make arrests."

He was in a radio car with an experienced cop at the wheel when a citizen stepped into the street, waving to them and calling out, "Officer! Officer!" The experienced cop pressed his foot on the accelerator.

"Hey, that guy's waving us down," Secreto said.

"It's alright. He'll call 911," the experienced cop said.

Secreto remained one of the true good guys as he made sergeant and ran the SNEU unit in East Harlem. He was then transferred to Central Park, which had gained sudden priority after the "airline pilot" incident with Chief Johnston. But the dumping ground was still a dumping ground as Secreto sought to put together a SNEU team there.

"Central Park, a lot of guys didn't make arrests," Secreto would recall.

He noted that the rookie Steven McDonald had made a minor collar—the primary significance being the willingness to make it.

"He made an arrest, so he came on my radar as a collar guy," Secreto later said.

Secreto approached Steven.

"Are you interested?" Secreto asked.

"Sure," Steven said.

The SNEU documented more than one hundred dealers in the park whom the unit arrested again and again. The dealers of the new drug called crack favored the Harlem end, sometimes selling "beat" stuff that was in fact ground-up pretzels. The hallucinogenic and THC dealers tended toward the middle area on the west side and Strawberry Fields, which was dedicated to the memory of John Lennon, who had been shot to death just across from the park in 1980.

Steven was posted for a time at the southwest corner of the park adjoining Columbus Circle, where dealers offered a little bit of everything. His presence caused them to move away, but they simply resumed on the other side of the circle, thereby crossing the boundary between the Central Park Precinct and Midtown North.

Steven was technically not supposed to venture outside his precinct. But he was finally unable to resist starting toward them. They moved away. He kept on, figuring he would check their IDs. He was interrupted when a young woman came up to him and said a man had just stolen her gold chain. She pointed to a nearby restaurant, where she said the thief had fled.

Steven entered and saw a man in the far corner trying to hide behind a menu. The young woman came in and cried out, "That's him!"

Steven went over and quietly asked the man to stand up. The man suddenly leapt to his feet, and Steven only then realized how big he was. Steven again found himself grappling with somebody, only not on a dark street but in a crowded restaurant, banging into tables and chairs, sending plates and glasses and cutlery to the floor.

Steven shouted for somebody to call the police. The man grabbed a knife, and the struggle turned desperate. Steven wondered why none of the people sought to assist him.

"Nobody helped me," Steven later told his younger brother Thomas. "Nobody helped me. I'm fighting with a guy trying to cut me."

Other cops came running in and helped Steven cuff the man. The customers and staff who had done nothing now gave him a standing ovation.

The arrest had been made in Midtown North, so Steven went with his prisoner to that station house, where a supervisor grumbled that the rookie had been poaching. The man was allowed to make a phone call and held out the receiver to Steven with the same hand that had brandished the knife. The man's mother was on the line crying and said her son was really a good boy and had a wife and kids of his own and had not been able to find a job.

The man was now also crying. Steven promised to stay with him through the whole booking and arraignment process. Steven's father had a decidedly different attitude when he heard about the collar.

"You should have shot him," David McDonald said. "What are you doing? Seriously, the guy's got a knife, and you're rolling around."

Steven continued to be a collar guy as well as a guy who showed initiative and reported for duty on time in proper uniform. He also was a married guy. And all that made him a good candidate to fill a vacancy in the precinct anti-crime unit, which had more regular hours than SNEU.

Anti-crime units work in plainclothes, surveilling suspects before they strike. The idea is to catch them in the act or immediately afterward.

To that end, Steven took it upon himself to begin reading the "61s," the reports filed for each crime complaint in the precinct. He studied the nature of the particular incidents, along with the time and location and the description of the perpetrators and whether they were armed. He looked for patterns and discerned one for bike thefts by males in their early teens.

On the afternoon of May 2, Steven and his fellow anti-crime cops followed a group of teens and watched them surround a kid on a bicycle. One of the teens reached in his jacket and produced what Steven realized was a black handgun.

"I couldn't believe it," Steven later said.

The cops jumped out, announcing themselves and commanding the teens not to move. Five of them obeyed. Two bolted, including the one with the gun. Steven and another cop gave chase, but the one with the gun managed to ditch it before they caught up to him. Steven later said that the encounter should have taught him a lesson.

"The lesson didn't take," Steven would note.

What stayed with Steven was what he saw later that night when he visited one of the teens at home. Suspects under sixteen were treated as juveniles and generally released to their parents' custody, unless they had a significant criminal history or had seriously hurt someone. The parents of one of the teens had already collected him when Steven discovered that they had not received some necessary paperwork. Steven decided to hand-deliver it to the teen's East Harlem apartment at the end of his tour.

As midnight neared, Steven went down a dark, fetid hallway on East 103rd Street. He knocked, and the apartment door opened to reveal a chaotic scene where the teen and four younger siblings were still awake. The parents did not speak English and gazed at Steven without expression as one of the kids translated his offer to help the teen. Maybe Steven could arrange for the teen to do volunteer work in Central Park? Or maybe sign him up with a basketball league? Or maybe just talk with the teen about what he might want to do with his life and how he might accomplish it? The teen could call him any time.

After Steven stepped back into the hallway and the door closed, he heard people inside the apartment laughing. He was undeterred in his sympathy and his impulse to help. He telephoned Patti Ann and recounted what he had seen and told her how incredibly lucky he and she were to have so much. She looked around their home, which looked like exactly what it was: a sparsely furnished one-bedroom apartment in Malverne.

"Okay…" she said.

He then told her that he gave the kid their home phone number.

"Are you crazy?" she asked.

No call came, and Patti Ann had other concerns after a visit to the doctor a few days later confirmed she was pregnant.

CHAPTER 3

Patti and Steven had not planned to have a family so quickly, but if she was overwhelmed by the sudden prospect, he seemed only delighted. He reassured her that they were in it together.

Steven continued to work anti-crime, but even with the unit's more family-friendly schedule, he too often arrived home after Patti Ann had gone to bed and too often awakened after she had left for work. He was watching the TV show *American Bandstand* on the morning of June 13 when he saw Belinda Carlisle perform "Mad About You." Patti Ann was out, and he wrote down some of the lyrics and left them on the kitchen table for her to see when she returned: "Mad about you...Lost in your eyes..."

The anti-crime team was going to a Mets game on the night of July 11, a Friday. Steven was scheduled to work the following day, and Patti Ann figured she was not going to see much of him until Sunday. She decided she would visit her sister, Julie, who was living in Yardley, Pennsylvania.

The Mets won 15–0, thanks to a pair of homers hit by Gary Carter, one a grand slam, both coming when their sergeant, Peter King, was at a concession stand. The other two cops in the unit had put in to take the next day off. Steven initially thought he might join them and call in sick when he awoke the next morning feeling under the weather.

He arranged to go with his fifteen-year-old brother, Thomas, to see the movie *Club Paradise*, a comedy in which Robin Williams plays a firefighter who retires on disability and opens a Caribbean resort. But Steven then had second thoughts. He had been doing very well in the department, making anti-crime and working in plainclothes after less than two years. He figured one way he could continue to distinguish himself would be to keep a perfect attendance record while others were quick to "bang out," or take a sick day.

When he spoke to Patti Ann on the phone, she urged him just to go ahead and stay home if he was not feeling well. He told her he was going in to work.

"I love you," he told her.

"I love you," she said.

He gave himself a pass on making the bed and washing the dishes, reasoning that he could do the chores when he got home, before she returned.

A light rain was falling, so Steven decided to take the car, an Oldsmobile Firenza, rather than the Long Island Rail Road and the subway. He put on the radio, and the Belinda Carlisle song "Mad About You" came on. He sang along, as if to Patti Ann.

The tune stayed with Steven as he parked outside the Central Park station house. Secreto of SNEU was there, nearing the end of a day tour made uneventful by weather that had deterred many of the drug dealers and their customers. Steven told Secreto about King missing both homers at the game, and they shared a laugh.

King and Steven set out in a green unmarked car. King was the sergeant, so he was in the passenger seat and Steven was at the wheel. They cruised the roadway and the footpaths wide enough to accommodate the vehicle.

The lower park was quiet, and Steven turned uptown, soon cruising with the Metropolitan Museum of Art on one side and the Reservoir on the other. They were approaching the Conservatory Garden when they spotted three young teens standing just off the roadway.

The trio matched descriptions of bike thieves in the 61s that Steven had studied. He saw them go still at the sight of the unmarked car. He lip-read one of them uttering two syllables: "Dee tees."

DTs was short for *detectives*, though the term applied to any plainclothes cops. Steven drove on a bit farther in what was just as obvious as a marked car to any criminal but spared anti-crime cops from being interrupted by everyday civilians with minor concerns. He turned into a driveway on the opposite side of the roadway. He continued up to a staff parking lot for Lasker Pool, deserted now because of the weather.

They stepped from the car, and King strode back down to the roadway. Steven began to circle around on a footpath that led into the trees. He figured he had a greater distance to cover and quickened his pace so they would both be in position to catch the teens in the act.

When he came to a clearing, Steven suddenly saw the teens. They had crossed the roadway and sought cover. They stood with their backs to him and were peering out at the roadway, likely to see if the DTs had doubled back in the car.

Steven was wearing his shield on a chain on his neck and had pulled it from under his polo shirt so it was in plain view as he approached the three. He didn't even think of taking out his revolver. He spoke in a low-key tone.

"Fellas, I'm a police officer. I'd like to talk to you."

The three turned and stared silently at him.

"What are you doing around here?" Steven asked. "Where do you live?"

The boys remained silent. Steven called out to the sergeant.

"Sarge, I've got them!"

Steven saw what appeared to be a bulge under the pant cuff of one of the teens. He bent down to feel what it might be and registered a sudden movement at the periphery of his vision.

Steven was looking up and beginning to straighten when the oldest of the three teens pulled the trigger of a .22 caliber pistol he had drawn from his waistband. Steven went down. The teen stood over him, firing just as the gunman had with Smiling Jim a half century before.

Only the teen did not miss. Steven was left lying in the dirt, bleeding from wounds to the neck, eye, and arm as the teens fled.

After the shockingly loud gunshots, all physical sensation had been surreally eclipsed by a tingling, as if the bullets had become thousands of hot pins and needles. Steven felt himself slipping away as his mind conjured what might have been his very last conscious image.

"Patti Ann," he would later report. "I saw Patti Ann."

Steven's face was covered with blood when Sergeant King came running up. King knew Steven was still alive only because his tongue was moving. The sergeant shouted into his radio.

"MOS shot! MOS shot!"

MOS stands for *member of service*.

Two young cops in uniform responded from the 23rd Precinct adjoining that end of the park. They drove up a wide footpath to the edge of the clearing and saw a plainclothes figure with a gold sergeant's shield on a chain standing over a sprawled figure.

Police Officer Denis Robberstad tried to stanch the bleeding as he and Police Officer John McAllister carried Steven to their car. McAllister drove with the sergeant beside him in the front seat. Robberstad sat in the back, his hand pressed to the neck wound as his fingertips sought a pulse, feeling for even the faintest throb of the life they were desperate to save. He detected none.

When they arrived at Metropolitan Hospital in East Harlem, the trauma team went to work. A tube went down Steven's throat, and a nurse began squeezing the Ambu bag attached to it. An IV line went into his uninjured arm. The bleeding was stemmed, and his wounds were examined. An X-ray was taken.

The doctors all but gave up hope when they saw the film. Steven's spine was nearly severed at C2, the second of the seven cervical vertebrae, the one targeted by an executioner's noose. Steven would not be able to breathe, much less move, on his own.

"The officer is not going to make it," a doctor concluded aloud. "The officer is dying."

CHAPTER 4

Minutes later, a shiny black Lincoln bristling with a remarkable number of antennas pulled up to the emergency entrance. An array of police and fire radios were crackling inside the car when the driver's side door opened. Out stepped a tall, gaunt man known as the Night Mayor.

Detective Brian Mulheren responded to all major incidents as City Hall's eyes and ears, deciding what warranted notifying the mayor. He proceeded into the emergency room and consulted with the doctors. He was told Officer McDonald was beyond saving.

Mulheren decided that there was nothing to lose and just maybe everything to gain by transporting Steven to what cops had long felt to be the premier hospital for trauma in New York and therefore the world.

"You might think he's not going to make it, but we're going to Bellevue," Mulheren said.

One nurse kept squeezing the Ambu bag, and another held an IV bag as a half dozen paramedics and cops brought Steven out to a bus-turned-mobile trauma hospital that Mulheren arranged for the Emergency Medical Service to dispatch. Mulheren also had the NYPD highway unit clear the FDR Drive and close off the entrances, so there was no traffic.

On the way downtown, Steven briefly began to regain consciousness. He heard sirens and voices and saw blurred, unfamiliar figures hovering over him, shifting places. They were strangers, yet intimate in their tone as they told him to take it easy, that he was going to be fine and other things they no doubt would have said no matter what his actual condition. He felt the breathing tube down his throat. The rest of his body felt nothing other than that tingling.

Patti Ann was with her sister sixty-five miles away in Yardley, and the NYPD was arranging for her to be notified and escorted back. Steven's parents and his brother Thomas were being brought in from Long Island. His mother had been home scrubbing the bathtub when they got the news that her son had been shot just as her father had nearly a half century before. She was keening in the old Irish way when the family boarded the police helicopter that swooped down to pick them up at a nearby ballfield, where Steven had often played as a boy.

"Steeeven!...Steeeeven!...Steeeeeeven!"

The helipad in Manhattan was moments from the emergency entrance at Bellevue on East 28th Street, just off the FDR Drive. Steven's parents and Thomas arrived just as the trauma bus rolled up and Steven was rushed inside. The doctors told them they could come into the trauma room for what would almost certainly be a final goodbye.

Thomas stepped up to the gurney where Steven lay, his head swollen, his skin brown from Betadine antiseptic wash, a ventilator attached to a breathing tube in his throat, a bandage above his right eye.

"Please don't die, Steven," Thomas said. "Please don't die."

Steven had regained consciousness, and he heard Thomas's voice and saw his brother's face materialize from the blur of strangers. Steven communicated the only way he could.

He winked.

And in that wink Thomas saw the surviving spark of the brother he idolized.

His sister Clare came in. She had been getting dressed to go out dancing when she got the phone call. She approached for what was supposed to be a final farewell, and Steven winked at her as he had with Thomas.

"He's communicating with me!" Clare exclaimed. "I'm not saying goodbye to nobody."

Patti Ann arrived at the hospital, having been brought there in a radio car relay by Pennsylvania state troopers, then New Jersey state troopers, then the NYPD. She passed through a crush of reporters and photographers and TV news crews outside the hospital and a multitude of cops inside. She was shown to a room and told a doctor would be there to speak with her, but she insisted on seeing Steven. She now gazed upon a figure that looked shockingly unlike the man she had married eight months before.

"When I saw Steven lying on the gurney in the emergency room of Bellevue Hospital, I knew our life would never be the same," she would recall.

But when she met the gaze of his one unbandaged eye, she knew he was still exactly Steven. He, for his part, must have been too overwhelmed, too lost in her eyes just to wink. He continued to go in and out of consciousness.

"Don't go under!" his father repeatedly called out as if from the sidelines of eternity.

Patti Ann was herself overwhelmed and returned that night to their apartment. She gazed around and realized that Steven had not tidied up as usual only because he assumed he would return before she did. She left the dirty dishes in the sink and fell exhausted into the unmade bed below the *Razor's Edge* poster.

When Patti Ann came back to the hospital the next day, she encountered a doctor who matter-of-factly used a word that struck her like a physical blow.

"Paralyzed?" she asked. "What are you talking about?"

"Oh, didn't they tell you?" the doctor replied.

Patti Ann continued on to the neurological intensive care unit on the seventh floor, where Steven had been moved. He had undergone a tracheostomy, in which a hole had been cut in the base of his throat and what is known as a cuff trach inserted down his windpipe. The end had an inflatable balloon that pressed against the walls of his airway, so the air from the ventilator did not escape from his mouth and nose rather than fill his lungs. The breathing tube that had been introduced through his mouth was now gone, but he still could not speak because the cuff pressed against his vocal cords and prevented air from passing over them. He was able to mouth four silent syllables.

"I'm paralyzed."

She was as mute as he was. Anything she might have said was distilled to tears.

Steven's family began to fill the small room and the press was around, and Patti Ann did not want to answer questions about Steven's condition. She escaped briefly again to Long Island, managing to nap until the early afternoon. A Nassau County radio car then drove her to the city line, where she was met by an NYPD car driven by Police Officer Robert Dalia of Highway Unit 3.

CHAPTER 5

In 1966, Robert Dalia had joined the NYPD as an eighteen-year-old trainee, one way a working-class kid could receive the equivalent of a college draft deferment. He had nonetheless received an induction notice from his draft board, complete with a subway token taped to the letter to ensure he could travel to the induction center on Whitehall Street in Manhattan. The NYPD promised to take care of it, first making sure he had not used the token. Any recruit who did so had to go buy a new token and affix it to the letter before being sworn in to the NYPD instead of the military.

After a stint as a trainee working the switchboard at the 23rd Precinct in East Harlem, Dalia became a full-fledged officer in 1968 and worked as a patrol cop in the 20th Precinct on the Upper West Side. That neighborhood would later become a realm of multimillion-dollar residences, but back then it was a domain of drug dealers and robbers known as "the wild west." The movie *The Panic in Needle Park* was set there, and Dalia had watched it being filmed.

Dalia was awarded the NYPD Medal of Valor for his actions when responding to a report of a robbery in progress at the Red Carpet Lounge on West 85th Street on the night of October 16, 1971. Four gunmen had gone into the bar intending to rip off a drug deal involving a kilo of heroin, only to find that the transaction had been completed two hours before. They emerged with a fully automatic military carbine, two sawed-off shotguns, and three handguns, and met the arriving cops with a fusillade. Rookie Police Officer Gary Hunt was shot six times—in the legs, hip, and abdomen—as he stepped from his radio car. His partner pulled him into the patrol car and sped downtown toward the hospital, radioing "My partner's shot! Eighty-fifth and Columbus."

Dalia and his partner arrived just as three of the robbers were scrambling straight toward them in an attempt to escape into Central Park. The robber with the carbine raked the radio car. Dalia's partner threw himself across the front. Dalia rolled out of the passenger-side door and sought cover at the back. He returned fire with his revolver and saw the robber with the carbine jump in the air.

"I shot that guy!" Dalia called to his partner.

The robbers retreated into a building, shooting off the lock to the front door. Dalia and his partner followed, positioning themselves on either side of the entryway. Dalia was reloading as he leaned out to peer inside. A shotgun blast punched a big hole in the door, just missing his head.

A blood trail inside stopped at the elevator. The cops continued up and soon had two robbers in custody. The third, the one with the carbine, had hidden atop a shanty on the roof. There was a sudden exchange of gunfire between him and one of the other cops, Police Officer Ralph Minetta.

The third robber rolled off the shanty, and Dalia joined Minetta in cuffing him.

"Ralph, did you shoot him?" Dalia asked. "Because I think I shot him down on the ground."

"Yeah, I think I shot him," Minetta said. "He dropped a gun."

Dalia searched the prisoner and found a shield case and what would prove to be a security guard badge.

"Oh, you're a cop?" Dalia asked. "You're a fucking cop, motherfucker."

Dalia then said to Minetta, "Ralph, come on, we're going to throw him over."

"No, you can't do that!" Minetta said.

Rather than toss the prisoner from the roof, the cops walked him down the stairs. An inspector decided that Minetta must have been the cop who shot the carbine-wielding gunman.

"I shot him, too, inspector," Dalia reported.

"No, you didn't, kid," the inspector said. "You thought you did. You didn't."

"Okay," Dalia said.

The wounded robber with the carbine gave his name at Roosevelt Hospital as Roy Williams. His fingerprints proved he was in fact H. Rap Brown, the Black militant who had famously declared that violence is as American as cherry pie. Dalia was in the squad room when detectives subsequently put Brown's clothes on a hanger and took photos. The idea was that when the time came, Dalia and the other cops would be able to testify accurately as to what Brown had been wearing.

"All of a sudden, there's a bullet, falls out of his jacket," Dalia would recall. *"Holy shit, what's this?"*

The only explanation was that the bullet had passed through Brown and been caught in his clothing. Ballistics proved that the bullet had come from Dalia's Smith & Wesson revolver, not Minetta's Colt. Minetta nonetheless got the full credit.

Dalia hoped for an opportunity to set things straight when he was called to testify at Brown's trial. He was on the stand for eight hours, and at one point defense attorney William Kunstler held up the carbine.

"Did you see my client with this?" he asked.

"Yes, I did," Dalia replied. "And I was shooting at him."

Kunstler inquired if Dalia got blood on his shirt while arresting Brown.

"Mr. Kunstler, you have to subpoena my mother," Dalia said. "Because my mother washed that shirt. She would know."

The jury found Brown and his three codefendants guilty of armed robbery, but not of attempted murder.

"Because they didn't know if he was trying to wound us or kill us; that was a jury in 1973," Dalia would recall. "That was basically an all-white jury, too."

An NYPD effort to push crime from the Upper West Side continued, and Dalia went with it, transferring to the 23rd Precinct in East Harlem. Violence remained as New York as bagels.

New York City had in effect told itself to drop dead, surviving the fiscal crisis only to become a killing ground with some two thousand homicides a year. Safety from being murdered or raped or robbed remained a prevailing concern in New York in 1982, as evidenced by a meeting between the 96th Street Block Association and an emissary from the 23rd Precinct. The police had expected a handful of citizens to attend. More than four hundred crowded in to hear what the NYPD was doing about crime in their neighborhood.

"As long as there are haves and have nots, we're never going to deter crime," said the emissary, Police Officer Charles Bonaventura. "We're just going to push it from one area to another area."

At the time, the 23rd Precinct had reduced prostitution on 86th Street by convincing the women to troll along the south side, which was then in the next precinct. Robberies had topped more than 1,800 a year in the

23rd Precinct and more than 83,000 citywide. The municipal budget had improved to where the department was able to pay overtime for cops to walk anti-robbery footposts in certain "target areas." The NYPD announced that this resulted in robberies being down 2 percent, but cautioned against expectations that the NYPD could significantly reduce crime.

"You can't change the behavior of criminals," NYPD Deputy Commissioner William Devine told the *New York Times*.

While robberies marginally declined in the target area at the downtown end of the 23rd Precinct, they spiked in the uptown end. Cops dismissed such strategies as "a Band-Aid on cancer," "shoveling sand against the sea," and "shoveling shit against the tide." Dalia said it was all just "checkers."

As in every precinct, a small number of cops in the 23rd made a great majority of the arrests. The others did only what was required, and their overall approach to policing was essentially *why bother?*

But, however pervasive that attitude might have been, however futile any effort might have seemed, there were still active cops such as Dalia. And being active meant they were making overtime.

A cop who was deemed to be earning too much was liable to be investigated. One in the 23rd Precinct had all his arrests in 1981 reviewed. The collars were all deemed "high quality," but he was still transferred to administrative duties, which included working the switchboard, as Dalia had as a trainee.

The notion that cops were just looking to make "collars for dollars" led the district attorney's office to be casual about demands on their time. Dalia had plans to go out after a four p.m. to midnight tour when his lieutenant informed him that a prosecutor had decreed that Dalia "must appear" in court first thing the next morning.

"Lieu, can we do anything here?" Dalia asked. "I'm going to be out all night."

"No, 'must appear.' The DA says 'must appear,'" the lieutenant replied.

Dalia had indeed been out all night when he arrived at the precinct at six a.m. the next day.

"Oh, the case is canceled," he was told.

Dalia had reached his limit with being a street cop. He drove home and made a phone call to a union delegate who had offered to get him into Highway 3.

CHAPTER 6

After six months training with high-speed pursuits and motorcycles, Robert Dalia began patrolling in radio car 2972, wearing the distinct Highway uniform: "crushed" hat with the inside wire removed and an enlarged brim, riding breeches with a light blue stripe down the outside of the leg, leather jacket, and high leather boots. He investigated accidents and enforced traffic regulations and ran escorts for everybody from a visiting president to the twenty-three-year-old wife of a gravely wounded officer shot by a teenager in broad daylight in Central Park.

"Twenty-nine seventy-two, meet Nassau, Southern State, Exit 17, Malverne," the dispatcher directed him.

Dalia had been raised at the border of Queens and Brooklyn. He had never even been east of the city line.

"What do I know about Long Island?" he later said. "Do I know what Malverne is?"

A Nassau County Highway Patrol car was waiting at the exit with Patti Ann.

"Come on, get in, we're going to Bellevue," Dalia said.

As Dalia proceeded toward Bellevue with Patti Ann sitting quietly in the back seat of his Highway car, one of the voices crackling over his radio reported that the mayor and the cardinal were at the hospital. Dalia hit the lights and siren.

Mayor Ed Koch had been out of town when Steven was shot, and it was not surprising that he had headed to Bellevue upon his return. But the cardinal's presence was unusual. Patti Ann sat in the back seat, terrified that it meant Steven had died.

On reaching the hospital, Dalia swung around to the rear to avoid the press waiting out front. Patti Ann entered expecting the worst, but she was told that Steven's condition was unchanged. Dalia followed as she was led into the family room to meet the mayor and the cardinal.

When Koch arrived a short time before, he had been struck by the remarkable steadiness of Steven's parents and siblings in such dire circumstances. The Night Mayor, Brian Mulheren, had quietly told him that the McDonalds were very religious, emphasizing the *very*. Koch had decided to call Cardinal John O'Connor, as he never had when responding to forty-three line-of-duty cop deaths since first taking office in 1978. Koch began breaking down in tears as he sought to explain the situation.

"I'll be right down," O'Connor told him.

O'Connor was blocks away and there in minutes. Steven's family was manifestly moved by his presence, thereby confirming Mulheren's assessment. Patti Ann now came in. She would later recount the cardinal's first questions to her.

"How long have you been married?"

"Eight months, Your Eminence."

"How many months are you pregnant?"

She had told only her immediate family and her closest friends that she was expecting. But Steven had told his fellow cops at the Central Park Precinct, and one of them must have told a reporter. The entire city now knew, the cardinal included.

"Three."

Dalia stood amazed by the whole scene.

"The mayor, the cardinal, the whole world is there," Dalia later said. "I'm thinking, 'What the fuck is this? It's a cop. Shot.'"

More than one hundred cops had died in the line of duty during the eighteen years Dalia had been with the NYPD, and a shot cop had come to seem like an unavoidable fact of existence in New York City. He was coming to realize that this one was different. Here was a handsome young cop, the son and grandson of cops, newly married with a pregnant wife, now fighting for his life after being shot by a teenager on a summer afternoon in Central Park.

Dalia was motioned over by Sergeant Jimmy Johnson from Employee Relations, the unit attached to the police commissioner's office that takes care of the family when a cop is hurt.

"Bobby, come here," Johnson said. "What kind of car you got?"

"I got a marked car," Dalia said.

"All right, I want you to go to Highway and get the sergeant's unmarked car," Johnson said.

"I can't do that," Dalia said.

"What do you mean you can't do that?" Johnson asked.

Dalia would later say in recounting this moment, "You know what that is, right? That's stealing the pope's car."

Dalia now told Johnson, "They will cut my balls off if I take that car."

"Don't worry about it," Johnson assured him. "When you get there, that car will be gassed up, washed, and waiting for you."

Dalia understood that his marked car heightened the chance that the press and others would spot and harass Patti Ann when she was already under so much stress. There was concern she might lose her baby as well as her husband.

"Where's the guy shot?" Dalia asked.

"In the head," Johnson replied.

He did not yet know that the more serious wound had in fact been in the neck.

"In the head?"

"In the head, three times."

Dalia figured the cop would almost certainly die, so his assignment would last at least until the funeral. He made a quick calculation.

"So in my head, I'm saying, 'I'll do overtime for three days, drive her to the funeral. I'm going to make a fortune,'" Dalia would recall. "That's how cynical I am."

Dalia drove Patti Ann home that night. She sat in the back.

"Quiet, polite, nice, young, sniffling," Dalia would recall. "I said, 'You can call me any time. I can be there at the drop of a hat.'"

When Dalia arrived at Highway 3 the next morning, the sergeant's car was waiting, gassed and freshly washed. A lieutenant on duty stood shaking his head.

"I don't know about this," the lieutenant said. "[The sergeant] is going to blow a shit fit when he finds out."

"Listen, I only take orders from the police commissioner," Dalia said.

"You don't want me to take the car, lieu, give me another car. It's going to fall on you."

At ten a.m., Dalia picked up Patti Ann with the unmarked car. She had told the cardinal the day before, "We'll survive this," but the doctors at Bellevue remained markedly less confident. The head of neurosurgery, Dr. Joseph Ransohoff, had been the medical consultant for the 1960s TV show *Ben Casey* and was supposedly a model for the gruff character. He lived up to his reputation as he examined Steven and concluded there was nothing to be done.

"He'd be better off dead," Ransohoff is said to have remarked out of Steven's earshot.

Steven remained in need of continual care, which would mean unending work for any nurses assigned to him. And he was deemed likely to die anyway. His nurses would then become the ones who failed to save a handsome young cop with a pregnant wife who seemingly had all of New York praying for his survival.

"No nurses wanted to take care of him," Nina Justiniano later said. "He was so high profile, so sick. The doctors were ready to give up on Steven. I guess [the nurses] figured they didn't want to be the nurse that was there when that happened."

But none of that stopped Nina and a fellow African American nurse named Jeanette Francis from volunteering. Nina in particular had made an effort to learn the workings of a ventilator. And they were not afraid of hard work. They were ready to demonstrate who was the real deal.

"We stepped up," Nina later said.

Nina had read about the shooting in the newspapers and knew that the suspect was Black and from Harlem. She took a question to Steven's mother:

"Steven got shot by a Black man, and his nurses are Black," Nina would recall saying. "Do you have a problem with that?"

Nina would remember that Anita McDonald gazed straight into her eyes.

"The doctors have given up on my son," the mother said, by Nina's account. "I want my child. Do whatever you can do to save my child. You got to save him. You got the power to save my child."

Nina looked straight back into Anita McDonald's eyes and recognized a mother's pain. Nina had lost a child of her own to crib death fifteen years before.

"It had nothing to do with her being white and me being Black," Nina said. "It was mother to mother. We connected as mothers."

Nina also discerned something rare.

"That woman did not have a racist bone in her body," Nina later said.

Nina felt that destiny was at work when she learned that both she and Steven's mother shared a birthday that very day.

"Mrs. McDonald was born the same day as me, July 19," Nina would later say. "We laughed about it. We were sisters from another mother."

Nina's mother had been a vibrantly religious woman named Willie Dean Stevenson, so named because her father was convinced he was going to have a son that he had named her before birth. She had come to New York in early 1952 as part of the Great Migration from the South. She arrived with tales of the Rosewood massacre of 1923, when white mobs rampaged through the Black town in Florida of that name, burning their homes, shooting and lynching anybody who did not manage to escape into the surrounding swamps.

Nina was later told that her mother left Jacksonville because she was pregnant and the wealthy family she was working for as a domestic was pressing her to have an abortion. Nina was born in New York. Willie subsequently married Owen Ray Parish, a truck driver from North Carolina, whom Nina would consider her father.

Parish delivered loads of cotton to New York mattress factories. He was also an iceman and would trudge up and down staircases with a huge block on his shoulder, chipping off pieces with an ice pick. He too often ended the day at a bar.

Nina's mother would tell her that the gospel said to honor thy father, even if he spent much of his time and money drinking and routinely returned drunk to four hungry children. He would roar laughing when he took out half of a torn $20 bill to show he still had some money.

"He would go to the bar, come home with that half a $20 bill," Nina later said. "He thought it was funny. We were starving to death."

Nina was still a youngster when she took it upon herself to attend Al-Anon meetings for the children of alcoholics. Her father's drinking remained a fact of her life, along with the absence of heat and hot water in their apartment on the second floor of a tenement at 212 West 141st Street, across from St. Charles Borromeo Roman Catholic Church.

"We had to get dressed in the kitchen with the oven door open," she would recall of winter days.

She would distinctly remember a sound from her childhood: "Listening to rats crawling in the wall..."

Part of the bathroom ceiling collapsed as the result of a water leak that continued to go unattended.

"The water was coming down so bad, if you wanted to go in the bathroom and sit on the toilet, you had to take an umbrella with you," she later said.

In a heatless apartment in a decaying slum, Nina was still able to delight in such things as a discarded clothesline that served just fine for jumping rope. She would later cite a lesson from her upbringing: "Think about what you can do, not what you can't do."

She did not allow circumstances to define her. She prevailed despite them, with faith in the Almighty and faith in herself, with the Spirit and her own spirit. She knew where she wanted to live someday when she walked down blocks where there were rows of individual homes.

"It was my dream as a child to live in a brownstone," she later said.

And Nina knew what she wanted to become when she attended the African American Day Parade. She watched a cohort of women in white uniforms march past with shoulders squared, heads up, eyes straight ahead, proud. They were from the Harlem Hospital School of Nursing, founded in 1923 by William Vassall of Brooklyn, who enlisted physicians and ministers and others to join him in the effort after his daughter, Lurline, was denied entry to Bellevue Hospital's program because she was Black.

"Gorgeous angels," Nina recalled of watching them parade by. "I wanted to be like them. I wanted to help people."

One thing Nina definitely did not want to become was a cop like those who periodically beat people on her corner with nightsticks.

"They called it a 'wood shampoo,'" she remembered. "They weren't nice. They were an occupying army."

She would add, "Mothers in Harlem tell their children the police are not their friend."

The first Black police officer in the NYPD lived three blocks downtown from Nina, on West 138th Street. Samuel Battle had attempted to join in 1910 only to be turned away, but he had tried again the next year and succeeded. He became instrumental in stopping the first riot to erupt in Harlem, which was sparked in 1935 by a rumor that a white store manager had beaten a Black twelve-year-old suspected shoplifter to death in the basement Kresge five-and-dime on West 125th Street. The boy was sixteen and uninjured, as the police sought to make known by distributing flyers showing him standing with Samuel Battle in uniform. The Manhattan district attorney blamed communist agitators for the unrest, and Mayor Fiorello LaGuardia commissioned an investigation. The result was *Negro in Harlem: A Report on Social and Economic Conditions Responsible for the Outbreak of March 19, 1935*. It determined that the disturbance was in fact "spontaneous" and resulted from "injustices of discrimination in employment, the aggressions of the police, and the racial segregation."

Little changed, and another riot erupted in 1943, after a police officer shot and wounded an unarmed Black soldier. The mistaken belief that the soldier had died led to violence, in which six people were killed.

Then there was the riot in 1964, when Nina was eleven. That erupted after an off-duty NYPD lieutenant shot and killed an unarmed Black fifteen-year-old named James Powell on the Upper East Side. Powell and some friends had been standing near their junior high school when a building super sprayed them with a water hose, reportedly saying, "Dirty n—rs, I'll wash you clean." Powell was among those who chased the super into his building. Nobody was harmed, and Powell was laughing when he returned to the street only to be shot and killed by Lieutenant Thomas Gilligan.

A group of cops subsequently found themselves being pelted with bottles and bricks not far from Nina's home. The cops included Police Officer Phil Romano, who had been a rookie on his very first radio run six years before when he and his Black partner, Al Howard, responded to a stabbing at Blumstein's Department Store on West 125th Street. A deranged woman had stabbed the Reverend Dr. Martin Luther King Jr. in the chest with a sharpened letter opener during a book signing. The ivory-handled weapon was protruding from King's chest, and Romano was credited with saving King's life when he reflexively stopped a panicked representative of the mayor's office from pulling it out. A doctor at Harlem Hospital later determined that the point was pressing against King's aorta, and any jostle would have proven fatal.

One of Romano's fellow cops now called to him as the riot turned against them.

"Phil, can you tell them what you did?"

Romano later said that the circumstances did not allow for much more than dodging the continuing barrage.

When it came to such day-to-day mayhem as burglary and mugging, people in Nina's neighborhood often tried to resolve the matter themselves. A teen known as Smokey went from taking drugs to robbing people. He persisted despite repeated warnings to stop from men of the neighborhood.

"He kept robbing people, and they killed him," Nina said. "They took care of it. And that was the end of it."

Nina went about with little fear of crime.

"I didn't have no problem," she remembered.

But, as street crime increased, older people in particular grew more fearful. And in October 1967, more than seven hundred Harlemites crowded into St. Charles Borromeo Roman Catholic Church directly across West 141st Street from Nina's building to express their concern.

"The muggings and rapes and the burglaries have reached the point that people must do something," one of the organizers was quoted saying.

NYPD Chief Inspector Sanford Garelik, then the department's top uniformed commander, was on hand. He pledged more and better police protection. The crime rate kept rising, along with distrust of the NYPD.

One person in uniform trusted by Nina and the rest of the neighborhood was the school crossing guard on her corner, who was said to be Billie Holiday's sister. A biographer might have noted that the sister's post was by chance a block from the West 140th Street brothel where the singer had been arrested at age fourteen along with her mother. Nina saw the sister as a living connection to the immortal icon who sang the haunting song "Strange Fruit."

Nina had heard her mother talk about lynchings in Florida, which had more lynchings per capita than any other state. And Nina saw photos of lynchings displayed at the National Memorial African Bookstore on West 125th Street. The shop was known in the neighborhood as Michaux's, after the proprietor, Lewis Michaux. A sign above the entrance read KNOWLEDGE IS POWER; YOU NEED IT EVERY HOUR. READ A BOOK.

One of the photos Michaux displayed was of Laura Nelson, who was hung from an Oklahoma bridge along with her fourteen-year-old son after a lawman was killed by an accidental discharge in a struggle over a gun. By some accounts the mob raped both of them. One of the books in the shop had a written account of what had befallen Mary Turner. She had been eight months pregnant when she was set upon by a mob after loudly protesting the lynching of her husband along with eleven other Black men in May 1918 in Valdosta, Georgia. The husband's capital crime was being friends with a Black man allegedly killed by a white man who had refused to pay him for work. A screaming Mary Turner was hanged and shot numerous times. Her baby was apparently alive when it was cut from her womb but killed when its head was crushed under a boot heel.

None of that was part of American history as taught to Nina at Benjamin Franklin High School crosstown in East Harlem. The faculty seemed to her to have scant interest in the students. One teacher punished her for a minor infraction by locking her in a closet. Drugs were everywhere.

Yet Nina remained focused on her goal. She told the guidance counselor that she was set on becoming a nurse.

"You don't have what it takes," the counselor told her.

Nina aced the entrance exam. She was waiting to be called when she became pregnant and had a boy she named Jason in 1971. He was ten months old when she awoke with a sense that something was terribly wrong.

"This dark came over me like somebody had injected ice in my veins," she would recall. "I knew he was dead before I looked in the crib. I felt it. I knew it."

But as she gazed into the crib, her mind could not immediately accept that the tiny, still form was Jason.

"He looked like a rubber doll," she remembered. "For that split second, I didn't believe it was my kid. I thought drug addicts had come in, taken my child, and left this."

She began to wail. She was heard a full long avenue block away.

"The cops came," she recalled. "They didn't say nothing."

The officers might have been so unfamiliar with crib death that they suspected Nina was responsible. They carried Jason out to a radio car. A neighbor told Nina not to worry, there were machines at the hospital that could save the baby.

As she rode in the back of another radio car, Nina met the gaze of the driver in the rearview mirror. She detected a flash of suspicion before the cop's eyes returned to the street.

The baby was already beyond saving as the result of what was technically called sudden infant death syndrome, which had only been identified in 1969. Nina also encountered suspicion in the silence of several neighbors who stopped speaking to her. She fell into a deep and prolonged depression.

"For six months, I didn't do nothing," she recalled. "One day, I just looked at my apartment and said, 'You got to clean up.' I started cleaning, and I've been cleaning up ever since."

In 1975, she achieved her childhood dream: She was admitted to the Harlem Hospital School of Nursing.

But the same fiscal crisis that prompted the cop layoffs also caused the nursing school at Harlem Hospital to stop taking new students and only train those who were enrolled before the shutdown. Bellevue had long since started taking Black students, but its nursing school was also shutting down, along with the rest of those at municipal hospitals.

Nina applied to the nursing program at St. Vincent's Hospital, a Catholic institution in Greenwich Village. She was accepted pending one seeming formality.

"I had to send a picture," Nina would remember.

She guessed why and put it off, but the school kept asking, and she finally sent it in. Her suspicions were confirmed when the school called.

"We don't think you could handle our nursing program," she was told.

The school did not refund her $25 application fee.

"At the time, a lot of money," Nina would recall.

She then learned of the Brooklyn Jewish Hospital School of Nursing. She applied but heard nothing back and figured the school had deduced she was Black from her Harlem address.

Then, three days before classes were due to start, she received a call. A school administrator told her that her application had somehow fallen between a desk and a wall and had just then been discovered.

"Would you like to come to our nursing program?" the administrator asked.

Nina began a three-year program so demanding that only 35 of the 105 students at the start would make it to the end. It was statistically far tougher to get through than the police academy, which was only six months.

"I didn't go out dancing the whole time I was in nursing school," she would recall.

Nina secured a federal Pell Grant toward tuition. She also applied to the Masons for a $286 grant to get through six months, subsisting on $1.25 for a slice of pizza and a soda each day.

"They sent me five hundred dollars," Nina remembered. "I was so happy about that."

Nine months into the nurse training came the capping ceremony, the equivalent of shield day when new cops receive their badge.

"It's just as big," Nina later said.

The ritual began at a candelabra. The director of the nursing program lit its seven candles, saying they represented the attributes of a true nurse: knowledge, skill, dependability, responsibility, happiness, love, and humanity. She then lit a candle held by each student. She ceremoniously crowned one student after another with a cap whose design was unique to their particular institution.

"No two schools had the same cap," Nina later said.

In the second year came the banding ceremony, during which a blue band was affixed to a student's cap. Those who made it to the third and final year would receive a black band that was universal to all nursing schools.

But to graduate, Nina had to get a perfect score on the math exam. Students only received two chances, and Nina fell short with a score of 98 on the first. She was studying so hard for the second while riding the subway that she rode past her stop to the end of the line.

"Miss, why are you still on the train?" asked a transit worker who came through to ensure everybody had gotten off.

Her future turned on answering every question correctly. One error and she would not become a nurse.

"That was my last chance," she recalled. "I passed, thank you Jesus."

She received the black band.

"In mourning for Florence Nightingale," Nina later explained.

It also signified that she was a registered nurse who had passed both the written and clinical exams.

"The real deal," Nina noted.

At graduation, Nina stood in her white uniform as proud as the nurses had been in that parade during her girlhood. The graduation ceremony at a Brooklyn temple was a dream come true that had one detail she had not foreseen regarding the male members of her family in attendance.

"Yarmulkes over their Afros," Nina remembered.

Nina took an oath that she boiled down to three words as a nurse's ultimate duty: "To relieve suffering."

She started at Peninsula Hospital in Rockaway, Queens, where any of the staff should have recognized the significance of the black band on her cap. A white phlebotomist nonetheless asked her if she was really an RN.

"You only got your RN because you're the right color," the phlebotomist said.

"Yeah, they gave me the Black test," Nina replied.

Nina then said, "Oh, you think the test is color coded? If anybody's the right color, it's you."

Her first day on the job was an overnight shift, starting at eleven p.m. She heard an aide call out at three a.m.

"There's a woman dead down there. You need to go down there."

Nina looked around to see who the aide was addressing.

"Then I realized he was talking to me because I was the only nurse," Nina would recall.

The woman was elderly, and Nina confirmed that she had neither pulse nor blood pressure. Her eyes were open, and Nina closed them. She called the doctor, who asked the time of death and said he would notify the family.

Nina would remember that it was a beautiful summer night outside as she began a ritual she would repeat again and again in the years ahead. Give the deceased a sponge bath. Insert any false teeth. Open a shroud kit and apply the enclosed chin strap. Cut off the hospital identification wristband. Fill out and secure the toe tag. Check the religion and cross the arms if the patient was Christian, palms pressed together if they were Jewish. Tie the arms and ankles in place. Wrap the deceased in plastic, with string tied at the neck, waist, and ankles. Slide the remains into an outsized bag, starting with the feet. Place any personal effects in a small bag.

It was all made easier by a serenity that followed death.

"It's a peace that comes over everybody," Nina later said. "When the angels come and get your spirit, there's a peace about you."

Nina decided something about the patients put in her care.

"The white girls assigned me the sickest, most incapacitated [patients] you could have," she recalled. "But that's okay. It made me strong."

Yet there were moments when they were all nurses first and foremost.

"When an emergency comes in, we band together like sisters," she later said. "We do what we got to do for that patient. Then we go back to hating each other."

She went on to work at a series of hospitals, including St. Vincent's, whose nursing school had rejected her after seeing her picture. She had locked that hurt away with all the others that came from being a person of color. She was thereby able to focus on her mission to help and heal.

"I loved the fact that I made people feel better at the end of the day," she later said.

As Nina saw it, the doctors concerned themselves only with the ailment. The nurses addressed the entire person. She guessed there might be a way to lift one particularly downcast patient's spirits. The hunch was proven correct when the patient spoke to a visitor afterward.

"She came in here, she washed my hair, I feel so good!" the patient exclaimed.

Such services were only what was expected when Nina was retained as a private-duty nurse with more moneyed patients. She learned as her mother had as a nanny for a family connected to the Gillette safety razor fortune that interplanetary travel was possible—it just took a brief walk or a few minutes by subway from Harlem to the Upper East Side.

"Oh my God, the difference from where we lived to some of those apartments takes your breath away," she later said.

But the grandeur of the surroundings only made the general discontent of some private patients all the more apparent. And many maladies and disabilities were beyond the immediate power of wealth to rectify. Nina concluded that the most important difference between people was not rich or poor, not even good or bad. She decided that people could either be happy or they could be miserable. She still felt the loss of Jason. And she continued to encounter bigotry. She now made a conscious choice on how to live despite all that.

"I chose to be happy," she said. "See the joy in things and be grateful."

Nina's happiness came easier when she had a second child, Ronda Clarke. She married a man named Wilfredo Justiniano, who helped her maintain her sunny outlook when she went to work at Bellevue in 1980. She served as what amounted to a battlefield nurse amid New York's constant carnage.

"That was a rough time," she would recall. "Lot of killing, lot of murdering, lot of drugs. We were in a lot of pain in the city at that time. The whole city was sick. A lot of racial tensions."

Rather than the mass civil disturbances of prior years, there was what former Mayor John Lindsay once termed "a riot in slow motion" created "by crime and poverty." Robberies and murders more than doubled between 1968 and 1982.

By 1985, Harlem had become so blighted that City Hall had begun auctioning off abandoned brownstones. Nina had grown up with a tenement dweller's awe of these once splendid private residences. And she suddenly had a chance to realize her childhood dream to live in one. The hitch was you had to pay the not inconsiderable sum of $500 just for the opportunity to make sealed bids on three properties, with no guarantee any bid would win.

Nina went ahead, and one of her bids proved to be a winning offer for a three-story residence at 28 West 130th Street. It was among twenty-eight adjoining buildings known as Astor Row, having been built by the ultra-rich family of that name in the early twentieth century.

More than a half century later, Nina wrote down an offer on a piece of paper: $29,999.

"I just picked it out of the wind," she would report.

Nina Justiniano's Harlem of resilience and pride was also a place of social ills bred by the inequities incubated in the wake of white flight. One result was Shavod Jones, known as Buddha because he had such fat cheeks as a baby.

Shavod had an arrest record dating back to when he was eleven, which was also the year he began psychotherapy. He was an inpatient at a psychiatric facility for three months when he was twelve. He spent a year at the Cedar Knolls residential school for emotionally troubled youths in suburban Hawthorne, Westchester County. He was expelled after he repeatedly ran away and attempted suicide, by his grandmother's account after another boy proposed homosexual sex. The Handicapped Office of the City Board of Education had deemed him a candidate for homeschooling and assigned him a teacher, but that required an adult chaperone, and one had not been arranged. He was told to meet with the teacher at a local library, but he never showed. He continued to be arrested for a variety of crimes, including twice for knifepoint robberies. His mother and grandmother had both gone to family court seeking to have him remanded as what was known as a PINS case, meaning a person in need of supervision.

"I beg them then, please lock him up because somebody's going to kill him or he's going to kill somebody else," his mother, Sharron Harris, later told the *New York Daily News*.

Family Court had declined to detain him as a PINS case because he was not present at the proceeding, as required by state law. Shavod was due to be sentenced for armed robbery on July 3 of that year, but it was postponed while an attempt was made to re-enroll him in the school for troubled teens. The sentencing was rescheduled for July 18.

Six days before the new date, Shavod was on a Harlem rooftop, test-firing a .22 caliber revolver that had been assembled in Florida and subsequently stolen and eventually ended up in his possession. He stuck it in his waistband under his shirt and set out with fourteen-year-old Ernest White and thirteen-year-old Carl Evans into the 840 acres in the middle of Manhattan that comprise the country's most celebrated urban park. Their intent was to steal a bicycle, but the weather reduced the possibilities and they had yet to accomplish their goal when a green Plymouth Fury came up the drive.

"That's a DT car," Shavod said, by White's subsequent account.

White further recounted how the three of them took a path away from the road, only for one of the cops to appear.

"The cop started searching my cousin Evans, and I heard *pow! pow!*" White would recall.

After the shooting, the teens had scattered. Shavod was spotted walking along the concrete shore of the man-made Harlem Meer by Police Officer Eddie Wagner and Police Officer Kenney Nietert of the 23rd Precinct. He approached the cops, dripping wet, looking like he had been swimming in his clothes. He told them he had just been mugged by a group of other teens, who threw him in the lake after stealing his gold chain.

The cops became dubious when Shavod pointed in what he said was the direction his assailants had fled. That would have meant they ran toward the sirens of the radio cars responding to the report of a cop shot. Shavod's tale soon unraveled. The other teens, White and Evans, had by then been picked up in the park, and they told detectives that Shavod was the shooter.

The gun was recovered from the waters of the meer with three spent cartridges in the cylinder. Shavod expressed a single regret as he sat in the precinct with Officer Wagner.

"I wish I had run into you without your gun or shield," Shavod said by Wagner's account.

Two days after the shooting and four days before Shavod was to have appeared in court for sentencing, a grammar school photo of him ran on the front page of the *New York Daily News*. His head was tilted to the side, propped on his upraised open right hand, a watch band on his wrist. His eyes were bright and he was smiling as if everything good were possible, at that moment, anyway. The headline read ONLY 15 YEARS OLD, HE'S CHARGED AS THE KID WHO SHOT A COP.

CHAPTER 9

That cop now lay in a bed at Bellevue, unable to talk, mutely mouthing, "I want to die...I want to die...I want to die."

Nina Justiniano managed to get Steven laughing with her line about not getting a paycheck for dead bodies.

She then commenced working sixteen-hour days to save him.

She began by bringing him out of the semi-stupor that had resulted from considerably more narcotics than he still needed.

Steven did have pain just below his ears. His neck could no longer support and shift the weight of his head. The roughly three pounds of brain along with seven pounds of eyes, skull, teeth, facial muscles and skin—a total of ten pounds—pressed down excruciatingly where sensation began.

But what Steven really wanted the drugs for was to escape.

"Proud, with a beautiful body, strong, handsome," Nina later said. "And to lose that at such a young age..."

Who would think that something so incidental as an itch on your nose could become a torment when you can't scratch it and cannot even call someone to do it for you? He not only could not walk, he also could not control his bladder or his bowels. And he was wracked by spasms.

When he closed his eyes and tried to imagine himself back before the shooting, he often suffered flashbacks to the immediate aftermath. He again saw faces he did not recognize hovering above him. He again felt the agony of having the breathing tube shoved down his throat. He again wondered why he could not feel anything else but maddening pins and needles. He again experienced the panicked confusion of not knowing why he was unable to move his limbs, why he was no longer in command of himself.

When he opened his eyes, he again knew exactly why. And a doctor who spoke to him and Patti Ann said that there was no hope it could ever be different, that he would remain paralyzed. Patti Ann began sobbing uncontrollably. Steven discovered that one other thing he could still do with her was cry. He had an overwhelming urge to reach out to comfort her. That made him feel all the more locked in his body.

Only when he managed to sleep was he able to hold Patti Ann and dance and run and play football. Then he would wake and become desperate to escape again. He still could not speak, but he could mouth his displeasure when Nina began to wean him off the drugs.

"Slowly, but surely," she would recall. "A little bit at a time."

He would ask for more and she would give him less, and he would demand more and she would give him even less.

"We fought like dogs," she would later say.

The struggle was continuing when the NYPD chaplain, Monsignor John Kowsky, arrived for what had become a daily bedside Mass. Steven seemed to think this would surely cause Nina to relent. She was not to be deterred.

"Oh, Father," Nina said. "Some things are about to happen here. We about to say some words in here."

Eventually, she cut off the drugs altogether. Steven continued making requests for more.

"I'm not giving you nothing!" she told him. "You're not getting no pain meds."

He had discovered that one sound he could make was to click his tongue off the roof of his mouth. He began using it to get her attention.

"Oh, you learned," she said.

The clicking turned insistent.

"Whatever you want, the answer is no," she said. "You are not getting it."

Insistent became urgent. She asked when he was going to stop taking drugs.

"When I can walk again," he mouthed.

"Suppose you can't walk. You think I'm going to be giving you these drugs?" she asked.

They continued to go back and forth.

"I'm going to go uptown, how about that?" Nina finally said. "Let me go up to Harlem, get some crack, and put it in your ventilator!"

Steven laughed again, along with several other cops who were in the room. He steadied but was soon back to repeatedly mouthing that he did not want to live, sometimes in tears. She would later describe him as "scared and depressed and sad."

"You still got your brain," she told him. "You can think, okay?"

He was also often *angry*.

"I want to take the bullet out!" he mouthed.

"Steven, we can't do that now," she told him, explaining that it was beyond the current ability of the surgeons.

"I want to take the bullet out!" he repeated.

His fury would subside, and he would sink back into grieving his living death. He was too manifestly transformed for the stages of denial and bargaining. Unable to proceed past depression, he would turn angry again.

Nina did not tell Steven that the doctors seemed to have given up on him. She would later say that the doctors ceased to order blood work and blood pressure medication and antibiotics.

"The doctors cut him off," Nina later said. "They cut off everything."

Nina would add that she and the night nurse Jeanette did their best to figure out what Steven needed. Only a doctor could order blood work, so they just had to guess the levels of medication.

"Me and the night nurse were flying blind," she recalled.

They scavenged what they could from elsewhere in the hospital.

"We did what we had to do," she said. "And we came through."

She understood that she was risking her nursing license. But she had made that mother-to-mother pledge to Anita McDonald. Nina and Jeanette continued doing everything they could.

"You lose your husband, you're a widow; you lose your parents, you're an orphan," Nina later said. "But there is no word that I know of to describe the loss of a child."

And Steven shared a rare quality with his mother.

"We would curse each other out, but in all our arguments, Steven never said one thing that was racial to me," Nina recalled. "In his darkest hours, when he was most angry, he never lashed out racially."

She added, "It was not in him at all. Trust and believe that. And I was with him at his darkest time. People show their true colors when they get to that point. He showed me his true colors, and it was not in him. And that's a miracle."

CHAPTER 10

The NYPD was not about to give up on one of its own. And, along with detailing Robert Dalia to drive Patti Ann, it assigned pairs of cops from the Central Park Precinct to assist Steven at the hospital in whatever way they might be needed.

"We were like backup for the nurses," Police Officer Dave Martelli later said.

Martelli was handsome and had a diamond stud in his earlobe, so Nina and everybody else called him Diamond Dave. He was a rookie who had been initially mystified when he saw the letters CPP next to his name on a list of precinct assignments that were otherwise designated by numbers.

"Sarge, what is this?" Martelli would remember asking his supervisor.

"Kid, you're going to the Central Park Precinct," the sergeant said. "Take your gun, throw it away, and put peanuts in your pocket."

But what happened to Steven was a reminder that even the CPP had its perils. And Martelli's assignment to Bellevue was an affirmation of a department tradition.

"They take care of you when you're injured," he later said.

Martelli and a second CPP cop would spend the full tour in Steven's room. Other cops would stop by to visit, and they would voice their feelings regarding the teenage gunman.

"They were very angry about it, and I can understand it," Nina later said.

But Steven also seemed to touch something else in them. She listened to them talk in Steven's presence, and she gained a different perspective regarding cops than was prevalent in Harlem.

"They had lives, too," she recalled. "They had families and people that were important to them in their lives."

She would add, "They were not mean and hateful. And Steven showed me that. I saw that through him. Steven was kind. I'm telling you, a kind man. I cannot tell you how kind that man was. A beautiful spirit."

Dalia would come in, and he sometimes seemed to forget that Nina was there. She did not know he was the cop who shot H. Rap Brown. But she definitely recognized his type as he told stories she took to be racially tinged about administering variations on the wood shampoo. He sounded much like she would have expected cops to sound.

"Bobby was a classic head-banging racist cop," Nina later said in offering her view. "I had to sit there and listen to him say how he beat my people."

Nina just continued tending to Steven's body and spirit in her own particular, unflagging way.

"And Bobby saw what I was doing," Nina said. "Bobby saw beyond the color of my skin. I think Bobby saw a human being deserving respect."

Nina concluded, "I turned Bobby around."

At one point, Dalia invited Nina to a party at his home.

"I was the only Black person there," Nina reported. "I felt a little uncomfortable, but it was okay, Bobby made sure I was okay."

On another day, the Patrolmen's Benevolent Association (PBA) expressed its appreciation for the efforts of Nina and Jeanette Francis by presenting them each with a string of pearls. They were also given PBA courtesy cards to present if they were ever pulled over while driving. Nina was not shy about using it when a cop stopped her for speeding on her way to Bellevue.

"I'm Steven's nurse!" she announced. "I'm going to take care of your brother!"

Upon returning home from another sixteen-hour shift, Nina remembered something she had intended to tell the night nurse. Nina was speaking to her from the phone in the kitchen when she heard sudden banging sounds coming from the bedroom. She went in to see her husband, Wilfredo Justiniano, flailing wildly on the bed.

"What is going on, what am I seeing?" she asked herself.

Wilfredo came out of it and said he had been having a nightmare.

"I was dying. I couldn't breathe," he told her.

She noted that his speech was slurred and his face was drooping. She brought him to the neurology department on the fifth floor at Bellevue the next morning. She left a written list of her husband's symptoms for the doctors.

"I went up to take care of Steven," Nina would recall.

She got a phone call.

"They told me my husband is very sick and had to go to the ICU," she remembered.

Wilfredo had been diagnosed with a brain tumor. He voiced a concern as he was about to undergo surgery.

"I don't want to be like your patient," he said, meaning Steven.

After the operation, the doctors were unable to revive Wilfredo, and they had to go back in. He regained enough awareness after the second surgery to know that he had suffered brain damage. He was by an ultimate measure in worse condition than Steven.

"Don't let me live like this," he told Nina.

She would recall that Patti LaBelle singing "On My Own" came on the radio as she was driving home that night.

"Tears down my cheeks," she would remember. "How is this going on in my life?"

She began going between Steven's current room on the sixth floor and Wilfredo on the seventh, in the neurological ICU.

"Because I had to," she later said. "The joke was I had two husbands."

Steven's mother joined her in praying for both.

"If you just have a little faith, you could get through it," Nina later said. "Because the world is full of pain, a lot of people try to avoid it, and you can't. Pain is going to find you no matter what you do."

And Nina did not just face pain. She addressed it with all of her ability.

"As a nurse my job is to relieve suffering," she later said.

By then, Steven had hung on long enough that the doctors concluded he would likely survive after all. The other nurses took an accordingly different view of caring for him.

"Now, everybody wanted to be his nurse," Nina remembered. "When Steven was dying, I worked pretty much three months with no day off. When he got better, all of a sudden, 'You're working too much.'"

Nina had become friendly with a white nurse who worked on the same floor, and they would sometimes grab coffee together during a break. The nurse had never expressed interest in caring for Steven, but now she approached his mother.

"One of the white nurses went to Mrs. McDonald and said, 'Steven needs a nurse who understands his needs,'" Nina would recall. "Mrs. McDonald wasn't having it."

The nurse seems to have mistakenly assumed that Steven's mother would not say anything to Nina.

"When Mrs. McDonald told me, I was shocked," Nina would recall. "Mrs. McDonald, she said, 'You think that's your friend. Let me tell you what she said about you.'"

Nina confronted the nurse.

"I told her, 'You're cut off, no more having coffee together,'" Nina recalled. "She started crying. That crying was tears of guilt and shame. She followed me into the room, trying to explain. I said, 'You can't explain that.'"

The nurse went to a supervisor, who responded by going to Nina with a dire threat.

"The worst words you can ever say to a nurse is, 'I'm going to have you canceled,'" Nina later said. "To say that is the worst that could ever come out of your mouth."

The supervisor was threatening that Nina would no longer be able to treat Steven.

"I had a flash of temporary insanity," Nina added. "I had to take her around the corner and tell her a few words. *You think you're going to cancel me?* I whispered in her ear that I would stomp her in the parking lot if she would ever even think of having me canceled. They would not recognize her when they brought her into the emergency room. *Take food out of my child's mouth, you're going to be among the missing.*'"

The staff noted that the often fierce supervisor was uncharacteristically subdued afterward. Several people came up and hugged and kissed Nina.

"What did you say to her?" they asked.

"I didn't say nothing," Nina replied.

A feeding tube had been inserted into Steven's stomach through his abdomen, but now he was able to eat. He could not feel the food going down when he swallowed, and that brought a fear of choking. He also could not register how much he had consumed. He had been robbed of the comfort of feeling full, that elemental bit of satisfaction that the depressed often seek through food.

Steven stopped eating, as if on a hunger strike against his fate, with full knowledge of how such a refusal had played out for IRA prisoners of the British in Northern Ireland.

"Steven could be quite stubborn," Nina noted.

Nina instructed Patti Ann to bring in a blender from home. Anything Steven refused to eat went right in it.

"You don't want to eat this sandwich?" Nina would ask. "No problem."

She would drop the sandwich in the blender along with whatever other food he rejected and hit the button. The result went in through the feeding tube. Steven just looked at her.

"You're not going to sit up there and self-starve," she declared.

She added, "God has a plan for you."

Nina could not tell what that plan might be beyond a singular obligation to eat and stay off drugs and keep living.

"You got a baby coming," she reminded him. "Your wife is having a baby and that baby needs a father."

She proclaimed a striver's strategy.

"Let's concentrate on what you can do," she said. "I don't want to hear about what you can't do."

On Labor Day weekend, a new priest arrived to say Mass in Steven's room. NYPD Chaplain John Kowsky had gone fishing. His usual fill-in, FDNY Chaplain Julian Deeken, also had holiday plans and sought out a fellow Franciscan friar, Father Mychal Judge.

"Do you think you could go to Bellevue Saturday and say Mass for Officer Steven McDonald?" Deeken asked.

"Sure, I'm free," Judge said. "Who's Steven McDonald?"

"Don't you read the newspapers or watch TV?" Deeken asked.

"I've been out of the country," Judge reminded him.

Judge had just returned two days before from a year-long stint in England. The Night Mayor, Brian Mulheren, picked Judge up in front of the friary on Saturday, the multiple radios in the car crackling with reports of the city's ongoing chaos.

Upon Judge's arrival at Bellevue, Steven and Patti Ann did not fail to notice that along with the traditional friar's habit and sandals, he was sporting an earring and a thin braid down the back of his neck. He began to say Mass, his voice warm and vibrant. The same spirit filled Judge's eyes, and Steven was suffused with a feeling that he thought had vanished along with the sensation in his limbs.

"Heavenly," Steven would later say.

At the end of the Mass, Judge broke into song.

And the Lord said let it be,
And the Lord said let it be,
Amen, all is well,
Let it be…

After Judge departed, Steven and Patti Ann looked at each other. They had never heard a priest just start singing in a Mass, and certainly not what sounded closer to the Beatles than a beatitude.

"We were like, 'Wow, is this okay he's doing this? Is that okay with the Church?'" Patti Ann would recall.

She was left with an unexpected and improbable feeling.

"It was almost like it was all going to be okay," she later said.

The next day, Patti Ann went to the friary and asked if Judge could come back sometime. He returned again and again, introducing the McDonalds to a prayer they had never heard.

Lord, make me an instrument of your peace…
Where there is hatred let me sow love,
Where there is injury, pardon…

Steven was still not able to speak and he mouthed a question.

"What prayer is that?"

"The Prayer of St. Francis," Mychal replied.

The words of St. Francis stayed with Steven as he entered his third month in Bellevue and Patti Ann entered her sixth month of pregnancy. She had begun to feel the baby move. Steven was never more acutely aware of what he could not do than when he was unable to reach out and feel the stirring in her tummy.

Despite the fervent prayers and love of his mother and Patti Ann, and despite Nina's particular nursing style of bolstering him and getting him to laugh, Steven was continuing to slip into despair. A fellow patient for whom every movement was an agony shuffled up to his bedside in an elaborate back brace.

Firefighter Ronald Bucca had been attempting to rescue a trapped fire lieutenant when he fell five stories. Fire officials afterward noted that Bucca had struck a telephone wire and a pair of cables on the way down, but speculated that his survival may have ultimately been due to his Army Special Forces parachute training. He landed on his hands and feet like some huge, muscular cat.

Bucca ignored what must have been his own excruciating pain as he made his way to Steven.

"How you doin'?" Bucca asked.

Steven would recall, "I couldn't communicate because of the gunshot wounds, but that didn't matter to him. He knew I was in a deep depression, dark moods, and he would spend time with me, trying to give me pep talks."

Bucca returned to see Steven day after day. Patti Ann gave Bucca a nickname that stuck: the Flying Fireman.

The city where Steven and the Flying Fireman both miraculously survived was also the city of the Miracle Mets, a team that was down to its last out and came back to beat the Boston Red Sox to win the World Series.

58 • Michael Daly

A ticker tape victory parade was planned the next day on lower Broadway. That also happened to be the day when the Boy Scouts of America were to give Steven an award for what some were calling the city's other great comeback. Steven was scheduled to accept the honor in a sixth-floor lounge at Bellevue in what would also be his first meeting with the press.

His father arrived at Steven's room before the event and was helping Nina get him into a wheelchair when Steven suddenly lost consciousness. His lips turned blue.

His father ran into the hallway shouting for help, but Nina understood right away that Steven's injuries must also compromise his body's ability to automatically pump an adequate supply of blood to his brain when he was abruptly positioned upright. He was experiencing an extreme version of the head rush that people can sometimes experience when they rise too quickly.

"Orthostatic hypotension," Nina later said. "Those are big words for low blood pressure."

Steven's consciousness and normal color were restored as soon as he was reclined, but Patti Ann had to accept the award on his behalf.

"We have our good days and our bad days, and this was one of the bad days," Patti Ann told the assembly in the lounge. "You've got to accept it. Steven can't be here today, but that doesn't mean he won't be here sometime in the future."

Eleven days later, on November 9, Steven and Patti Ann marked their first wedding anniversary. Monsignor John Kowsky was unable to come to Bellevue, and Father Mychal Judge was asked to fill in. The priest launched into an impromptu talk on the joys of love and marriage that soon had everyone in tears. He began to fear that he himself would lose his composure when he spotted a Notre Dame pendant a visitor had brought. He started to sing.

"When Irish eyes are smiling…"

Steven and Patti Ann and the others began to laugh through their tears, and all was well, for a few moments anyway. But Steven continued to turn despondent as Patti Ann proceeded on into her seventh month of pregnancy. The moment came when Nina set a stool beside the bed and pulled the privacy curtain closed and called to Patti Ann.

After feeling the baby's movements against his cheek, Steven began to experience a nascent stirring of his own. He might not ever be able to do what other fathers did with their children. But maybe there was something he could do. Maybe he could become an instrument of peace as in the Prayer of St. Francis.

"That's when he started thinking about forgiving that boy," Nina later said. "When he felt the baby move around and stir in Patti Ann's belly, Steven decided to give up that hate, that anger, that feeling sorry for himself."

But no sooner had he begun to consider forgiveness, no sooner was hope gained, than it began to slip away. Flashbacks of the shooting were joined by flash-forwards. He had always seen himself playing catch with his kid and going to the beach and doing all the things he had wanted to do with his own, too often absent dad. All those imaginings now became impossibilities.

"You're thirty years old, you need somebody to wash your face, wash your behind, feed you," Nina later said. "You can't go to the bathroom without help. That would make anyone bitter. A lot of people would have wallowed in self-pity for the rest of their life."

Nina reminded Steven that even as the days and nights in the hospital blurred together with no promise of him getting better, each distinct minute was a minute closer to when he would become a father.

"Come on now, Steven, you're not going to wallow in that self-pity," Nina told him "You ain't got time to wallow."

Steven again and again willed his limbs to move. Nothing. He filled with fury, at what had happened, at that teenager named Shavod Jones who had left him without even the ability to vent his fury with clenched fists or a raised voice. Nina was still able to detect it in his eyes and in the mouthing of his words.

"This poison, this resentment—let it go, Steven," she urged him.

Steven still could not talk, and Nina got him laughing once more when she told him that this inability made him the perfect confidant.

"I can tell you all my business, and you can't repeat it!" she informed him.

One thing that had been much on her mind was her winning bid for the brownstone. She now confided in Steven that she was pondering a strategy.

"Hold on to this building until the neighborhood change," she told him.

That meant sealing it up and continuing to pay taxes with the presumption that the streets would become safer. Some simple and emphatic advice came from a cop who had been left paralyzed, on a ventilator, and still unable to speak after being shot by a symbol of Harlem's seemingly intractable ills.

"Go for it," Steven mouthed.

Nina later said, "And I went for it. That was our little secret."

CHAPTER 12

That November, Steven was joined at Bellevue by three of six officers who were shot while seeking to arrest a murder suspect.

At the end of October, on Halloween, four drug dealers had been found executed in an apartment on Southern Boulevard in the Bronx. The ballistics matched those of a gun fired at detectives during a high-speed chase as they sought to arrest a twenty-year-old named Larry Davis for the robbery of a Harlem man. Davis managed to get away and continued to elude capture as he became the prime suspect in the quadruple homicides and three other killings committed with the same .45 caliber pistol during drug rip-offs. Detectives formed a task force to track him down. They repeatedly came close to capturing him, only for him to slip away.

On November 19, the detectives tracked Davis to a six-story building on Fulton Street, in the Bronx. They summoned the assistance of the Emergency Service Unit (ESU) in making the arrest. ESU is a unique combination of SWAT and rescue. When people need help, they call the cops. When cops need help, they call ESU.

Those who responded included one of the two female members of ESU, forty-year-old Police Officer Mary Ellen Nugent Buckley. Mary is the daughter of Irish immigrants and was raised in the South Bronx, the Irish poor having preceded the Black and Hispanic poor. Her mother had been sixteen when she lost her own mother to tuberculosis back in Ireland, and four of her siblings had died before she turned eighteen. The mother had been left with no desire to go back to the Emerald Isle.

"She said she knew nothing but misery there," Mary would later say.

The most heartbreaking loss had come in America when Mary was two. Her six-year-old brother, Terrence, was struck by a car while playing with her other brother, Ed, outside their Bronx apartment building.

"Ed was eight at the time," Mary would recall. "Terrence ran out in front of the car. Ed remembers seeing his head in the wheel well of the car and a police officer just standing there. I wonder if he would have been saved today. EMS is so good now, but sometimes it is better not to be saved."

Terrence was taken to the old Lincoln Hospital.

"He didn't die right away," she would recall. "My mother was told to go home and rest a bit. She said she was on the couch and saw a white bird rise from the floor. Just then my uncle knocked on the door to tell her Terrence had passed and she should come and kiss him while he was still warm."

Mary figured that the hardness of her mother's earlier life explained why she was not one to otherwise hug or kiss.

"It wasn't her thing," Mary later said.

Mary was eighteen when she showed the makings of New York's Finest.

"It's a warm South Bronx night in the summer of sixty-four," a neighbor, Jerry Horn, would remember. "A group of guys in their late teens and early twenties, from Cypress and Brook Avenues, are standing in a circle on the sidewalk in front of a storefront club house on East 141st Street. In the middle of the circle is a man…He's stocky, in his thirties, and almost completely blind. He's being taunted by the members of the circle. He's prodded, pushed, and teased from all sides. He gets frustrated and angrier with each jab and poke taken. The laughter of the bullies grows as he lunges for them in vain. The younger guys watch what's going on and do nothing—myself included. Finally, mercifully, someone enters the circle and puts their protective arms around Judge. 'Stop it, that's enough!' she yells. That someone was Mary Ellen Nugent. A hero of mine since that day."

Twenty-two years later, Mary joined her fellow "E-men" in meeting up with detectives from the 41st Precinct, one precinct over from where she had stood up to the bullies.

"When we arrived at the front of the building we saw detectives running in ahead of us," she would recall. "That isn't how we operate. We have certain procedures that we follow.

"Some detectives ran up towards the roof and some to the second floor. I have no idea why. We have heavy weapons and vests while they have much less. I think they were frustrated because he kept slipping out of their hands.

"The apartment was on the first floor in the back right corner. Someone did open the door. There was screaming right away. His sister, I think. It was her apartment. Davis ran to the bedroom in the back."

Detective Thomas McCarren stood framed in the doorway and called out to Davis. Davis's toddler nephew then emerged from the bathroom.

"Which put him in between us and Davis. So Davis decided that it was a good time to start shooting because we wouldn't shoot back."

A .45 caliber bullet hit Mary directly in the mouth.

"It did feel like slow motion," she would later say of what had seemed to be her last moment. "I could feel the bullet cutting my lip. It was a very violent thing to happen to my body. I felt like there was ice in my veins. I could feel the ice branching out. I was in my own world even though I could hear the shooting. I thought I was going to die on some stranger's floor."

Mary experienced a greatly accelerated equivalent of the five stages of acceptance.

"About a half second for each. Denial, anger, etc. It was, 'Oh no, oh crap, oh well, etc.'"

She thought of her daughter, Fiona, who was conceived and born during the police layoffs and was now about to turn nine.

"I asked God not to let me die while she was so young."

And somebody else flashed to mind.

"I actually did think of Steven McDonald, because I thought the bullet went straight back to my spine."

Mary had somehow survived and remained in full command of her limbs when she arrived at Bellevue. The doctors said she would still need surgery, and a fellow female officer told her that she should go ahead and have a good cry.

"My mother said 'Don't cry. If you start you will never stop,'" Mary would recall.

Mary was able to celebrate her own daughter's ninth birthday at the hospital. The following day was Thanksgiving, and Fiona was back at Bellevue, in the cafeteria with her mother and two of the other wounded Bronx cops and their families, as well as Steven and Patti Ann, along with Nina and Father Mychal. Mulheren the Night Mayor had organized a turkey dinner.

Also present was the actual Santa from the Macy's Thanksgiving Parade, successor to the one Steven had seen two decades before as he stood curbside with his uniformed father. Mary's face was still discolored and swollen. She had a literally wounded smile as she posed for a photo with Fiona and Santa.

"All I want for Christmas is my five front teeth," Mary told him.

Fiona later wrote Santa a letter.

"She said she believed in him because he was a miracle and her mother being alive is a miracle, and he didn't have to bring any gifts, but if he wanted to, he could leave some," Mary would remember.

Mary was discharged from the hospital the following week, pending a return to have her jaw wired. There remained the manhunt for Larry Davis and that drama briefly had the city's attention. A captain called Mary on December 6 to say Davis had surrendered.

"It felt good," Mary said simply.

CHAPTER 13

Meanwhile, opening arguments in Shavod Jones's trial had begun the day before Thanksgiving. Steven would have been the star witness had he been able to appear in the courtroom and speak. The prosecutor told the jury that if necessary, Steven could be videotaped answering yes or no questions with a nod or a shake of the head. His testimony was not needed. A jury of eight women and four men convicted Jones of attempted murder after two hours of deliberations.

"I had no desire to go to the court," Patti Ann later said. "I just remember being upset hearing that the doctor that got on the stand said that Steven would never be the same. You still had the hope that eventually one day he would have gotten out of the [wheel]chair, but the doctor was adamant that this is not going to happen, this is the way he's going to be for the rest of his life."

Patti Ann's due date was nearing, and Nina made sure that a delivery kit was in any vehicle that transported her in the event the baby arrived before expected. Nina understood that to lose this child was to lose hope, for this was Steven's one and only chance to be a father.

Whatever kind of father he might be able to be.

As Christmas approached, Steven prepared to make his first venture outside the hospital and attend midnight Mass at St. Patrick's Cathedral. He wanted to thank the city for all its love and support and decided this might be the right time and place. He could mouth the words beforehand, and Patti Ann could read a transcription aloud from the lectern.

Mulheren the Night Mayor figured how to ensure Steven was attached to a functioning ventilator the entire time. But a winter storm swept into the city, and with it came the possibility that he could catch a dangerous chill in the icy rain and biting wind.

At midnight, Steven and Patti Ann watched the Mass on the television in his room.

"My top religious news story of 1986 is at Bellevue hospital at this very moment," they heard the cardinal say. "Police Officer Steven McDonald has been lying in a hospital bed now, for more than five months, with his bride of thirteen months constantly at his side, always praying with him."

The cardinal asked rhetorically what made this news.

"Many police officers have been shot," he noted.

He sought to explain why Steven was different.

"It's almost as if all the world's suffering can be summed up and placed in that hospital bed with Steven McDonald."

The cardinal reported that Steven and Patti Ann's faith had never faltered, "Not for one single instant."

"Time after time, their doctors have told them that humanly, there is no hope, medically, there can be no progress. Time after time, Steven and Patti Ann had insisted that a miracle will take place. To me, this is the miracle. This is the meaning of Christmas."

Even as Steven felt the urgency of impending fatherhood, his prolonged hospital stay continued to blur days into nights. And when his mind turned anxious, it was intensified by the enforced physical stillness. Nina put on music and told Steven that the little bit he was able to tilt his head from side to side was still enough to move to it.

"We going to bounce to the music," she told him.

Steven made a tentative attempt.

"Look at that white boy, ain't got no rhythm," she said. "Come on, Steven, with the beat now…Come on, you off the beat."

They laughed together and kept bouncing. He was soon *on the beat* with her, keeping time, that little bit of motion as in sync with the rhythm as if he were dancing again.

"He could *bounce*," Nina later said.

Between bouncing sessions, Steven would pass the long hours by watching videos. The newspapers correctly reported that he played his favorite, *The Quiet Man* with John Wayne and Maureen O'Hara, again and again. He received a surprise visitor.

"Steven, she's here," Nina said.

"Who?" Steven asked.

"Maureen O'Hara!" Nina replied.

The actress had heard of Steven's passion for the movie. The woman whom Steven had seen on the screen countless times now stepped up to his bedside.

"You ever seen a boy in love?" Nina later asked. "I think this was his second love. That day lifted that man up to glory."

Steven watched *The Quiet Man* yet again, only this time with O'Hara perched beside him. The movie came to the scene where she slaps John Wayne.

"I hit him so hard, my arm hurt for a week," she told Steven.

The real-life heroine to Steven and Nina and the cops and everybody was Patti Ann. She was a constant presence, all the more a marvel for being pregnant in the midst of everything.

As the delivery date approached, Patti Ann could have arranged to have the baby at Bellevue, but she decided to stay with the Long Island ob-gyn she picked at the start of her pregnancy. The big moment was near when the doctor told Officer Dalia to take her shopping and get her to walk around. Dalia drove her to a mall, and they roamed from store to store before heading to her mother's house.

Early the next morning, Patti Ann called Steven at Bellevue to say she had gone into labor and was heading to Mercy Hospital on Long Island with a family friend who had been filling in as a Lamaze partner. Steven waited and wondered and prayed.

At 3:36 p.m. on January 21, 1987, the phone in Steven's room rang. Six months and ten days after the shooting, he had a son. He and Patti Ann had already decided on the name Conor, after the main character in the novel *Trinity*, his favorite book as listed on his NYPD recruit questionnaire. She had been using the name at Bellevue during the toughest times, even before they knew the baby was a boy.

"Steven, you have Conor coming," Patti Ann would tell him. "You got to keep going."

Mulheren the Night Mayor had arranged for a video fax link to the nursery, but the images on the device's small screen were too blurry for Steven to make out anything but exasperatingly vague forms. The police surgeon Gregory Fried then arrived with a video that he had made in the nursery with Patti Ann's blessing.

On the same screen where he had watched *The Quiet Man* and dozens of other movies, Steven now beheld *the boy*. Steven mouthed a single word when Fried asked him how he felt.

"Overwhelmed."

The front page of the next morning's *New York Daily News* announced SON A JOY TO BEHOLD. Steven remarked to Nina that he had not actually beheld his son. He understood that would not happen until Patti Ann had recovered enough from the C-section delivery to bring Conor in.

On the morning of the fourth day, a Saturday, Patti Ann's doctor figured she was strong enough but warned her not to carry anything. That included Conor, so Dalia carried him as they proceeded from the unmarked car into Bellevue. They were nearing the elevator to Steven's room when Dalia decided it would be better to risk having Patti Ann carry the baby than for Steven's first sight of the boy to be of another cop holding the son he himself would never be able to hold.

Steven had not guessed the surprise in the works, even when Nina departed from the usual morning routine of letting him go back to sleep after he was fed and dressed. Nina had instead gotten him up and into a wheelchair that she then parked facing the window. He had gazed out at the East River and drifted off when he was roused by tickling at his ear. He opened his eyes.

There was Conor, looking so much like him, his tiny arms and legs moving as they had been when Patti Ann's tummy was pressed to his face, but now right there before him.

"It was as if I could move my own arms and legs again," he would recall.

He mouthed a single word.

"Wow."

CHAPTER 14

O n the very day that Conor McDonald was born, Shavod Jones was given the maximum for a juvenile in such circumstances, three and a third to ten years in prison.

"Nobody really knows me," Shavod had told the judge when asked if he had anything to say. "They just know who they say I am."

Those words of Shavod. The Prayer of St. Francis. The love for and of Patti Ann. The wisdom of Nina. The reality of his son. The reality of what he could never do with Conor. The question of what *could* he do as a father.

Steven's worries swirled and churned and tumbled even as the physical weight of his immobilized head continued to cause him excruciating pain. He could bounce a bit to music with Nina Justiniano, but when sitting up he still had difficulty shifting the burden on the top of his spinal column. He could only mouth a request to have himself reclined.

Nina continued to assist him with a physical ordeal that few could imagine. It included the agony of having a trach cuff periodically replaced just above where sensation began. There was also the indignity of a procedure known as the bowel program every other day that began with a nurse setting things in motion with a digit. And the arms that would not obey his commands were periodically seized by involuntary spasms, causing them to flail uncontrollably, making it impossible to sleep.

The solution with the arms was to spread them out and tie them down with bedsheets. And there he would lie in cruciform at the still and tumultuous center of an intimately epic struggle against anger and despair.

After the spasms passed, Nina would set his arms back at his sides. Steven's internal thrashing and grappling would continue, and Nina had the sense of witnessing a battle for something essential.

"The spirit of the city," she later said.

When hope faltered, he sometimes asked Nina to pull his blanket up over his head so he was enveloped in darkness. He would drift off and forget where he was and panic when he awoke.

The department surgeon Fried was present on February 3, when Monsignor Kowsky came into the room and announced that it was St. Blaise's Day. Blaise is the patron saint of those suffering throat ailments, and Kowsky gave Steven a special blessing. Fried was Jewish but was inspired to test a theory he had.

Fried told Steven that if they increased the input of the ventilator, they should be able to deflate the balloon in the trach cuff enough that air would pass over his vocal cords while he still got enough oxygen. Steven agreed to let Fried try it.

A rasping whisper soon followed.

"Hello," Steven said.

Fried dialed Patti Ann at home and put the receiver to Steven's mouth. She picked up to hear three rasped syllables.

"I love you."

The voice was faint, but she recognized it right away.

"It was him," she later said.

A short time later, Cardinal O'Connor came to visit. Steven greeted him with his newly regained ability to speak.

"It's a miracle," the cardinal exclaimed.

The true miracle for Steven was Conor, who continued to amaze him each time Patti Ann brought the boy into the room. She would set Conor on the bed beside Steven's head, and he would feel the movements directly. Steven would breathe in the new baby smell.

The scent of gunpowder at the shooting had been as acrid as hate and anger. The new baby smell was as sweet as possibility itself, and a decision now emerged distinct from the tumult of Steven's thoughts and emotions. He knew what kind of father he was going to be. He appeared to Nina to acquire a glow as he whispered words that reached her as if shouted from a mountaintop.

"I want to forgive him."

CHAPTER 15

Conor McDonald's christening was set for March 1, which would also be Steven's thirtieth birthday. Steven decided that it would be the right time for the letter of thanks to the city he had planned to offer at the cathedral on Christmas Eve.

And now he had something more to say.

Every new day brought ordeals and frustrations that challenged Steven's decision regarding the person responsible for it all. The morning of the christening presented the added task of being dressed appropriately. A suit coat would have been difficult to put on him, and a ventilator connection occupied the place where a tie's knot would have been drawn. Patti Ann instead brought a nice green shirt and an easily stretched pale yellow argyle V-neck sweater. His outfit was completed with slacks and polished shoes.

As the time neared, Steven was set in a wheelchair rigged so the ventilator would move along with him. He was wheeled into the Chapel of Our Lady Helper of the Sick in Bellevue Hospital. His head was propped up with two small pieces of wood. A silver fount was set on a large plywood tray affixed before him.

Steven's brother Thomas, now sixteen, and Patti Ann's sister Julie stood as the godparents, each holding a lit white candle. Patti Ann cradled Conor in a white baptismal gown as the cardinal performed the rite. Conor cried out as the water trickled over his forehead. Steven smiled. Patti Ann then lifted Steven's hand and traced the sign of the cross on Conor's forehead.

A number of cops were in the line for communion, and several were moved to join family members in touching Steven's cheek or kissing his crown.

The room was too small to accommodate the attendant media mob, so it was decided that Steven's statement would be delivered in the larger

Protestant chapel next door. Steven could still not speak above a whisper, and his dictated words had been typed on three sheets of paper and handed to Patti Ann. She now began to read aloud.

"I became a police officer to help the people of New York in any small way I could," the statement said. "My father and grandfather before me had the same dream. When I first wore the badge of a police officer, I was so proud to and hoped that I would be able to live up to its tradition of courage and compassion."

It went on, "There is no group of men and women who care as much about this city as the men and women of the New York City Police Department."

It continued, "On some days, when I am not feeling very well, I can get angry. But I have realized that anger is a wasted emotion, and that I have to remember why I became a police officer. I'm sometimes angry at the teenage boy who shot me."

Patti Ann seemed to have difficulty reading these words. She steadied herself and kept reading.

"But more often I feel sorry for him. I only hope that he can turn his life into helping and not hurting people."

Then came the transformative sentence that did indeed bring pardon to injury, faith to doubt, light to darkness.

"I forgive him and hope that he can find peace and purpose in his life."

For a stunned moment, the only sound was the working of Steven's ventilator.

The letter proceeded to thank New Yorkers for "helping me more than I ever could have helped them, as much as I tried," adding, "Our lives have been touched by new friends, who have brought us hope in times of despair, joy out of tears. Let me tell you, there is more love in this city than there are street corners."

The letter recounted the remarkable visit from Maureen O'Hara. "She became a good friend, and we are so happy she is here to witness the christening of our baby boy."

O'Hara stood nearby, crying real tears along with Mayor Ed Koch and even the reporters. They listened as Steven's letter again expressed his gratitude for the city's love, going on to say, "But I ask you to remember this: I chose the life of a police officer with all its risks."

Steven's fondness for the Mets did not keep him from echoing Lou Gehrig's famous farewell speech at Yankee Stadium in 1939: "I believe I am the luckiest man on the face of the earth."

The letter ended with "I only ask you to remember the less lucky, the less fortunate than I am and who struggle for the dignity of life without the attention and without the helping hands that have given me life."

Steven could do nothing to stem or wipe away his tears, and a nurse dabbed the corners of his eyes. The sound of the ventilator continued, each mechanical huff a reminder of the magnitude of what Steven was forgiving. The chapel then filled with applause.

But Steven's decision to forgive his assailant was met with silence among many of his fellow cops across the city. They did not want to voice even a word of disapproval for a comrade who had been so grievously wounded.

"It wasn't up for a lot of discussion," recalls retired homicide detective

Walter "Call Me Bill" Clark, who later became the model for two of the main characters in the TV show *NYPD Blue*. "It was a sensitive subject."

The policewoman who had been shot in the mouth by Larry Davis was among those cops who had no problem with Steven's decision.

"I was fine with Steven forgiving the boy who shot him," Mary Buckley later said.

She added, "As far as me forgiving Larry Davis, I may have been able to forgive him for shooting me since that was his 'job.' Good guy versus bad guy. However, he lied about me, and that was pretty unforgivable."

She figured he "probably assumed I was one of the guys until he heard the news the next day. Smart enough to know that I would be a sympathetic figure, he said I ordered the other officers to kill him. 'Kill the Black n—r' were the words he accused me of saying. My daughter was very upset and asked me if I really said that. She was nine years old. I have to say it is not a word that I use. So it's not just what he did to me, it's what he did to my family. I wasn't filled with hate, but I didn't feel the need to say I forgave him. No one asked me if I did, anyway."

Steven remained one of their own, as hundreds of them made clear as they marched past a TV camera set up on the route of the St. Patrick's Day parade a fortnight later. Steven had marched in his first parade as a cop four months before the shooting, and he had gone up Fifth Avenue literally following in the footsteps of his father and grandfather in earlier years. He watched the 1987 parade on television from Bellevue, hearing cop after cop after cop say his name as they passed the microphone.

"Steven...Steven...Steven...Steven."

On April 21, crowds of civilians lined the route as Steven departed Bellevue in the same rolling emergency room that had brought him there from Metropolitan Hospital ten months before. He was taken to a nearby heliport, and an NYPD helicopter flew him to LaGuardia Airport. He was there loaded onto a plane belonging to Craig Hospital, a rehabilitation facility outside Denver, Colorado.

JOURNEY OF HOPE the next morning's front page of the *New York Post* proclaimed.

People had begun calling Steven McDonald a hero.

"He was my hero long before July 12, 1986," Thomas later corrected.

At Craig, Steven underwent seven months of physical therapy that helped him better cope with what could not be changed. He learned to maneuver a mechanized wheelchair, steering it around orange plastic cones by puffing and sipping on a pair of plastic straws attached to a computerized motor. Patti Ann was told to give it a try, so as to better understand the difficulty of what he was working to master.

Five days before Thanksgiving, Steven flew to Kennedy Airport on a jet provided by FedEx.

"If I could have, I would have gotten down and kissed the ground, because I love New York," Steven told reporters.

Little Conor came toddling up to him, having taken his first steps while his daddy was away learning how to move, too.

Waiting a few feet away was a specially equipped van that Colorado cops and firefighters had chipped in to buy. A ramp at the back hoisted the wheelchair so Steven could roll in. He finally headed toward home—a year and a half after he left to work a four-to-midnight.

Only he was not returning to the one-bedroom apartment. Two Wall Street executives had purchased the McDonalds a $200,000 home in Malverne, just down the block from Patti Ann's parents. The house had needed to be remodeled to fit Steven's particular needs, and the PBA had held a benefit at the Jacob Javits Convention Center attended by eight thousand. Dozens of neighbors and friends and fellow cops had donated money and labor. The refurbished house's features included a roll-in shower and a lift to get Steven to a second-floor bedroom.

A California company had installed a computer system called Home Automation Link, or HAL, coincidentally the same name as the one in the movie *2001: A Space Odyssey*. This completely benevolent HAL could be programmed to recognize Steven's voice and convey commands via a wireless microphone affixed to his wheelchair. Steven was no longer able to regulate his own body temperature, but he would be able to adjust the thermostat in the house. He would also be able to control the lift, open and close doors, turn the lights on and off, and operate the TV.

Those who had pitched in, along with hundreds of other well-wishers, were waiting with welcome home signs and balloons when a whoop of sirens announced that the McDonalds and their police escort were almost there.

The NYPD Emerald Society Pipes and Drums struck up "The Minstrel Boy" and "The Wearing of the Green." Mayor Koch was also there, and he again had tears in his eyes when he presented them with a golden key to their new home.

"It's too cold for a speech," Koch said. "God bless this house. We're annexing this ground to New York City."

Steven was wearing his shield from a chain around his neck, just as he had been when he approached the teens in Central Park. He had fully regained his ability to speak and now addressed the mayor and the crowd with an NYPD radio code.

"I'm ten ninety-eight," he announced.

That meant available to resume patrol.

PART
II

CHAPTER 1

On February 28, 1988, a gunman dispatched by a jailed drug dealer stepped out of the early-morning darkness and shot twenty-two-year-old rookie Police Officer Edward Byrne three times in the head as he sat alone in a radio car, guarding the home of a witness.

More than ten thousand cops turned out for the funeral, standing six deep in formation outside a Long Island church, the biggest such showing in memory. Their very number demonstrated their outrage that a comrade so young had been murdered that way.

"It could have happened to anyone out there, any time," said Officer Pete Maginnis, also twenty-two. "We can't let it happen again."

Steven McDonald was there, in dress uniform, though putting on the jacket had been a considerable challenge. His helpers at home had finally deduced that the thing to do was extend his arms as straight up as possible, slide the sleeves over them, then bring the rest of it back over his head and down behind him.

Steven now began to roll in his wheelchair past block after block of fellow officers whose feelings about forgiving anybody who shoots a cop could have only been hardened by this latest killing. The sight of him nonetheless appeared to stir something deep in them—the finest in the Finest. One cop and then another and then another and soon all of them began to applaud, their clapping muffled by their white gloves.

Eighteen days later, Steven was able to join his fellow cops in the St. Patrick's Day parade. He began the route with Patti Ann and Conor, now fourteen months old, but she and the boy only went the half dozen blocks to the cathedral. They remained in the cardinal's residence as Steven continued on.

Here was a day Irish eyes really were smiling, and none more brightly than Steven's, even though he had yet to completely master steering the wheelchair over long distances and veered more than he would have liked. At moments he grew short of breath from puffing on the steering straw, but he kept on.

A dour side of the Irish presented itself when the Hibernians in charge of the parade complained that Steven was slowing up the march. They cited a regulation that banned floats from the parade and decreed that this included motorized wheelchairs.

"They said that Steven was a float," an incredulous Patti Ann later reported.

That October, two police officers were shot to death in separate incidents on the same day. Chris Hoban, age twenty-six, was working undercover narcotics when suspicious drug dealers made him hold up his arms to be searched.

"He looked like he was being crucified," his partner later said of this moment before the dealers shot and killed Hoban.

Two and a half hours later and fifty blocks uptown, Michael Buczek, age twenty-five, and his partner had just responded to a report of a woman with stomach pains. They were emerging from the lobby of the woman's building when they encountered two men who were just coming in. The cops sensed something and called for them to stop. One of the men suddenly opened fire. Buczek fell, mortally wounded.

Hoban and Buczek received a joint funeral in a Brooklyn church even though they had not known each other. Steven attended, but the sight of two coffins covered with the NYPD flag being carried from Our Lady of Perpetual Help hardly encouraged forgiveness among the twelve thousand cops who stood at attention outside.

"We were at war," Detective Malcolm Reiman would recall. "It was a war in the streets then."

Reiman would add, "I came on this job to catch the predators. I could not understand or accept forgiveness for a cop shooter."

Yet, there was Steven McDonald, again in his dress uniform, determined and unwavering, still impossible to condemn, even at a double police funeral.

The following month, Steven wheeled himself into a Bronx courtroom for the first day of the Larry Davis trial.

Davis had already been tried and acquitted for the quadruple homicide that had sent the detectives searching for him in the first place. He was now charged with shooting the six cops as they sought to arrest him.

"The drama of the trial was heightened by the pervasive sound in the courtroom of the rasping wheezes of the respirator attached to [Steven] McDonald," the *New York Times* reported.

The lead defense attorney, radical activist William Kunstler, understood that Steven's presence represented a threat to his strategy. Kunstler complained to reporters outside the courtroom of "indecent…police histrionics," saying Steven was there to "constantly remind the jury of police victims."

The same year Steven was shot, a group of corrupt cops in the 77th Precinct in Brooklyn had been indicted for robbing and shaking down drug dealers. Kunstler now alleged to the jury in his opening arguments that Davis had only been acting in self-defense against a similar "gang of corrupt police officers" who had first enlisted him to sell drugs when he was just fifteen. Kunstler said that after the scandal in the 77th Precinct, the cops in the Bronx who had been using Davis "became worried about him because he might tell on them or would run away with their money."

"The police will never admit that they were ever in league with Larry Davis or that they fired the first bullet," Kunstler said, telling the jurors that he was going to lead them through "the murky world of police corruption."

He promised, "You'll see how the police treat young third-world people in the depressed communities of our city."

A reporter asked Steven why he was there, and he only replied that he planned to attend every day. His presence was his statement. He represented what police officers risk, what could have happened to any of these wounded cops. Those rhythmic wheezes of the ventilator filling every momentary hush was a sound from the vivid world of police sacrifice.

The next day's newspapers reported Kunstler's charge that Steven was a "pawn" of the PBA. *New York Daily News* columnist Gail Collins wrote that "there cannot be two more different cop-shooting cases."

"This case is not about what happened to Steven McDonald," Collins opined.

The then PBA president, Phil Caruso, may have lost his nerve and asked Steven not to return to the trial.

The hush in the courtroom was absent any whooshing when Mary Buckley stepped up to the witness stand.

She would remember that the anticipation was the worst part of testifying, because she feared her words might be twisted into something that would hurt the case.

In a tone the *New York Times* described as "quiet but firm," Mary testified that when she and the other cops entered the apartment, Davis had dashed into a rear bedroom. She remembered Detective Thomas McCarren calling on Davis to surrender.

"The next thing I heard was a shot," she testified. "And the same second I could feel it almost like a knife cutting through my lip at first, and then I don't know if I could describe it as an explosion or a jolt, but it was so violent."

She recalled telling herself, "This is it" and "You are going to die on a stranger's floor." Her thoughts had gone to her young daughter.

"I didn't want to leave her," she said.

Mary recalled that as she was rushed into the hospital, "I kept feeling the back of my head to see where the bullet came out. It felt like I had a hole through my mouth."

She testified that she had since undergone 135 hours of dental work.

"A lot of pain," she noted.

The prosecutor sought to counter the defense contention that Davis had only fired in self-defense.

"How many shots did you hear before you were struck by gunfire?" the prosecutor asked.

"I was struck by the first shot," Mary replied.

"The very first shot?" the prosecutor asked.

"Yes," Mary said.

"Are you certain of that?" the prosecutor asked.

"Absolutely," Mary said.

Mary periodically looked over at the jury box. She would recall, "One of the jurors was wearing a Spuds McKenzie T-shirt and fell asleep while I was testifying."

Mary was not allowed to attend the trial while other witnesses were testifying, but she was permitted to sit in during the summations. She only then learned that a forensics expert had testified that a hole from a shotgun slug was in a dresser drawer in the room where Davis had been. The expert indicated that the shot had been fired from inside the bedroom.

"We had all testified that we weren't in the bedroom," Mary later said. "I know I got shot right away, but I don't see how anyone could have gotten into the bedroom. There were only three shotguns. Everyone was backing out."

Mary now watched Stewart hold up the drawer.

"If they lied about this, they lied about everything," Stewart said.

After deliberating for five days, the jury found Davis not guilty of the top charge, attempted murder. Davis was convicted of weapons charges, including possession of the .45 caliber pistol that had been used to shoot Mary. But that was little comfort to her and the other cops.

"After the trial I was angry," she later said. "I felt I had been a good police officer and treated people with respect."

And Mary still could not forgive Davis for having said she used the N-word and for that having reached her daughter.

"So, it's not just what he did to me; it's what he did to my family," she later said.

Mary's daughter, Fiona, was now twelve and wrote a letter to the defense lawyers.

Dec. 2, 1988
Mr. Kunstler and Ms. Stewart,
    I am Mary Buckley's 12-year-old daughter. Please stop lying! I know for a darn fact that my mother's not a druggy (drug dealer.) If she was, do you think we'd live in a rut like downtown Yonkers? . . . You liars had some kids in my class believing that I lived in a drug house. I never thought seventh graders could be so stupid. Damn you to hell!

> Your archenemy,
> Fiona B. (signed)
> FIONA BUCKLEY

On December 15, Davis appeared for sentencing on the weapons charges. Steven was among more than six hundred off-duty cops who demonstrated outside the courthouse, demanding that Davis receive the maximum. Steven did not believe that personal forgiveness meant escaping punishment for possessing weapons that wounded six fellow cops.

"We bleed—Davis walks," several signs read.

Mary was inside the courtroom along with four of the other wounded cops when Davis rose to address the court.

"Give me the same sentence you would give your own son in similar circumstances," he said. "The prosecution is trying to get you to do what they could not, convict me and sentence me because I defended myself."

Kunstler argued that Davis should get the same six-month sentence given subway vigilante Bernhard Goetz, who had also been acquitted of attempted murder but convicted of possessing the gun with which he shot four teens in 1984.

The judge described Davis as "a violent, gun-carrying acknowledged crack and cocaine dealer" who had kept weapons and narcotics in the apartment where his sister's two young children lived. Davis was sentenced to a term of five to ten years.

"He still got away with what he did to us," Mary would later say.

Mary had taken the sergeant's promotional exam, and her name had reached the top of the list when she had still been out sick, undergoing an extended nightmare of reconstructive oral surgery. Any number of people had advised her to put in for a disability pension and get three-quarters of her salary, tax-free, for the rest of her life.

"People kept telling me I should apply, but I didn't want to," she would remember. "I told them that I would apply if Davis was acquitted. I really didn't think that would happen."

When the acquittal actually came to pass, Mary was a sergeant who had returned to patrolling a city where homicides had gone from 1,582 the year that she and Steven were shot to 1,672 in the following year and up to 1,896 in 1988, despite the efforts of thousands of cops. She retired ten months after the acquittal and was required to turn in her sniper's rifle. Through the scope on that rifle, she had protectively witnessed everything from hostage situations to President Ronald Reagan's appearance at the Statue of Liberty's centennial on July 4, 1986.

"I was surprised at how bad I felt," she later said of relinquishing the weapon. "I had to go out and walk around for a while. I guess it was the finality of it that got me."

At the annual NYPD Medal Day, Mary was awarded the Combat Cross. The aftereffects of being shot went beyond dental repair and deeper than she initially knew. She got a measure of that when she was parking her car and heard another car backfire in the distance.

"Right away, I could smell gunpowder," she would recall.

A fuller and more surprising measure would come years later, when she went to see the 1996 movie *Courage under Fire*, in which Meg Ryan plays a soldier who is killed in action during the Gulf War.

"Fiona had seen it and said it made her think of me," Mary would recall. "The funeral scene got to me. Meg Ryan had a daughter about the same age that Fiona was in 1986. They did the flyover, and I guess it was the little girl—whatever—I started to cry so badly that I had to get up and leave the theater and go to the lobby. I was sobbing, and I am not one to cry. It was about ten years after, and I was shocked at my reaction."

During the decade in between, she continued to help others. Her cop days done, she enrolled in nursing school. She then saw a help wanted ad in *Nursing Spectrum* magazine for St. Francis Friends of the Poor, founded by a trio of Franciscan priests who had converted three SRO hotels in Manhattan into residences for the mentally ill. The state had largely emptied out the psychiatric institutions on the theory that the patients would fare better in the community, which in New York City meant they ended up on the street or in the subways.

"I thought being in the PD was pretty good as far as experience with mental health was concerned," she later said.

She was hired.

"They took a chance on me, and it worked out well for all of us," she reported. "I love my St. Francis people. Both the priests and the tenants."

Mary enjoyed working with the chronically mentally ill, particularly with the schizophrenics, perhaps partly because they were the ones most in need.

"I think schizophrenia is sadder than cancer," she later said.

She looked back at the life that might have ended on a stranger's floor of a Bronx apartment.

"When I was a young woman, I assumed I would marry a cop or a fireman, have two or three kids in a house in Rockland County, and go back to work when they were in school," she said.

She had in fact married a cop, then divorced and married again and had a daughter. But she had not kept to what had seemed preordained. She had not just become somebody's wife.

"Years later, I realized that I was an NYPD sergeant with my own car and house. I had grown up to be the man I always thought I would marry."

CHAPTER 2

In an effort to save Shavod Jones, Steven sought to arrange a meeting with his assailant. Steven told doubters that he viewed it as following up on a case, just as veteran cops often do.

"As far as I'm concerned, I'm still on the job," he said. "I've got seventeen years until I retire."

He added, "This is a terrible thing, but something good can come out of it. I don't want it to destroy two lives. I don't want him to think his life is over because he's done this to me."

Shavod's lawyer had drowned on a trip to Brazil, but his wife, Regina Darby, was also an attorney, and she had taken over the case.

Steven asked a friend to deliver some stationery and stamps to Darby along with a note to Shavod he had dictated.

"Let's carry on a dialogue. Please write if you have time."

Steven received a call from Darby saying that she did not think it advisable for Shavod to respond, as he had an appeal pending. Darby suggested she might be able to arrange a meeting between Steven and her client's mother.

A day and time were set. Sharron Harris was seated in Darby's office when Steven arrived. The blankness of her expression suggested to Steven that she viewed him as an enemy who was responsible for her son being in jail. She remained silent as Darby spoke.

"Mrs. Harris would like to know your intentions," Darby said.

Steven had not imagined that he, as the victim, would be asked what motives he might have beyond offering forgiveness. He replied that he hoped to speak with Shavod, perhaps counsel him, keep him from being claimed by the streets.

Steven looked at Sharron, whose eyes went from Darby to the wall.

"Something good can be made out of something bad," Steven said to her. "Shavod can start over and make something out of his life."

She said not a word to him.

"They couldn't trust me," Steven later said. "My intentions were misunderstood. It was like, 'What bad am I up to now?'"

By then Steven and Patti Ann had joined writer E. J. Kahn III in producing *The Steven McDonald Story*, an as-told-to account of the shooting and the two ensuing years. A subsequent edition acquired a new chapter that began with Shavod's grandmother, Leonora Jones, calling Cardinal O'Connor's office several weeks after Steven met with Shavod's mother.

Leonora said she wanted to meet with Steven. "Diamond Dave" Martelli drove him in the van on Palm Sunday to where she worshipped, the Convent Avenue Baptist Church in Harlem. Steven went in a side door to avoid reporters and photographers who had gotten word of the meeting. He noted that a painting of Jesus Christ hung between pictures of Abraham Lincoln and John F. Kennedy. Images of the same three hung on the wall of the room at home where he underwent his continuing physical therapy.

"Personal heroes," Steven later said.

As the parishioners came in for the service, many paused to welcome Steven. The choir had begun to sing when an elderly woman approached.

"I'm Leonora Jones," she said. "Shavod's grandmother."

"Hello, Mrs. Jones," Steven said. "I guess you know who I am. I'm hard to miss."

He saw her lower her head as if with guilt over his condition. He tried to dispel it with a smile and words to match the spirit that filled the church.

"I'm happy to finally meet you," he said. "You're a fine woman."

She answered with a smile of her own, but it quickly faded as he watched her eye the entirety of him in the wheelchair, being kept alive by the air whooshing into a hole in his throat via a blue translucent tube. She shook her head almost imperceptibly.

"Oh God," she said.

She managed another smile and sat. She looked at him repeatedly during the service, but did not speak to him again until the end.

"Shavod really is a good boy," she told him. "He needs help."

"Yes, I know," Steven said.

"Can you help him?" she asked.

"I can."

"Please try."

Steven gave her his phone number.

As Steven rolled out past them, worshippers applauded him just as cops had at young Eddie Byrne's funeral. A teen who looked just a little younger than Shavod had been when he shot Steven was by the door, holding a box of floppy disks.

"You like computers?" Steven asked.

"I love 'em," the teen said.

"Keep loving 'em, and you'll make it," Steven said.

"Officer McDonald, thanks for being a good Christian," the teen said.

"That's nice of you to think so," Steven said.

Two months later, the phone rang in the McDonalds' home just as Steven and Patti Ann were preparing to head out to a fundraiser. Patti Ann's sister, Katie, had come to babysit Conor, and she answered.

"It's Shavod Jones," she said.

Steven would recall that everyone in the room save little Conor went silent and still. Somebody held the phone to Steven's ear.

"Officer McDonald?"

Steven heard rap music and jailhouse noise in the background. He did not immediately reply.

"Officer McDonald?"

The voice was softer than Steven would have expected. He would later compare it to that of a lost kid.

"Yup, this is Steve. Shavod, is that you?"

Steven heard somebody else shouting.

"Give it up, Buddha. Off the phone now!"

Steven knew that Buddha was Shavod's nickname.

"Are you okay to talk?" Steven asked him.

"I'm okay," Shavod said.

Steven then asked, "Shavod, what can I do for you?"

Steven was now the one who got no reply.

"Shavod?"

"I don't really know how to say it," Shavod finally said.

Shavod paused.

"I'd just like to say that I'm sorry for everything that has happened."

Steven was not immediatcly sure how to respond.

"I understand, Shavod," Steven finally said.

Steven then could think of no talk other than small talk.

"What are you doing to keep busy up there?"

Steven saw Patti Ann give him a look as if he had lost his mind.

"I work with my hands," Shavod said. "They have a shop up here. Some machinery. And I work with wood. But, I'd rather be someplace else."

"What do you mean?" Steven reflexively inquired.

"I'm getting along all right, but it's not like being home."

"You know your grandmother loves you. You know we've been doing some talking."

"I know."

Steven saw Patti Ann point to her watch.

"Shavod, I'm going to go now," Steven said. "I got to give a speech."

"Okay."

"But I want you to know that when you get out, I'll be there for you. You've got some good family who want you to make it. And you've got me, too."

"Thank you, Officer McDonald."

Shavod got off the phone. Steven started rolling toward the door and the waiting van.

"Come on, Patti Ann, we'll be late," he said.

She touched his face. He felt the softness of her hand.

"That wasn't easy for him, you know," Steven told her, adding "And I know it wasn't easy for you."

"I love you, Steven," she said. "I love you."

Some days later, one of the nurses Steven needed around the clock answered the phone and told him Shavod Jones was calling.

"I was wondering when you were going to call me again," Steven said. "I hope this is not some big con job. If you're going to change your life, it's going to take more than calling up a guy in a wheelchair."

Shavod told Steven that his family had sent him the as-told-to book.

"I cried, Mr. McDonald," Shavod said. "I cried when I read your book."

"Thank you for reading the book, Shavod. But crying's not going to help either one of us."

"Yeah, I know, but I feel so bad."

Steven suggested that when he got out Shavod could help build a new Boys Club being planned for Harlem.

"It would make your grandmother happy," Steven said.

"Is Patti Ann okay?" Shavod asked.

Steven did not reply.

"And your boy, Mr. McDonald?"

Steven said, "I love them more than my own life."

Shavod said, "Yeah...well, I won't bother you anymore now. Thanks for letting me call you. I'm going now."

"Goodbye, Shavod."

The conversations with Shavod were recounted in the chapter added to the new edition of *The Steven McDonald Story*. The additional pages concluded with Steven wondering aloud if he would want Shavod to become Conor's friend and maybe join the McDonalds at Christmas. Steven allowed that he was unsure if it would be fair to his wife and son to treat his would-be killer as a member of the family.

"But I have a feeling that our relationship has only begun," Steven said. "I have a feeling that if Shavod can begin his life again, then maybe there's even hope for me."

Such hope proved insufficient for the movie and television folks who had initially expressed interest in Steven's story.

"Producers ask, 'What's the payoff? Does he get up and walk at the end?'" Steven's lawyer and close friend, Peter Johnson, said. "They want a happy ending."

Steven did not get up and walk, but he did sometimes patrol Central Park in the van with Bobby Dalia. They had a police radio and were responding to a report of a crime in progress one night when Dalia had to put on the brakes. Steven came rolling forward from the rear of the van and slammed into the back of the driver's seat.

"Buckle that fucking thing up!" Dalia called out reflexively.

"I can't," Steven responded.

Steven and Dalia were not patrolling Central Park on the night of April 19, 1989, when a heinous crime further signaled the city's unraveling. A young woman was sexually assaulted and battered nearly to death while jogging near where Steven had been shot three years before. She was comatose when she was rushed to the same hospital.

Four days after the attack, Steven asked a detective to call the victim's family and inquire if he could visit. The family knew Steven's story and said he would be welcome.

Steven entered Metropolitan Hospital for the first time since he had been carried in at the edge of death. He spoke quietly with the victim's parents and two brothers. The family then took Steven in to see her.

Steven used the plastic straws to steer himself to her bedside. She remained in a coma, her ventilator whooshing in syncopation with the portable, battery powered one on the back of his wheelchair.

"Tubing lines coming out every place you could imagine," Steven later said.

Father Mychal Judge had come with Steven, and he placed a hand on the woman's battered head and blessed her. They all then formed a semicircle around the bed, and everyone joined hands save for the immobilized Steven.

The person on either side of him touched his unfeeling hands. Mychal led them in the Our Father and a Hail Mary, followed by the Prayer of St. Francis.

The woman awoke from her coma twelve days later with no memory of the attack. Five teenagers would be found guilty and would have already served their sentences when, in 2002, a convicted sex murderer confessed to being the sole assailant. Supporters of the Central Park Five would contend that they had been railroaded. More than a few cops would remain convinced that they were guilty, no matter what the DNA and other evidence indicated.

Steven stuck to a simple, often unpopular principle voiced in the prayer at the victim's bedside. Mychal watched it guide him through everything that hardened the hearts of those around him in the days ahead.

"Forgiveness," Mychal said. "We must forgive, or we cannot be."

Mychal noted of Steven, "This is the highest form of forgiveness I know of. You can say it, but to live it every day, when vengeance seems natural..."

Mychal added, "There's something deeper there than you and I know."

Mychal told the story of St. Francis inviting two of his young followers to join him in preaching the gospel. They walked the length of the town, and one of the followers said he thought they were going to preach the gospel.

"We just did," St. Francis told them.

Steven continued to preach with his simple, silent presence at police funerals and memorials and ceremonies. He and Mychal seemed to be the gospel come to present-day life on the many nights they traveled the city together. Mychal knew the name of seemingly every homeless person they encountered, Steven would offer a warm smile and kind words from his wheelchair.

"How are you doing?" he would ask.

The two sometimes paused by the water's edge at the foot of Manhattan, the twin towers of the World Trade Center rising behind them, the Statue of Liberty's upraised torch shining across the harbor. They also led pilgrimages of peace to Northern Ireland and of faith to Lourdes.

Steven and Mychal did differ over which mayoral candidate they favored in the 1989 Democratic primary. Mychal was fond of David Dinkins, who during World War II had been turned away from a Marine Corps recruiting station because he was Black and had simply gone to another station and then another and then another, until one finally accepted him. Dinkins had continued to persevere upon his return to civilian life, getting along by going and going and going along. He became a state assemblyman and then the city clerk. He was now seeking to become the city's first Black mayor.

Steven supported the incumbent, Ed Koch, who had been a constant presence at the hospital after he was shot and had been unceasingly supportive. Steven and Koch had formed a personal bond that was reaffirmed when they saw each other at every police funeral and academy graduation. Koch had Steven join him at the 1989 St. Patrick's Day Parade. Nobody was calling Steven an unauthorized float as he went up Fifth Avenue in a wheelchair with Conor in his lap, a smiling Koch marching at his side. Steven and Patti Ann agreed to make a campaign commercial in which they spoke of Koch as a friend of the cops.

Three weeks before the Democratic primary, a sixteen-year-old named Yusef Hawkins went to see a used car listed for sale in the then largely Italian American neighborhood of Bensonhurst in Brooklyn. A group of white thugs set upon Hawkins because he was Black and imagined he had come to date a local girl. Hawkins was beaten and fatally shot twice in the chest.

The murder added power to Dinkins's argument that he was a unifier whereas Koch was a figure of division. Dinkins beat Koch and went on to narrowly defeat the equally divisive Republican candidate, former prosecutor Rudolph Giuliani, in the general election. Steven had become a Dinkins supporter after the primary and attended his inauguration. Steven was particularly taken by a passage of the new mayor's address that described the city as a "gorgeous mosaic."

Steven echoed it ten days later, when he gave a speech of his own at an auditorium in Queens to a group of ninth grade students with learning disabilities. The students sat rapt as the lone figure in a wheelchair spoke from the stage.

"The real American has not yet arrived; he is in the crucible. He will be the fusion of all the peoples," Steven said.

Steven was paraphrasing the writer Israel Zangwill, whose play *The Melting Pot* coined the phrase and enthralled President Theodore Roosevelt at its 1909 opening.

"Don't listen to the people who are heartless, who don't care about you, who say you have no role to play," he said. "They are wrong."

Steven went on.

"The city needs everybody. You guys may not believe that, but it's true—everybody. People in wheelchairs, people who struggle."

New York had already seen its first Black police commissioner, Benjamin Ward, under Ed Koch. Ward had started as a patrolman in a largely Irish precinct in Brooklyn during the 1950s and had not been given a locker for three years, so he had to travel to and from work in his uniform. He was the deputy commissioner for community relations in 1972 when Police Officer Phillip Cardillo was killed in a Harlem mosque while answering an apparently bogus call that an officer there needed assistance.

An ensuing standoff ended after police allowed those inside—the killer almost certainly among them—to leave on the promise they would later present themselves at a nearby station house. The promise was not kept, and Ward was widely blamed for essentially letting a cop killer go. The deal was in fact brokered by Chief of Detectives Albert Seedman on orders from the top brass at headquarters, who may have themselves been acting at the behest of then Mayor John Lindsay.

Ward went on to be appointed commissioner by Ed Koch. He was extremely bright but became more widely known for his drinking than for his thinking. He was said to have shown up inebriated at a PBA gathering and urinated in a police helicopter as he departed. He vanished for three days at the time of what became known as the Palm Sunday massacre in 1984.

Police Officer Joanne Jaffe and her partner had been the first two cops on that scene, responding to a report of "people asphyxiated" on Liberty Avenue in Brooklyn. The cops entered a first-floor apartment to discover ten people shot to death, two women and eight children. One of the murdered women was sitting in front of the television with a spoon and some pudding still in her hands. She had been feeding a thirteen-month-old girl, who was on the floor, covered with blood. The baby's wailing signaled that she was alive.

Jaffe stood by the front door, holding the baby as more cops arrived, along with detectives and supervisors of ascending rank.

"I was in love with her," Jaffe would later say.

She asked the detective squad commander, Lt. Herbert Hohmann, if she could continue taking care of the baby. He checked with the Administration for Child Services (ACS) and reported the answer.

"No."

Jaffe sat with the baby in an unmarked car as it sped along the rain-slicked Belt Parkway, seeking to shake a press photographer. A front-page photo the next morning showed the baby nestled in Jaffe's arms in the back seat, sucking on a pacifier.

THE ONLY SURVIVOR, the headline read.

Jaffe left the baby in a Coney Island apartment with a foster family that had been arranged by ACS. She eventually went on to adopt the girl.

Ward proved to have been on a multistate bender with a mistress that ended with his car breaking down on the New Jersey Turnpike and asking an NYPD highway unit to come get him. He remained commissioner for another three years.

Upon taking office, David Dinkins appointed the city's second Black police commissioner, Lee Brown, who had run the police departments in Atlanta and Houston. Brown was a nonnative New Yorker, and his frequent travels earned him the nickname among cops Out of Town Brown.

Ten people were shot to death in an eight-hour period as New York began 1990. The year would see 2,245 homicides, an average of more than six a day. Thirty-nine children were shot to death. One was killed two days after his fifteenth birthday when he declined to exchange high fives with another teen on his family's doorstep in Brooklyn. His twin sister was just on the other side of the door, reaching to open it, when she heard him shout his last words.

"I got shot. I got shot. I'm going to die. I'm going to die."

A dozen youngsters were killed by stray rounds that summer, four in less than a fortnight. A trauma team at one Brooklyn hospital had just lost a fight to save the life of a three-year-old with a head wound when a one-year-old, also with a head wound, was brought in. They lost that fight as well.

But it was the September 2, 1990, killing of a twenty-two-year-old tourist from Utah that really roused the press. Brian Watkins had come to New York to see the US Open and had been in a Manhattan subway station with his family when they were set upon by a crew of teens. He was fatally stabbed as he moved to protect his mother after she was struck in the face and kicked in the chest.

DAVE DO SOMETHING! the *New York Post* demanded on its front page.

Dinkins was taken to task for not attending young Watkins's funeral in Utah. He privately said that he would then have had to explain why he did not attend the half dozen every day for murdered New Yorkers. The killing continued, and mothers in the tougher neighborhoods took to having their children sleep in a bathtub, instructing them to dive for the floor if they heard gunshots during their waking hours. A mother in a Brooklyn housing project noted that "stray bullets have no name" and said people in safer neighborhoods ought to "put themselves in our shoes for ten minutes."

"They should know how it feels to watch your children's pencils shake when they try to do their homework with the sound of gunshots outside," she said.

Two weeks after the Watkins killing, *Time* magazine ran a cover story titled "The Rotting of the Big Apple." The accompanying article reported that 58 percent of New Yorkers surveyed said they would rather live someplace else, and 60 percent worried about crime constantly.

"A surge of brutal killings has shaken the Big Apple to its core. Frightened residents now wonder if Gotham's treasures are worth the hassle," the magazine reported.

The following month, Dinkins announced a crime-fighting plan he called Safe Streets, Safe City. He released a fifty-seven-page report accompanied by a 535-page police manpower study.

"We will not wage war by degree," Dinkins declared. "Our strategy calls for an assault on all fronts."

The year ended with 2,245 homicides in New York, a record nearly tied in 1991, which logged 2,225. The 75th Precinct in Brooklyn had so many homicides that there was a whistle hanging by the log book that somebody blew each time there was a new one. That included a shooting in November 1991 at Thomas Jefferson High School, whose alumni ranged from actor Danny Kaye to Goldman Sachs CEO Lloyd Blankfein. A fourteen-year-old sophomore fatally gunned down a fellow student and critically wounded a computer science teacher. Among the witnesses was a teen who still had a bullet in his head and another in his shoulder from shootings outside the school. He was a friend of the sixteen-year-old victim and knelt beside him.

"He kept saying, 'Get me up.' The more he talked, he kept losing his voice," the witness later told a reporter. "He pointed toward his chest. I unbuttoned his collar. There was a hole in his neck."

Three months later, Dinkins scheduled a visit to the school to speak to the students about escaping the cycle of drugs and violence, with himself as a role model. He was due to arrive in seventy minutes when a fifteen-year-old shot to death two fellow students in a hallway a dozen strides from where two police officers were standing. The cops had been posted there after the earlier fatal shooting of the sixteen-year-old and the wounding of a teacher.

As the two latest victims were carried out, hundreds of students filed into the auditorium to hear their mayor.

"You have got to learn from this," Dinkins said. "You must learn from this. So please help me. Help your principal. Help yourselves."

The principal, Carol Burt-Beck, had determined that another four dozen of her pupils had been killed outside of school since she arrived there in 1987. She had established a "grieving room" where students could mourn lost friends.

"Anybody could just come up to you and shoot you," a fourteen-year-old named Eddie Alvarez told a reporter. "I've just grown used to it because I've lived here all my life."

CHAPTER 5

Throughout a city where gunshots set pencils trembling in the hands of children, Steven McDonald visited schools.

"This is probably the best place for me to be," Steven told a reporter one day as he rode in the van through Brooklyn. "A lot of these kids have relatives or friends who have been shot...And for me, it's a chance to dispel myths about cops, especially white cops."

One of his favorite questions came at an elementary school.

"How do you open your Christmas presents?" a youngster asked.

He also spoke at Bishop Loughlin High School, which his father had attended a half century before, then almost entirely white, now almost entirely minority. He rode onto the stage for the first of two assemblies in the auditorium with his shield on a chain around his neck. He sat as a solitary figure as he again delivered his message of forgiveness and of being thankful for what you do have.

"You may be thinking, 'What does *he* have to be thankful for?'" Steven said. "You'll just have to take my word for it. The words aren't always there, but I hope through my presence I've shown you that life is good."

Steven was addressing teens whose daily existence outside school called that into question. And they did not seem generally inclined just to take anybody's word for anything, including the word of a white quadriplegic cop on a ventilator

After a question-and-answer period in which there were neither, Steven sat in the faculty lunchroom. He, as usual, declined to eat in public lest he be embarrassed by the messy procedure that necessitated him being fed like a baby.

At the second assembly, Steven chose not to go up on the stage, but to remain down where the students sat. The awareness during lunch of being the only one not eating inspired him to speak of the many things people might not consider about his daily existence. He could not feed himself. He could not wash himself or dress himself or even scratch his nose. He could not tell hot from cold. He had continual spasms. He often had nightmares.

Steven then spoke of the teen who had shot him.

"He has had to struggle every bit as much as I have," Steven said. "Prison has not been a good experience for him. I hope when he returns to the community, he will never return to those destructive ways."

Steven was clear that his attitude didn't make him remarkable.

"I don't think I'm anybody special," he said.

He gazed at these kids who all had struggles of their own.

"I look up to you," he said. "I applaud you."

He smiled.

"Although I can't move my hands," he said.

The kids responded with their own hands, giving him a standing ovation.

"My love goes out to you!" a girl cried out.

"How could you forgive someone who's done this to you?" one boy inquired. "I couldn't."

Steven replied, "When I was shot, I was dying, and my family and I said all sorts of prayers. I wanted to be forgiven then for my sins, and if I was to be forgiven by God, I had to forgive Shavod Jones."

He added, "It hasn't always been easy to do that, but if I'm going to live my faith, if I want to get to heaven, this is what I must do."

CHAPTER 6

Steven was still exchanging letters with Shavod. Steven dictated his to a nurse. He signed them "Steven" with a pen held in his mouth, the handwriting slightly tremulous, but clear, the S upper case, the t crossed. He suggested that he might visit Shavod in prison.

Then Shavod asked Steven to lobby on his behalf with the parole board. Steven knew he would have considerable influence, but that only made the decision more difficult. Steven was not at all sure Shavod was ready to be returned to a city that had grown only more chaotic and violent.

Steven decided not to do as Shavod asked. The phone calls and letters from prison stopped. Steven also heard nothing more from the grandmother, whom he described to a reporter as "a sweet, kind woman." He keenly regretted not being able to do as he knew she wished.

"I don't think they were happy," Steven said.

Steven continued to travel the city, preaching his gospel of love and forgiveness with words and simple presence wherever he was inspired to visit. His roster of drivers now included a cop who would become closer to him than anybody who was not a blood relation. And that was indirectly thanks to Commissioner Brown.

Police Officer Jon Williams was a rookie who had grown up in a section of Hempstead tougher than most people imagine when they think of Long Island, and he had no family police connections. He was working in the 79th Precinct in Bedford-Stuyvesant, Brooklyn, when he was unexpectedly summoned to report in civilian clothes to Sergeant Jimmy Johnson at headquarters. Johnson was the same employee relations supervisor who had assigned Dalia to Patti Ann four years before. But Williams arrived knowing none of that. He also had no idea why Johnson took him in to see the police commissioner.

"I'm really confused at this point," Williams would remember.

Brown solved the mystery.

"I have a good friend of mine, Detective Joe Smith, lives not far from you," Brown said. "He's going to need someone to take him back and forth to radiation treatments. Do you think you can do that?"

"Sure," Williams said.

Johnson presented Williams with the keys to an unmarked car and gave him the detective's address. Williams received stellar reviews from the detective and his family when the two-month assignment ended.

"Why go back to the 79th Precinct?" Johnson asked Williams. "Have you ever heard of Steven McDonald?"

"Yes, of course," Williams said.

Johnson then posed a question to Williams as a person of color.

"Do you have any problem being around white people on a continued basis?"

"No, not at all," Williams replied.

Williams soon after met Johnson at the McDonald residence. Steven was on the back deck, as he often was when at home in nice weather. Williams would soon learn that Steven loved to sit with his eyes closed, the sun on his face. But at first introduction, Williams knew so little that he held out his hand.

"Awkwardly, I put my hand out to shake his hand, not realizing the extent of his paralysis," Williams would recall. "He was like, 'You can touch my hand.' I touched his hand and he told me, 'It's okay.' I was so happy to be in his presence, and I felt sorry for him. It just really hit me he couldn't move anything but his head, and he told me, 'It's okay. No really, it's okay.'"

They talked for two hours, and Williams began to learn that Steven's primary concern was always about others, not himself.

"All he wanted to know was how am I doing, 'How's everything going? How's the job? How's your family?'" Williams would recall.

In a pause, Steven made a simple remark that was life altering for Williams.

"Here's this guy with everything in my mind to be upset about and he's telling me, 'Doesn't this sun feel good?'" Williams remembered. "I said, 'Yes, it does.' At that moment is the first time I took pleasure in little things like the sun, the wind, the rain. Before that, I never took notice."

Steven told Williams as he was leaving, "It's a pleasure to meet you. Get home safe."

Williams would later say, "There was a connection there. It was the beginning of something. Just the look in his eyes when he looks at you with that big Irish smile."

Williams became one of the regular drivers under the tutelage of Diamond Dave Martelli, who had stayed on with Steven after the Bellevue days.

"This is our brother," Martelli said of Steven. "If you don't think you can develop that same brotherhood, in all honesty I don't think this can be the place for you."

Williams had already felt that bond at the first encounter, and it strengthened with every tour.

"The more I got to work with him, the more I got to know him, to find out what a pure spirit he was," Williams would remember.

Steven's impulse on encountering differences was to point out similarities. That included when Williams, a Baptist, accompanied the devoutly Catholic Steven to Mass.

"He said, 'Same union, different locals,'" Williams would remember.

Steven was clearly very proud of his family heritage in what he considered the greatest police department in the world, but he also spoke of the importance of the NYPD including an ever increasing percentage of people from all backgrounds.

"He would tell me that was the way the NYPD will grow and reflect the community," Williams said.

Williams noted that Steven sought out specific schools to address.

"He felt it was important to speak to the kids that needed to hear the message most, because if someone had spoken to Shavod Jones and made him feel special about who he was in his life, then Shavod Jones might not have done this to him," Williams later said. "He felt it was important to speak to these kids and let them know, 'You are very special.'"

At the same time, Steven was thinking of his fellow cops.

"That was a big part of this motivating factor: 'Let me speak to these kids, because it could save another police officer from that angry child,'" Williams would later say.

Steven carried that concern when he visited the precincts.

"And let them know how he felt about them and tell them to be safe and say, 'Look at me, you do not want to go home like this. Be safe. Remember your tactics,'" Williams recalled.

Williams added, "He would speak at schools in the morning and go on to address the four to midnight roll call. He had it all covered."

Steven was able to connect with both cops and community in times of contention.

"Only Steven could do that," Williams said. "He would walk—so to speak—on both sides. He traveled with the truth."

Steven brought love and received it in return without seeking it.

"He didn't promote himself, but everyone knew him, and once they spent time with him and saw that smile, they loved him," Williams said. "This was Steven, and when I realized who I was in the presence of, I knew it was just my honor and privilege to be with him."

On off hours, Steven would sometimes ask Williams to swing by a pond near his home.

"Go get the bread. Let's go feed the ducks," Steven would tell him.

Williams would recall, "That was one of his favorite places. He would go and just watch the ducks eat the bread. It was so peaceful there."

Before going off duty, Williams would give the nurse a hand in getting Steven settled for the night. Williams would then return to his own life.

"Leaving the house, I would pull over and I would cry," Williams recalled. "I'm getting ready to go home and take a shower and see some friends, and I just helped carry him and put him in bed, and that was how he was going to spend the night."

Williams's own personal worries were put in perspective.

"Steven made me realize I didn't have a care in the world," he later said.

Over time, he came to another realization.

"Steven is happier than a lot of people," Williams said.

Steven said to him, "Jon, I'm not able-bodied, but I feel like I am better in this wheelchair than when I wasn't."

Williams ceased pulling over in tears and feeling guilty. He began lingering longer with Steven after he could have just gone off duty.

Williams also spent time with Conor, who had turned three when he first arrived. Williams took to showing Conor how to play sports over the ensuing years, as Steven would have if he had been able.

"He was my dad's arms and legs," Conor would later say.

Steven, Conor, and Williams would often go to a local high school athletic field. Williams would sometimes just toss a football to Conor in the cul-de-sac outside the McDonalds' home.

"Steven would come out in the chair. 'Throw it over his head, Jon, make him run for it,'" Williams remembered. "We would get a good laugh."

Steven would call out "Boy-o!" to Conor and began calling out "Jonnie!" to Williams as a greeting.

"Steve-o!" Williams would exclaim.

Where Steve-o and Jon-nie would have fist-bumped like brothers from another mother, they were inspired to express fraternal affection in the same manner Boy-o had been showing love for his dad since he was able to climb up the wheelchair. A very long day had come to an end when Williams leaned forward. They rubbed foreheads.

"The first time, [it was] unspoken words, 'I got you, brother,'" Williams would recall. "He was like, 'I got you, too, brother.'"

Steven later furthered Conor's social education by asking Williams to take him to that rough part of Hempstead where he had started out. The lesson was that very good guys also come out of very bad neighborhoods such as those that had produced Shavod Jones, for whom Conor struggled to find forgiveness.

"He just wanted to punch the guy in the nose that did that to his dad," Williams later said.

As the 1991 St. Patrick's Day parade approached, a group of handicapped children ages six to thirteen sought permission to join in. The parade committee barred them.

"If you can't walk, you can't march," a parade official supposedly said.

Steven announced he would not participate in the parade if the children were not included.

"The Irish American community has been the victim of prejudice in the past, and it's sad and almost frightening that the community is perpetrating prejudice against its own members," he declared. "They should know better."

Governor Mario Cuomo stepped in and invited the handicapped children to march at the front of the parade with him and the New York State Police. Steven joined them while Dinkins opted to relinquish the mayor's traditional place at the front so he could show solidarity with another group that had been targeted for exclusion.

The parade committee had also barred the Irish Lesbian and Gay Organization (ILGO), but a contingent in the line of march announced it would welcome the group. Dinkins was jeered as he made his way up Fifth Avenue, a shillelagh in hand, the ILGO around him. The mayor's security detail opened umbrellas to ward off tossed beer cans, but Dinkins was nonetheless doused by the contents of several.

This happened far enough back in the procession that Steven was initially unaware of it when he reached the route's end. He did not yet know that the day was anything but a good one—for him and especially for the children who joined him.

"The parade meant everything to me, and it meant everything to them," he said.

He allowed, "I'm really tired. It takes a lot out of me."

One of the children, nine-year-old Sarah Cronin Williams, immediately understood as few others did.

"I'm tired of smiling," Sarah reported.

Six months later, in August 1991, a car in a motorcade accompanying the head Hassidic rabbi in Brooklyn's Crown Heights struck two Black children, killing one, seven-year-old Gavin Cato. A riot erupted and continued for three days before police finally quelled it. Dinkins heard that a Jewish man had been stabbed, and he rushed to the hospital. His arrival interrupted the trauma team's routine, and they skipped the step where the patient is examined for other wounds. The man reportedly died as the result of an injury that initially escaped their notice.

A subsequent state report documented the lack of a swift and effective police response to the disturbances. Commissioner Brown soon left town altogether, saying he needed to care for his ill wife and would be teaching at a college in Houston. Dinkins replaced him with First Deputy Commissioner Raymond Kelly, an Irish American born and raised in New York. Kelly's father had been a milkman, and his mother worked as a checker at Macy's, watching over the changing rooms. The future commissioner had served in his teens as a balloon handler at the Macy's Thanksgiving Day Parade. He had spent three years as a Marine rifle platoon commander in Vietnam but still managed to become an NYPD sergeant at age twenty-six. He was a forty-three-year-old NYPD captain in 1985.

As Kelly rose higher in the ranks, New York descended further into chaos. Dinkins hoped that Kelly, along with a master plan that included hiring 2,103 new cops, would make Safe Streets, Safe City more than just a catchy phrase.

CHAPTER 7

*B*oom! Boom! Boom!

The pounding on Thomas McDonald's bedroom door came on a morning he was on leave from the Navy, having followed Steven in becoming a corpsman. Thomas had been out partying with his best friend, who was back from the Marines. They were now roused from sleep.

"Let's go, fuck-os!" bellowed a voice.

The voice belonged to one of Steven's drivers.

"What? What's going on?" a groggy Thomas asked.

"You're going to take the test!"

"Test?"

The driver led Thomas and his buddy out on the street. Steven was in his van with coffee and egg sandwiches.

"Let's go, fuck-os," Steven said. "Let's go take the test!"

After three often agonizing years on a ventilator, after all the department funerals and despite the seemingly uncontrollable violent crime, Steven still thought the NYPD was a good option for his kid brother.

"He'd signed us up, didn't even tell us," Thomas later said.

Thomas and his friend now found themselves taking the police test given that morning at Jamaica High School in Queens. Thomas was one of the top scorers. He still figured on remaining in the Navy as he returned to duty during Operation Desert Storm.

The conflict ended after five weeks, but Thomas's unit remained crammed aboard the amphibious transport dock USS *Denver* off the coast of Kuwait for six months while others returned to a victor's welcome and a ticker tape parade up the Canyon of Heroes in New York. An edict against dumping in the Gulf caused the garbage to build up onboard and turn fetid in the 130-degree heat, which became nearly unbearable when the ship's air-conditioning broke down, save for a section reserved for officers and the electronics. Only a near mutiny prompted the commander to allow enlisted personnel to sleep for two hours a day on the floor of the cooled quarters.

"It was such misery," Thomas later said. "A prison bid is what I did."

When Thomas finally returned, Steven and the McDonald clan were at the airport with balloons and welcome home signs.

"The whole airport stopped and applauded," Thomas would recall.

The six months of misery had confirmed for Thomas that the NYPD was the way to go after all.

The hitch in hiring the 2,103 new cops was that the city could not afford them. The mayor's office sought to go ahead with what it privately called "a gimmick with a capital G." The new cops were sworn in at Brooklyn Tech High School at what was officially recorded as "11:59 and 59 seconds P.M., Tuesday, June 30, 1992." They were thereby hired in the last second of one fiscal year, but would not start being paid until the first second of the next, giving the city twelve months before it had to start kicking in toward their future pensions.

The recruits who took the oath at one second before midnight included Thomas McDonald, now twenty-one. The seating was alphabetical, so he was next to two brothers also named McDonald.

"Andrew McDonald, Sean McDonald, Thomas McDonald," Thomas later recounted.

These other McDonald brothers—who were not related to Thomas and Steven—learned from their father that adversity was no excuse for taking the easy way in life. John McDonald had come to New York with his family from Dublin eighteen years before, when Sean and Andrew were just tykes. Andrew would later say, "Sean and I got our strength and sense of purpose from him. He emigrated from Ireland with nothing to his name. He got by with a work ethic and good moral standard. He had suffered his setbacks in life. He was laid off from his job with the airlines around the time my mother got breast cancer."

Their mother's condition had worsened.

"He dropped everything to make sure she was taken care of and could die at home in Ireland. He lost everything as the cancer took her. Sean was eleven, I was seven. We returned to New York homeless—we stayed with my uncle and his three grown children in his two-bedroom apartment.

"Times were tough. Sean and I knew what it was like to miss a meal. We knew about Christmas without gifts. We knew what it was like to shop for school clothes at the Salvation Army."

Andrew noted, "Through all this, my father didn't resort to crime. He asked family for as much help as they could provide and fought through adversity. That is why Sean and I grew up to be good people."

Andrew went on, "Growing up in New York City in the 1970s was rough. It was a different place back then. Crime was everywhere. Jobs were hard to come by. It didn't matter how smart we were, Sean and I didn't have the means to go to college—it just wasn't an option. We needed money to pay the bills."

Sean had started working at fourteen in a deli, as had Andrew.

"We didn't choose a life of crime," Andrew noted. "We didn't try to get over on other people, take what we wanted from people weaker than us. We worked and became reliable members of society."

When they entered the academy, these other McDonald brothers resided in Astoria, Queens, where Thomas was now living. He and Sean were in the same academy company, so they rode the N train in together each day. Sean finished with a 96.5 average, among the top 10 percent of his class. He wore a gold shoulder braid at the graduation in Madison Square Garden.

Steven was asked to address the gathering. He spoke of duty and integrity and compassion and making a difference in the lives of others while risking your own.

"Be prepared for the second-guessing of your split second, life-or-death decision," he advised them. "Rely on your police training."

Thomas would remember a moment at the graduation when his mother and father stood on either side of Steven. His mother was the daughter of a shot cop, and she had a son who was a shot cop and now a second son who risked becoming a shot cop. She and her husband seemed less concerned than might have been expected.

"They both said, 'We always worried about Steven; we don't worry about Thomas,'" the family's newest cop would recall.

Steven getting shot had made Thomas less liable to romanticism, less likely to see the best in everybody, however much he still worshipped his older brother. Thomas had made a promise to himself: "Nobody is getting the drop on me. I am not going to put my mother through that again. That's not happening. And, I'm not going to end up in a wheelchair.'"

Thomas started his rookie year at the 23rd Precinct, which was adjacent to where Steven had worked. Cops from that command had found Steven and rushed him to the hospital. And they had caught Shavod Jones.

The 23rd Precinct was also where Shavod lived, and that led to some assumptions. Thomas got ten feet inside the door of the station house on his second day when the commanding officer, Bob Curley, came up. Curley was an outsized Irish cop out of central casting, complete with a big mustache.

"I know why the fuck you're here," Curley said. "Everybody knows why you're here."

Curley then asked what he wanted to do other than be there in the event Jones came out of prison.

"I want to be an anti-crime cop like my brother and be a detective," Thomas told him.

"Listen, kid, I'll make you a deal," Curley said. "You work hard for me, I'll give you whatever you want."

Thomas set about making collars at drug spots. He was on a foot post when he heard a female officer begin screaming over the radio.

"Central's going, 'What's your location?'" Thomas would recall. "She's like, '*Arrahhrrr!*' In the background, I can hear a fight going on. A guy in the background is yelling out where he is."

Thomas checked the street signs for his own location.

"I look up and I'm right across the street. *Oh shit*," Thomas would recall.

He ran over and dashed past the screaming female officer to help a rookie male housing cop restrain a struggling robbery suspect.

"Hey, you're Steven McDonald's brother," the male cop said. "I'm Kevin Gillespie."

Gillespie said he and Thomas had been in the same academy class. But it had been one of the biggest ever. Thomas did not remember him.

Soon after, Thomas was told over the radio to "ten-two the house"—report to the station house. The commanding officer, Curley, gave him some news.

"Listen, Shavod's getting out."

Curley said there had been "a big meeting" that included the police commissioner and officials from parole.

"It occurred to me nobody in the room knew you worked here," Curley told Thomas. "I had to say something."

Kelly wanted Thomas transferred immediately to avoid any possible encounters. Curley said that Thomas was a hard worker and should not be penalized because his brother had been shot.

"Why punish this kid twice?" Curley asked.

Kelly asked where Thomas might want to work.

"He wants to be in anti-crime like his brother," Curley said.

"Get him an interview for Street Crime," Kelly said.

Street Crime was plainclothes like precinct anti-crime, but ranged city-wide and was one of those relatively rare elite units that really was elite. Its motto was "We Own the Night." Joanne Jaffe, who adopted the baby from the Palm Sunday massacre, had worked there as a sergeant from 1986 to 1989, then as a lieutenant from 1991 to 1993. Everybody had to be interviewed and approved by the commanding officer, the legendary Richard Savage, then a captain, on his way to inspector.

"I used the selection process as a secret tool," Savage once told a reporter. "I looked at arrest activity. They had to be highly recommended by their commanding officer. I also looked for warning signs: I wanted people with no departmental charges in the police trial room, no prior shootings, and no civilian complaints."

Thomas was accepted. The unit's base was on Randall's Island, which has entrances to highways connecting to Manhattan, the Bronx, and Queens, with Brooklyn easily accessible. Thomas began going from hotspot to hotspot.

"Whatever the worst precinct was the month prior, that's where you go next," he later said.

Newcomers had to pass a probationary period, and the other two members of Thomas's initial team of three were soon gone. He passed and set about being the best Street Crime cop he could be, along with others who were doing the same. He once made three gun collars in one tour.

"And I was nothing special," he later said.

Thomas was in the vicinity of the 75th Precinct in Brooklyn when a call came over the radio that housing anti-crime was in pursuit of a robbery suspect armed with a gun. He assisted a housing anti-crime cop with a Fu Manchu mustache in making the collar.

"Hey, Tom McDonald, what's up, bro?" the other cop said.

"Hey, what's up?" Thomas said.

"It's Kevin Gillespie, remember?"

Thomas only then recognized the academy classmate he had last encountered at the scene of a robbery outside a Harlem housing project.

"Oh shit, what's up, bro?"

"It's good to see you. What is it about us and housing robberies, man?"

"I don't know."

In October 1993, a crowd at another upper Manhattan housing project turned rowdy when police began towing away double-parked cars. A twenty-two-year-old with no criminal record tossed a thirty-pound bucket of dried spackle off a roof, and it struck twenty-five-year-old Police Officer John Williamson six stories below. Some in the crowd cheered, though several later said they did so before realizing that Williamson had been seriously injured. He was rushed to a hospital, where he was pronounced dead.

In the aftermath, people in the neighborhood created a sidewalk shrine in Williamson's memory with flowers and candles set on a table covered with a white cloth. Mayor David Dinkins suspended the towing. Rudy Giuliani, who was running against him for mayor again, accused Dinkins of caving in to "urban terrorists."

"If you want to get your way, kill a police officer and cheer about it," Giuliani said.

Giuliani then declared, "There is no excuse to double-park."

Maybe it only looked like Giuliani's campaign van was double-parked later that month when he leaped out to shake some hands in a more prosperous part of Manhattan. He was not so foolish as to promise to make people safe from violent criminals. But he was pledging to rid the city of "quality of life" violators such as panhandlers and street vendors and his bugaboo, the "squeegee men" who sought a handout after washing car windshields unbidden.

Giuliani now stopped to ask a peddler selling earrings on the sidewalk if he was licensed. The peddler displayed a Department of Consumer Affairs permit, and Giuliani continued on.

"Watch out, we have a quality of life problem!" one of his entourage then cried out.

A homeless man was sitting on the pavement ahead. Giuliani skittered past him and proceeded to a subway entrance at East 86th Street. He there greeted people returning from work.

Most, if not all, of the New Yorkers who ascended the steps to encounter Giuliani likely knew him as the law-and-order candidate. Not even the people on his staff were aware that he would not exist at all were it not for parole. Simple math showed he had been conceived while his father, Harold Giuliani, was on parole for armed robbery, and there were no conjugal visits in those days. Had his father remained incarcerated, there might have been another little Rudy, but not this one. Giuliani was seven when his father decided the family would join the white flight to Long Island.

"I think [my father] felt, 'Who knows what could happen to a kid growing up in Brooklyn?'" Giuliani later said.

Giuliani nonetheless attended Bishop Loughlin High School in Brooklyn, which Steven's father had attended and where Steven himself would later speak. But Giuliani returned to Valley Stream at the end of the day. He subsequently became an assistant US attorney in Manhattan. He then went to work for Deputy US Attorney General Harold Tyler during the Ford administration.

"Rudy spent an awful lot of time watching press conferences," Tyler would later say. "You could see his eyes really glitter as he followed every move."

In 1981, Giuliani himself was named associate attorney general, the number three spot in the Department of Justice. He subsequently sought and secured a demotion to US attorney for the Southern District in Manhattan. He thereupon took over a case in progress against the ruling commission of the Mafia and made a name as a mob buster. He had many press conferences as he also pursued high-profile cases against politicians and Wall Street executives.

He was too driven to just accept his narrow defeat in his 1989 run for mayor. He was now back at it in 1993, promising to clean up the city with a fervor that caused some to call him "Mighty Whitey."

The election was a month following the spackle-bucket killing. Dinkins was slightly ahead until the votes from predominantly white Staten Island came in. The Staten Island turnout had been especially heavy because the ballot also had a referendum on whether the borough should move to secede from New York City.

Giuliani won by thirty thousand votes, the closest mayoral race in city history. He announced that he was appointing William Bratton, then the Boston police chief, as his top cop. Bratton had previously run the New York City Transit Police with considerable success, thanks largely to a stout subway cop who had proven himself a crime-fighting genius policing the underground in a homburg hat, a Mickey Mouse T-shirt, and pink high-top sneakers.

While the new mayor gave press conferences, it was Jack Maple who would transform the City of New York.

Police Officer Steven McDonald as a rookie. *(Courtesy of the NYPD)*

Steven in the time before the shooting.
(Courtesy of the McDonald Family)

Steven being carried from Metropolitan Hospital on the way to Bellevue, July 12, 1986. *(New York Daily News)*

Steven in his Bellevue Hospital bed, with Patti Ann and his mother and father. *(Getty)*

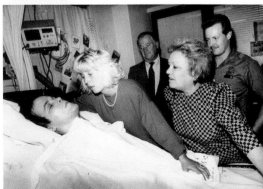

Nina Justiniano in full uniform. *(Courtesy of Nina Justiniano)*

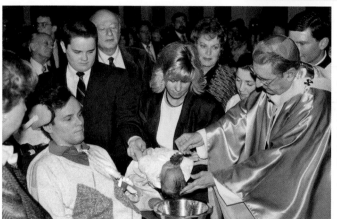

Conor's baptism in the Bellevue Hospital chapel. Thomas is holding Conor's hand. Maureen O'Hara is in the background. *(New York Daily News)*

Steven in dress blues. *(Getty)*

The other McDonald brothers: Andrew (left) and Sean. *(Courtesy of Andrew McDonald)*

Steven, Patti Ann, and Conor going up Fifth Avenue at the Saint Patrick's Day Parade. *(Courtesy of Patti Ann McDonald)*

The promotion kiss. *(New York Daily News)*

Sanny Liu and Angelina at the memorial observance for Detective Wenjian Liu and Detective Rafael Ramos. *(Author Photo)*

Steven, Patti Ann, Conor, and Katie, with Murphy. *(Courtesy of Patti Ann McDonald)*

Steven's funeral. *(Getty)*

Jack in the Oak Bar...
(Larry Williams)

....and in a Times
Square donut shop.
(Larry Williams)

Vertel Martin. *(James Hamilton)*

The Decoy Unit: Jack in pink sneakers, Elizabeth in a Yankees jacket. *(Bruce Davidson)*

Jack Maple, cave cop. *(Courtesy of Brigid O'Connor)*

Jack with Joanne Jaffe. *(Courtesy of Brigid O'Connor)*

Bratton, Miller, and Jack's ghost at CompStat. *(Courtesy of the NYPD)*

The shootings continue...
(Courtesy of the NYPD)

Police Officer Brendan Maple
at academy graduation.
(Courtesy of Elizabeth Sheridan)

The Jack Maple Comp-
Stat Center. *(Courtesy of
Brigid O'Connor)*

PART
III

CHAPTER 1

The December 13, 1945, edition of the *Brooklyn Eagle* presented a full-page map with numbered dots representing fifty-one violent crimes committed in the borough over a fortnight.

THIS MAP SHOWS WHERE CRIMINALS STRUCK HERE IN WAVE OF OUTLAWRY, the headline read.

Dots 6 and 7 corresponded to two crimes that had inspired a previous headline:

PURSE THIEVES CAUSE THE DEATH OF TWO WOMEN, ONE OF THEM DEAF MUTE

HUNT FOR ASSAILANT HINDERED BY VICTIM'S INABILITY TO TALK

SPINSTER OF 85 DIES AFTER BATTLING BOYS FOR 75C, ROSARY

Dot 6 was the spinster, Josephine Delamane Foster, a retired secretary who lived on President Street in Park Slope in Brooklyn. She had been venturing out to a corner newsstand when a group of teens knocked her down, with fatal results. Their meager take was described in the headline.

Dot 7 was a fifty-four-year-old deaf-mute woman, Isabel McCormick of Ralph Avenue in Brooklyn. Her family did not know she had been attacked until three days later, when she fell so ill that they rushed her to Bushwick Hospital. Doctors quickly determined that she had an infected knife wound.

Only then did Isabel tell her husband and two daughters that somebody had suddenly stepped out of a dark alcove, stabbed her once in the abdomen, and fled with her purse as she was returning home three nights before.

Isabel was near death when detectives arrived. They did not know sign language, and she was unable to communicate any other way. The family told them that she had indicated that she did not know her assailant. She is said to have run an extended right index finger from left to right across her forehead, signing that her assailant was Black.

She died without explaining why she had kept the attack secret, but the knife wound and that gesture with the right index finger were apparently enough for the detectives to accept it was a robbery-murder. They did not seem to pursue the case any more vigorously than they did that of the Park Slope spinster who died the same day. The spinster's niece was prompted to call the office of NYPD Commissioner Arthur Wallander and complain that nothing was being done to catch her aunt's killers. Wallander was a long-time cop who had been appointed to the top spot just a month before. He seemed determined to establish himself and make a mark. The front page of the *Brooklyn Eagle* on November 10 read:

WALLANDER PROBES LAXITY IN HUNT FOR BORO MUGGERS

POLICE CHIEF ACTS ON CHARGE BY VICTIM'S NIECE

Wallander ordered 203 additional cops assigned to Bedford-Stuyvesant, where three of the mapped killings had occurred, Isabel McCormick's among them. Along with twenty-five uniformed radio car teams, there was also the precursor of the Street Crime Unit, a squad of particularly able cops clad in street clothes. They were deployed in trios in unmarked cars to crime hot spots. The result was not a single robbery in the targeted area. And when crime spiked elsewhere in the borough, the unit was deployed there with similar effect. The NYPD seemed to be on the way to systematically addressing crime.

But the first of a series of scandals caused the department to shift focus from crime to corruption, and Wallander's crusade to end "police laxity" was soon all but forgotten. Detectives seem to have paid little if any attention after Isabel McCormick's widower, Francis McCormick, also a deaf-mute, was found sprawled beside the fountain at Columbus Circle in Manhattan with a fatal head injury in 1949. The death was apparently designated a CUPI, "case under police investigation." No actual investigation seems to have been conducted.

One family member, not yet born, would come to believe that Francis was murdered by the same person who knifed Isabel as the result of a love triangle. That family member was Jack Maple, and a half century later he would deploy cops across the whole city using dots on maps such as the one in the *Brooklyn Eagle*. The strategy would become transformative when he insisted that cops address each crime as if the victim were a family member.

Isabel McCormick was Jack Maple's grandmother and would figure in his creation of the NYPD's first cold case squad. Isabel and Francis had first met when both attended St. Joseph's School for the Deaf, founded in the Bronx by the Society of the Daughters of the Heart of Mary. Boys there were taught printing, a trade considered particularly suitable because the noise of the presses would not bother them. Girls learned cooking and dressmaking. The students are said to have been close or perhaps closer than family to each other, bound by the prejudice against them and by an inherently intimate language.

Francis had gone on to work in the composing room at the *Brooklyn Eagle*. Isabel had ended up in an abusive common-law relationship with a man she met at a dance, Peter Cassiola. She could not hear the music but loved to move to the vibrations and was uncommonly beautiful.

Cassiola fathered her two daughters. He had full powers of speech and mocked her as a "dummy." He apparently viewed learning sign language as unnecessary when he could communicate what he wanted to say with his fists.

Then came the day Isabel had a chance reunion with her former school-mate Francis. She could communicate with him, and he treated her with respect and also knew the sting of being treated like a "dummy." He was by all accounts a wonderful man. He was someone with whom she could rightly make a sign that involved raising the hand palm out with the thumb, index finger and pinkie extended while the ring and middle fingers were curled down:

"I love you."

Isabel took her two daughters—then ages two and seven—as she fled the years of abuse. Francis McCormick married her and raised her children as his own. The couple bought a radio so the girls could listen to spoken English in a home where the first language was necessarily sign. Isabel still loved to dance to vibrations. She also relied on vibrations to wake early, placing an alarm clock under her pillow.

Jack later figured that his grandmother's initial failure to tell anybody about her wound made sense if she hoped to spare her daughters from learning a terrible truth: She had been stabbed by their biological father. Isabel also may have worried that Francis would report it and the arrest of her abuser could lead to sensational newspaper stories that her husband himself might be asked to typeset about a love triangle involving two deaf-mute people. She knew enough about the prejudice against "dummies" to imagine how that would play, especially if there were two girls born out of wedlock. And then what would the nuns in her parish say?

Those same concerns would have only become more acute after the wound was discovered. And she would not have been the first, nor the last, white person to avoid identifying her actual assailant by saying she had been attacked by some unknown Black man.

Jack's mother, also named Isabel, went on to marry a decorated veteran of the Battle of the Bulge who worked as a guard with the Railway Express Agency until its demise and then signed on with the US Postal Service. They had seven kids: three girls and four boys. Jack was the oldest son.

At some point, Jack's father, George Maple, had occasion to dig up Isabel's baptismal record and saw that her biological father was not Francis McCormick, but Peter Cassiola. George took it upon himself to do some further digging and learned Cassiola was in the hospital after suffering a debilitating stroke.

A nun-instilled sense of obligation compelled Isabel to visit Cassiola in the hospital. She brought Jack, who was then in grammar school. Jack would remember being unsure why they were there, for he had a distinct sense that his mother did not like this man. She told Jack that the man was criminally insane and dangerous.

Jack would only later learn the man was his grandfather. Jack would become convinced that Cassiola murdered both his grandmother and his step-grandfather.

Young Jack stored the visit as a puzzling memory as he continued on in Holy Child Jesus Catholic Academy, five blocks from his home in working class Richmond Hill, Queens. He would later speak of more viscerally determinative experiences, most particularly getting the small box of crayons when other kids in the neighborhood had the big box and always being cast as a beast by the manger in the school Christmas pageant. He would recall peering through the eyeholes of a papier-mâché donkey head at the classmates chosen to play Joseph and the Three Wise Men and then gazing out at the audience, none of whom were gazing back at him.

He sensed no destiny greater than that of a perpetual beast as he glimpsed the future at the 1964 World's Fair in Flushing Meadows Park. The twelve-year-old Jack, who would later change the whole city with numbers and a computer, took no particular note of IBM's exhibit, "Mathematica: A World of Numbers...and Beyond."

What Jack would most clearly remember from the fair was not getting one of the Belgian waffles that others enjoyed as they strolled past. His father was raising a big brood on a civil service salary, and he refused to buy them even cotton candy.

"My father said it had worms in it," Jack's sister, Anna Marie, would recall.

That year, Jack went to the deli across the street from his home and asked for a job. Anna Marie would remember, "He was hired on the spot. His first assignment: quality control of the pickle barrel."

He was soon promoted to stock boy and announced to his parents that he wanted to contribute half of his wages to the household. They told him that the only thing they wanted was for him to do well in school.

One problem for Jack was that he read slowly and deliberately. He would recall getting a sick feeling in his stomach at eight p.m. on Sundays, when he heard the music for *The Ed Sullivan Show* come on television. It signaled that come morning it would be Monday, and he would once again be the only kid who had not done his book report.

But when Jack set a particular goal for himself, he was capable of almost preternatural focus. He surprised even himself when he aced the Specialized High School Admissions Test, which determines who is admitted to the city's top four high schools. He gained entry to Brooklyn Tech.

He was still the son of a Richmond Hill civil servant, so turning sixteen meant that his father began rousting him from bed on Saturday mornings for the tests that would really determine the course of his life. He took the whole range of civil service exams, including those for the post office, the NYPD, the FDNY, city sanitation, even the Transit Police.

In the meantime, a neighborhood friend who had somehow managed to get a job at the 21 Club in Manhattan arranged for Jack to work there as a men's room attendant. Jack was one kid in the neighborhood who knew the rumors about Paul McCartney being dead were false, because he had seen the Beatle at a urinal.

Jack reported that many celebrities were cheap when it came to tips, but the supposedly tightfisted Richard Nixon had shaken his hand and presented him with a $20 bill. Jack used it to take his siblings to the candy store across the street.

"Get whatever you want!" he told them.

Anna Marie would remember, "We left with fistfuls of goodies on Nixon's dime."

During his 1969 campaign for reelection, Mayor Lindsay pledged to fight violent crime and disorder by hiring four thousand new cops. He upped the number a few days later to five thousand, and the NYPD list reached Jack's name when he was halfway through his senior year at Brooklyn Tech. Jack had further demonstrated his ability to focus on a goal when he became the first senior there ever to make the football team as a walk-on. But the season had just ended and he dropped out, figuring a night school diploma would serve him just as well as an NYPD trainee.

Had he been called by fire or sanitation, Jack would have had to worry about the draft and Vietnam. Police trainees received a draft deferment.

In February 1970, one day before he was supposed to begin training as a city cop, Jack was notified that it was not to be. He would later learn that Lindsay had quietly instituted a hiring freeze that only came to public attention when one of his aides let it slip in an interview.

Jack was out of school, out of a job, and out of a deferment. He started work at UPS.

Two months later, he got a call to become a trainee with the Transit Police Department (TPD), at the time still a separate agency under the state Metropolitan Transportation Authority and therefore unaffected by the city freeze. The TPD was also underground in the subway's perpetual gloom. And George worried that his son might turn down the opportunity in the hopes of joining the NYPD whenever it began hiring again.

George was then working nights at the main post office across from Penn Station in Manhattan, and he invited Jack to join him there. George had fought in America's bloodiest single engagement of World War II and would joke that he had twice received the Bronze Star only because he turned out to have been advancing when he thought he was retreating. He was a hero in his son's eyes, and Jack was stunned and silently angered to hear his father speaking meekly about men in neckties he termed "the big bosses."

At midnight, George led Jack down to the underground tracks. The train from Dover, Delaware, arrived, and Jack followed his father to where a baggage crew began unloading coffins. George informed him that this was the latest delivery of young men from east of the Mississippi River who had been killed in Vietnam.

"Do you want that to be you?" George quietly asked.

On November 2, 1970—nine days after his eighteenth birthday—Jack became a trainee cave cop, as those who patrolled the subways were called. They were also called the "Oh" police. That was because if a girl excitedly asked if they were a cop and they replied they were with transit, the response would likely be something like a deflated "Oh."

Jack was one Oh trainee who did not need to worry about meeting girls. He married Karen Brunetz, his high school sweetheart. She worked in Jahn's ice cream parlor, which offered the Kitchen Sink Sundae, a huge bowl of thirty scoops with a dozen toppings that made a Belgian waffle seem like just a nibble.

After nearly three years as a transit trainee answering phones and working the radios and handling paperwork at Brooklyn criminal court, Jack entered the Transit Police Academy. He graduated four months later, on March 15, 1974. A *New York Daily News* photographer took a picture of him kissing Karen outside the ceremony at New York City Community College in Brooklyn. Jack was holding her with both hands, and her right leg was raised as she leaned into him.

"Smack! A Little Lip Service," the caption read. "Transit Patrolman John Maple gets emphatic congratulations from his wife, Karen."

By his twenty-first birthday, Jack Maple seemed destined to live out his days exactly as might have been predicted by the nuns who cast him as a beast by the manger. He was married and had begun the twenty-year count to a full pension. He had taken out a mortgage on a two-family frame house on the same tree-lined block where he had been raised. He walked past the deli where he had once served as guardian of the pickle barrel on his way to serving as a guardian of the subway.

After a brief training period in Brooklyn, Jack was assigned to District 1, based in the station below Columbus Circle in Manhattan. The subway from Richmond Hill did not go directly there, and Jack had to hike crosstown to the intersection where his maternal step-grandfather had become a CUPI.

Unlike their city counterparts, cave cops patrolled alone with no reliable way to summon backup, as their radios were often useless underground. Every transit rookie experienced a moment when they faced a lawbreaker bigger and stronger on a moving train between stations. They then found out who they were at their core.

Jack's moment involved a hulking man who was threatening subway passengers. Jack began wrestling with the man and radioed a desperate call for help.

"You're coming in broken up, go to a landline," came the reply from the transit dispatcher.

Jack managed to snap on the cuffs and get his prisoner off at the next station, where he called in the arrest once he found a working pay phone. He dissuaded the cops who responded from taking his prisoner to "the Room." This was a remote chamber in the Times Square subway station with a slanted ceiling that was spattered with blood from beatings. Battered prisoners were sometimes stuffed in one of a row of dented wall lockers for a few hours.

Jack further parted from the prevailing view of subway justice when he entered his command to see a captain beating a handcuffed prisoner. Jack stepped up and removed the handcuffs.

"Hit him now, captain," Jack said, knowing the captain could not report him without admitting what had precipitated it.

On another tour, Jack got a lesson in caution when he misjudged the length of a four-foot iron pipe wielded by a deranged man on a subway platform. Jack was struck in the head and fell onto his back. The man was raising the pipe to strike again when Jack drew his gun and fired five times just as he was losing consciousness. Another cop had happened on the scene and also fired. They would never be told whose bullet had proven fatal.

Whenever a cave cop was seriously injured, the top brass of the Transit Police hurried to the hospital. Chief Robert Rapp entered as the trauma team was cutting away Jack's clothes to reveal he was wearing women's panties.

Jack had just awakened and voiced exactly what he had felt that morning after the absence of clean underwear of his own caused him to put on his wife's.

"Actually chief, they're quite comfortable," Jack said.

Rapp was by then under investigation for falsifying crime statistics to make the subways seem safer, particularly overnight. He was soon after fired and replaced by former NYPD chief of department Sanford Garelik, who had addressed the Harlem gathering of concerned residents in a church across from Nina Justiniano's building seven years before, promising to provide more and better police protection, which never came. Garelik had since retired and served one term as the New York city council president. He had been defeated in 1969 by Paul O'Dwyer, brother of Bill, the onetime police commissioner and mayor who had suddenly been appointed ambassador to Mexico when a corruption scandal reached City Hall.

As he became chief of the Transit Police in 1975, Garelik made another pledge to reduce crime, also promising not to fudge the numbers. Jack was put in a new citywide plainclothes unit in which cops worked with partners, just as in the city police. Most of the cops in the unit opted for a plainclothes uniform of jeans and fatigue jackets, which made them immediately recognizable to the crooks.

At eleven a.m. on August 20, 1975, the onetime beast in the manger was outside a subway entrance at the edge of Bryant Park on West 42nd Street clad in a canary yellow jumpsuit and what he later termed "Elton John sunglasses." He was finally in a play where he could cast himself in whatever role he chose. He was approached by two men who offered to sell him marijuana.

Jack told the men to come down into the subway so they would not be seen by the police. They agreed and had negotiated a transaction involving twenty-one ounces when Jack announced himself as a cop.

Jack made two mistakes. He drew out his gun just to intimidate but he was not ready actually to use it. And he held it too far away from his body.

One of the men suddenly grabbed Jack's gun with both hands. The man would later be identified as thirty-four-year-old Cyril Morgan of the Gowanus housing project in Brooklyn. He was as strong as he was fast.

Jack clapped his other hand on the gun and pulled with all his strength against the tugging, furious force. The handle began to twist in his right hand until it slipped from his hooked fingertips. The barrel swung toward him and the black hole of the muzzle loomed before his eyes.

His left hand was on the cylinder and he tried to freeze it and prevent the gun from firing. He felt it begin to rotate. Jack summoned everything inside himself and with all his desperate might managed to move the barrel a half an inch to the right. There came a roar. An orange and blue flame from the muzzle seared his right cheek.

The bullet missed, but the barrel now jerked back to the left. He felt the cylinder begin to rotate again. Panic again charged his arms and he managed to push the muzzle a half inch to the left. There came a second roar and this time the blue and orange flame seared his left cheek.

Jack continued to wrestle for the gun with Morgan, and one or both of them lost their footing. They ended up rolling on the concrete with the gun pressed between them. Jack blindly felt the curve of the trigger guard and managed to work his forefinger inside.

Jack could not tell which way the barrel was pointed, but he knew Morgan was stronger and would soon regain control of the gun.

"I'm exhausted," Jack later said. "I pulled the trigger. He's shot and he screams."

Morgan reared up, bleeding from a chest wound. His hands had fallen away from the gun, and he was pummeling Jack with both fists when other cops came running up, his partner among them. The partner had been watching from a distance as the drug deal was made and had given chase when Morgan's pal took the struggle as an opportunity to flee.

Morgan was taken to Bellevue Hospital and listed in fair condition. Jack, with a muzzle flash burn on each cheek, was taken to St. Clare's as a precaution.

CHAPTER 3

Night had fallen as twenty-three-year-old Jack Maple walked along Central Park South in his bloodstained pantsuit on his way to catch the subway home to Queens. His cheeks were stinging as he went by the Oak Bar in the Plaza Hotel. He passed along the five-by-four-foot windows set a throne's height from the sidewalk and peered into a dimly lit realm to see elegantly clad figures whose lives seemed free of the worries and hazards that ruled his own.

"It looks like nothing bad could ever happen in there," he would recall.

Upon his arrival home he undressed and saw that the blood had seeped through to his skin. He washed it off in the shower and he would remember watching the water turn pink as it swirled down the drain.

Earlier on the day of the shooting, another transit cop had fatally shot a fourteen-year-old after the teen allegedly flashed a knife at a man in the East 96th Street station in Manhattan. The Manhattan District Attorney's Office was openly dubious about both incidents. A prosecutor named Joseph Morello visited the scene of Jack's shooting. Jack's account was corroborated by a bullet hole in an overhead subway sign.

"He's actually telling the truth," Morello remarked.

The transit bosses had an overriding concern, and a supervisor dispensed with any queries as to the particulars of the shooting or how Jack was feeling.

"Maple, you were off post!" the supervisor announced.

In the days ahead, Jack was consigned to clearing the homeless from the underground passages at Grand Central Terminal. The task had proven perpetual, as they would no sooner be ejected than they would return.

Jack assembled more than a dozen of them together on the main concourse across from the iconic information booth, beneath the famous vaulted celestial ceiling on which the constellations were accidentally depicted backward. Passengers of the subway and commuter trains bustled past the gathered unfortunates as Jack proposed to his charges that they show who they really were. His assumption that they included a number of veterans proved correct when he called for them to fall in and come to attention.

"About face!...Forward march!"

Somebody called them "the bum army," as Jack led them to the street. He asked them to stay out of the terminal henceforth when he was working, save for an occasional drill. A good number of them complied.

Meanwhile, the subway had such a bad reputation that on another day a European couple who had been robbed at gunpoint in the street refused to go down the steps with Jack to make a report because the underground was too dangerous. The truth was, the vast majority of crimes were committed aboveground. Jack did chance upon the occasional subway felony, and he was able to collar subterranean pickpockets with the aid of a compact spyglass, or monocular, that he took to carrying. But generally, criminals used the trains like everybody else, as transportation to and from work.

Jack had taken the same oath as the city cops, and he possessed the same powers of arrest under the same laws. He saw no reason to remain at the bottom of the steps and just watch criminals ascend. He would follow them up to the street, and his suspicions were very often confirmed. The result would be an arrest, which would lead to overtime, which had become an obsession with the cost-cutting transit bosses. He also made periodic off-duty arrests, which generated even more overtime.

A captain called Jack at home to threaten him with dire consequences if he kept it up. He was summoned to Transit Police headquarters in a building above the Jay Street subway stop in downtown Brooklyn. Jack was ordered to work the radio rather than go on patrol.

Halfway through the tour, Jack was instructed to return to his usual duties in Times Square. The supposed suggestion was that he should take the brief time as a "house mouse" as a warning. He surmised the real reason while he was waiting for a train in the station below headquarters.

Jack had learned from watching crooks that people who are together but pretending not to be still tend to move at the same pace and rhythm. That appeared to include two men who approached on the platform.

Jack tested his observation when a train pulled in. He stepped aboard and then back off, as in a well-known scene from the movie *The French Connection*. Both men did the same and got on again when Jack did. They were still pretending not to be together and still following Jack when he met up with his partner in Times Square.

"Internal Affairs is following me," Jack told him. "They think we're going off post."

Jack had not yet taken his meal break, a time in each tour when he was allowed to venture past the top of the subway stairs. He would then briefly metamorphize from cave cop into an officer beyond the jurisdiction of the Transit Police and not under the command of the NYPD, but with full powers of arrest in both realms.

"Jack Maple, policeman to the world!" he would sometimes declare.

During this particular meal period, Jack and his partner had started down West 42nd Street—known as the Deuce—when they saw four men robbing a sailor. The shadows from the Internal Affairs Division (IAD) looked on as Jack and his partner managed to arrest three of them.

After the prisoners were through the system, Jack sought out the transit chief of patrol at headquarters. Jack recounted the robbery collar on the Deuce.

"I had IAD following me, and one guy got away," Jack said. "They didn't go to help me. I think they should be arrested for nonfeasance."

As Jack anticipated, IAD denied they had been following him. He did not want to get his partner entangled in whatever was to come next, and he requested to go back to uniform, which likely would have happened anyway as punishment. He was transferred to District 20 in Queens, where his reputation for being wild preceded him.

"I'm going to be checking up on you," a sergeant warned him.

"I hope you carry an extra set of cuffs, sergeant," Jack replied. "Because I'm going to be busy here."

Jack was assigned to a fixed post in front of a token booth on an elevated platform at the Southern Boulevard station. A large sporting goods store below had been gutted by a fire, and a pair of NYPD radio cars were keeping watch for looters. Jack checked the scene with his monocular and saw a burglar inside. He hurried down to the street and alerted the city cops, but the building was sealed, and there seemed to be no immediate way to gain access.

Jack then saw an FDNY rig approaching. He flagged it down, and the firefighters lent him a twenty-foot ladder. Despite a fear of heights, he clambered up to the roof and soon was descending with the burglar in custody.

After processing his prisoner overnight and into the next day, Jack was back at his post on what happened to be Thanksgiving. An inebriated man came through the station beating a young boy.

When Jack intervened, the boy proved to be deaf-mute. Jack had never learned sign language from his mother and was unable to communicate with the boy. Jack was able to question the drunk, who reported that the boy was his son but lived in a group home for children. The man had taken his son out, ostensibly for the holiday, and the home had given him $10 to buy the boy a turkey dinner. The man had instead spent the money on drink and had turned abusive.

In those days, transit cops had to book their prisoners at NYPD precincts, so Jack was not back to his own command until he had completed the twenty-four hours needed to process the arrest of the inebriated abuser. That also meant considerable overtime.

"Where's Maple? He's in a lot of trouble," a lieutenant was saying when he entered.

"That's me," Jack announced.

"You're in trouble. You're getting overtime," the lieutenant said.

"No, you got it mixed up," Jack said. "I'm not in trouble. The guy that beat the kid, he's in trouble. I'm not in any trouble at all. I didn't do anything wrong."

Perhaps because he associated the deaf victim with his murdered grandmother, the incident was a crystallizing example of what Jack learned to be the ultimate difference between being a cop and guarding the pickles or stocking the shelves at the corner deli.

"The great thing about being a cop is when you're right in what you do, no one can tell you not to do it," he would later say. "When you're a stock boy and they say, 'Don't stock the shelves like that, do it like this,' even though it's screwed up, you've got to do it. You know when you work literally in any other business, you have to do it."

Jack was given a new fixed post directly in front of District 20's main facility in the Parsons Boulevard station. He had been there all of an hour when he heard screams coming from a nearby stairway. He dashed over and saw a fellow transit cop's son being mugged while on the way to visit his father at work.

The transit bosses responded to Jack's arrest of the mugger by transferring him to District 12 in the Bronx. This was the equivalent of the NYPD's "highway therapy," in which troublesome cops became "roads scholars" assigned to the command most distant from their home. He now had to commute from Queens to the Bronx.

"I was someone they had now pushed against a wall," Jack later said. "I didn't do anything wrong, I made excellent arrests, but they were going to break me. They were going to make a point of this."

As it happened, the trip required Jack to switch from the A train at 42nd Street and Eighth Avenue to the West Side IRT trains a block crosstown at Seventh Avenue. That meant walking the Deuce on the way to work.

"Now, with my back against the wall, I have nothing to lose," Jack later said.

Jack began making arrests during his Deuce commute. He would spot a pickpocket or recognize somebody he knew had an outstanding warrant or encounter a dealer who offered to sell him drugs.

"I am not who you think I am," Jack would tell the dealer.

Jack's even tone and steady gaze would cause the dealer to recognize his mistake.

"I am who you think I am now," Jack would then say.

CHAPTER 4

The bosses had a predictable reaction to Jack's flurry of arrests.

"What the fuck are you doing?" a supervisor asked.

"Listen, I don't know if this is a setup or not," Jack replied. "I see all these crimes being committed, and I don't want IAD to arrest me for nonfeasance if I don't take action. I have to take action."

On a day that Jack actually made it to the Bronx, the captain in charge of the district approached.

"So, you're Mr. Maple. You're the person everyone is afraid of," the captain said. "Look at you. You're a kid; you're a baby."

The captain assigned him to the 238th Street stop on the IRT, the end of the line. The station is elevated and exposed to the winter cold. A sergeant came by every half hour to give Jack a "scratch," signing his memo book to confirm that he was on post and not seeking shelter.

Between scratches, Jack arrested a farebeat who claimed to be a cop but proved to be a Bronx burglar. Jack notified Internal Affairs, as is required in all cases where someone impersonates a police officer. He then notified the sergeant that he had made a collar.

"Can't you give him a summons?" the sergeant inquired when he arrived.

"I already notified Internal Affairs," Jack said. "Want me to call them back and say you want me to give him a summons so I can go back on post? Or do you want to talk to Internal Affairs? Whatever you want to do, I don't care."

Jack was transferred to District 1 in Manhattan, perhaps because he would be easier to keep an eye on but also likely because he could travel from his home in Queens to its main facility in Columbus Circle without that walk across the Deuce.

He continued making arrests, each of which brought him to the Early

Case Assessment Bureau (ECAB) on the second floor of the Manhattan criminal courts building. There arresting officers waited interminably for one of the junior assistant district attorneys to make a quick initial review of the charges.

One wag had made footprints on the wall of the windowless waiting room, as if he literally had been climbing it. Some cops sought to catch what sleep they could on plastic chairs bolted to the floor. Others stretched out in the hallway, where the heavy sleepers were roused like dozing derelicts in the morning.

Cops would be left aching, and the overall message was that they did not deserve any better. The usual response should they register any objection to conditions there was "You're getting overtime, aren't you?"

Some cops were in fact there just for the overtime, and they were able to get a little more from one of the women who typed up the complaints. She would put a case folder further down in the pile if you brought her coffee and maybe lifted her spirits a little.

Jack was one of the relatively few dedicated cops—from the transit, city housing, and Port Authority police departments as well as the NYPD—who pursued crime as not just a job but as an avocation.

"Ten percent do 90 percent of the work," Jack often noted.

He took to passing the long hours reading nautical magazines such as *Boating* and *Yachting*. His body remained in ECAB, but his mind was sailing the sparkling seas in one of the highly rated vessels.

When the name Maple was called over the public address system, Jack would go in to see an assistant district attorney, whose routine questions included whether the prisoner had made any statements. Most cops would say no, so as not to be bothered. Jack asked early on what statements were the best to obtain. He was told that the ones written and signed by the suspect were strongest in court. The next best were those that the suspect dictated and then signed.

Jack thereinafter sought to obtain a written statement following every arrest. He did not resort to threats or abuse. He developed a repertoire of ploys and found that one approach often worked with robbers.

"I don't want to hear about this robbery," Jack would say. "We got you on this one. I want to know about all the other ones you did."

"I didn't do any others," the suspect would respond.

"If this is really the only one, write that down and I'll show it to the DA," Jack would say.

Jack made intentional mistakes in the dictated statements, then had the suspects cross out the errors and initial the corrections. That demonstrated that the suspect not only could read but had read these particular words. He strengthened one statement written by taking his prisoner out the back entrance to Manhattan criminal court and across a small park to a Chinese funeral home to get it notarized.

In the late 1970s, Jack was put back in plainclothes, working midnights. That meant going after lush workers, cave crooks, such as Nate Napper and Six-Fingered Gibson, who specialized in relieving dozing straphangers of their money. Some would pretend to be checking on the victim's welfare while slicing his pocket with a razor. The most adept just used their extended fingers to ease out the wallet. Some had been at it for so long their DOBs were before the start of the twentieth century.

"They would see you at night and you would see them," Jack would recall. "The rules of the game were 'I get you right, I get you right. Otherwise…'"

One night, Jack spied two of the better lush workers circling a man who was sleeping on a center bench on the lower level of the Lexington Avenue station. The lush workers saw Jack and watched him board a departing train.

At the next stop Jack commandeered a cab and had the driver speed back to the Lexington Avenue station's entrance. He dashed down two levels and reached the lower platform before he could likely have made it back by a returning train. He started down the outer edge of the platform so that the row of successive columns hid him from the lush workers' view. He caught them in the act and got another lesson in the importance of adaptive and creative strategy.

Jack was then assigned to the central robbery unit, working plainclothes throughout the city. He spent hours at home in front of a mirror, studying the shapes various guns make when concealed under various items of clothing. He got to where he could tell not only when a person was carrying a gun but also what kind of gun it was.

On seeing, let's say, a faint triangle of a particular size at the waistband of someone wearing a sweatshirt, Jack would step up and, in one sudden motion, hold up his shield to identify himself as he clamped his hand down on what he knew to be an automatic pistol of a large caliber.

"If you have your hand on their gun, they can't shoot you with it," he once explained.

He sometimes strolled past a shop on the Deuce just beyond the subway steps that sold holsters, among other things. More than once he watched a customer take out a gun and try it in a holster. He would make the arrest when they returned to the street.

Meanwhile, Jack filed an official grievance alleging that he was being pressured not to perform his sworn duties out of concern for overtime. He was coming off a midnight tour when he was informed that the department's second in command, Deputy Chief Anthony Bouza, wanted to meet with him immediately.

"So, I'm on overtime again as they're bringing me down to talk about overtime," Jack later noted.

He hopped a train and got off at Jay Street.

"Who do I see, but a pickpocket I have a warrant for," Jack would recall. "So, I lock him up."

Jack arrived at headquarters with a handcuffed prisoner who was sure to generate even more overtime. He sat the prisoner down.

"This isn't a booking facility," one of the headquarters staff said.

"Yeah, but it's convenient," Jack replied.

Jack left the pickpocket in the care of the staff. He proceeded on in to see a onetime rising star of the NYPD who billed himself as "Socrates with a gun" and employed a vocabulary that suggested he spent considerable time with a thesaurus.

Bouza had been the NYPD's Bronx commander in late September 1976, when Muhammad Ali faced Ken Norton at Yankee Stadium. A group of off-duty cops staged a rowdy demonstration outside, protesting deferred pay raises and a new work schedule. Bouza later said that he was busy deploying on-duty cops to keep the off-duty ones from blocking the bridge when groups of teenagers began robbing and terrorizing the fight-goers seeking to gain entrance.

"My problem at Yankee Stadium was not with off-duty cops who were demonstrating; my problem was with the gangs of feral youths who ran wild there," Bouza told the press.

The NYPD made it clear that his best option was to retire. He departed in what was widely viewed as disgrace and became a "double dipper," augmenting his $26,000 NYPD pension with a $45,000 salary as the new deputy chief of the Transit Police, for a total of $71,000.

When Jack entered Bouza's office on the second floor of headquarters, Socrates with a gun was wearing a tie and a suit with pencil-thin lapels, in contrast to the wide ones generally favored at the time.

"He looked at me like I was something attached to the bottom of his shoe," Jack would recall.

Bouza invited Jack to sit down.

"I've been waiting a long time to meet you, Mr. Maple," Bouza said.

Jack had not forgotten how his war hero father had been intimidated by the big bosses, and he was determined not to be. But he was still only a twentysomething cop, and Bouza was just one rank below the biggest boss.

Jack saw a computer printout on Bouza's desk and figured it was likely a summary of his arrests. He dared to hope that the list of felony after felony would mean something.

"You are the most immoral person I have ever met," Bouza then said.

Jack was stunned.

Bouza continued, "You are taking bread out of people's mouths here."

Jack managed to keep his voice respectful, though he no longer saw a big boss.

"Chief, can I speak to you man to man?" Jack asked.

"Yes, Officer Maple," Bouza said.

"Are you sure?"

"Yes."

"You're sure you're sure?"

"Yes."

Jack spoke with the steadiness of knowing that he was absolutely in the right and that Bouza was absolutely in the wrong.

"You got some balls saying that to me..." Jack began.

Now Bouza was the one who was stunned.

Jack went on. "You left the NYPD in the biggest disgrace other than corruption for a high-level supervisor in its history. You were there at the Ali-Norton fight in Yankee Stadium when they had what they called a police riot and a regular riot. And you did nothing. You came over here to double dip. You get a pension from the NYPD, and you get a full salary here. And you have the audacity to tell me that I'm immoral? You should be ashamed of yourself."

Jack continued, "You know, we have a contract that we go by. You make a contract with me that I have to go to 42nd Street and work. You know that a lot of times I'm afraid of these people on 42nd Street. I really am. But somehow, I find the courage to face them, right? And I'll be goddamned if I'm going to be afraid of a guy wearing a Ricky Nelson suit down here."

Jack would remember Bouza gesturing toward the computer printout.

"Well, you do make excellent arrests," Bouza then said by Jack's account.

Jack wondered if it was possible that this big boss was actually afraid of him.

"I will never bother you. I think you're a good officer now," Bouza continued. "Do you have anything else to say?"

"Yes, I do, Chief," Jack said. "Hold on to them suits. They're going to go back in style someday."

The overtime grievance took Jack to the biggest boss, Chief Sanford Garelik. He was a triple dipper, collecting pensions from the NYPD and the City Council and now his Transit salary. He seemed surprisingly afraid of Jack from the first moment of their encounter.

"About the overtime, you know there is no problem," Garelik said.

"That's not true, Chief," Jack said. "You're lying right now. And you know it."

Garelik did nothing more than sputter.

"You're wondering how I have the balls to talk to you like this," Jack said. "The nuns in grammar school told me a man with a clear conscience has the strength of ten men. I have a clear conscience."

He later reflected, "You can't be afraid of the consequences when you know you're right."

He decided that one reason these big bosses had actually been fearful of him was the possibility that he might go to the press.

"They're afraid if you're that strong, who else are you going to tell?" he said, adding, "It's not like being a stock boy."

Jack further reasoned, "Anybody that wants you to compromise like that is a coward anyway, because they're compromising so much every day. So, if you're strong with them, they are going to be afraid of you."

Jack continued making arrests. He was strolling in plainclothes on West 47th Street when he was approached by a teen who offered to sell him several gold chains that had broken when they were snatched. The bust was accompanied by a bit of good luck.

"He had actually robbed somebody in the subway," Jack later said.

Jack offered the teen a reprieve if he told him where he and his friends usually sold stolen gold. The kid pointed out one of the jewelry stores that lined the street, and Jack launched an impromptu undercover sting that ended with the manager's arrest. The bosses sputtered. But they subsequently used the same strategy—dubbing it "Priority Yellow"—in response to a 40 percent spike in chain snatches in the subway.

Various arrests did indeed lead to more overtime, and Jack continued to pass more long hours at ECAB reading boating magazines. He took particular interest in a no-frills thirty-five-foot motorboat made by Bruno & Stillman of New England. The deck was coated with gritty concrete-colored epoxy, and two manhole covers served as engine hatches, making the boat look like a floating piece of the Deuce. And it seemed all the more the boat for him when he read that it was especially steady in rough seas.

His local bank expressed serious doubts that a cave cop who took home $225 a week could afford a $15,000 boat loan. Jack explained that he had rented out his house and sold his furniture and moved with his wife into a basement apartment in anticipation of living on the boat.

"We sleep in a single bed," Jack said. "That's how my wife got pregnant. Are you telling me she got pregnant and she's got no place to sit, and you're not going to give me a loan?"

Maple took possession of his boat in Portsmouth, New Hampshire. He started up the engine, and he was living out an ECAB fantasy as he took the boat on a quick test run in the harbor. A crowd gathered and cheered as he spent the next hour and a half trying to dock it.

That was enough for one of his three crew members, a mental patient between commitments. He decided he may be crazy, but he was not that crazy.

"I'm leaving," he announced. "You can't make the dock, you ain't going to make New York."

Jack and his two remaining mates—a fellow cave cop and a legally blind pet store clerk—somehow made the three-hundred-mile journey, running aground only once. He secured a berth at a marina in Howard Beach, Queens, that had a splintered dock and several half-submerged boats.

Jack was back at work on the B train two nights later when a young man in a black leather jacket took a deep huff from a paper bag smeared with glue. The young man then spat in Jack's face.

"You can't do that," Jack told him. "I'm a yachtsman."

Within the Transit Police, Jack had two possible routes for advancement at that point. One was by a competitive civil service exam. He took the sergeant's test in 1977 and began a years-long wait for his name to come up on the list.

The other route was a promotion to detective. That was done at the discretion of a board of big bosses. He figured there was no way they would ever give him a gold shield, even though he had made four hundred quality arrests.

On September 9, 1979, Jack appeared on the cover of the *New York Daily News* Sunday magazine standing on the prow of his boat. He wore an admiral's getup from an earlier era, complete with gold brocade and epaulets far grander than any police chief's outfit.

MOVE OVER MILLIONAIRES, HERE COMES ... THE STREET SMART YACHTSMAN
COMMODORE VANDERBILT HAS A NICE SORT OF BOAT.
SO DID ARISTOTLE ONASSIS. BUT NEITHER COULD COMPARE WITH THE
MOTORBOAT KNOWN AS MAPLE'S YACHT

The article inside featured photographs of two boats. The caption read: "Status symbols: J.P. Morgan had one (right.) So does Jack Maple (above.)"

Jack originally named the boat *It*, but decided to send IAD into a tizzy by rechristening it. He spelled out the new name on the stern with black electrical tape: *Quaalude*.

Jack took to cruising the islands: Rikers, City, Hart, Wards, Randall's, Roosevelt, Governors, Coney. He was crossing Brooklyn's Dead Horse Bay when he encountered a knucklehead in a speedboat who erupted into the nautical equivalent of road rage.

Jack responded by laughing. The knucklehead grew only wilder and pulled up alongside, uttering dire threats.

"I'll come on that boat and kick your ass," the man said.

"If you board this boat, I will arrest you for piracy," Jack said.

The man no sooner boarded the *Quaalude* than he was facedown in handcuffs. Jack notified the Transit Police of the arrest from a pay phone at the marina.

"I have one under for piracy," he reported.

CHAPTER 6

The yacht. The "hang on to them suits" line to Anthony Bouza. The affidavit notarized at a Chinese funeral parlor. The reporting of IAD for nonfeasance. The wife's underwear in the emergency room. Those and all the other Jack Maple stories seemed to have added up to a guarantee that the bosses would never give him a gold detective shield. He figured his chances of promotion remained zero, even after Sanford Garelik and Bouza were fired, apparently for failing to reduce subway crime.

But in December 1980, the seeming impossible happened. Jack would decide that all those stories may have in fact been the reason he was made a detective.

Every transit boss who had started out as a cave cop knew what it was to be mocked and derided when booking a collar at an NYPD station house. Those transit bosses who had come from the NYPD were well aware of how their former colleagues viewed cave cops. They also had likely ended up underground after either disgrace or disappointment at the NYPD. Garelik's successor as transit chief, James Meehan, had held several high level NYPD positions before giving up hope of getting the top spot there. Meehan then came to share transit's longtime experience with the NYPD.

"They were pissed on by the city cops," Jack said.

And the Transit Police had no particular cave cop they could cite who was the stuff of legend.

"The Transit Police had no hero," Jack noted.

He said of those who now gave him a gold shield, "Even though they despised me internally, I gave them a personality that they didn't have."

He quickly added, "And I don't mean to be a braggart or anything. But the only way I can figure why they didn't kill me is that I gave them a personality so that when they were at a cocktail party and the [NY]PD bosses were complaining about this cop and that one and that one, they could say, 'Yeah, we got this fucking guy Maple who's running around…'"

He concluded, "So that in some way made them feel equal to their peers on the city police."

At twenty-eight, Jack became the youngest detective in the department. He had a tendency to gain weight, and that had not been helped by subsisting largely on a cop's fast food fare. He decided that his new and unexpected station in life required a more dignified image than that of a fatso who grimaced because his pants were too tight and dumped talcum powder down the legs so his thighs would not rub themselves raw. He embarked on a diet of thirty cups of coffee a day supplemented by an occasional bite of fish.

In just over a month, Jack dropped from 225 pounds to 160 pounds. His waist melted from a size 40 to a size 30. He had three designer suits fitted to his new physique. He also purchased a homburg hat and a dozen bow ties.

"I always felt the bow tie had a classic look," he said.

In his fifth week as a detective, Jack chanced by the Plaza Hotel and the plate-glass windows of the Oak Bar that he had once passed with blood spattered on his chest and a muzzle flash burn on each cheek. This time, he had just completed a day tour, and he was wearing a pin-striped three-piece suit, a white shirt, and a bow tie with red and gray stripes. He had stopped earlier in the day at the flower stand in the Union Turnpike subway station, and he had a red carnation in his lapel as he came to the Plaza's entrance. He slowed.

"Good evening, sir," the uniformed doorman said.

The doorman was speaking to him as if he belonged there.

"Good evening," said Jack

Jack went up the marble steps.

A few cushioned strides across the carpet, and Jack was in the Oak Bar. The coolness of the dim lighting was balanced by the warmth of the polished wood. The voices in the room were a contented murmur.

"The first time I walked into the Oak Bar and sat down, I knew that was where I should always be," Jack later said.

Throwing a $20 bill on the bar, Jack ordered a Chablis on the rocks. The bartender ignored the bill and rang up the drink on a check. Jack would remember, "The bartender looked at me like I was nuts for putting the money up. I never made that mistake again."

Jack slipped the $20 bill back in his pocket. He sipped wine and engaged a corporate lawyer in what he would later call "chitchat." Jack would recall, "He said he made a lot of money, but he didn't have the time to enjoy it. I said to him, 'You give me the money, and I'll send you postcards saying what a great time I'm having.'"

In the days ahead, Jack returned again and again to this realm removed from all worry. His life began to orbit between the Oak Bar and the subway. He was leaving the bar when he decided to stroll on through the hotel lobby and came upon the Palm Court. He sat down at one of the tables, and a waitress took his order of a coffee and chocolate cheesecake. The waitress seemed to know the exact moment he wanted a second cup of coffee. And just as he felt a desire for a glass of water, she came up to fill his glass.

"Their timing is perfect," Jack would report.

Soon, Jack was also a regular at the Palm Court. He followed one particularly bad day in the subway by slipping the violin player a $5 bill and asking him to play a tune from when Jack and his wife, Karen, fell in love, "Lara's Theme."

"Of course, he looked over, saw I was settled, and *then* picked up the violin and played," Jack would remember.

Only once did the Palm Court seem less than perfect. On that night, a waiter asked Jack to hurry with his coffee because the comedian Alan King was scheduled to film a movie scene there.

"I was very annoyed," Jack later said. "I told him Mr. King had to wait."

After each evening at the Plaza, Jack would hop the subway back home to Queens. Karen had given birth to a baby girl the same month the yachtsman cover story came out, and they had lived on the boat until they noticed their daughter was able to walk fine on board but got wobbly ashore. They moved back into the house, where little Jacqueline found her land legs. Jack would play with her and scold the dog and watch television.

From the bay windows in the living room, he could look out on the tree-lined street. An occasional teenager in designer jeans passed on his way to score angel dust in Forest Park. Sometimes, a car came up the block, stopped at the intersection, and drove on. There were no people in evening clothes. There were no limousines or hansom cabs.

"Before, I thought my house was Tara in *Gone with the Wind*," Jack later said.

During one of his evenings at home, Jack saw a commercial for a company called the Money Store. He scribbled down the phone number that flashed on the television screen, and picked up the telephone. He would remember, "I knew I was in trouble when they were overly friendly."

Jack hung up and he forced himself to stay away from the telephone. But every time he went to District 1, he passed through the Columbus Circle subway station, where two other District 1 cops had been killed that year, both with their own guns in separate incidents. One had been so thrifty that when he brought a sandwich to work each day, he saved the tin foil, smoothing and folding it for future reuse.

Finally, the temptation of the Money Store proved too great for Jack. He stopped at a pay phone.

"I tried not to call, I really did," Jack later said.

Two days later, Jack went into the Money Store branch on Long Island. He signed a paper that put his house up as collateral, and he picked up a check for $20,000. To this he added an $8,000 pension loan.

He then began stopping at a Citibank branch every few hours to see if the two checks had cleared. Finally, at the branch on Lefferts Boulevard, he slid his plastic card into the computer and saw a wonderful number flash onto the display screen: $28,000

Jack Maple was ready to roll.

CHAPTER 7

In keeping with his new wealth, Jack now washed down his $4.50 slice of cheesecake at the Palm Court with a $110 bottle of Dom Pérignon champagne. After years of patrolling Times Square and watching well-dressed people pour into the theaters, Jack went to see a Broadway show. He chose *42nd Street*, and his favorite tune was "We're in the Money." Another night, he went to the River Café at the base of the Brooklyn end of the Brooklyn Bridge. There, he tried sushi.

"I didn't let anybody know I didn't know what it was," Jack later reported.

When summer came, the Oak Bar, the Palm Court, and the other spots on Jack's itinerary filled with people who had Hamptons tans. Jack spent hours sunning himself on the dock in Dead Horse Bay where he now kept the *Quaalude*. Off duty, he took to wearing open-necked white shirts, gray slacks, and soft black loafers without socks.

"No socks—that's the very preppie thing," he later said. "I was dressed casually elegant."

On duty, Jack stayed with the bow ties and sported a straw boater. This, of course, drew some comments from his neighbors.

"They'd ask me, what was I, undercover?" Jack would recall. "And I'd say to myself, 'If they only knew how undercover I was.'"

The wardrobe also proved to have a certain effect on felons, and Jack was able to arrest fifteen of them in a month without so much as a tussle. One was a purse snatcher big enough to make good on a threat to do him serious bodily harm. Jack pointed out that he was wearing a $400 suit and $100 shoes. He then held open the door of his unmarked car. The purse snatcher slid meekly into the back seat rather than risk the consequences of a wrinkle or scuff.

After a trying shift in the subway, Jack could boost his spirits by stopping into the men's room at the Plaza to freshen up and shave. He would then splash himself with Zizanie cologne and leave a dollar tip for the washroom attendant. He would sometimes sit in the lobby and leaf through the same yachting magazines he read in ECAB, only they now fit his surroundings.

"I really believe when I was born they messed up and put me in a civil service bassinet by mistake," Jack said.

And all Jack had to do to support this wonderful life was again slide a plastic card into one of the Citibank computer terminals. Jack would remember, "I was like a Citibank junkie."

During one trip to the computer, Jack hit the button for account information and saw that his fortune had dwindled below $2,000. He checked into the Plaza for the weekend, went to a Broadway show, and stopped for a late-night sandwich at the Stage Deli, where he encountered Raquel Welch. The following morning, he had several slices of chocolate cheesecake in the Palm Court and took a final stroll through the hotel lobby before heading home.

The next day, Jack went to the Citibank branch in Kew Gardens, Queens. He slid in his plastic card and hit a button. The green numbers that flashed on the screen reported his total personal fortune: $12.

In the days that followed, Jack was seen in such spots as a doughnut shop on Eighth Avenue and a lunch counter in the Times Square subway station. One afternoon, he took his daughter to McDonald's in Queens. He had a cheeseburger and fries while she raced around the playground.

"This is some fall, from the Palm Court to the playground at McDonald's," Jack observed.

His wife had suspected that he was living beyond his means, but he had been able to conceal from her the full extent of his extravagance. The future now promised little more than years of payments to the Money Store on an annual salary of under $30,000, and he confessed all.

Karen was a practical woman, and after she had thrown the television through the front window, her temper cooled. She directed Jack to begin his penance by painting the inside of their house.

"I like painting, I love it, I really do," Jack said.

But the view outside the repaired widow was still 108th Street in Queens, and Jack was still Jack.

No longer able to afford to be a man-about-town, Jack continued to be one of the town's most able defenders. And as his bank account reached bottom, his name rose toward the top of the sergeant's list. He was among those promoted in April 1982.

As with all the new sergeants, Jack was returned to uniform and assigned to the Tactical Patrol Force (TPF), which was composed of cops just out of the academy who worked eight p.m. to four a.m. He passed on to them what he had learned from almost nine years as a cave cop.

"I could teach them everything nobody taught me," he later said.

He was briefly assigned to Brooklyn, where his young charges included twenty-one-year-old Irma Lozada. She came in ten minutes late for roll call but insisted that by her wristwatch she was on time. He just looked at her, imparting a silent lesson not to play cute with a boss when you are in the wrong. She reset the watch that he correctly guessed she had turned back.

"What time does Mickey say now?" Jack asked.

Jack was then reassigned to another TPF group in District 1 in Manhattan. He also taught these rookies all he knew about spotting guns and pickpockets and the importance of not looking afraid even though you are.

"The people that we the police arrest are usually about ten times tougher than we are," Jack said.

He added, "The best thing I find is to make them laugh. You make them feel that what they did is not that bad, so why fight?"

He also taught what was his guiding principle from the start.

"Treat every crime as if the victim was your mother," he told them.

Or maybe your maternal grandmother, in Jack's case.

The rookie to whom Jack felt most like kin was Police Officer Vertel Martin, the five-foot-three, 110-pound great-niece of Josephine Baker, the Jazz Age dancer and singer who became a superstar in Paris doing the Charleston in a banana skirt. Vertel had been the only blood relative among the dozen members of the "Rainbow Tribe," which Baker assembled by adopting children of seemingly every race and religion.

Her fellow transit cops gave "yeah, sure" nods when Vertel spoke of living in a fifteenth-century chateau in southwestern France. Yeah, sure, people paid admission to see Baker and the rest of the Rainbow Tribe. Yeah, sure, hundreds of thousands attended her aunt's funeral in 1975, paid for by Grace Kelly.

Jack felt certain the stories were true even before he chanced upon a Josephine Baker biography in a bookstore near Columbus Circle. One of the photos showed little Vertel in the chateau kitchen.

"What was your aunt like?" somebody asked her.

"She was a fucking bitch," Vertel replied.

After the chateau, Vertel had lived with her immediate family in one of the rougher neighborhoods of Queens. She would speak with some anger about being consigned to clean the house and wash dishes while her brothers went off to work with their father in his landscaping business. She left home at sixteen and later worked as a detective at Alexander's department store. More than one shoplifter was thwarted when she suddenly appeared from behind a clothing rack.

"That's one advantage about being little," she later said. "You can hide."

She got a taste for what felt to be her true calling, and she took the test for the Transit Police. Her father and brothers had been in scrapes with the law, and she did not tell them her career choice until she had been sworn in.

"It's just not a police family," she later said. "They don't have a high regard for the profession. They don't regard it as a profession. They regard it as an evil."

In the academy, Vertel was one recruit who loved the physical conditioning.

"I always felt fat and ugly, and that made me feel stupid," she would recall.

That now began to change.

"I saw my body develop," she would remember. "I started getting muscles. I really started looking excellent."

She had little trouble with the academics, especially an "urban culture" class in which an instructor handed out a glossary of street slang.

"To me, they were just saying every day, normal talk," she later said.

At her graduation in July 1982, Vertel was the only woman and the only African American to receive one of the five guns that are awarded for excellence. She reported to TPF wearing shield 2821 and an extra-extra-small bulletproof vest. The smallest regulation shoes were a size and a half too big, so she wore three pairs of socks.

"I put in shoe pads, too," she later said. "That part worked, because they made me taller. I had all kinds of stuff in them shoes."

As she began to patrol the trains, faces would break into what she calls a "what-is-she-doing-in-uniform smile." Others flashed an "isn't-she-cute-smile." She would recall, "What's really devastating is when I get on a train and some piece of garbage laughs like I'm some kind of joke. That's where I had to learn restraint. Growing up in the neighborhood I grew up in, I'm used to going up to somebody and saying, 'Get out of my face.' "

There were also the young men who responded to Vertel more as a woman than as a police officer.

"It has to be this shade of blue," she noted. "It just makes me look ravishing. They see me and they turn into lovers. They say, 'You're the best-looking woman police officer I've ever seen.' You know how many women police officers there are? That's heavy. That's really enough to catch your heart. Being a good-looking police officer is a bitch. You wake up the instinct in a man."

One young man followed her from car to car. Vertel later said, "You can't shoot him, you can't beat him, you can't give him a summons. What are you going to say when you get down to court? 'This man thought I was beautiful, and I had to straighten him out?' "

After a few more such incidents, Vertel stopped smiling on duty. She said, "I don't know how it is with the men, but I can't smile, because that means weakness. They start thinking, 'Look at this little cop.' "

She adopted a deliberate, square-shouldered stride modeled partly on characters in television Westerns. She began tucking her nightstick under her arm.

"I used to walk like a girl," she said. "I used to hold my nightstick very effeminate. Now I give the bad walk. I hear people say, 'Yeah, that bitch thinks she's bad.' "

At the 137th Street station, Vertel ordered a man to stop holding a subway car door open. The man stepped off and punched out the window where Vertel was standing. She strode onto the platform to see the man standing with his family, now with a baby in his arms.

"Put the baby down, and let's go," Vertel told him.

The man handed the baby to a woman and punched Vertel, who responded by hitting him on the head with her nightstick. The man remained upright.

"I knew it was war then," Vertel would recall.

The man's family joined him in pouncing on Vertel. Punches and kicks came from all directions. She felt a hand tugging on her gun. She grabbed her holster with one hand and clutched a fistful of the man's shirt with the other. She would remember thinking, "You got to hold on," and praying to God, "Please, don't let me let go of this mother…"

Finally, she heard the sound of other cops running onto the platform. She laughed.

"The troops are here," she told herself.

Vertel cuffed the man. She was taken to Columbia Presbyterian for cuts and bruises.

"Getting a beating on 137th Street was the best time I've had on this job," she later said. "Because I knew I was going to survive. That only made me walk that platform more bad."

She acquired a heavier nightstick, which proved as effective as she needed it to be when a six-foot man tried to strangle her. She arrested other men for rape and for robbery. She jumped on the back of one hulking suspect who ran down the platform with her as she shouted, "Stop, police!" She eventually brought him down and cuffed him. He turned almost conciliatory.

"They're big and bad out there, but you get them inside behind bars, they're different," she reported. "I get a lot of apologies."

In the Chambers Street station in Manhattan, she found herself facing an unruly crowd.

"That's the first time I realized how little I was," she later said.

She hopped up on a turnstile with her nightstick in hand.

"And I said, 'All right, let's have some order here,'" she would recall. "They looked at me like Superwoman just arrived on the scene. I don't know where that voice came from. I had to dig deep for it. After I took my heart out of my mouth, I patted myself on the back."

Rather than make the long trip home to Queens when she got off at four a.m., she sometimes slept on a cot at the district. The other cops became accustomed to the sight of her scooting about in white slippers. The route would take her past the lockup, and the prisoners often broke into whistles and shouts of "Hey, mama!" They seemed to particularly like the braided "tail" of hair that she grew down the back of her neck.

"I was gonna dye it blue, but I don't think the job's ready for that," she said.

CHAPTER 9

Jack also supervised rookie Wayne Richardson, who grew up at the eastern end of Long Island.

"I had never seen a hoodlum before, just on TV," he said.

In February 1983, Wayne was in the Rockefeller Center station when a citizen approached him to tell him he had just seen somebody rob a jewelry store. Wayne went up the subway steps with the citizen, who then pointed to a young man on the far side of Sixth Avenue.

"That's him! That's him!" the citizen said.

A snowstorm had hit the city, and Wayne discovered a blood trail as he chased the young man. He slipped repeatedly, but so did the fleeing suspect. Wayne finally caught up with him and cuffed him as a city radio car appeared.

"We got it," one of the city cops said. "We'll take it."

"Nope," Wayne said.

The blood was from deep cuts in the suspect's hands. Wayne searched him and found several watches that still had price tags.

"This is a good one, $49.50," Richardson said as he examined one of the tags.

"That's $4,950," another cop said.

The watch proved to be a Rolex. Wayne's prisoner was twenty-one-year-old Stoney Battle of Brooklyn, who had suffered the cuts when he and seven other young men from Brooklyn smashed the window of a jewelry store on Madison Avenue. They had grabbed some $60,000 in watches before scattering.

Battle refused to name his buddies, who had made similar smash-and-grabs at a number of other jewelry stores. Wayne called Jack, who managed to persuade an assistant district attorney to put him, Wayne, and Vertel Martin on special assignment to pursue the case.

"Jack had the DA thinking it was his idea," Vertel would recall.

Jack warned the assistant district attorney that the Transit bosses might object to the arrangement, which was without precedent.

"Don't let them intimidate you," Jack said.

For the duration of the assignment, Jack was back in plainclothes, which for him were not so plain, having added black-and-white spectator shoes to his bow tie and homburg. He figured they would need an unmarked police car, so he just took the keys to one at headquarters.

"It caused a real ruckus, because he didn't tell anybody," Wayne later said. "They thought somebody stole it."

The manager of the jewelry store received an anonymous call saying Rennie Smith was one of the other thieves, and a records check showed that somebody with that name had been identified in several similar crime complaints. Jack and his rookies parked down the street from Smith's home address and watched several people come and go. One particularly hapless-looking individual emerged and ambled around the corner. Jack and his rookies followed and pulled up to the curb alongside him.

"Get in the car," Jack said.

The individual, who would prove to be named Harvey, complied. Jack asked the young man what open court cases he had, on the assumption that there were some. Harvey named some relatively minor possession of stolen property charges. Jack said he could talk to the district attorney's office on Harvey's behalf if he told them who had been hitting the jewelry stores. Harvey named seven young men besides Stoney Battle, including Rennie Smith, whom he described as the ringleader.

Without arrest warrants, Jack and his rookies could not just go storming in as they proceeded to pick up each of the seven. Jack heard a baby fussing inside Smith's apartment and asked the suspect to come out so they could talk.

"I got a cold, and I don't want to get the baby sick," Jack said.

Smith opened the apartment door and stepped into the hallway.

"Congratulations, Rennie, you're under arrest," Jack said.

Jack summoned his repertoire of eliciting statements, and Rennie confessed, as did each of the others, with the exception of Battle. They seemed shocked that anybody had come after them. Jack then pressed them to say what they had done with the watches. The fences they named included a schoolteacher who moonlighted in a Canal Street jewelry store. The fence had paid the suspects $500 for watches worth nearly ten times that and then sold them at a considerable discount. One of his customers was a vice president of EF Hutton, who was wearing the Rolex in question when Jack and his rookie cave cops showed up unannounced at his office in the World Trade Center.

"When Sergeant Maple talked, EF Hutton listened," Jack said afterward.

At one point, Jack went with Vertel to speak with an NYPD detective squad boss. The lieutenant had a dish of candies out on his desk, apparently for anybody to take, but became incensed when Vertel did, perhaps because she was Black, perhaps because she was a cave cop, or maybe because she was both.

"Get the fuck out of my office," the lieutenant told Vertel and Jack.

"*Your* office?" Jack said. "This office belongs to the people of the City of New York. *You* get the fuck out of this office!"

Jack had been skipping lunch, though less to lose weight than to save enough money for another appearance at the Oak Bar. Many of his fellow officers sought to escape the stress of the streets in gin mills. Some had become alcoholics. And as he sipped a single Chablis, Jack decided that his friends would have done better to have had a fling at the Plaza.

"It would be hard to be an alcoholic at $4.50 a pop," Jack said.

He would later say that he found that just a little imbibing—and no more—at such a moment brought him a certain clarity. It may have been what scientists have more recently described as the facilitating effect a modest amount of alcohol can have on creative thinking by imparting a slight relaxation in cognitive control.

"I wasn't thinking of the world," he later said of his various such ruminations. "I was thinking of running my squad in my own little world as best I could."

His single drink done, Maple rose with neither the means nor the inclination to have a second that might have clouded the creative clarity imparted by the lone one. He left the Oak Bar and stopped downstairs in the men's room.

"How have you been?" the attendant asked.

"I haven't been around for a while," Jack said.

Jack then left his usual dollar tip and departed, smelling of Zizanie cologne as he continued his work.

CHAPTER 10

The watch caper done, Jack returned to uniform with Vertel Martin and Wayne Richardson, but with an added twist that had come to him in the Oak Bar. He announced that all the rookies assigned to him would henceforth be patrolling in dress blues, complete with the white gloves usually worn at department ceremonies. He deployed what he termed the White Glove Squad with orders to lock up any lawbreakers they encountered.

The mere sight of the White Glove Squad was soon causing street criminals of Times Square to scatter. Jack's approach elicited cries of "The sarge is out!" The cry carried not only respect but also an odd and surprising affection. He seemed to make the career criminals feel they were part of the drama that was New York, and the script called for them to behave, at least while he was on patrol.

On the night of May 9, 1983, Jack stopped a nineteen-year-old from Queens who was carrying chukka sticks, a pair of twenty-four-inch lengths of wood joined by a chain. The teen told Jack that he had bought the illegal weapon at a store on the Deuce. Jack went there and seized not only two hundred sets of chukka sticks, but also one hundred canisters of tear gas, and forty brass knuckles, along with switchblades, knives and stilettos.

"We want to clean up the subways and bring the people back to 42nd Street," he was quoted saying in a New York *Daily News* story about the bust. "We want to serve notice on the criminals that when they see the white gloves, they should take off."

On breaks, Jack would sometimes enter the vacant Candler building on the Deuce. The twenty-four-story structure had been built just before World War I by Coca-Cola magnate Asa Griggs Candler. Maple would ascend to a balcony just below the summit and sip coffee as he gazed down at Times Square and predicted it would all be transformed someday. He would often

162 • MICHAEL DALY

take off-duty strolls through the blighted crossroads that he promised would again be the realm of families and tourists.

"It's going to be the Emerald City," he would say.

However secretly proud they may have been, the Transit Police bosses joined the NYPD brass and the Manhattan district attorneys in taking the view that Jack Maple was trouble. Transit Police Chief Meehan was heard to ask a question: "What the fuck is going on?"

In 1983, Jack was exiled to District 34, a woebegone terminus in Coney Island, the end of the line in seemingly every sense.

"The cops were really demoralized," Jack would recall. "They hated the job. They hated themselves. The sergeants hated them. They were miserable."

After roll call, he moved to break the spell of self-loathing, boss hating, and misery. He took five of the cops on the Cyclone roller coaster.

"Two trips in uniform," he later said. "I paid."

He then directed his squad to their assigned trains, on which they embarked closer to giddy than gloomy. He began spending part of each tour on patrol with one of the cops, observing what they did and showing them how it could be done better. The end of the tour presented a problem for young cops not ready just to go home.

"They get off at four o'clock in the morning and there's no place to go," Jack later said. "They're twenty-two years old, and they've got all these hormones."

Jack bought a case of Dom Pérignon champagne.

"So instead of drinking beer on the boardwalk, they're drinking champagne on the boardwalk," Jack later said.

By then, Jack's marriage had unraveled, the Money Store having proven also to be the Divorce Shop. He took a special interest in rookie Police Officer Elizabeth Sheridan, both as one of the more promising cops and as a young woman with a smile that was all the more dazzling in the subway gloom.

Elizabeth was the Brooklyn-raised daughter of a bus mechanic. Her father had started out as a driver, and on Sundays, Elizabeth and her three sisters would ride in the back of his bus in dresses and patent leather shoes. She had gone from high school to typing and filing for a publishing house to serving as a secretary for a moving company to working as a bank teller to processing purchase orders for a chain of movie theaters. Some of her coworkers were women who had been suffering the same low-paying drudgery for decades.

"I looked at them and I said, 'I'm not going to end up that way,'" Elizabeth would recall.

In January 1982, she enrolled in the academy. The years of office work had left her barely able to struggle through the physical training. She began exercising at Bath Beach Body Building Center, doing bench presses and curls until she couldn't move.

On the first day of firearms training, the revolver proved to be heavier than she expected, and she had difficulty fitting her hand around the grip. She lined up the sight with the target and slowly squeezed the trigger.

"I hit it. I couldn't believe it," she would recall.

She was soon an expert shot and began bringing her gun home.

"Put it away somewhere, and don't take it out," her father told her.

In July 1982, Elizabeth was assigned to the downtown Brooklyn command. A five-foot-four former secretary who had always been afraid to ride the trains at night now patrolled the subway as shield 3351.

"Most people stare until I leave the car," she later said. "They laugh, and that gets me mad. They said, 'That's protecting us?' They said, 'Can I ask you a question?' and I already know what the question is. It always starts out, 'What would you do if some guy came up to you...?'"

At the Sheepshead Bay station, Elizabeth ordered a hulking derelict off the D train for urinating in a car. As she escorted him onto the platform, he turned and grabbed her nightstick. She drew her revolver and called on her radio for help. The radio was not working. And Elizabeth found herself in a standoff.

"I thought to myself, 'I can't shoot this man,'" she would recall. "I thought, 'I'm going to get that stick back.'"

Slipping her revolver back in its holster, she leaped at the derelict and knocked the nightstick out of his hands. The derelict then wrestled her onto her back. The citizens on the platform scurried away as she struggled to get back on her feet. She threw one punch after another.

"I didn't want to stop hitting him," she later said. "I was so wild."

When other officers arrived twenty-two minutes later, Elizabeth was standing over the derelict with the nightstick in her hand.

"That was the first fight I ever had with somebody," she later said. "I thought, 'I really hit this guy.' I didn't think I had it in me. A lot of other cops said, 'Why didn't you shoot him?' I said, 'You had to be there.' After that, I could tell someone what I would do if a big guy came up to me. I tell them, 'I'm out here to win.'"

In the days that followed, Elizabeth found that she walked with a bit more confidence and that she gave a command with a touch more authority. She saw a six-foot-two man take a portable radio from a passenger, and she quickly removed the man from the train and put him in handcuffs.

"It was easy," she later said. "It was too easy."

The next day she reported for duty and discovered that her uniform hat was missing. She was unable to go on patrol without it, and the lieutenant detailed her to answer the telephones at the front desk. That was a little too close to being back in the moving company office. She would later say, "I was there for half an hour, looking at the clock, thinking, *I got to get out of here*. It was like forever."

Finally, somebody came up with the hat, and she asked for permission to head for the subway.

"I got my hat, and I got out of there," she later said.

With Jack as her sergeant, Elizabeth came to love police work all the more. And Jack became all the more smitten with Elizabeth. But Coney Island was still literally the end of the line, and he heard there was an opening for a sergeant in the citywide plainclothes task force. He went to see Meehan in the office that Garelik once occupied.

"You're an unguided missile," Meehan told him.

"I'm not an unguided missile," Jack replied. "I'm a guided missile with a flight plan."

"Keep your nose clean; we'll see what happens," Meehan replied.

Jack took this to be an Irish way of Meehan saying that he was going to give him the plainclothes spot. That seemed confirmed when Meehan held out his hand. Jack reached to shake it and accidentally knocked over a small statue that Meehan kept on his desk. It fell to the floor and rolled under the desk. Jack knelt down to retrieve it.

"I hope nobody walks in here now," Jack said. "It looks like I'm kissing your ass after I did so good."

CHAPTER 11

In May 1984, Jack joined the plainclothes task force. The unit sometimes used an office in the Times Square station that also housed a closed circuit television system. Dozens of cameras offering various views of the station were connected to banks of monitors.

"All monitors will be closely watched," Sanford Garelik had been quoted saying when he unveiled the new system in 1978. "That is the key. If a screen is watched closely, our officers will be notified to respond and they will respond immediately."

The cops assigned to the facility were generally on restricted duty for medical or disciplinary reasons, and they grew predictably weary of just staring at a wall of small screens. Those who were not reading or doing crossword puzzles seemed to be in a somnolent state.

"Look! She's naked!" Jack called out.

The cops snapped awake and quickly looked from screen to screen.

"Oh, you missed it," Jack said.

On September 21, 1984, Jack learned that a cop who had worked for him as a rookie during his first days as a sergeant in Brooklyn had been killed. Irma Lozada had been working plainclothes anti-crime at the Wilson Avenue station at 3:50 p.m. when a lone teen named Darryl Jeter snatched a passenger's neck chain aboard an arriving train. Jeter had turned nineteen that day.

"Maybe he was shopping for his own birthday present," NYPD Police Commissioner Benjamin Ward later said.

Lozada watched Jeter flee onto the platform and dash down the stairs to the street. The now twenty-five-year-old cop may have once sought an excuse for being late for roll call by setting back her watch fifteen minutes, but when it came to actual police work, she did not hesitate for a second.

The station overlooks the Most Holy Trinity Cemetery. Lozada knew from other robberies that thieves sometimes cut through an overgrown lot adjacent to the cemetery administration building. She circled around the other way and encountered Jeter striding toward her in the weeds.

Jeter was nearly a foot taller and maybe seventy-five pounds heavier than Lozada. She sought to throw him off guard by telling him that she was searching for a lost dog. He turned to look. She used the moment to draw her gun and take out her handcuffs.

As she moved to cuff him, Jeter suddenly grabbed her gun, just as Cyril Morgan had grabbed Jack's gun at such a moment nine years before. Jeter pointed it at Lozada's face and fired. She went down with a serious but survivable wound.

Jeter began to stride away but reconsidered and turned back toward her. She held up her shield as if it might protect her.

"Wait!" he would recall her begging. "Wait!"

At the last instant, she turned away from him. He shot her in the back of the head.

Lozada had become separated from her partner, and she was not found until 7:10 p.m., more than three hours after the shooting. The city's first female police officer killed in the line of duty lay still, holding her shield, her handcuffs at her feet. Her watch had kept on ticking.

One of the crowd of gawkers was overheard saying he had seen somebody fleeing in the direction of a building on the far side of the lot. Transit Detective Vinnie Carrera began going from apartment to apartment, and a woman told him she had been looking out her back window when she saw a teen clambering up the rear fire escape.

The woman subsequently identified Jeter from a photo array. He was arrested and told detectives that he had sold the gold chain for $70 to a neighborhood fence known as Candy Man. Lozada's gun was found in Jeter's room.

Jack and the alumni of the White Glove Squad were back in dress uniform for the funeral. They joined 3,500 other cops who assembled five deep along six blocks in a light drizzle outside Holy Name of Jesus Church on the Upper West Side of Manhattan. Children from the Holy Name School joined the cops in standing at attention when the Transit Police Emerald

Society's pipe band slow-marched the flag-draped coffin up to the church entrance. The Transit Police chaplain, Father John King, gave the eulogy and told the mourners that the name Irma means bright colors in Spanish. He spoke of her as a rainbow.

"A glorious arc of color made of tears and sunshine," he said.

After the Mass, the cave cops due to work that day returned to the gloom of the underground.

Chapter 12

On plainclothes patrol, Jack noted that more and more groups similar to the band of Rolex thieves were riding the subway from Brooklyn and the Bronx into Manhattan. Only these thieves had not come to loot jewelry stores.

What would become known as wolf pack robberies were now all the rage, and each night saw posses of young people prowling mid-Manhattan for what they first termed shopping and later called vicing and wiling. The first to spot a promising target shouted "Baw!" Another youngster had to second the motion by calling out "Set it off!" whereupon the whole posse jumped in. Certain members specialized in such things as choking the vic, as victims were called, or ripping his pockets. They termed it wiling because they employed their wiles, but the police and the press and even some fellow teens mistakenly called it wilding.

Jack understood that the strategy behind "multiple perpetrator robberies" was based on the same assumption as in the jewelry store smash-and-grabs: If one or two of them got caught, the cops would not bother going after the others. And, however many the police did catch, the cases tended to go nowhere.

In court, the victim was often unable to say exactly who had done exactly what in the sudden blur of blows and kicks. The accused then had an excellent chance of going free.

The occasional desperate junkie or old-school solo mugger was still out there. But more than half of the street crime in midtown was now being committed by posses that Maple would see troop off the trains and head for the steps leading to the street for another night of hunting for vics.

In January 1985, the Transit Police received a state grant to fund a decoy squad to combat these wolf packs. The NYPD's Street Crime Unit had long

NEW YORK'S FINEST • 169

used decoys, with one of them, Richard Buggy, getting robbed 103 times in a three-year period ending in 1976. A robber then slashed the throat of another decoy, Robert Bilodeau, as he sat in a Times Square doorway, posing as a derelict in 1979. The city police subsequently restricted the deployment of decoys to particular patterns of specific criminals. The NYPD did let the Transit Police borrow a team of city decoy cops for the same Priority Yellow campaign that Jack had inspired. NYPD decoy Officer Rita Kalowitz was robbed six times in the first month, earning her the nickname Ripped-Off Rita.

Another female officer came to Jack's mind when his bosses asked whether he wanted to become a sergeant in a new, all-transit decoy squad. He convinced them that it would only work if the twelve members of his team did not look like cops.

"And of course, the only reason why I said that is because I wanted to be with Elizabeth," Jack would recall.

Jack had yet to win Elizabeth Sheridan over when he left Coney Island. He figured that if he got her into the new decoys, he might not only cut crime but also increase his chances with her.

Jack understood that he was unlikely to do either if the decoy squad proved to be just another state funded anti-crime project in search of a press release. He knew that Elizabeth and the rest of the team would have to top the record of Ripped-Off Rita's crew.

To counter the strategy of the posses, Jack would concentrate on grabbing most if not all of the wolf pack members at the scene. He would then track down any who did manage to get away, just as in the Rolex caper. The decoy "victim" and the backups would note which crook did precisely what. The crooks would then face a strong possibility of conviction and would be much more likely to cooperate. And to wrap it all up, Jack and his team would get written confessions from all those they grabbed.

On April Fool's Day 1985, the new Transit Police Decoy Squad prepared to embark on its first tour.

In a back room at the unit's Brooklyn headquarters in the Lorimer Street subway station, Jack set out seventy-two pieces of fake gold jewelry, twelve watches, nine cameras, six radio-cassette players, fifteen wallets, ten handbags, six briefcases, and three pairs of sunglasses. Police Officer Carol

Sciannameo picked three chains and a fake Rolex watch. Elizabeth took several chains, a fake Seiko watch, a wallet, and a handbag.

"How about a camera?" somebody asked.

By two p.m., the rest of the cops had reported. Elizabeth looked like a high school kid in a Yankees jacket. Officer Julie Eubanks wore a black do-rag. Officer Richie Doran came in a black leather jacket and a brown cap that his mother wore while working at a Sizzler steak house. Officer Ronnie Pellechia wore jeans and a blue hooded sweatshirt and looked remarkably like a plainclothes cop.

"I didn't know what everybody else would be wearing," Pellechia said.

After roll call, the cops deployed in groups of three and four. Pellechia, Eubanks, Doran, and Elizabeth strolled to the LL line. Elizabeth had never carried a purse before, and she clutched her black leather bag as if it were a football. Jack came up and slipped the strap over her shoulder.

"It's done like this," Jack said.

When the train rolled in, the four cops stopped talking and became strangers. Elizabeth was the decoy, and she sat by a door with her "gold," her pocketbook unclasped. The others scattered through the car and kept a furtive watch.

At East New York, they followed Elizabeth off the train and toward the A line. The only person who accosted her was a middle-aged woman.

"Excuse me, but your bag is open," the woman said.

"Oh, uh, thanks," Elizabeth said.

The group trolled back and forth between East New York and Hoyt Street. Elizabeth displayed her jewelry, and read Nevil Shute's *On the Beach*, and struggled not to laugh when she glanced at Doran. A teenager wearing Cazal glasses studied Elizabeth and turned to a friend.

"The bitch might not have but $100," the teenager said.

In the late afternoon, the group headed into Manhattan to "play" the rush hour. They got off the A train at West 42nd Street, and Eubanks assumed the lead. Elizabeth trailed him toward Times Square. The two remaining cops drifted behind as backups.

At the Times Square station, Eubanks led Elizabeth past a change booth. She paused to buy a token, and a teenager in a gray leather jacket bumped her from the front. She felt a slight, fishing line sort of tug on the shoulder strap of her bag. She glanced to the right and saw a second teenager, this one in a brown leather jacket, remove her wallet. The two teenagers then scooted toward the stairs.

"Julie," Elizabeth said.

Eubanks was a hefty six-foot-four, and he swept the teenagers up in his arms before they could react.

In a nearby police room, the Decoy Squad's first two catches identified themselves. The one in the gray jacket identified himself as Ernest Smith, sixteen, of Bedford-Stuyvesant. He had $3.05 in his pants pocket. The one in the brown jacket said he was He-Allah Broadhead, also sixteen, of Coney Island. He had no money.

"I'll be seventeen soon," He-Allah said.

"When was the last time you were arrested?" Jack asked.

"Never."

"Never?"

"I was in family court."

"For what?"

"Running wild."

"What else did they call it?"

"Robbery."

"What else?"

"Burglary. Assault."

"How about a chain snatch?"

"Yeah, once. But I didn't do it."

Elizabeth gave a good performance as a shaken complainant and identified He-Allah as having lifted her wallet. He-Allah said, "Come on, miss. What did I do to deserve this kind of treatment?"

Doran searched He-Allah's leather jacket and found a Macy's price tag. The jacket had been marked down from $235 to $100.

"Since you stole this on sale, it's only a misdemeanor," Jack said. "At the regular price, it'd be a felony."

"I bought that jacket hot, but it's my jacket," He-Allah said.

When Doran went off to call Macy's, He-Allah said that the jacket actually belonged to his sister. He insisted that he did not know Ernest and that he had just come off a train from Brooklyn when he was arrested. Eubanks asked why he had stepped into the token line.

"I got on line because I'm mentally disturbed, and I got no other place to go," He-Allah said.

A few minutes later, the results of a computer check on He-Allah came in. Jack read aloud each of the ten arrests, including two for robbery. He-Allah sat silently on a wooden bench and gazed at the list. Then he took a deep breath.

"I didn't do nothing," He-Allah said. "I didn't put my hand in no bag. I gave up my life of crime."

Jack put his arm around He-Allah.

"I don't think you're a bad guy," Jack said.

"I'm not," He-Allah said. "I'm nice."

Jack smiled. He tried another of his ploys to elicit a statement.

"I want you to look me straight in the eye and say 'I didn't do nothing' ten times," Jack said.

He-Allah smiled.

"See," Jack said. "You're laughing already."

"I'll pay whatever penalty," He-Allah said. "Do what you want with me."

With a shrug, He-Allah rose to pose for a mug shot. He turned his tweed cap backward, cocked his chin, and puffed out his chest.

"What grade are you in?" Jack asked.

"Ninth."

"Who's your homeroom teacher?"

"Homeroom teacher?"

"I thought you said you were in the ninth grade."

"I am, but I been out of school for years."

When Ernest was questioned, he also insisted that he and He-Allah did not know each other. The cops determined that the address he had given them was a burned-out building and that he actually lived in the same housing project as He-Allah. Ernest's only visible reaction was to flick his cigarette.

"I just want to go home," Ernest said.

The following day, the teams reported a series of near-hits. Jack suggested that the cops might be looking around too much. He told them to watch their body language and to make sure the bait was not too "sweet."

He reminded them that criminals seem to have some instinctive sense that grows more acute in the final instant.

"There's something the victim does or doesn't do that sets them off," Jack said. "You have *to be a victim*. You have to believe the role you play. If you believe it, everybody's going to believe it."

The decoys began making collar after collar. A group of four robbed Elizabeth, who had augmented her student look by carrying a literary text and a philosophy book.

"I had a couple of Supreme Court books, but I figured I better not bring those," she said.

The one who actually took her wallet was nine-year-old C-Allah, known as Little C.

"How tall are you?" Elizabeth asked.

"Four-foot-five," C-Allah said.

"How much do you weigh?"

"Seventy pounds."

"What grade are you in?"

"Sixth. I mean fourth."

C-Allah extended his fingers and slipped his hand out of the handcuffs.

"Hey, look at this!" he exclaimed.

The biggest of the four was named Derriah. He said that he had a prior arrest for attempted murder. He also announced that he was the father of two children.

"How old are they?" Wayne Richardson asked.

"Three and two," Derriah answered.

"How old are you?"

"Fifteen."

At a nearby desk, Elizabeth was on the telephone to Derriah's mother. Elizabeth hung up and said, "She says his being arrested is a blessing. She doesn't want him, and she doesn't like him."

Derriah said, "If my mother slap me, I hit her back."

When the juveniles asked for water, the cops filled Styrofoam cups. The juveniles asked for more, and each made distinguishing fingernail marks in the Styrofoam so he would not end up drinking from somebody else's cup.

In keeping with the latest fashion, three of the juveniles had a pair of eighteen-karat teeth bearing their initials. C-Allah said he was going to outdo them all.

"I'm going to get my whole name straight across," C-Allah said.

Officer Joe Quirke inquired if the four had any goals.

"Yeah, I got that," one named Robert said. "Jewelry."

"Not *gold*," Joe said. "*Goals*."

"I just want to be rich," Robert said.

Derriah expressed the same ambition and repeated a saying among his home borough's robbers:

"Manhattan make it, and Brooklyn take it."

Jack questioned his collars about how they chose victims and such tricks of their trade as "throwaways," a second jacket they pulled on just before a robbery and discarded as they fled.

"You just pick up the basic things," eighteen-year-old Mark Ross from Brooklyn said. "Crime is crime."

Mark added, "Every time you go to rob, you do get that nervous feeling. You say, 'No,' but the money makes you say, 'Yeah.'"

As with all the prisoners, Jack asked Mark to write a statement. Mark detailed in small, neat letters that he and his friends had come from Brooklyn looking for vics. Jack patted him on the back.

"You have nice handwriting," Jack said.

Jack added *throwaway* and *vic* to everything else he learned in a field of study he put to immediate and continued use.

"Crookology," he called it.

CHAPTER 13

Jack's decoys continued to make so many collars that IAD investigated whether he was engaging in entrapment. He was cleared as the unit made even more arrests, often setting up in the last car, which was known as the party car. There was only one door anybody could enter while the train was in motion, and a single lookout could keep watch for cops while everyone else could smoke pot or play a boom box and dance without immediate concern. But the more feloniously inclined also took advantage of the opportunity to rob anybody who aroused their interest.

If there was no music, Police Officer Billy Carter would sometimes set his boom box blasting and work his hips in what he termed "the dick dance." His fellow undercovers would join in with their own style or maybe roll "joints" with loose Lipton tea. One particularly successful decoy was an apparently drunken businessman wearing a "Hello my name is..." sticker on his suit jacket lapel.

"Vic," it read.

Who could resist robbing a vic named Vic?

One night, robbers decided to target a transvestite and discovered that the vic was Police Officer Billy Courtney, instructed by Maple to wear a dress and a wig. Billy had added the bra on his own.

Asians were often targeted because thieves believed they would not go to the police. Decoy Police Officer Yee Bong Tso was robbed again and again.

Jack was always working right alongside his cops, sometimes sporting a wild, bushy beard and an old-fashioned police overcoat with a choker collar, his sergeant's shield pinned upside down on his chest. Or he just wore a Mickey Mouse T-shirt. His usual footwear continued to be his pink high-tops.

For Christmas 1985, Jack's decoys went shopping for him on Orchard

Street. The cops bought him a black zip-up sweater that had a series of white Playboy bunny heads around the middle. Jimmy Nuciforo later noted that it was the height of fashion.

"Among thieves," Jimmy said, adding, "at the time."

Jack completed his fashion statement with camouflage pants. He wore a sable fur hat.

"Like a Cossack," Jimmy noted.

In the final minutes of 1985, they were in Times Square. Jack watched wolf pack after wolf pack arrive by subway and chant "Forty-deuce! Forty-deuce!" as they proceeded into a crowd of more than one hundred thousand that had gathered to watch the world-famous ball drop. The 1,300 city cops on hand included the mounted unit, which had a number of horses at West 47th Street and Broadway. Jack was there with his crew, all of whom had better ideas of what to do on New Year's Eve.

"Nobody wanted to be working," Jimmy later said. "But that was Jack."

The decoy was Officer Jerry Lyons, posing as an inebriated business-man, tie undone and askew, revealing a gold chain. Jack set him by a subway entrance.

"At the top of the stairs," Jerry later said. "It had to be on the stairs, because we're transit, right?"

As the countdown to the New Year neared, Jack watched a trio of young men begin eyeing Jerry. Jimmy Nuciforo was chatting with a young woman from Virginia who asked if she could have her picture taken with him. He showed her his police shield.

"I'm going to have to be quick, we are going to make an arrest," Jimmy said.

Jack was already closing in when one of the three young men reached with his left hand to snatch the gold chain from Jerry's neck. The man's right hand was on a gun inside his coat, and Jack clamped his own hand on top of it.

"Gun!" he called out.

As they wrestled, Jack's shirt pulled up to expose his own gun and the man tried to grab it. Officer Carol Sciannameo jumped in.

Another of the three young men moved to escape, and Vertel grabbed him around the waist. He kept moving until Jimmy joined her in bringing him down. Jimmy then began wrestling with the third man. A gun fell out of the man's pocket, and Jack retrieved it.

Elizabeth and the other backups swarmed in. Newly promoted NYPD Sergeant James Waters—later to become chief of counterterrorism—saw the tussle and responded with some mounted cops. Jack and his decoys were covered with horse manure when they rose with their handcuffed prisoners.

"You know how manure's got that straw in it?" Jimmy Nuciforo later said.

As they took their prisoners down into the subway, Jack's crew could hear the crowd begin to count aloud the final seconds. Bands of thieves who remained in the Square sent up a chant of their own.

"Three!" went the crowd.

"Snatch gold!" went the thieves.

"Two!"

"Snatch gold!"

"One!"

"Snatch gold!"

"Happy New Year!"

In the first moments of 1986, the thieves turned their chant into action, snatching gold chains and removing watches and taking wallets and otherwise robbing dozens of people. One celebrant started the year with a robber's hand in each front pocket, later saying the two sets of groping fingers felt like a pair of big, wriggling fish.

All cave cop arrests at the time had to be logged in with both the Transit Police and the NYPD. Transit assigned each case a control number. Jimmy figured that since theirs came just as the ball dropped, they would be recorded as the first case of the year, as CN00001.

"But it was 00005," he would remember.

Four other transit collars had been logged in before theirs. And there were no doubt many more logged by the NYPD, though there would have been hundreds more in Times Square alone if every crook had been caught. Eight people were murdered in the city on New Year's Day, the first a Baltimore handyman shot to death at twelve thirty a.m. in a robbery while visiting family for the holidays in Brooklyn's 75th Precinct. The unrelenting carnage and chaos led many city cops to feel that their efforts were ultimately futile.

The common expression returned: "Just shoveling shit against the tide." The police had always been much better than the press at treating uncelebrated murders as important, but some detectives were now speaking of "misdemeanor homicides."

Jack's crew remained in high spirits as they made collar after collar, with periodic dancing to a boom box in the party car. Every decoy knew what it was to be targeted. The backups witnessed each robbery firsthand. Every perpetrator was apprehended and interviewed, and almost every one wrote a confession. None of the cops tried to skate with just a clearance. All of them felt they were doing police work as it should be done.

"Cops can have a good time, they can do a great job, and they can be very effective," Jack later said.

Looking back, everybody in the decoy squad agreed that the best New Year's Eve they ever had was the one where they stood in Times Square covered with horseshit, complete with straw.

J ack figured that what his squad accomplished should have qualified all of them for promotion to detective. But the decoys remained part of a city-wide plainclothes task force. That meant there was a point system deciding who would get one of a limited number of gold shields. He was required to prepare evaluations for each member of his squad with an "activity" formula that promised to be doubly unfair. The cops within his unit would get points for being robbed and taking the collar, but not for serving as backup. And cops outside his unit would get the same points for grabbing somebody who beat the fare.

Jack sought to balance it out by quantifying other factors, such as number of interrogations and decoy operations in whatever capacity. He was thereby able to secure shields for some of those he judged most deserving, but many went unrewarded.

Even though Jack demonstrated a remarkable ability to retain and cite statistics, he had a visceral dislike for rating cops this quantitatively.

"It was all about numbers," Elizabeth later said. "He *hated* evaluations."

The experience left Jack all the more ready to return to the detective division himself. He figured that the strategy was well-enough established that it could run without him. He also had won Elizabeth's heart, and they were on their way to getting married and having a son.

So in the spring of 1986, Jack knotted together his pink high-tops, which had become scuffed and worn during a year of "running it." He tossed them over a utility wire in Union Square, from which they continued to hang as he returned to wearing spectator shoes along with a suit and homburg, as befit his new position as a detective supervisor.

As it happened, the Union Square subway station was the headquarters of Transit Police District 4. Four plainclothes cops from that command

were at the center of a growing scandal involving false arrests for supposedly attempting to pickpocket and grind against female passengers. The
cops in question had been making the bogus collars to gin up numbers for
the very evaluation system Maple detested. The falsely arrested included
an African American off-duty NYPD officer. His lawyer alerted John
Miller, the city's premier TV crime reporter. Miller is the son of a newspaper columnist whose pals included Frank Costello, a Mafia boss so polished he was known as "the Prime Minister." Costello's wife was Miller's
godmother.

Miller had followed his father into the news business, becoming an
on-air reporter for a local TV station while still in his mid-teens. He dashed
from crime scene to crime scene in New York's bad old days. While his high
school buddies spent their Saturday nights sneaking a beer or a joint, Miller
was covering multiple homicides in the Bronx. When his buddies went to see
the movie *Looking for Mr. Goodbar*, fifteen-year-old Miller had been at the
scene of the actual 1973 murder that inspired it.

In December 1985, Miller reported from the crime scene after another
mob boss, Paul Castellano of the Gambino family, was shot to death along
with a bodyguard in the street outside Sparks Steak House in midtown Manhattan. Miller then covered the resulting rise of the new Gambino boss,
strutting celebrity gangster John Gotti, who had the brash allure of the devil
himself in a $3,000 suit and a haircut that a barber next to his Mafia social
club touched up every day.

Miller was the same age as the cop at the center of the story when he
responded to the scene of Officer Steven McDonald's shooting eight months
later. But along with that tale of forgiveness and of what is at the core of the
best cops, Miller now covered a story of cops at their worst in the person of
the four from District 4. He heard grumbling that decoy transit cops had
also been making bogus arrests. And the sheer number of decoy collars initially convinced Miller that the rumors must be true.

Miller then met Jack and decided the reason the arrest numbers were so
high was that this fat cave cop was a policing genius.

"I went from 'Fuck them!' to 'Fuck me!'" Miller would recall.

In the meantime, Jack had noted that a new scourge was driving crime
to record levels aboveground as well as below. Jack had first encountered it

several months before, while riding an uptown IRT train. He entered the car just as a young woman in the company of a child finished smoking something with a glass pipe. She then sat there with red, glassy eyes while a tiny plastic vial rolled empty at her feet with the rocking of the train.

Jack was soon seeing little vials seemingly everywhere, some discarded empty, others containing little white chunks when taken from the pockets of thieves. The emergence of crack triggered a surge in violent crimes, though it failed to prompt one detective in Jack's new command to spoil a perfect record of never making a single collar.

"He's just not into making arrests," another detective explained to Jack.

Meanwhile, despite Jack's continuing efforts, some of the stars of his decoy crew had still not made detective. They included Vertel and Wayne. The fall of 1986 saw them working in District 33 in Brooklyn.

Wayne usually walked Vertel to her car at the end of a tour, but on the night of September 4, he was going to the gym in Manhattan. She told him not to bother.

"So I bid him bonsoir, and I went to the parking lot," Vertel would recall. "There was a uniform cop standing at the front gate, so I said hello to her, and I went on in. My car was parked toward the rear of the lot, in a real dark section. I get in the car, and always look around because it's spooky."

She saw a head bobbing up and down in front of this van parked next to her. The hood of the van went up.

Vertel got out of her car and saw a battery next to the van. She took out her shield.

"Police. What's up?" she asked.

The man just looked at her and began to walk away. She started after him.

"Police. Come here," she said.

The man just kept walking. Vertel grabbed him with her right hand and turned him around.

"Yo, man, I'm the police," Vertel said. "What're you doing? Stop!"

The man knocked her arm away. He became agitated.

"Yo, man, get out of here!" he yelled. "You're not arresting me!"

Vertel could smell alcohol on his breath. She grabbed the man. He began punching her. She held on to him. He kept punching, punching, punching.

"Your adrenaline's pumping, and you're fighting," she would remember. "I must have been scared, I guess."

Vertel called out for help and then told the man, "Calm down. This is only a misdemeanor. Don't worry about it."

The guy kept punching. She grabbed him by the shoulders, saying, "You're not gettin' away. So forget about it. You're gonna get arrested."

She had long before made a resolution that when she decided to make a collar, she was going to make the collar, no matter how big they were, no matter how hard they fought.

"So we're tussling and stuff and carrying on, and all of a sudden, I see it. He reaches into his back pocket and flicks a knife, and I see the shininess of the blade. I'm looking at it, and I'm saying, 'I'm in a jam now.'

"I didn't even think about my gun. I was thinking, 'Why is he pulling out a knife? Why is he getting violent? Why is he getting crazy? Why is he trying to hurt me?'

"I figure I got to pull this guy off balance, because I don't want him to be shafting me. I back up and pull him off balance, but then he swings the knife up. I threw my left hand up to block.

"I was talking to the guy, like trying to talk some sense to him because I couldn't see any rationale for this. I was saying, 'Calm down. What are you doing that for? Calm down.' I was even telling him, 'It's only a DAT [desk-appearance ticket].'

"I saw the blade coming down, and it seemed like in slow motion, because I had time to think of so many things. I said to myself, 'I'm gonna die,' because I knew this guy was overpowering me, and I knew there was nothing I could do to him physically.

"I was starting to rationalize in my mind why this couldn't happen to me, and then Irma Lozada passed through my head. I knew she died in a lot, and I was in a lot, and I started thinking about lying on the ground bleeding to death. I started thinking, 'If he kills me here, nobody's gonna find my body until later, and he's gonna get away, because it's dark back here.' I said, 'I don't want to die like this in this dirt.'

"I was thinking so many things, I guess it took my mind away from action. In fact, I almost forgot I had the gun for a moment. The only thing that jolted me back to reality was the feeling of the blade on my skin.

"He came down real hard with the knife and hit my hand. I still had my shield in my hand, and you could hear the clink when the knife hit it. And then I felt, like, a little prickle on my finger. I'll never forget that prickle. That's when I reacted. I knew it was time.

"I just went and grabbed my gun out. I remember saying in my mind, 'This is a textbook situation.' I was thinking, 'The textbook says give him a warning.' And I gave him a warning.

"I said, 'Don't move. Don't move.'

"He kept coming down with the knife, and I could feel the force coming down like he wanted to hurt me... That's when I said that I couldn't do anything else. I shot him. Boom. It was loud.

"At first, I thought I missed. It didn't have any effect. I could still feel the force coming down. I said, 'Why is he still fighting?' But finally, I could feel him weakening. I stepped back, and he said, 'You didn't have to shoot me, man.'

"Then he dropped the knife and whoomp, he fell down. He was struggling even then, and I wrestled his arms and put them behind his back. It wasn't bleeding that much. You could see the hole in his shirt. He was yellin' and screaming he was in pain. 'I'm gonna die, I'm gonna die.' All this kind of stuff.

"The uniform cop ran over, and I said, 'I just shot this guy. Get some help. Get an ambulance, you know what I mean?'

"She called a ten-thirteen [officer in need of assistance]. I don't know why. Everything was over with.

"I remember hearing a whole lot of footsteps, like you can hear the troops are coming. And they were comin', too, boy. They were breaking from everywhere. The thing I was most concerned about was that they saw that knife, that nothing happened to that knife.

"[A supervisor] ordered me off to the side. The guy was yelling, and then after a while he was quiet, and I thought he was going to die. Everybody was, like, 'Yeah, well, where was the car? Over there? All right, somebody do a sketch of the crime scene. Rope off this here.' And this guy's laying there.

"I'm saying, 'Damn, somebody ought to help this poor motherfucker,' because I didn't want him to die. That's not something to die for.

"Then EMS [emergency medical service] came, and they surrounded the guy and started doing that medical stuff. The funny part was, I wasn't even in shock. I thought, 'Damn, after you shoot somebody, you're supposed to be traumatized and stuff.' But I wasn't. I felt that the guy tried to kill me, or at least tried to hurt me, and he got his just deserts.

"Then they brought me over to District 33 and put me in a room there. [An officer] came in and said, 'Yeah, I ran the sheet on the guy. He's on parole for robbery.' [Another officer] called and said the guy made a confession at the hospital. The guy's statement was that he showed me the knife. That was his term. 'Showed.' About two in the morning, I saw the DA. You could tell he was angry he had to come out at that time of night.

"Usually, when you shoot a guy, you shoot him to kill him. I didn't feel that's why I shot the guy, though. And I said that. I didn't shoot him to kill him. I just wanted him not to kill me, you know what I mean?

"I finished in there about four in the morning and I went back to the parking lot and got in my car. I felt like a hero to myself. You know, it's a good feeling when you come out of a situation like that alive. You feel good because you didn't do anything wrong. When you're right, you're right, and there's nothing more powerful than that.

"I got home, like, five o'clock in the morning. I turned on the radio, and I lay down and heard them talking about the shooting…It was very sketchy, just a couple of words. Then I turned the radio off and went to sleep for a few hours.

"I must have been in a little bit of trauma, because at nine o'clock I went and got, like, five videos and just sat there and played videos. And then I said, 'Let me go in,' and I went to work.

"When I was driving in, I turned the radio on, and there was nothing said about [the shooting]. I guess so much had happened in the course of the day that it became old news.

"I got to work, and I found out the guy didn't die. It was funny: People were getting mad at me because the next day I came right back to work. They said, 'You should seek psychological services,' and all that. 'You should go sick.' Why should I do that? I didn't do anything wrong.

"They have a shrink department. They were calling me up and they said, 'You really should come down and talk to us, because a lot of times you really don't know.' I said, 'I know. I know me.'

"I just wanted to hurry up and go see my partner and talk about it. You know, I have a tendency to think I'm bigger than I am. I'm actually only a little girl, believe it or not. I went back to police work and making collars."

Ten months later, Martin was promoted to detective. She took out the case file on Irma Lozada, who had been killed two years almost to the day before her own encounter in another Brooklyn lot.

"I looked at the crime scene pictures," she would recall. "And I saw her body just laying there in the dirt with all this broken glass around. I was saying, 'Yeah, she had a little body, like me.' I was saying, 'Damn, what if that was me?' I'm not religious or anything, but I believe in God. I believe He covers my back, you know?"

CHAPTER 15

In the meantime, Jack had taken the lieutenant's test. He had initially said he was too busy actually fighting crime to study department procedures. But a non-cop friend convinced him that there was a huge difference between sergeant and lieutenant and that the promotion would better enable him to implement his ideas.

"The Emerald City, Jack," his friend reminded him.

Jack again proved capable of almost preternatural focus. He scored number one on the lieutenant's test by such a margin that the bosses figured he must have cheated. He was, after all, a half a wack job who just had a high school equivalency diploma. He was ordered to take the test again. He scored even higher.

"That changed my life," Jack later said.

One result was that a chief who had scored number one on all his tests contacted Jack and said the department was creating a new citywide unit targeting pattern robberies. The chief asked Jack to lead it.

"Fine," Jack said. "Let me pick who I want."

The chief agreed, and Jack became the commanding officer of what was called the Repeat Offender Robbery Strike Force, the RORSF.

Among the cops Jack brought into the unit was one he would come to consider a second son, twenty-five-year-old Fermin "Sonny" Archer. Sonny had started out as an unarmed school safety officer, working at the now defunct Eastern District High School in Brooklyn, one of the first in the city to have metal detectors, meaning that kids began each day getting scanned for weapons. The student body was described as 99 percent minority. More than three thousand kids were crammed into a facility meant for two thousand. Only 20 percent graduated. One-third were absent on an average day. A Spanish teacher was knocked unconscious when he told a student not to smoke during a fire drill. There were periodic riots, one quelled by a hundred cops. Archer had departed by the time a school safety officer was fatally beaten by a dozen students with bats and chains. The officer reportedly radioed for help, but his fellow officers did not respond.

Sonny was big in heart, big in courage, big in determination, big in honor, and just plain big—six-foot-three and 240 pounds. He seldom smiled, for reasons that become apparent when he did: He instantly went from scary to looking like a huge teddy bear. He had a way of speaking without uttering a word and replied with just a dubious look when Jack offered his vision of the future as they stood on West 42nd Street near Seventh Avenue.

"Someday, people will be going to Times Square in tuxedos and evening gowns," Jack said.

A reminder of the present state of things came as a man snatched a woman's pocketbook nearby and disappeared around the corner. Sonny proved to be as fast as he was big. Jack was moving to join the chase when he heard a cry that he would come to recognize as the sound of Sonny catching up with somebody.

The challenge for the RORSF was to predict where a subway robber would strike next. Jack focused on how he was going to cover the city's subway system and its 472 stations with twenty-four cops. And the unit was prohibited from investigating robberies that had already occurred, which the detectives considered their exclusive purview.

At the River Café, Jack sat with a view of the Statue of Liberty and the spires of downtown Manhattan, sipping a single champagne cocktail. He would later speak of again experiencing the clarity that came with just a little imbibing, and no more.

His thoughts harkened back forty thousand years from cave cops to cave dwellers.

RORSF headquarters was in a space the Transit Authority leased on the first floor of an aboveground building. One interior room had fifty feet of wall space as uninterrupted as if it were in the subway, and Jack announced that the unit would use the wraparound expanse much as hunters of prehistoric times employed the walls of caves.

The cops Jack had chosen included the former decoy who had dressed as a transvestite. Bill Courtney was the son of a city cop as well as a punk rock fan and an off-duty regular at CBGB with a fondness for the Dead Kennedys. Jack now instructed Courtney to prepare a map on which they could record all subway robberies. Jack never said anything about being inspired by the 1945 crime map in the *Brooklyn Eagle* that had included his grandmother's fatal stabbing. If he had seen a clipping of it, the map likely figured in his thinking at some level. Or maybe the similar intent and the importance placed on each victim was simple coincidence.

Courtney contacted a young woman he was seeing who worked with computers, though the data processing Jack sought was closer to that of prehistory than of the high tech eventually to come. Courtney figured that a dot matrix printer might be a handy way to generate 472 attached sheets of paper that were each headed by the name of a particular station, with space below for entering details of whatever crimes transpired there. The result wound around all four walls and extended into the hallway.

"The Charts of the Future!" Jack exclaimed.

CHAPTER 16

Had Jack used the sheets just to record the location of the many robberies, the result would have not been much different than the pin maps he had seen in virtually every city police command.

"They basically just tell you that crime is out of control," Jack noted.

The 1945 crime map in the *Brooklyn Eagle* was not much better.

The dots were numbered, but you had to check the corresponding summary in a compendium of fifty-one crimes over a six-week period.

The Charts of the Future immediately conveyed the particular type of robbery as well as the time of day, number of perpetrators, and other pertinent details. The collection of crime data was overseen by Jack's second in command, Vertel Martin. She had made sergeant, having celebrated her promotion with a party at the club Chez Josephine on West 42nd Street, owned by one of her famous aunt's non-biological "rainbow children." She was now tasked to update the Charts of the Future with data collected at eight a.m. daily.

"Every day," Jack said. "Every station."

Jack still talked about always wanting the big box of crayons as a kid, but he needed just three basic hues and a half dozen single digits to impart his fifty-four feet of printer paper with the gift of prophecy.

Green, blue, and red denoted which time period a robbery occurred. Numbers from one to six designated the particular type of robbery: (1) with a gun, (2) with a knife, (3) strong arm, (4) wolf pack, (5) bag snatch from between trains, (6) token booth. A 5 with a concentration of green on a particular stretch of the Seventh Avenue line, for example, made clear with one glance the power of the Charts of the Future.

"You could just see it," Jimmy Nuciforo would recall. "It jumped out at you."

The green made unmistakable a pattern for bag snatches from between train cars during the four p.m.-to-midnight shift. A quick review of the applicable crime reports showed that each involved a male who targeted women on the platform as he leaned out from between the cars of a departing train. He appeared to have made more than one hundred snatches, and the Transit Police had already issued an internal alert saying he operated on the local track along the Seventh Avenue line. Jack's map showed that the snatches in fact occurred on the express track at the five stops between 14th Street and 96th Street on the Seventh Avenue line in Manhattan.

Back in 1981, twenty-year-old Herman Cephas had employed this strategy to snatch as many as two hundred bags, at one point committing 15 percent of all felonies in the subway. He had strengthened himself by hanging on to a parking meter with one arm and using the other to catch kids who tried to run past. But his style involved leaning out parallel to the platform and then rising so as to lift the purse up and over the victim's shoulder.

This new mega-snatcher simply reached out and grabbed, relying on the force imparted by the train's momentum to tear it free of the victim, often breaking the strap in the process. The danger was that the victim would be pulled off balance and either strike a pillar or the side of a moving car, with possibly fatal results.

Jack deployed the two dozen cops in his unit to ride the trains between the five stations every day for a week between two and seven p.m. But the new snatcher may have taken the same precaution Cephas had, riding in one direction and then the other to look for any possible cops.

Though there were no new bag snatches, Jack's crew did repeatedly notice a spindly character riding between the cars despite the rule against it. The man had appeared to be about to strike on several occasions, but reconsidered. The cops checked the mugshots of known robbers and identified him as Leroy Lawrence of the Bronx.

On the chance that the surveillance might prompt Lawrence to change his usual routine, copies of his picture were given to detectives to include in photo arrays they showed victims and witnesses in other parts of the subway system. That resulted in an off-duty cop identifying Lawrence as the man who had snatched a woman's bag from a moving train at a downtown station on another line.

Jack and a team headed up to Lawrence's sixth-floor apartment in the Bronx, ready to make the first major arrest resulting from the Charts of the Future. They had just knocked on the front door when Jack heard the sound of somebody scrambling to the back and opening a window. He shouldered the door and reached the window in time to see Lawrence make a remarkably daring leap from a small balcony onto a fire escape one apartment over and one floor down. The cops Jack had waiting in the back found that a wall prevented them from reaching where Lawrence descended. He made a successful getaway.

Later that day, Jack was approached by a Transit Police chief.

"You know, we're very disappointed," the chief told him.

"Don't worry about it," Jack replied. "Because when the screenplay is done, I make the leap also, and I catch him on the fire escape."

Soon after, Lawrence was arrested for something unrelated and also arraigned on the outstanding robbery charge. Jack had more immediate success with dozens of other robbery patterns. The Charts of the Future became all the more effective with the introduction of colored stick-on dots big enough for notations of essential details.

Thanks to the charts, Jack and his cops zeroed in on a small crew of robbers who had been operating at a station at the tip of downtown Manhattan. The cave cops hid in the shadows at either end of the station and caught the crew in the act. One of the robbers managed to escape on foot into the tunnel leading under the harbor and on into Brooklyn. Jack could have just cleared the case and left it at that, but he continued to employ the principles of the decoy days. He cajoled the captured crooks into giving up the name of the escaped teen.

Jack and another cop pulled up just as the teen was arriving home from a long and no doubt unnerving walk through the dark tunnel from Manhattan.

The teen saw them and dashed up his stoop. Jack and the other cop chased after him, and his mother met them at the apartment door wearing a T-shirt with you can't touch this emblazoned across the chest. The other cop had his gun out when he pulled open a closet door and for an instant seemed about to shoot a bag of laundry he mistook for a crouched human form.

"Put your gun away," Jack ordered.

Jack tried a bathroom door and discovered that the teen had run inside and locked it behind him, as a much younger kid might have. Jack laughed, and at the next moment the teen burst from the bathroom, wild-eyed, considerably bigger and stronger than either cop, seeming to be fury personified.

The other cop was drawing his gun again, and Jack moved to prevent a shooting by grabbing the teen around the waist. Jack hung on as he and the teen rebounded off furniture and a wall and ended up on the floor, struggling. Jack then whispered in the teen's ear in an improbably intimate tone.

"I'm not mad if you're not mad."

The startled teen seemed to forget his rage for just the moment Jack needed to handcuff him. The teen's anger soon after reignited, and Jack showed him a foil-covered suppository he was carrying to alleviate an attack of hemorrhoids.

"You see this?" Jack asked the teen. "I'm an old man, and you beat me up, and now I'm bleeding out of my ass, and I now have to use this."

The teen hung his head.

"I'm sorry," he said. "I didn't mean to hurt you."

On a subsequent robbery case in Brooklyn, one of Jack's cops called him to say that the prosecutor wanted to reduce the charge to petit larceny. Jack became the first squad boss in memory to appear in person at the district attorney's office regarding what was viewed as just a routine minor case. He tested the prosecutor with a little fib.

"This guy was the ambassador from Nigeria that got robbed," Jack announced.

The prosecutor stammered and said it would be a robbery charge after all.

"So, it's different then, it's different on who gets robbed?" Jack said. "I caught you, you little scumbag!"

CHAPTER 17

The difference in response depending on who gets victimized was dramatically demonstrated on the night of April 19, 1989, when a twenty-eight-year-old investment banker who had been out jogging in Central Park was sexually assaulted and savagely beaten nearly to death.

The police had received reports of several less serious random assaults by a group of teens that night in the same vicinity, and city detectives decided that they had also attacked the woman, who became known as the Central Park Jogger.

From what Jack could tell from the early press accounts, the NYPD actually seemed to do what should be done in the aftermath of a wolf pack attack. Five teens were rounded up and charged after making videotaped confessions.

Only later did Jack learn that thirty or more teens had been seen going into the park. That meant that twenty-five or more had not been identified and picked up. And DNA of the semen recovered from the victim did not match any of those who had been arrested.

Had the NYPD checked for recent similar sexual assaults, the detectives would have learned there had been a brutal one in that section of Central Park just two days before by a lone assailant. The young victim was being severely beaten when her screams drew a passerby to the scene, causing the attacker to flee. She told a detective in this earlier case that her assailant had a stitched cut on his chin, and a check of local hospitals produced a name, Matias Reyes. But nobody had linked that case with the Central Park jogger after the detective who identified Reyes was transferred and the earlier victim reportedly moved away. The earlier case was closed.

The connection was only established long afterwards by Nancy Ryan of the Manhattan District Attorney's Office with the assistance of Reyes himself. Reyes confessed to both attacks, and his DNA matched that from the jogger case. He further admitted to numerous other sexual assaults, twice attempting to blind his victims with a knife. He also pleaded guilty to murdering a pregnant woman in the presence of her young children. He would deny any association with the teens who came to be called the Central Park Five.

Those revelations were years away, a number of which the Five spent in prison. What Jack did know in the days immediately following the attack on the Central Park Jogger was that in other cases the city police too often continued to focus on getting a clearance rather than on catching all the crooks involved. The posses roamed the streets much as before, although the "revitalization" of Times Square did lead them to shift their primary hunting ground from midtown to Greenwich Village. But when a posse struck underground, Jack and his crew went after every member, no matter what the race or background of the victim.

That included the case of a thirteen-year-old Hispanic girl who was stomped and sexually assaulted in a Harlem subway station just a few days after the Central Park attack. The next dawn saw Jimmy Nuciforo, now a detective, roust a fourteen-year-old named Melvin from his bed. Melvin confessed in his mother's presence to having joined a posse of females in the attack. He had committed the sexual assault while the posse held the victim down on the train platform.

"Melvin, you going to make people think there's something wrong with you," the mother said.

Nuciforo and his unit went on to pick up all the other participants, including a thirteen-year-old who said her name meant "gift from God" in Swahili. She was friendly with some of the Central Park Jogger posse and took exception to the news coverage.

"It's not *wilding*," she said. "It's *wiling*."

Gift from God had a semicircular scar from being bitten on the cheek and a line of stitches where a razor had sliced her ear in half. One of the other cops asked her if the local boys like girls who are hard.

"If you hard, you don't need boys," she replied.

The attack on the Hispanic youngster never made the newspapers, though some girls attending Gift from God's school on the Upper West Side hit the front page when they went beyond robbery and assault to sticking women in the behind with push pins.

PUSH PIN POSSE, the headline read.

J ack Maple lived with Elizabeth Sheridan for a time in Williamsburg, then a high-crime section of Brooklyn save for the stretch of Withers Street where they lived. The block had long been the turf of the Mafia, in particular the crew made famous by the book and movie *Donnie Brasco*. It was also home to Bamonte's restaurant. The proprietor, Anthony Bamonte, told Maple that he would not have to worry about his car if he parked it on the block. Everything went fine until a night when there were no spots and Jack parked just around the corner. By the next morning somebody had broken into the car and stolen the radio, an act that was so common across the city that some people had taken to putting signs reading NO RADIO and ALREADY CLEANED OUT on their dashboards.

"I said *on* the block," Bamonte told him.

Jack and Elizabeth subsequently moved to Bay Ridge, where they awoke one day to discover that a burglar had visited the apartment while they slept. A gun was missing from the bedroom closet, which meant the burglar must have walked right past them holding it.

They had a son they named Brendan, but Jack remained unrelentingly and overwhelmingly Jack. He and Elizabeth parted ways. He rented a studio apartment in a walk-up in Upper Manhattan and passed his off hours taking long lone walks through streets he had policed beneath.

"Mostly, I had been under Manhattan," he noted.

One night, Jack met the newsman John Miller for dinner. Miller suggested afterward that Jack join him at a onetime Austro-Hungarian neighborhood bar that had become a particular kind of celebrity hangout.

"Come on, we're going up to Elaine's."

Elaine's was much as it had been in its working-class days, but the walls were filled with framed book jackets and the tables were occupied by big-name writers and actors and artists and singers and composers and moguls and the occasional Nobel Prize winner. The owner, Elaine Kaufman, had once supposedly told someone who asked for directions to the men's room, "Turn right at Michael Caine."

Less illustrious souls were left to stand at the bar or consigned to the Siberia of an adjoining room. Those who did not know Kaufman would have assumed that to be the fate of an overweight cave cop from Queens.

But Kaufman was also proudly from Queens. And her time with truly great ones of every calling enabled her to recognize genius in many forms.

All Jack had needed for full acceptance at the Oak Bar and the River Café was proper attire and the price of a drink. Elaine's required something else.

"People with talent, and it didn't matter what," Miller later said. "[Jack] gained admittance into the A list very quickly."

For a little more than he would pay in some cop haunt, and a little less than he would pay in the Oak Bar, Jack could chitchat with people at Elaine's who were as accomplished at acting and writing as he was at catching crooks. But he still faced the problem of finding love again. He appraised his chances.

"Short, fat, balding, and ugly in the age of AIDS," he said. "I have the girls right where I want them."

At transit headquarters, Jack encountered a pretty officer by the coffee cart. Brigid O'Connor seemed aloof, unobtainable, and generally in keeping with what Jack had come to expect from a particular sort of Irish American woman.

"I said, 'Miserable, huh?'" Jack would recall. "Oh yeah, she was Irish."

Jack had never backed down from the most ferocious crooks, but his nerve failed him completely when it came to asking such a woman for a date. He needed a plan, and he soon devised one that began with him showing her a personal ad he had composed.

Detective Lieutenant looking for spirited Irish redheaded beauty 25-35 who possesses the following assets: (1) No public displays of affection. (2) Proficient at the silent treatment. (3) Guilt-ridden when having a good time. (4) Favorite sayings: "What's the use?" "Why bother?" (5) Least used words: "I'm sorry." (6) Cranky in the morning. (7) Phrase most often elicited: "What's the matter?" Invariable

198 • Michael Daly

response: "Nothing"...Extra credit for mood swings. Freckles a plus. Great smile a must.

On reading this, Brigid blushed, and Jack heard her say, "That's me." He went ahead and put the ad in the *Irish Voice*, and Brigid asked about the eight women who immediately responded. He spoke to each one, which afforded him eight excuses to talk to Brigid.

In the meantime, burglars had twice cleaned out his studio rental. He told Brigid that he had decided to move, and she allowed that she was renting out a basement apartment in her house on a beach block in Belle Harbor on the Rockaway Peninsula, known also as the Irish Riviera.

Where he had once wandered solitary through the upper East Side, Jack now strolled with Brigid along the beach in Queens. They were on one walk when he pretended to discover a bottle that he had in fact planted at the water's edge an hour before. The bottle contained a scroll of paper, and Brigid unrolled it to see a drawing of a stick figure wearing a bow tie.

"She smiled, and I think it was even at me," Jack later said.

On the second Saturday in February, Jack donned a tuxedo and escorted Brigid to the Fourth Annual Valentine's Day Dinner Dance of the Transit Police Women's Association. They stopped afterward at Elaine's.

"The only girl I talk to beside Brigid is Elaine," Jack affirmed.

Jack rose to the A++ list at Elaine's after two beefy wiseguys of the John Gotti Jr. variety came in early one evening.

"Dressed in their *good* tracksuits," Miller noted.

The pair would not have been seated at all had it been later, but Elaine went ahead and gave them a table for two under a bust of George Plimpton. They looked over at Jack and Miller, who were at a table for four in a choicer location.

"Cops suck," one of the wiseguys said, intentionally loud enough to be overheard.

Jack suggested they pipe down and watch their manners.

"I'll kick your ass," one of the wiseguys said.

Jack smiled.

"Let's see how that goes," Jack said. "Then, I'm going to lock you up. I'm not taking you to the 19th Precinct. I'm taking you down the stairs into District 1 past homeless guys and piss smell."

"I been to Rikers," the wiseguy said. "I fucked guys like you up the ass."

On hearing that, Elaine had enough.

"You two guys shut up," she said.

She called to the waiter to give them their check and ordered them to leave.

"Hey, he started it," one of the wiseguys said, pointing to Jack.

"I thought you guys weren't supposed to rat on anybody," Jack scolded. "I thought you weren't supposed to give anybody up."

CHAPTER 19

As Jack sought to address subway robberies with the Charts of the Future and his twenty-four cops, his bosses were detailing hundreds of transit officers to pursue a strategy conceived by George Kelling, a highly paid academic who had co-authored a famous magazine article that put forth the broken windows theory.

"Social psychologists and police officers tend to agree that if a window in a building is broken and is left unrepaired, all the rest of the windows will soon be broken," Kelling and James Q. Wilson had written in 1982. "This is as true in nice neighborhoods as in rundown ones. Window-breaking does not necessarily occur on a large scale because some areas are inhabited by determined window-breakers whereas others are populated by window-lovers; rather, one unrepaired broken window is a signal that no one cares, and so breaking more windows costs nothing."

Kelling was given a six-figure consulting contract. One result was that the Transit Police launched Operation Enforcement in the fall of 1989, seeking to address subway equivalents of broken windows such as farebeating and panhandling.

"Though Operation Enforcement was largely a police operation, its primary goal was not to fight crime but to restore orderliness to the subway," Kelling subsequently wrote. "Disorder, unpleasant in itself, breeds crime, and just as importantly, breeds the fear of crime."

The police supervisors who implemented this strategy measured success by the tally of arrests, summonses, and ejections. They would pose a question that would be echoed a decade later, when the NYPD became overly obsessed with numbers.

"What's the count?" a supervising captain famously demanded every morning.

Kelling questioned the innate value of plainclothes units such as RORSF that focused not on disorder but on crime.

"We do not start with an assumption that because there are such units we must find a purpose for them," the report said. "Despite war stories about the success of those operations, there's no evidence that they succeeded."

The result of Operation Enforcement was that felonies in the subway rose by 15 percent between its launch in April 1989 and the same month in 1990. Or, as Jack put it, "The crime was up double digits every fucking month."

Kelling blamed the rise in crime on a rise in disorder as a result of opposition from civil libertarian groups. He suggested that his approach might have been scrapped as a failure had the Metropolitan Transportation Authority not named what he called "a staunch broken windows man" as the new head of the Transit Police, William Bratton of Boston.

Like Jack, Bratton was the son of a postal worker and grew up in a working-class neighborhood. Bratton had wanted to be a cop for as long as he could remember. He was not yet two when he slipped away and gave his mother a terrible fright as she frantically searched, finally finding him standing in the middle of the street, directing traffic. He spent many hours during his grammar school years in a branch of the Boston Public Library that happened to adjoin the local police precinct, reading again and again a child's history of the NYPD called *Your Police*.

"We must always remember that whenever we see a policeman, he is your friend," the book said. "He is there to protect you."

Bratton had enjoyed a happy childhood. His memory of *The Ed Sullivan Show* was of a time on Sunday night when his homework was done and the family all watched it together. Bratton's favorite show was *Dragnet*. His desire to become a real-life cop stayed with him as he graduated high school in 1966.

Unlike big and bustling New York, Boston did not give a police exam regularly. And Bratton had to wait until he was twenty-one before he was even eligible.

In the meantime, the Vietnam War was escalating, and Bratton chose to enlist rather than be drafted, even though this meant a three-year commitment. The difference was that he could choose his assignment, and he of course put in to become a military policeman.

He was offered a chance to go to officer candidate school and start off as a lieutenant, but he stuck with the MPs. He was made a dog handler.

In Vietnam, Bratton and his dog walked the perimeter of the US Army's biggest base. He had a brief brush with combat during the Tet offensive, when Viet Cong sappers struck the sector next to his, killing a fellow dog handler.

Upon his return, Bratton still had to wait until early 1970 before the Boston police gave a test. He nearly missed it because his car broke down in a blizzard, but his sister saved the day and got him there on time. He passed and was sworn in on October 7, 1970, a day after his twenty-third birthday. He was living his boyhood dream as he stood outside Boston's Symphony Hall, directing traffic.

Bratton's ambitions did not end there, and he was determined to rise through the ranks. He studied a full year for the sergeant's test, even carrying flashcards to review during lulls on duty. He scored number one on the written portion, second overall.

As a new sergeant, he trained as a hostage negotiator. He was responding to a report of shots fired when he suddenly found himself five yards away from a gunman who was holding a woman hostage.

Bratton had his own weapon pointed at the gunman, and a standoff ensued. A defining moment came when Bratton lowered his gun to his side, telling the gunman he was not going to harm him. The gunman then lowered his own gun. The incident ended with the hostage safe, the gunman under arrest, and nobody being hurt.

By chance, the offices of the International Brotherhood of Police Officers overlooked the scene. Its president witnessed the whole thing and subsequently made Bratton the organization's person of the year. Boston's police commissioner assisted in the award presentation.

Bratton went on to become a lieutenant and to command a model policing zone that was testing the theories of Bob Wasserman, an academic who had become director of the Boston Police Academy and then the department's director of operations. Wasserman was an early advocate of community policing, and he viewed Bratton as a fresh young face of the modern cop at a time when the department was under intense criticism.

In a big shake-up of the top brass, thirty-two-year-old Bratton was elevated in one jump from lieutenant to second in command. He moved into a grand office in police headquarters and put up a sign a friend had given him: YOUTH AND SKILL WILL WIN OUT EVERY TIME OVER AGE AND TREACHERY.

A reporter asked what Bratton hoped would be his next step. He said he hoped to someday be commissioner.

On reading that, the present commissioner reacted as a cranky old Irish guy might.

"Oh, he would, would he?" Commissioner Joe Jordan reportedly said.

Jordan demoted Bratton and consigned him to an office in a distant station house on a floor otherwise occupied only by lockers. Deliverance came in the form of an offer to run the MBTA Police, the Boston area's much maligned and downtrodden transit cops. Bratton built up their training and equipment and self-esteem. Boston's onetime "Oh" police became "Oh!" police.

"The Cinderella department," Bratton called it.

In the meantime, the head of the Boston transit system, Robert Kiley, had left to become the new head of the MTA in New York. Kiley subsequently hired Wasserman and George Kelling to study—among other things— whether the New York Transit Police should be merged with the NYPD. Wasserman and Kelling recommended that he keep the departments separate, perhaps in part so they could use the Transit Police to test their theories regarding community policing and broken windows. They also urged Kiley to appoint Bratton, an avowed proponent of both approaches.

In April 1990, Bratton was appointed the new head of the Transit Police. Jack saw a news clip of his new boss.

"He was wearing a Ralph Kramden bus driver's hat," Maple would recall. "He was saying he was going to knock down crime. I said, 'Okay, let's see.'"

Jack huddled with his second in command, Sergeant Tommy Burke.

"I want to write a plan to knock down crime in the subway and get it to this guy," Jack told him.

Jack conducted surveillance to determine a pattern of another kind, this involving a coffee pot at the office of Chief of Detectives Mike O'Connor in Transit Police headquarters. Jack learned that Bratton stopped by to fill a cup there around the same time every day. Jack asked O'Connor to pass on to Bratton a ten-page summary of his crime-fighting plan. Jack understood that O'Connor could have just presented the ideas as his own to impress the new chief.

"A lot of people would do that," Jack later said. "They would have erased a few names and put their own name on it."

But O'Connor, nicknamed Iron Mike, was an honorable soul. He did warn Jack that if the ideas had merit, Bratton might claim them as his own.

"I don't give a shit," Jack replied.

A s it happened, one of William Bratton's great strengths as a leader was a determined belief in giving credit where credit is due. He also was not afraid to put promising ideas into immediate action.

At a breakfast meeting, Jack went over his proposals with Bratton.

"The reason they brought me here is to reduce crime," Bratton said.

"If we go by this plan, it's going to happen," Jack said.

Jack's proposals included moving his entire RORSF team into the detective division, from which they could investigate robberies as well as identify patterns, debrief prisoners, go after accomplices, and debrief them about other crimes, while checking everybody for warrants.

Bratton was indeed a staunch broken windows guy, and Jack proposed intensifying the effort against farebeats, but only as an integral part of the larger plan. Jack wanted to be at once more aggressive and more measured.

In Jack's plan, anyone who had identification and no recent farebeating stops or outstanding warrants would just be given a summons and allowed to continue on their way.

"The strategies have to be enforced equally for all, but good people need a play," Jack later said. "It's a sense of fairness that you want out there."

And taking someone into custody unnecessarily removed the cop from the scene. Giving a good person a play had the added reward of leaving the cop in place.

"Not only a sense of fairness, but you want to catch more bad guys," Jack added.

In his view, the tally of actual bad guys caught fairly was the count that mattered when enforcing "quality of life." He said the goal should be not so much to preserve order as to lock up bad guys and otherwise make their lives miserable.

206 • MICHAEL DALY

"The broken balls theory," Jack said. "It's not about broken windows; it's about breaking balls."

He also said, "Fixing broken windows on a house that's falling down is like giving a facelift to a cancer patient."

Jack opposed "sweeps" such as those that would lead to the excesses of the stop-question-and-frisk era to come.

"I'm not a big fan of throwing people on the wall," Jack would later say. "What I want is, 'Here are the rules I play by. You're going to be stopped for these violations. We're going to do the warrant check. We know you're a member of a gang. We know you've been known to deal drugs. We know you're on parole or probation. These are the other things we can do.'"

He emphasized, "You want these things to be done very, very professionally, because you don't want a besieged community here."

He knew that actual bad guys who got a summons were far more likely than others to just throw it away and fail to show up in court. They could now expect an early-morning visit if they did.

Previously, transit had assigned forty detectives—more than were in RORSF—to a joint NYPD-TPD warrant squad. But the transit warrants were just left to form huge piles.

With Bratton's approval, Jack now formed a unit that he dubbed the Fugitive Investigative Strike Team (FIST). He instructed Vertel to get the transit warrants. She called the NYPD lieutenant who had been in charge of the joint squad.

"I'm sending a couple of detectives with boxes," she told him.

"You better send a couple of trucks," the lieutenant replied.

Vertel later added, "He wasn't lying. There were hundreds of thousands."

Vertel prioritized them, and FIST began venturing out before each dawn to arrest people with outstanding transit warrants.

Jack would go on pickups, and he once encountered a white pit bull when hitting the apartment of a convicted drug dealer in Brooklyn.

"Get 'em!" the drug dealer commanded.

Jack noted that the dog had a black circle around one eye that made him look like the pooch in the Our Gang movies.

"It's Petey!" Jack exclaimed. "Petey, come here!"

To the dealer's considerable consternation, the dog went up to Jack, wagging the stub of his amputated tail.

The newly constituted Central Robbery squad settled into another unused space in the parole building on West 40th Street in Manhattan. Maple took to living in the new robbery headquarters as a kind of crookologist in residence. He would sometimes amble casually through the squad room between his office and the shower, bare legged, clad in nothing but a Burberry raincoat.

"Who's that?" asked a prisoner who was being questioned by one of the detectives.

"That's the boss," the detective replied.

"That's your boss?" the prisoner asked.

The former RORSF cops who were now newly minted members of the detective division dressed the part, which meant Sonny Archer had to buy a suit. The salesclerk at the clothing shop measured him and determined he would require a 54 large jacket but had only a thirty-two-inch waist. No suit could accommodate those dimensions.

"Can't do it," the salesclerk said.

Archer ended up buying two suits and discarding half of each.

Under his suit jacket, Sonny wore a 9mm semiautomatic pistol, Bratton having decided to replace the .38 caliber revolvers that had long been standard for the transit police as well as the NYPD. Cops of the city's various departments had been clamoring for the change since the killing of twenty-two-year-old NYPD Officer Scott Gadell in 1986, fourteen days before Steven was shot. Gadell had emptied his six-shot revolver in a gun battle and was frantically reloading it one cartridge at a time when the gunman walked up with a nine shot, magazine-fed semiautomatic pistol and shot him in the forehead. Bratton's decision to arm transit cops with 9mm semiautomatics that could hold as many as seventeen rounds signaled that he was willing to risk a firestorm of criticism should anything go wrong. He was also giving the cave cops a reason to feel that the subway was above the surface world—by one measure, anyway.

Sonny became one of the first transit cops to fire a 9mm in the line of duty when Jack's squad moved to arrest a suspect in the gunpoint robbery of two armed revenue guards of $28,000 in cash receipts they had collected from token booths. The cops had made the identification by tracing a beeper dropped at the scene. They had proceeded from the manufacturer to a wholesaler and eventually to a retailer not far from Jack's office. The transaction had been in cash, but the store had a paper record that simply said "Mr. Shafeeq."

The lone convicted felon with that surname was Abulawali Shafeeq, who had been paroled the previous September after serving six years for robbery. Jack's squad was staking out the Brooklyn rooming house where Shafeeq resided when they saw him approach. Sonny and Detective Jawann Olajide-Stuckey strode up from either side as he began to ascend the stoop.

"Police! Don't move!"

Shafeeq whirled around with a pistol in his hand.

"No, don't you fucking move!" he said.

With that, Shafeeq fired once at Sonny. Stuckey opened up from the other side, and Shafeeq wheeled toward him, firing twice.

Stuckey had always found gunfire jarring at the pistol range, but these shots seemed to make no sound at all. He registered only the muzzle flashes as he and Sonny and their suspect all blazed away in the early-morning darkness.

Five bullets hit the man, and Shafeeq kept coming down the stoop, still firing. Stuckey sought cover behind a tree and squeezed the trigger until his pistol was empty. Shafeeq continued to advance straight at him, seemingly as intent on killing as on escape.

Sonny then fired the last round in his clip. The bullet shattered Shafeeq's leg, and he went down as if he had been tackled. Stuckey's hearing returned with the man's scream.

Sergeant John Dove appeared from a backup car and asked if anybody was hurt. Sonny patted his chest and reported he was fine. Stuckey felt something trickle down past his right eye, and he raised his hand to his face. His fingers came away covered with blood.

"I said, 'Look at me, I think I'm hit,'" Stuckey would remember.

Stuckey took a step back and leaned against a car. Shell casings littered the pavement. Gunfire had torn a chunk out of the tree. His Philadelphia 76ers baseball cap had two bullet holes in the brim.

"Like the cowboy pictures," Stuckey later said.

Then the tree and the hat and everything else began to blur and dim. Stuckey found himself not just bleeding but blinded. He now had only sound to guide him, and he heard somebody shout into a radio.

"Ten-thirteen! Officer down! Officer shot!"

Detective Billy Courtney was there and helped Stuckey into the back of an unmarked car. Courtney drove as Stuckey lay on the seat and listened to the siren wail and the radio crackle with questions about the shooting. He sat up and tried to clear his eyes, but he was unable to see anything more than vague forms. He lay back down as the car sped through Brooklyn.

Courtney braked to a stop outside the emergency entrance to nearby Interfaith Hospital. Courtney dashed inside, but the ER was being phased out, and the only doctor in evidence was sleeping under a table.

Courtney roused the doctor, and Stuckey felt himself being lifted onto a stretcher and wheeled inside. Hands began taking his blood pressure and other vital signs. Nobody responded when he called out that he was blind. He was still waiting for a doctor to examine his eyes when he heard somebody suggest that Interfaith was not properly equipped for this sort of injury.

"Then I heard a doctor say, 'He's not stable, and I won't be responsible if you move him,'" Stuckey would recall.

A voice told Stuckey that he had to sign a waiver absolving the hospital of responsibility if he was moved. Stuckey said he could not see the form, and Sonny stepped up to press a pen into his hand. Stuckey blindly affixed his signature and felt himself wheeled back out to an ambulance.

Stuckey heard what sounded like hundreds of sirens as he rode toward the Brooklyn Bridge. An ambulance attendant said it was the biggest motorcade he had ever seen other than when the president was in town.

"I wasn't in any pain; I just couldn't see," Stuckey later said. "I kind of felt guilty. I thought, *Maybe I'm not hurt enough for all this attention.*"

Stuckey then felt a jolt, and he was pitched to the floor. A detective explained that the ambulance had careened into a construction barricade. Stuckey felt himself hoisted back onto the stretcher as they sped up the FDR Drive to Bellevue Hospital. Stuckey was wheeled into a second emergency room and hooked up to a machine that monitored his vital signs. Cops and medical people began hitting him with questions from every direction. *How old are you? Where's your ID card? Were you shot in the head, officer? Where's your gun? What happened to the other guy?*

Somebody rinsed Stuckey's right eye, and suddenly he could see again. He gazed up and fixed his full attention on the monitor overhead and the numbers giving his heart rate and blood pressure. He would remember telling himself that he was fine as long as those electronic digits stayed steady.

A nurse then did something else to Stuckey's right eye, and his vision blurred back toward blindness. The electronic digits disappeared, and the fright apparently caused his blood pressure to plummet. The monitor he could no longer see began beeping an alarm.

"I thought, God, I must be going out," Stuckey would recall.

Any number of hands were suddenly working on Stuckey, and he felt somebody cutting off his clothes. The alarm ceased. He would remember, "I kept asking, 'How bad is it?' The nurses would say, 'Not bad.' I heard cops say, 'He has entrance and exit wounds. He looks f—ed up. He took one in the head.'"

Another hand came out of the dimness, and this one clasped Stuckey's own. The hand belonged to a PBA delegate whose gentle voice quietly told Stuckey not to worry. Stuckey's eyes could not distinguish gender, much less race, but he could surmise from the voice that the delegate was male and white.

Stuckey was himself Black. He now was in a world of sound, and all he heard were the quiet tones of the cops who had come to see how he was doing and the bustle of the medical people bent on helping him. Those around him seemed as blind to his color as he was to theirs, and he experienced a moment when race appeared not to matter.

"I really felt for the first time in my life that I was just a person," Stuckey would later say.

The PBA delegate stayed with Stuckey as he was wheeled off for a CAT scan. Stuckey lay on a cold steel table and listened to the hum of a machine. A doctor studied the films and informed Stuckey that nothing had pierced his cranium. A bullet had struck him by the right eye but had caused no serious injury. An operation would be needed on the left eye to remove bullet fragments and tree splinters. Some plastic surgery might also be required.

"I remember thinking, *I'm ugly to begin with*," Stuckey would remember.

"I must have said it out loud, because somebody said, 'Maybe if you have plastic surgery, you'll look better.'"

A dozen hours after the shooting, Stuckey was discharged from the hospital. He was still essentially blind, and he would have many hours in the days ahead to fit together the pieces of all that had happened. He determined that his brief moment of sight in the emergency room had ended when the nurse removed his contact lens and his eye swelled shut. He learned that a search of Shafeeq's room had produced two sawed-off shotguns and a homemade bomb.

Shafeeq had survived and had been taken to Kings County Hospital, where he had undergone surgery for wounds to his leg and abdomen. Jack went to speak to him and leaned close to Shafeeq's left ear.

"Hey, you fuck," Jack began. "You want to know how we found you? You dropped your beeper at the scene."

The monitor spiked, *beep beep beep.*

Ten days after he was wounded, Stuckey appeared before a grand jury wearing what he called his Ray Charles glasses. He recounted what had happened and went back to the waiting area only to be summoned again several minutes later. He expected some follow-up questions.

Instead, the prosecutor said that the grand jury had voted to indict Shafeeq for attempted murder of a police officer. The forewoman added that the jurors hoped Stuckey's vision would return. He then heard them all break into applause.

"I thought, *Maybe I should be hurt worse; all this and I'm not in pain,*" Stuckey later said.

In the weeks ahead, Stuckey's vision did indeed begin to improve. He went in to see the doctor, fully aware that he was a candidate for the fabled "three-quarters" tax-free disability pension, the equivalent of his full salary. The cops who had applied for it included former NYPD Chief of Department Robert Johnston, the same boss who had been so outraged by a drug dealer's offer in Central Park that he ordered rookies, including Steven McDonald, sent there. Johnston got "three-quarters" by claiming he had suffered hearing loss when two firecrackers exploded several feet from his ear at a Rolling Stones concert two years before.

But in the way of Sergeant Mary Buckley, Stuckey told the doctor he was only interested in going back to work. He spent the next six months slowly recovering all but 10 percent of his eyesight. He returned to duty again able to tell white from Black, but not forgetting that there had been at least a moment when all questions of race had ceased to exist.

"For me it was like that Martin Luther King thing," Stuckey says. "You judge a person by his character."

Jack and his crew kept at it, and crime in the subways tumbled, just as he predicted. Bratton made him special assistant to the chief, enabling him better to implement the full scope of his plan. His wiles led to a 15 percent drop in subway crime overall as reported crime on the surface declined by only 4.4 percent. Wolf pack robberies underground plummeted from 1,200 a year to just twelve.

After twenty-one months, Bratton announced that he was resigning as chief of the Transit Police to become superintendent of the police in his hometown of Boston. He asked Jack to come with him as his chief of operations.

Jack resigned from the Transit Police and traveled to New England for the first time since he had gone to collect his yacht. His pink high-tops continued to hang from the wire in Union Square, a symbol for a few in the know of the strategies that could successfully address crime in New York.

PART
IV

CHAPTER 1

The Christmas tree lighting at Rockefeller Center is an annual tradition that goes back to 1931, when construction workers in the early stages of the project put up a twenty-foot balsam fir. They decorated it with cranberries and paper garlands and tin cans.

A Rockefeller press agent was inspired to hold the first official tree lighting two years later. The event was repeated annually, save for during the blackout period of World War II.

On December 2, 1993, tens of thousands were packed into the plaza and the surrounding streets for the moment when New York is always at its magical best. Mayor-elect Rudy Giuliani was there, as was William Bratton, who would soon be taking command of the NYPD.

Jack Maple was also in attendance, and Bratton introduced him to several chiefs as his choice to devise and implement new strategies for fighting crime. Jack's presence did not keep several chiefs from chuckling at the thought of a cave cop telling them how to do anything. Jack said nothing, but he remembered a line uttered by the Joker in one of the Batman movies.

"Wait 'til they get a load of me!"

In a single unprecedented leap, Jack went from transit lieutenant to the NYPD deputy commissioner for crime control strategies. He set to studying the workings—and shortcomings—of the NYPD. He learned that Narcotics only worked eleven a.m. to seven p.m. and was off on weekends. The warrant squad did not get started until seven thirty a.m. and also had weekends off, as did Major Case and Robbery.

"Unfortunately, the criminal element worked nights, they worked weekends," Jack later said.

The community policing officers were allowed to pick whatever shifts they thought might be most effective in their respective communities.

216 • MICHAEL DALY

"The vast majority worked ten in the morning to six at night, with weekends off," Jack reported.

On the days Narcotics was working, it considered low-level street buys to be a waste of time.

"We want to make the big ones," a Narcotics commander told Jack.

"Where do you live, Clarkstown or one of those places?" Jack asked. "Let's say one of these low-level scumbags was standing in front of your house every morning, selling drugs? Do you think you would be on the phone to the fucking Clarkstown cops? And if they said, 'Gee, don't you understand, they're just low-level guys, we are waiting for the big case' and the big case would be over in a year, do you think that would be okay as your children are stepping over crack vials on their way to school?"

"You know, you're right," the commander allowed.

When it came to burglaries, Jack discovered that the department was not investigating any break-ins where the stolen property was valued at less than $10,000 in Manhattan or less than $5,000 in the outer boroughs, which for some victims would amount to their life savings.

"We're saying, 'If you're poor, we're not going to investigate anything,'" Jack said. "And nobody cares about catching accomplices, because the case is cleared with one arrest."

To help Bratton assemble a new staff, Jack met with various promising commanders at a modest Brooklyn facility with a grand name that held personal significance.

SHEEPSHEAD BAY YACHT CLUB read the sign in front of the place not far from Dead Horse Bay and the Barren Island Marina, where Jack kept the *Quaalude.*

Jack accepted a department car but declined a driver. He radioed the operations desk on one of his first nights cruising the city.

"This is Commissioner Maple, anything going on?"

Operations was accustomed to keeping big bosses apprised of such matters as traffic backups and water main breaks that might impede their travels.

"All's quiet, commissioner," came the reply.

"How about any homicides? You got any homicides?"

"Well, we got two in Brooklyn."

"How about the Bronx?"

"We got two there, too."

"How about Manhattan?"

"We got one, but it's above 125th Street."

Meaning it was in Harlem.

"But all's quiet?" Jack asked.

"All's quiet, commissioner."

Bratton echoed this appraisal when Jack came into his office toward the end of the first week.

"You know, things are pretty quiet around here," Bratton said by Jack's recollection.

"Quiet?" Jack replied. "There's fucking thirty murders so far. They don't tell you stuff."

Jack would later note, "Police departments do that with commissioners. They know the commissioner is sort of like a temporary resident. They've seen them come and go, and think when they deprive them of a lot of the information, they have more control over them."

Jack got on the phone with the operations desk.

"I want to know every murder, and I want to know every time we fire a gun and hit somebody," he said.

"Do you know how many times that is?" the person at operations asked.

"Yes," Jack said. "There were 1,946 murders last year. And I know we were in forty-four shoot-outs. We hit seventy-eight people, killing twenty-five."

His ability to immediately summon such precise numbers caused some to figure Jack was a kind of wacky nerd from the underground, or maybe a law enforcement equivalent of Rain Man. But Jack had simply taken the view that treating every crime and every victim as equally important began with knowing exactly how many there were.

At headquarters, Jack decided that the chiefs seemed considerably more concerned about corner offices and reserved parking spots than about robbery and murder. He sat in one interminable meeting where commanders talked about overtime and gas in the precincts and just about everything but what they should be focused on.

"I've been sitting there for an hour and a half, and nobody's used the c-word," Jack said.

There was an uncomfortable hush.

"You know, *crime*," Jack said.

Operations at least showed some spirit in the way it responded to his standing order to be notified.

"They were cute, I got to hand it to them," Jack would recall. "If a murder happened at ten at night, they would wake me up at three in the morning and tell me we had a murder. I like that. You got to admire that."

Jack would respond to the scene no matter what the hour. He was often notified when he was at Elaine's, and he would rise from one of the better tables and drive off to the city's latest murder. Detectives working in the rougher precincts on what would have been considered a "misdemeanor homicide" would see a deputy commissioner arrive.

"They weren't used to that," Jack later said.

On February 5, Operations notified Jack of a police-involved triple shooting in a Brooklyn beauty parlor. Off-duty Police Officer Arlene Beckles had been under a hairdryer whose roar drowned out the shouts and screams when three gunmen burst in. She needed only to open her eyes to know that she would meet all but certain death if she did anything other than cower. But she also saw the terrified faces of civilians she had sworn to protect.

Beckles took a deep breath and rose, still wearing the smock.

"I really counted myself out," she would later say. "I really didn't think I had a chance. There were three of them, and there was just me. I should say God and me."

Beckles would later say she was not sure why she stepped to the side as she rose still wearing the salon smock. Detectives would conclude that she instinctively used that first dire instant to place herself, and therefore the gunmen's bullets, away from the Saturday night crowd of civilians sprawled around her. She used the next moment to call out the warning she had been trained to give, even in such a terrible predicament.

"Police! Don't move! Drop your weapon!"

The lead gunman turned toward Beckles, weapon in hand. He and his partners had most likely picked this salon for much the same reason that some men were still grumbling that women could not cut it as cops. He must have been the most surprised crook in the world when this tiny woman fired through the smock and shot him in the face.

The two remaining gunmen opened up and Beckles returned fire, wounding both before she ran out of bullets.

A gunman she had shot in the hand rushed her and knocked her down and placed his pistol to her head. He pulled the trigger. She heard a click as it misfired. He tried to unjam it and pulled the trigger a second time. She heard a second click as it misfired again.

"He states he is very upset at this because his gun was new," a detective would later note in a report.

The second and third gunmen fled. The lead gunman leaped up and grabbed Beckles. She was still struggling with him when a transit sergeant raced in.

"I'm a cop!" Beckles cried out.

The sergeant helped subdue the gunman and asked Beckles if she was all right. She nodded and proceeded to recover two weapons from the floor, even then mindful of such small matters of procedure as keeping her fingers outside the trigger guards.

The detectives responded and found Beckles sitting in a blood-soaked salon smock.

"I'm just shaken up," she said.

Jack arrived to inspect the scene.

" 'Twas beauty that shot the beast," he said. "Three times. In a beauty parlor."

Bratton soon after presented Beckles with a detective shield in a kind of battlefield promotion.

Other police-involved shootings were more problematic, and Jack learned that Operations was often sparing in the details when he was notified.

He responded to one scene in Queens having only been told that two felons had been killed after their car was pulled over following a shooting.

"Don't worry boss, this looks pretty good," a detective told Jack.

The detective allowed that the cops who approached the car were unaware that the gunman in the shooting had somehow slipped away. The windows were tinted, and one of the cops used his flashlight to smash the one in the right rear so he could see inside. The flash of light and the sound of breaking glass had apparently caused his partner to imagine he was being fired upon. He had begun shooting and killed the two felons inside. No gun had been recovered.

"So when do we get to the good part?" Jack asked.

On that night and on many other occasions, Jack was joined by John Miller, who had taken a six-figure pay cut to go from an ABC News correspondent to NYPD deputy commissioner for public information. Miller now arrived with Jack at crime scenes that not even local news covered. The individual detectives almost always treated homicides with due attention, but in the past that had too often translated into what amounted to a shrug in the upper ranks. The highest levels of the department were now signaling that every murder counted.

Jack was back at one of the better tables at Elaine's, once more experiencing the clarity from just a little champagne, when he reached for a napkin and took out a pen. He prepared to list the strategies he would need to accomplish in the whole city what he had achieved in the subway.

"I'm thinking, *What is it in strategies that we need?*" Jack would recall. "I put down we need *intelligence.* Then, *What kind of intelligence do we need?* We need the *accurate, timely, intelligence.* I said, *All right, so that's the crime that we got to know right away.* And then I said, *What are we going to do then, when we get there? Well, then we got to put the cops where the crime is.* So I put down *deployment.* Then *rapid deployment.* And then I said, *What are we going to do there with the tactics?* And then you got to *follow up.*"

He considered all the units that only worked Monday to Friday. And, if the Transit Police had been derided as cave cops, he figured the NYPD in its present form was the Weekday Police. *Follow-up* would have to be seven days a week, twenty-four hours a day. *Relentless.*

With that, he completed a list on the napkin of four simple, up-from-the-underground principles for reducing crime: (1) Accurate, timely intelligence. (2) Rapid deployment. (3) Effective tactics. (4) Relentless follow-up and assessment.

Neither Rudy Giuliani nor William Bratton seemed to share Jack's belief that he could cut violent crime in half within two years.

"Bratton at that point did not see the dramatic crime [reduction] in the cards," Jack would recall. "Giuliani didn't see it."

Bratton did make a public promise to reduce the fear of crime. The front-page headline of the *Daily News* read: TOP COP WILLIAM BRATTON: I'LL END THE FEAR.

Bratton and Jack were summoned to City Hall by Peter Powers, the deputy mayor for operations. Powers had known Giuliani since they both attended Bishop Loughlin High School.

"You guys are going way too high profile," Powers said, according to Bratton's subsequent account in his book *Turnaround*. "This business with the press and the TV shows and the interviews and the front-page profiles, these are going to cause problems."

Powers went on, "We need to be aware of these stories. The mayor is very concerned. We will control how these stories go out. The mayor has an agenda, and it's very important that everybody stay on message and that the message comes from the mayor."

Jack did not care about the message or whose photo was on the front page or who was going to get credit for what. He was only interested in getting back to turning *what is* into *what should be* and saving lives with principles he had been developing since his first days as a cave cop. He was silent until he and Bratton were going back down the City Hall steps.

"Commissioner, have I thanked you for this job lately?"

At Elaine's, Miller had a question for Jack.

"So, how are we going to do it?"

Jack replied, "It's going to be an easy one, as long as we have absolute control."

Jack was not talking about message and image control, such as Powers cited and Giuliani demanded. Jack was talking about operational control, such as he had when running his crew in the subway. Miller gave him a look.

"What are you thinking now?" Miller asked.

Jack recalled the same movie line that had come to him at the Christmas tree lighting.

"John, did you ever see the fucking Joker in Batman?" Jack replied.

The NYPD was about to get a load of the onetime cave cop many in headquarters would come to call the Jackster.

Timely intelligence proved to be considerably more challenging with the NYPD than when Jack had Vertel Martin and Bill Courtney begin each day by collecting all the pertinent details of every crime in the subway.

Jack Maple now sought to have city cops in every precinct do the same. He did not even ask for a daily tally.

"I said, 'I gotta get this crime weekly,' and I was in for a fight," Jack later said. "They said it couldn't be done."

He also wanted the weekly numbers compared with the same week the previous year. He was told it was absolutely impossible.

"Do a hand count," Jack ordered.

Jack learned that a sergeant named John Yohe in the chief of patrol's office had been collecting monthly robbery reports from the precincts. Yohe was at his desk when a stout figure in a bow tie and two-tone spectator shoes appeared.

"I'm like, 'What the hell is this?'" Yohe would remember.

Jack told Yohe that he had been on a long hunt.

"He'd been all over the department trying to get numbers," Yohe would recall. "They were saying, 'We're going to need to put a pilot program together. It might take six months, it might take a year.'"

Yohe now told Jack, "I got an idea. Let me get back to you in a couple of days."

Jack asked, "Days? Not weeks? Not months?"

Yohe decided that there was no reason why he could not simply enter the other numbers just as he did the robbery stats. He and a team that included Sergeant Eugene Whyte set about getting the tallies.

"We got to get these numbers," Yohe would tell the cop in charge of each precinct's tally.

"We don't have them yet," the cops would say, often adding something like, "The captain went home."

Yohe would respond as a representative of a deputy commissioner.

"You better call him at home and get him out of bed."

One early problem was accuracy. Yohe called a command that reported fifty-seven rapes in a week, an increase of over 2,200 percent.

"We meant to say we had one," the cop at the command said.

"Why did you type fifty-seven?" Yohe asked.

"I don't know," the cop said.

Yohe ended up adding a notation to the weekly compilation: "All results are preliminary and subject to future analysis and revision."

Jack warned that murder counts could change, as the victim might not actually die until sometime afterward.

"So you had to make sure to add all the bodies every day," Jack later said.

At police headquarters, John Yohe and Eugene Whyte and other cops on Jack's geek team continued entering numbers from the precincts and comparing these latest tallies of 1994 with those of the previous year. A blizzard began closing in on the city on February 8, and they quickly had to save the data on a 5.25-inch floppy. The file needed a name, and it could be no more than eight characters.

"Compstat," they wrote.

The most literal translation was "comparative statistics," but those who were there knew the real meaning.

"It means, 'It's fucking snowing and we got to go home,'" Whyte would later say.

Yohe wanted to keep working, blizzard or no, so he packed up an NYPD laptop. He figured he would do best not even trying to go home to Long Island and return by morning. He instead headed for his grandmother's home in Brooklyn. The snow was already so heavy that the subway ran only part of the way, and he had to trudge the rest through growing snowdrifts.

They finished assembling the data on February 13. Jack wanted it printed in book form, and they worked through the following night to get it done.

"Valentine's Day," Yohe noted.

The cover read: "Weekly Crime/Arrest Comparison Report: Report Covering the Week of February 7, 1994 through February 13, 1994." And in red it warned: "These Figures Are for Internal Use Only—Not to Be Released to the Public or Other Agencies."

Whyte ensured it was a limited edition of twelve copies, each bearing an individual secret mark to distinguish it from the others in case it was copied and leaked either inside or outside the department. Should somebody find an error, the whole process could be called into question.

From there, Jack set to demonstrating how important crime stats could be if used as a tool the proper way.

"And I was very proud of myself with my little book, and I went around to different chiefs," Jack later said. "Now there start to become rumbles within the department. That, you know, I'm making all this work, and they're printing all these books, and it's overtime in headquarters. And, you know, what's the use of it?"

Bratton asked Jack, "Did you put people on overtime?"

Jack would remember telling Bratton, "Yeah, we were printing these books up, and this is what we need to do. How [else] are you going to know where the crime is?"

Jack would later say that Bratton deserved considerable credit for letting him go ahead despite resistance during the first months.

Among the main grumblers was the head of Bratton's transition team, Bob Wasserman. He was the academic who had figured in Bratton's early rise in the Boston Police Department and now was assisting him in New York.

Jack would recall that he was in Bratton's office when Wasserman told him, "You know, we don't think you really need these books like this. You know every three or four weeks is fine."

Jack afterward grabbed Wasserman.

"What the fuck would you know about crime?" Jack asked. "What the fuck would you know what we need?"

At the same time, Jack had come to understand that headquarters was governed by such ponderous bureaucratic protocols as an unwritten rule that meetings were to be held in the office of the highest-ranking party.

"I saw we were never going to get anything done like this," Jack later said.

Jack began just dropping in unannounced to speak with the various chiefs each day: Chief of Department John Timoney and Chief of Patrol Louis Anemone as well as Chief of Detectives Joe Borelli and others. Jack would show them his numbers and give them his latest ideas.

"I also had to win them over one by one," Jack later said. "So when the big meeting came, I had the fucking votes."

Jack would see Bratton as many as eight times a day for maybe two minutes at a time to keep him apprised. Jack penned no reports or memos beyond that napkin in Elaine's.

"I never wrote a piece of paper," he later said.

Jack's own office was originally next to Bratton's on the fourteenth floor, but that was then given to Janet Lennon, the special counsel hired on Wasserman's recommendation. Jack settled into an out-of-the-way suite on the ninth floor.

"Which was actually quite lovely," he later said.

He made sure there was no sign on the door.

"So nobody knew how to get there," he later said. "It looked like they were walking into a closet, but when you walked in, I had a beautiful suite. I had a big office with a big shower. It was exactly what I wanted...I wanted a little mysterious thing."

At a headquarters conference, Jack used the c-word and said there should be crime maps in each precinct showing robberies and shootings and murders. And he wanted it all updated daily.

"Do you know how long that will take?" he was asked.

Jack had asked one of his people to average how long it took to make the daily tally over the course of a month in the city's busiest precinct, the 75th.

"Yes," Jack said. "Eighteen minutes."

He was yet again asked if he knew how many murders there were, and he yet again replied 1,946. He then posed a question to them.

"Do you know how many shootings there were? Does anybody know?"

No answer came.

"There were 5,933," Jack said. "Of those 5,933 people shot, how many different shooters do you think we have out there? Two thousand? Three thousand? Thirty-five hundred?"

Jack noted that between the NYPD and transit and the housing police, the city had thirty-seven thousand cops to catch at most a tenth as many shooters.

"Let's go get them," Jack said. "Come on, this should be a fucking grounder. I walk around and I see these signs up, 'Welcome to the NYPD, the greatest detectives in the world.' It's not like we have 2,500 cops to address thirty-seven thousand shooters. It's the other way around."

A representative of Chief of Detectives Borelli informed Jack that he could have monthly numbers, but not weekly. Jack went to Borelli's office.

"Listen, I need the information from the detectives weekly," Jack said.

"You know, you're lucky I like you," Borelli said.

"No, Joe, you got it wrong," Jack replied. "A lot of people have been fucking disappearing around here. You're lucky I like you."

The grumbling continued among the academic element in headquarters. Jack would sum up their view as "The fucking transit cop with the night school diploma thinks this is so simple. He's oversimplifying this really complicated issue of crime and, you know, social behavior and all this other horseshit."

Wasserman again complained about Jack to Bratton.

"He was the guy that said to Bratton, 'You know, Jack's going around here coming on too strong with people,'" Jack later recalled. "I grab him on the side and I say, 'Hey, fuck-o, if you have a problem with me, you tell me, you understand? Bob, don't get in my way.'"

Jack noted that Wasserman had previously served as chief of staff of NYPD Commissioner Lee Brown.

"Bob, when you and Lee Brown were here, this was the murder capital of the fucking world," Jack now told Wasserman. "You understand? I'm not going to let that happen here now."

Wasserman had continued to work with George Kelling, co-author of the broken windows theory, serving as high-priced consultants. Jack viewed them and their ilk as know-nothing hustlers.

"So he's been on this gravy train with Kelling, and they're geniuses at this," Jack would later say. "We in policing say we're professionals. Anybody that says they're professional, they're not really sure of it...In order for us to make us feel like we're professionals, what do we do? We hire the Kellings and the Wassermans and these other characters. So they come and they write a report and they bring you to the Kennedy School and they give you an award..."

Jack imagined it as a scene from his favorite movie, *The Wizard of Oz*, saying, "There are many men who are professionals. The only difference between them and you is they have a *diploma*!"

One difference between Jack and his predecessors at the executive staff meetings was that he had *numbers*. The usual routine prior to Jack had been for a borough commander to come in and give a general briefing.

"There'd be a couple of softball questions about overtime, nothing about the tactics or anything else," Jack later said.

When the Manhattan South borough commander came in, the numbers told Jack there had been an uptick in robberies in the 5th Precinct.

"A lot more heroin out there," the borough commander said by way of explanation.

"No kidding? Really?" Jack said. "Where is it? Where is it coming in? Who's dealing it? How do you know they're the heroin addicts that are doing the robberies? Have they been debriefed?"

"Uh...ah...uh...ah..." the borough commander said.

Jack had just shown some of what else he had along with numbers.

"They had never been asked a follow-up question before," Jack later said.

Jack learned that every borough command had a monthly meeting of precinct commanders regarding robberies and red light summonses. Robbery, not homicide, was then considered the bellwether crime. And red light summonses were used to estimate the revenue the city could expect.

Jack and the new chief of patrol, Louis Anemone, decided they would attend the next meeting. They learned that it was in Brooklyn North, just across the river. The hitch was that it was scheduled for one p.m., when Anemone was otherwise engaged. The obvious solution was conveyed to the borough commander.

"Standby for a telephone message. You are hereby summoned for your borough robbery meeting to be held at One Police Plaza at eleven hundred hours..."

Jack and Anemone hoped to hold the meeting in the command and control center on the eighth floor, but they were told that it was reserved for emergencies.

"Yeah, two thousand people killed a year is not an emergency," Whyte later remarked, channeling Jack and on the way to becoming a Maple disciple.

Miller was happy to let them have the briefing room officially used for press conferences. The meeting was opened to anybody in headquarters who had an interest, as well as the press.

"I was told to put up signs in the elevators," Whyte would recall.

The room was packed when the Brooklyn North commander and his precinct heads arrived.

The initial precinct commander was chosen at random. He began a presentation as if he were addressing a community meeting: how many square miles in the command, how many civic groups.

"How many GLAs?" Jack demanded.

That was grand larceny auto, not a number the precinct commander was likely to have handy.

"How about your robberies?" Anemone asked. "Tell me about your robberies. How many patterns? What hours in a day do your guys work?"

Those were answers the commander should have had, but he was either rattled or unprepared—likely both. Anemone threw up his arms.

"That's it!" he said.

He rose and announced he had heard enough. He told them to come back next week. He used the c-word.

"And we're going to talk about *crime*," he said.

Anemone gave Whyte a wink as he strode out with Jack. The performance was all the more effective because Anemone was in uniform and known as a street cop, truly one of NYPD's own. Jack had not wanted anybody to dismiss it as just coming from some cave cop.

When Brooklyn North returned the following week, Inspector Joe Dunne of the 75th Precinct was up first. Dunne had learned from the earlier meeting what to expect, and he had come prepared with immediate answers to every possible follow-up question. He was soon after promoted to the new Brooklyn North borough commander, in charge of all patrol cops, as well as detective squads, warrant squads, and narcotics units within his realm. The result would be a drop in crime 50 percent faster than in the rest of the city.

The two Brooklyn North meetings demonstrated that precinct commanders could be shamed but could also shine. Every borough command was subsequently summoned in rotation. Jack and Anemone began playing bad cop/bad cop every Wednesday and Friday.

"We'll call it the crime control strategy meeting, or the crime meeting," Jack said.

Jack's numbers crew had become confident enough in the stats that they began printing up enough books for each precinct, updated every Monday. But they had no funding for any of it, and the crew had to scrounge what it could at night from unlocked offices at headquarters.

"We'd take their ink cartridges and replace them with empty ink cartridges," Whyte would recall.

They sought funding through a federal Innovation in Government Award and gave their program the name that to them meant "It's fucking snowing and we got to go home."

One of Bratton's senior aides made it a little more eye catching by inserting a midcap: CompStat.

CHAPTER 4

C ompStat also became the new name for the crime control strategy meetings. What those who faced it would come to register mentally as *COMPSTAT!!!* was originally set for nine a.m. But several commanders complained that the traffic was tough at that hour and that they often had appointments around that time, anyway.

"Fine. We'll do them at seven a.m.," Jack said.

Chief of Department John Timoney complained during one of Jack's visits to his office that the three-hour sessions were too long. Jack began his response by closing the door.

"John, we go to these press conferences, and we stand like potted plants between Bratton and Giuliani," Jack said. "I'm asking for two meetings a week, three hours a meeting, six hours. And we spend more time than that at press conferences that we don't even talk at. Now what do you think is the most important thing here?"

"Fuck, I hate you, but you're right," Timoney said.

In the meantime, Jack had been receiving briefings from Narcotics and detectives and a variety of specialized units such as the Career Criminal Squad.

"They're giving me the jerk-off, dance for company briefing," Jack would recall.

At one such briefing, Jack asked for an estimate of the number of murders that were narcotics related.

"I don't know, 25, 30, 35 percent of them are narcotics murders," he was told.

"Explain to me how we solve them," Jack said.

"Well, you know they're very hard to solve."

"Do we ever get narcotics together with the detectives to go in and make surgical buys so they can take out these guys? Forget about the big cases, the cop murders."

"No, we don't do that."

Jack asked what might happen if a narcotics team with a sergeant was placed in each homicide task force. He would recall, "Of course, the detectives told me they were already coordinating, which was a lie."

With that came a more sweeping and, in his view, equally false assurance.

"At the same time, the detectives were saying they were out catching everybody," Jack would remember.

When Jack asked about a particular case, the detectives would say, "We have an active investigation."

"What does that mean?" Jack would inquire. "Tell me exactly what it means. You got up in the morning, you went to work? What did we do to catch this guy?"

Jack knew that detectives too often did little more than file a form known as a "want" when they got a photo ID on a suspect. Some twenty-eight thousand wants had accumulated in the various precincts without being acted upon.

"So, I bring in two ringers from the Transit Police," Jack would recall. "I bring in Sonny Archer and Jimmy Nuciforo."

Sonny had become the most talented manhunter Jack knew, proving to be a kind of computer whisperer—more than just a whiz—when tracking suspects. Nuciforo was now so well versed in the ways of a determined and resourceful investigator that Jack had given him his detective's ring from his own time as one. Jack dispatched the pair along with Vertel to the 75th Precinct, which had reported 126 homicides in 1993, the highest murder rate in the city. They had orders to take a stack of wants and not come back to the office until they had made at least thirty collars.

"He wanted us to go out and show them how it's done," Nuciforo would recall. "We knew absolutely they weren't going to be happy to see us."

After a predictably sullen welcome at the station house, the ringers were directed to a filing cabinet containing the wants written on index cards. A sign hanging on the wall read WELCOME TO THE 75TH PRECINCT—HOME OF THE GREATEST DETECTIVES IN THE WORLD.

They selected cards mainly for homicide cases and were joined by Vertel as they went to work. The very next day they arrested a murder suspect the 75th Precinct detectives had been unable to locate.

"You know how I found the guy?" Sonny asked. "I looked in the phone book."

The ringers worked out of their car but sometimes needed a computer to track down a suspect. And to that end would slip into Jack's office around three a.m. Sonny would set to winnowing key details from the NYPD's nineteen databases.

Jack caught them early one morning.

"What are you doing here?" he demanded.

Archer tried to placate Jack by showing him a picture of one of the guys they were seeking. Archer always started a hunt by getting a photo. That way, he could recognize the man if they located him and avoid such embarrassments as locking up the wrong guy or maybe talking to the guy you want and not realizing it is him.

"I know where this guy is," Archer told Jack.

"Unless you can put cuffs on this photo, you didn't get him yet," Jack said. "Get the fuck out of this office."

The ringers continued to grab one suspect after another. They started at five a.m. and more than once had arrived at the 75th Precinct with a new prisoner when the detectives came in at seven thirty a.m.

"We'd be sitting in the squad room," Nuciforo recalls. "They hated us. *Hated* us."

One man they sought had been homeless when a family took him in. He had rewarded their kindness with robbery and rape.

The ringers went to see the suspect's mother. Archer brought along a handbag, saying it belonged to the suspect's girlfriend and they hoped to get it back to her.

The mother said the girlfriend had just given birth at Brookdale Hospital.

The ringers hurried there, hoping to see the suspect, but when they peered in the neonatal unit, all the new dads were wearing surgical masks. Archer then spotted a mole on one man's cheek just above the mask. It matched a mole in the suspect's photo.

By the end of the week, the cave cop ringers had converted fourteen violent felony want cards into collars.

"Imagine if we had sent some real detectives to do the job," Jack told Borelli.

Gene Whyte was preparing the latest homicide tally for CompStat when he noticed that a prostitute had been found hog-tied and strangled with a pink towel in the New York Inn near Times Square. He recalled a similar murder four months before in which a prostitute on a Lower East Side hotel had been murdered in the same way, also with a pink towel.

The captain at Manhattan Homicide remained dubious that there was a pattern, even after a third prostitute was hog-tied, strangled, and left for dead in a hotel. The only significant difference in the most recent killing was that the attacker used a clothesline rather than a pink towel.

The prostitute who survived the similar attack described her assailant as having a pock-marked face and carrying an orange gym bag. She said he had asked her to twirl before him like a ballerina and back up toward him with her arms outstretched in front of her. She complied, and he suddenly tied her ankles and pulled out a pearl-handled silver pistol.

"We're not at this time convinced it's the same person," the homicide captain said. "But we feel it's serious enough to alert the public, in particular ladies who may be involved in prostitution."

Jack had a question for the captain at CompStat.

"Are we saying we suddenly have several people who are out there strangling prostitutes?" Jack inquired.

Jack reasoned that there may be other women who had survived attacks and suggested that detectives canvass Manhattan prostitutes. They soon found a woman who had been raped in an elevator and then sodomized on a rooftop by a pock-marked man with an orange gym bag.

She was urged to alert the police if she saw him again. She did exactly that not long afterward, and police arrested a thirty-three-year-old man who worked at the information desk at the American Bar Association. He was carrying an orange gym bag found to contain a pearl-handled silver pistol, along with clotheslines, bondage magazines, and Kool cigarettes, the brand of the butts found at the murder scenes. The suspect was shown a photo of one of the strangled prostitutes.

"That's the one I killed in the New York Inn," he said.

He told police he had "a ballet foot fetish" and had been on the prowl for his next victim when he was arrested.

"I already killed two women," he told detectives.

Beyond particular murder cases, Jack had also been working on ways to curb the continual flow of illegal firearms into the city. He had himself still put nothing in writing beyond that first list of four principles on the napkin at Elaine's. But people at headquarters prepared a document dated March 7, 1994, that offered a first public look at the Maple approach, giving credit where credit was demanded, if not due:

"Police Strategy No. 1: Getting Guns off the Streets of New York. The Honorable Rudolph W. Giuliani."

The briefing room reverted to being used for a press conference where Giuliani and Bratton stood surrounded by 4,400 guns, a third of the total seized during arrests the previous year. The event had originally been slated for City Hall, and Giuliani had initially insisted "no guns" through his communications director, Cristyne Lategano. Giuliani was apparently concerned that a photographer might snap a picture of him holding a gun. He was still embarrassed by a 1986 picture from his time as the Manhattan US attorney of him dressed as a supposed Hell's Angel on an undercover crack buy.

But Giuliani was persuaded that the event would be less theatrical if it were held at police headquarters, where the seized guns belonged. He could not have been pleased by the headline in the next day's *New York Daily News*, which read TOP COP TARGETS ILLEGAL WEAPONS. But the headline in the *New York Times* was GIULIANI OFFERS PLAN TO CURB GUNS.

"A gun arrest should be seen as an opportunity to find out the full scope of the conspiracy that brought the gun here to New York City," Giuliani was quoted saying.

Under the plan, the citywide street crime unit would focus on guns, beginning with the 75th Precinct. A dozen cops would be added to a joint Firearms Task Force to further coordinate city and federal efforts.

The detectives in the city's thirty-eight robbery squads would be required to follow up on all gun cases by debriefing suspects with an eye toward developing informants and identifying suppliers. And of course, every gun collar would be mapped.

That very night, an employee at an arts and crafts store in the 77th Precinct in Brooklyn buzzed in two men, one of whom proved to be carrying a sack full of guns. The employee objected when the men proceeded to use the premises for a gun deal. The man with the sack of them allegedly began firing one of his wares, killing the employee and wounding three other people, including himself by accident.

Jack sent his ringers, Jimmy Nuciforo and Sonny Archer, to the 77th Precinct detective squad to collect case folders for a number of homicides there, to be reviewed at an upcoming CompStat. The first files they checked were so skimpy they would be sure to infuriate Jack, and the ringers decided to give the squad commander a break.

"Boss, we pulled these; there's almost nothing in them," Nuciforo told the commander. "Got any we can look at and bring back?"

"Maple ain't nothing but a transit lieutenant to me," the squad boss said with contempt.

The squad boss was saying that whatever rank Jack now held in the NYPD, he was still just a cave cop.

"All right," Nuciforo said.

Upon their return to headquarters, Nuciforo recounted the conversation to Jack. Nuciforo came in the next morning and saw the squad boss sitting in Jack's office.

"Jimmy, tell me what he said about me yesterday," Jack asked Nuciforo.

O n March 10, 1994, Shavod Jones was paroled. He had served seven years and was now twenty-three. He was free for all of twelve hours when a squad of a dozen parole officers arrived at the apartment in the Taft Houses in Harlem that he shared with his grandmother, mother, brother, and sister. The state had discovered that it failed to add twenty months in penalties that he had received for multiple assaults on correction officers and for fighting with other inmates. He was taken away in handcuffs and returned to prison.

"In all my years, I have never seen as much hate in a man's eyes as I saw in his," a parole officer later told a reporter. "He looked as though he wanted to kill someone."

Steven McDonald's brother Thomas was still with Street Crime and was in the Bronx five nights later. Andrew and Sean McDonald, the brothers who had been sworn in at midnight with Thomas but were unrelated to him and Steven, had both been assigned to the Bronx after graduation. Andrew was in a patrol car when he heard a fellow cop give a desperate call for help over the radio: "I'm shot! I'm shot!"

Andrew told his partner, "I hope that's not my brother."

Sean had been assigned a solo footpost that night to keep people out of a condemned building on Edward L. Grant Highway. He was now twenty-six, and his field training sergeant had called him "pure gold," saying, "You'd tell him to do his job and he did it, never complained." He was married and had two kids, ages three years and eighteen months. They were asleep with a babysitter at their home north of the city. Their mother, Janet, was augmenting Sean's cop salary by waitressing.

Two girls happened to see a robbery in progress as they passed a clothing store called the Filo Boutique, around the corner from where Sean was posted. They passed the news in Spanish to a man on the street. The man was Dominican and spoke only a few words of English, but he recognized the uniform of the NYPD when he spotted Sean down the block. A few syllables of broken English were all the man needed to send Sean up to the store.

Sean peered through the glass, seeing no obvious signs of trouble. The door was locked, and he had even less reason to suspect danger as the two men inside buzzed him in. Sean already had a reputation as one of the 44th Precinct's sharpest cops, and he thought to put his foot in the door. He could see two men in the store, but he had no way of knowing that the owner and his wife lay bound in the back.

Sean cautiously remained halfway in the doorway as he called over one of the men and searched him for weapons. Sean then ordered this man to stand facing a wall with his hands up on it. Sean summoned the second man. But before Sean could search him, the second man pulled a gun. Sean's service revolver was holstered, and the most he could do was grab the man's weapon. A life-or-death struggle ensued.

The first man then stepped away from the wall and blindsided Sean with a punch so hard it caused him to lose his grip on the gun and tumble out onto the sidewalk. The second man began firing, hitting Sean five times from behind, in places where his bulletproof vest offered no protection. Sean pitched face-first onto the cold pavement. The two robbers stepped over him and fled in a black Isuzu with $70. Sean managed to make the radio call for help that Andrew hoped was not his brother.

At Columbia Presbyterian Hospital, Andrew stood ashen-faced outside the trauma room as doctors and nurses did what they could for Sean. Their father, John, arrived from Queens, wearing a bright green sweater and speaking in a brogue that Sean had often imitated around the station house. Their father remained composed as the department surgeon Gregory Fried spoke.

"We've lost him," Fried said.

John's response was as quiet as faith and dignity.

"God rest his soul," John said.

He softly repeated something that stayed with anybody who heard it.

"He was a lovely boy," he kept saying. "He was a lovely boy."

John worked as a doorman. He said that the NYPD was much more than a job to Sean and Andrew.

"My boys always wanted to be police officers," he said. "They had the calling."

He turned to his surviving son.

"Andrew, we have to be strong," John said. "This is a part of life."

John said of Sean's kids, "And what are we going to do with the children? What's going to happen to them?"

Janet McDonald arrived, the state police having picked her up at the restaurant where she worked. She was still in her uniform under a white ski jacket. The sight of her caused a crowd of cops to go silent as she strode down a long hallway leading to the trauma bay. An improbable sound accompanied each step.

"Oh my God," somebody whispered. "Those are her tips."

She had been working for tips while her husband was risking his life, and the coins in the pockets of her white apron jingle, jingle, jingled. The jingling stopped as she entered the trauma room, and then there came a cry of pain and deepest grief. Her Sean lay dead on a gurney, covered with a white blanket.

Janet bent over him and kissed his forehead, where he had suffered a deep gash when pitching face-first onto the sidewalk. She cradled his head and whispered to him.

"I love you."

Her hands eased away, covered with blood from the two bullet wounds behind his ear. She paused and then wiped her hands on her jacket.

"I'll never wash that jacket again as long as I live," she would later be quoted saying. "It's there for life."

She was led into a small room, where she was joined by Giuliani and Bratton. Anger burned through Janet's dark grief, and she seemed suddenly lucid as she spoke of the killers.

"You've got to get them."

In her own terrible pain, she voiced the fear that this might happen to somebody else.

"You can't let them kill another cop," she said.

Jack was up in the Bronx listening to Chief of Patrol Louis Anemone address a group of cops assembled on a grassy traffic island near the murder scene. They included Steven's brother Thomas.

"Go find these guys," Anemone said. "Go get them."

One of the cops who spread out into the streets discovered the getaway car parked a few blocks away. Inside was a .38 caliber Smith & Wesson revolver that would prove to be the murder weapon.

An auto registration check led the police to a man who said he had recently sold the car to twenty-six-year-old Javier Miranda. Detectives arrested him outside his apartment.

A second suspect, twenty-one-year-old Rodolfo Rodriguez apparently learned the police were after him. He strode into the 34th Precinct station house and surrendered.

On St. Patrick's Day, Sean McDonald was laid out in a Queens funeral home. He was dressed in the uniform that he had hoped his three-year-old would see him wearing for the first time when he took the boy to the parade. His uniform hat had been set over his stilled heart. A satin heart hung above him, emblazoned with the word *Daddy*.

Bratton was one of the first to arrive at the wake. He offered a prayer at the coffin, then turned to Janet, who had Andrew beside her in solemn attendance.

"They're not going to be in a position to kill another cop," Bratton told her.

There was still the cop they had killed.

"Everybody's brokenhearted," a mourner said to Janet.

"I know," she replied, in tears. "He's got a beautiful little boy to follow in his footsteps."

Thomas McDonald was working that day but came by the wake before heading back out, rejoining the Street Crime Unit's effort to get guns off the street.

Steven was also there in dress attendance. He prayed before the coffin of the thirty-sixth New York City cop to die in the line of duty since he was shot. Afterward, he steered himself up Fifth Avenue in the parade. Spectators called out to him, their shouts joining the skirling bagpipes.

"Steven! Steven! Steven!"

The NYPD Emerald Society Pipes and Drums played again two days later, outside Most Precious Blood Church in Astoria. The pipers played "Amazing Grace," and ten thousand cops saluted as Sean McDonald's flag-covered coffin was borne inside. Steven sat with his eyes fixed straight ahead. His brother Thomas was there.

Janet McDonald went up the steps with Sean Jr. The sun was shining, but the wind brought a chill.

Inside the packed church, Janet sat in the first row between Andrew and his father. The Reverend Frank Capellupo declared, "Heroes and hope are what today is all about."

Bratton offered an epitaph: "Sean McDonald, New York City police officer, shield number 11686, hero of the city."

At the conclusion, Andrew carried Sean Jr. outside, and the boy gazed up as NYPD helicopters flew overhead in tribute. The drums struck up a mournful rhythm, and the band slow-marched the hearse down the street.

After the burial at Pinelawn Memorial Park, Thomas McDonald joined Andrew McDonald for dinner. They were now bound by so much more than the shared surname that had put them together at the swearing in. They were both kid brothers who idolized an older brother. And both those older brothers had fallen victim to bullets in a city where there were estimated to be as many as two million illegal guns.

The killing of Andrew's brother was another challenge to the message of forgiveness offered by Thomas's brother. Cops and others who would never have said anything directly to Steven would at moments speak their minds to Thomas.

"My brother has heard it from some people," Steven allowed. "Some people think I'm not sincere. Even in my own family, some people find it very difficult, because they've been hurt very badly. They ask, 'How could you forgive him?' "

The most common sentiment among cops toward cop shooters was expressed by Sean's widow when she attended a court appearance for the two men accused of killing her husband.

"Please, God, please let the death penalty go through," she told a reporter. "They have to have some kind of fear."

CHAPTER 7

On March 23, 1994, a double nonfatal shooting in a famous Manhattan bridal shop received considerably more press attention than the Brooklyn arts and crafts store murder a fortnight before.

Two gunmen entered the Vera Wang Bridal House in the Carlyle Hotel on the Upper East Side and demanded a watch and jewelry from a Maryland couple who were shopping there with their two daughters to get a dress for the older girl. The father resisted. One of the gunmen shot both the man and his wife with a silver semiautomatic pistol before fleeing. The wounds were not life threatening, but the younger daughter's cry was widely reported:

"I hate this city!"

Even in a low-crime area such as the Upper East Side, the detectives had apparently failed to identify a pattern of five prior robberies over the previous months. But now it was in the newspapers and on TV news in a big way. A whole task force of detectives was seeking to identify and arrest a duo the press was calling the Silver Gun Bandits.

The pair struck again on June 28 in an elevator at the Peninsula Hotel. That gunpoint robbery was recorded by a surveillance camera, and police released the footage. Somebody recognized one of the bandits and tipped off the police.

As is customary in high-profile cases, a press conference was scheduled to announce the arrests. John Miller knew Mayor Giuliani would want to attend and tried to reach his counterpart at city hall. But Giuliani and his staff were at a Yankees game and did not respond until fifteen minutes before it was supposed to start. Miller offered to delay it, but a Giuliani staffer told him to go ahead.

After the press conference and the predictable media reaction, Miller got a call instructing him to go to Gracie Mansion and await the mayor. An aide

244 • MICHAEL DALY

advised him simply to apologize and not offer any excuses, no matter how justified.

Giuliani's arrival was announced by a slamming car door and a shout.

"Where's Miller?"

Giuliani entered in a rage.

"What the fuck happened?" he asked.

Miller did as the aide recommended, but Giuliani pressed for an explanation. Miller told him exactly what happened. Giuliani suggested darkly that somebody at police headquarters was placing their agenda ahead of his agenda.

Jack's sole agenda remained reducing crime. And to that end he used his credit card to buy enough acetate for each precinct to make crime map overlays. These aboveground Charts of the Future were displayed with overhead projectors at the biweekly CompStat meetings.

The size and importance of CompStat grew to where Jack was accorded the eighth-floor command and control center. The big wall screens there were capable of displaying computerized maps that became true Charts of the Future, showing the latest data in an instant.

The basic principle was the same as with any such pin map, be it in the 1945 *Brooklyn Eagle* or at the transit RORSF: Just as a dot was a dot, each crime was equally important. And, as Jack taught his rookies when he was a sergeant, every crime should be treated as if the victim were a family member. A robbery on Livonia Avenue in toughest Brooklyn flashed on the screen no differently than one in a fancy Manhattan bridal shop. The entire department was marshaled as Jack's squad once had been. The cops went where the crime was.

"Relentless," Jack would say again and again.

One hitch in CompStat that affected the rougher neighborhoods was that the existing software prevented the display of more than one crime at a location. The street geek John Yohe managed to overcome it by using longitude and latitude rather than address.

"I basically tricked it," Yohe later said.

Multiple shootings at one trouble spot would now appear as separate incidents. And woe to the commander who could not answer truthfully in the affirmative the queries from Jack and Chief Louis Anemone. *Did you deploy uniforms at hours that match the crime? Did they patrol the hallways and stairways and rooftops as well as the elevators? Did they check the building for anybody with open warrants? Did they arrest and debrief those people and check for anybody on parole and whether they were abiding by all the conditions? If they were not, was that used as leverage for information?* All of this was for crimes that previously would have prompted little more than a shrug from the department.

Commanders were pushed to be inventive, and if somebody lost two Yankees tickets in a robbery, the commander was liable to be asked if his cops had checked on game day to see if anybody used them. And commanders could forget all the traditional excuses for not taking action. Jack inquired about drugs in a housing project at the Brooklyn/Queens border. The commander said he had been unable to get undercovers in to make buys.

"Tomorrow morning, fatso here is going there in a Hawaiian shirt," Jack said—Fatso being Jack himself. The commander ensured that the dealers were in handcuffs by dawn.

On occasion, a commander would be less than truthful at CompStat. One said his people were debriefing everybody who was arrested. He could not explain why records confirmed that for only three hundred out of four thousand arrests in that precinct.

Some of the exchanges sounded a little like Jack interviewing C-Allah or one of the other wolf pack kids.

"Captain, what did you do about those robberies on the upper right of the map?"

"I called the robbery squad, commissioner."

"Oh yeah? Who'd you talk to?"

"McGinty."

"What day was that?"

"Tuesday."

"Let's call the robbery squad and see if McGinty was working Tuesday."

"You know, I might have spoken to Garrity."

Jack found that the commanders who lied were generally no better at it than your basic subway robber. He more than once used the same line when urging them to fess up.

"Come on, tell the Jackster," Jack would say.

On one occasion, Jack and Anemone anticipated that a particular

Brooklyn commander would need some encouragement to be forthright at CompStat. The commander was making his presentation and answering questions when people started laughing. The commander turned and saw that instead of a crime map on the screen behind him there was an animation of Pinocchio, the nose having grown longer and longer as he spoke.

Every Thursday, Bratton and Jack met with Giuliani at City Hall. Jack had noted at his first mayoral meeting that Giuliani was holding up his pant cuffs with paper clips.

"This is a no-frills crew," Jack said afterward.

The paper clips soon disappeared, but Giuliani persisted in a habit of gazing downward and then suddenly raising his head and looking straight at you. Jack assumed that this was intended to be intimidating, but he just gazed right back at the mayor. Jack managed not to laugh.

At the meetings, Bratton and Jack were able to report continued progress against crime. Narcotics and other divisions of the weekend police had adjusted their shifts to the hours criminals keep. The example set by the ringers Archer and Nuciforo spurred the detectives to be out there catching ever more suspects in cases the press barely noticed.

But Giuliani rebuffed Bratton's requests to make public the decline in crime. Bratton saw no reason not to discuss the improved numbers when addressing a private gathering of private sector executives. Word of it reached City Hall, and a mayoral aide called Miller.

"What the hell is he giving out good crime stats for?" the aide demanded to know.

At headquarters, the chiefs were beginning to admit that Jack just might be onto something. Maybe.

"Well, the homicides are starting to come down," Chief of Detectives Joe Borelli allowed. "But, you know, summer's coming."

"No shit, Joe, there wasn't a summer last year?" Jack replied. "You should go against last year's numbers."

When summer came, Thomas McDonald and the Street Crime Unit were deployed to Bedford-Stuyvesant, the neighborhood that had reported the most homicides and shootings in the two previous months. It was only coincidentally where Jack's maternal grandmother had been murdered in a crime spike that prompted the creation of the precursor of the Street Crime Unit in 1945.

A half century later, Thomas and his comrades concentrated on the 79th Precinct, a square-mile area where there had been six homicides and two dozen shootings the month before.

Street Crime made 120 gun arrests that first month. Narcotics also pitched in along with other elements of the former weekend, now 24-7, police.

"Over the next three months, there was one homicide and a half dozen shootings," Thomas later said. "The next six months, they didn't even register on the radar of the city's crime."

In early September of 1995, Thomas McDonald and his partner were deployed in upper Manhattan. They got a radio call to telephone their command as they were driving near Metropolitan Hospital, where Steven had first been brought after he was shot nine years before. Thomas sat in the car while his partner went to a pay phone. Thomas guessed from the partner's expression when he returned what the call had been about.

"That motherfucker got out, didn't he?" Thomas asked.

"Thomas, I was told we got to get out of here right now," the partner said.

The department did not want to risk a chance encounter between Thomas and Shavod Jones. Thomas would recall "really steaming" as he sat in his lower Manhattan apartment three days later. His beeper started "going crazy." One of the numbers was for a fellow cop working up in the 26th Precinct, and Thomas called him.

"Bro, where are you?" the cop asked.

"I'm at home," Thomas said. "Where are you?"

"Shavod just broke his neck," the cop said. "Shavod Jones, Buddha, he broke his neck. We got him in the back of a bus right now"—a bus being an ambulance.

Shavod had been out for all of three days when he climbed on the back of a Honda 500 motorcycle driven by a friend who popped a wheelie. The friend lost control, and the motorcycle hit two parked cars, one occupied by a team of parole officers assigned to keep watch on him. Shavod was rushed to St. Luke's Hospital, but the injury proved fatal.

Steven was in the van with Diamond Dave Martelli at the wheel when word came that Shavod had been killed. Martelli was still with Steven nine years after the shooting, among those who drove him in the van from place to place.

"A lot of schools, tons of schools, high schools, elementary schools," Martelli would recall. "Sometimes, we'd do two in a day. We went to every neighborhood everywhere."

Martelli, like fellow driver Jon Williams, had seen the impact of Steven's message of forgiveness.

"He brought even these tough kids to tears," Martelli would report.

Sometimes, Martelli would drive Steven home for a brief rest and then take him back out to an event or a function in Manhattan.

"People wanted to be with him," Martelli later said. "People wanted to see him. They wanted to hear him."

Martelli would be standing next to Steven when admirers held out a hand to shake his hand, making the same mistake Williams had on meeting him.

"I'd try to subtly correct them," Martelli would remember. "They'd say, 'Oh my God, I forgot. I'm sorry.'"

Martelli witnessed how Steven would return home exhausted only to face the ordeal of being hoisted into bed, having his arms secured in a kind of nightly crucifixion and trying to sleep when it was never easy, no matter how drained he might be. Steven would sometimes seek escape by having comforters piled on his head, but when he drifted off he was liable to wake without immediately knowing where he was, unable to throw them off.

He would then set off the next morning. He was having increasing trouble with the muscles he could control, as his neck had not only to support the weight of his head but brace against any bumps or potholes the van hit. The department tried changing the suspension and the tires on the van, but a pothole could still bring agony.

Martelli and Steven's other caretakers knew it all as intimately as if they were family. Martelli and Jon Williams had proven their devotion in a particular way; they had refused to take any overtime while caring for Steven, no matter how many hours were involved.

"I never even put in for it," Martelli later said. "I just felt it wasn't the right thing to do. I'm not making overtime on this guy's back."

And Martelli, like Thomas and others who adored Steven, could attest that it is easier to forgive somebody who hurts you than it is to forgive somebody who hurts someone you love.

"In watching Steven living this life, I basically just wanted to go strangle this kid," Martelli would say of Shavod.

On hearing that Shavod had died, Martelli told Steven, "I'm glad that guy's dead."

Steven replied, "Dave, come on, that's not right."

Steven had not spoken to Shavod in five years, but he had recently told a reporter that he hoped he and his onetime assailant might become a unique team.

"I don't think we've ever seen anything like what I envision, the two of us, together," Steven said. "Maybe Shavod and I will go to schools together and speak to kids. It'd be an amazing sight."

Patti Ann had told the reporter, "Steven really, truly believes that. People get upset with him. You know, like, 'Come on, Steven, wake up!'"

Steven was now devastated by Shavod's death.

"I'm almost as bad off now as the day I was shot," Steven was reported saying.

Steven also said, "I'd always hoped I could say the right words to touch his heart and soul."

Steven reflected Father Mychal's theology that there is God in good just as there is the devil in evil when he said, "There was goodness in [Shavod's] inner being."

Steven later learned that Shavod had spoken to his mother of calling him "when I'm ready."

A reporter asked Steven if the death might afford him a kind of closure. Steven said, "Shavod Jones is always going to be a part of my life. I'm paralyzed from the neck down. I'm dependent on a ventilator. Is there closure? I'd say no."

Some consolation came when Steven learned what Conor said in his third grade class after the daily prayer was followed by any intentions the students might want to offer.

"I just said, 'I pray for the boy that shot my dad,'" Conor would recall.

Conor was later asked if his classmates joined in praying for Shavod Jones.

"Yeah, they did," Conor reported.

Conor may have just been following Steven's example that day, but there was much of his father in him. Conor even walked like Steven. And that had to be innate.

"He never saw his father walk," Patti Ann noted.

CHAPTER 9

In one of the weekly meetings at City Hall, Giuliani complained to Bratton and Jack about press reports that another city was making more gun arrests than New York. Jack explained that the NYPD was making so many gun collars that crooks were less likely to carry them. Jack said that when crime is down, arrests also go down.

"No!" Giuliani exclaimed. "When crime goes down, arrests go up!"

Jack had determined that as much as 30 percent of the city's crime was tied to drugs. He told Giuliani that they could certainly send arrests way up if they deployed roughly the same percentage of the city's thirty-seven thousand cops to wipe out narcotics.

"You want to knock out crime?" Jack asked, according to Bratton's recollection. "We can put ten thousand people into the Narcotics Division and take this place out. There will be no more crime."

"Well, I don't know about that," Giuliani said. "I'd think we'd have to talk about that."

Back at police headquarters, Jack set to putting together the specifics of what he dubbed Operation Juggernaut. Some of the brass dismissed the idea as wacky, muttering in much the same tones as when they discussed Jack's style of dress.

When the plan was set, Jack unveiled Operation Juggernaut in all its details to Giuliani in the command and control room. The presentation included a video with a rousing soundtrack and images of cops raiding drug spots and busting dealers, followed by images of children of every ethnicity playing in what truly would be safe streets in a safe city. Giuliani seemed genuinely pleased. He approved an extra $1 million for the corrections budget to cover the accompanying increase in arrests.

"It's money well spent," Giuliani said. "Let's do it."

Jack privately remarked, "I think Rudy has a boner."

As preparations were being made to launch Operation Juggernaut at the start of 1995, the strategies already in place promised to end 1994 with a record double-digit reduction in crime. The department had indeed gotten a load of the Jackster, and no chief was likely to mock him at the upcoming Christmas tree lighting at Rockefeller Center.

But Bratton and Jack missed the event after twenty-six-year-old Police Officer Ray Cannon was shot interrupting a robbery at a Brooklyn bicycle shop. Jack rushed to the scene. He was told that Cannon and his partner, Officer Kevin Murphy, had responded to a 911 call of a robbery in progress. They entered Frenchie's Cycle World to see a man in his thirties with two teens by the cash register.

"Everything's fine," one of the three called out to the cops. "There's been a mistake. You can go home."

In the next instant, the man in his thirties opened fire with a 9mm pistol. Cannon went down. Murphy returned fire, killing the gunman before taking cover by the front entrance and radioing for help. Officer James Hunt and Sergeant Michael Cafarella of the Housing Police arrived.

"The perps are still in there, and my partner's shot," Murphy told them.

Hunt peered into the store and saw the shot cop's arm stretched out from behind a metal rack.

"I said, 'I got to get him out,'" Hunt would remember.

Cafarella and Murphy covered from the doorway as Hunt started into the store. Hunt was crouched and had his gun out, and he knew that at any instant one of the robbers could jump up and start blasting. He kept working his way in until he reached the outstretched arm. He came around the rack to see Cannon lying unconscious with two bullet wounds to the head.

Hunt now had no choice but to holster his gun.

"I couldn't pull with one hand," Hunt would later explain.

Hunt began pulling Cannon toward the door, but the wounded officer's gun caught on a rack. Hunt took what threatened to be a mortal moment to free the weapon and resumed pulling, only for Cannon's radio to catch. He freed the radio and got Cannon to the doorway.

"Working my way in wasn't too bad," Hunt would recall. "Coming out was a little tough."

Cafarella continued to keep cover as Hunt and Murphy got the wounded cop behind a parked car. They undid the belt holding a gun that Cannon had never had a chance to draw. They uncinched the bulletproof vest that had offered no protection against head wounds.

"We waited for the ambulance and prayed," Hunt later said.

One of the arriving paramedics kept looking over his shoulder at the store, and the cops decided that he did not need any distractions. A cop drove a radio car into the line of fire and the added cover let the medic concentrate on the wounded Cannon. Hunt helped get Cannon on a stretcher, and the ambulance sped away as more and more cops arrived.

Emergency Service cops went into the shop and found one of the teens bleeding on the stairs leading down into the basement. The other was hiding under boxes.

"Last night we was planning the robbery," one of them later wrote in a confession. "My uncle said he wanted a bike. So [he] asks me and my brother to go."

At Brookdale Hospital, Giuliani and Bratton spoke with Hunt and Cafarella. The two cops insisted that they had done no more than what any number of cops would have done.

"You just do it," Hunt later said.

The doctors fought to save Cannon, summoning too much experience with gunshot wounds.

"Massive, massive injuries," a doctor said of this case.

At 7:54 p.m., Cannon was pronounced dead. His twenty-five-year-old wife, Laura, arrived a few minutes later, looking small and lost as she pulled up to the emergency entrance in the back of an unmarked car. She walked with a chaplain up the concrete ramp. She numbly brushed her brown hair from her face and went inside. She was brought into a small room and told that her husband had died. Her muffled cries came through the wall.

"I was brought to the hospital never expecting to hear those five words that will haunt me for the rest of my life: 'We did everything we could,'" she would later say.

The city's latest police widow went in to see her husband, and afterward Giuliani joined Bratton in offering what comfort they could. Cannon's father, Raymond Cannon Sr., had also arrived.

"His whole life he wanted to be a police officer," Raymond Sr. would later tell a reporter. "He knew the risks. We all knew the risks. But he was living the life he wanted to. He loved the job. He loved his fellow officers, and they loved him. He was probably one of the fairest officers on the New York Police Department."

Hunt and Cafarella stood quietly outside the conference room.

"It doesn't matter what happened on the scene," Hunt said. "This guy is dead."

Hunt looked down at the floor and shook his head.

"It's a shame," Hunt said.

Murphy came out of a side room in a thermal undershirt, looking shaken. He hugged Hunt hard enough that his knuckles whitened.

"Thanks a lot, man," Murphy said. "Thanks a lot."

Murphy stepped back, and the two men stood silently before each other, their eyes saying more than could ever take form in words. Murphy then left, and Hunt took a deep breath. He sighed softly before returning with Cafarella to the street.

The funeral was at St. Patrick's Church in Smithtown, Long Island. The fifteen thousand cops in attendance of course included Steven.

The presiding priest had married Ray and Laura just four months before.

"Inside the uniform of that one good cop was one great human being," the Reverend Joseph Schlaefer told the mourners. "He had a deep-rooted joy about life and an ability to find humor and an eagerness to be there if anybody needed him...One of his expressions was 'I'm in, I'm here, let's go.'"

Bratton offered a simple eulogy: "Raymond R. Cannon Jr. Appointed Oct 15, 1990. Badge No. 20811. Assigned to the 69th Precinct, Sector Boy. Partner Kevin Murphy. Hero of the city. Hero of our times. He will be missed."

Giuliani also spoke, saying that a fellow officer had told him Cannon was "the best cop in the precinct." Giuliani wondered aloud why the finest of the Finest always seem to be the ones to die.

"Because they're the ones that come forward," Giuliani said. "They're the ones who take the risk. They're the ones who always without questions are ready, willing, and able to do their duty."

In a written statement to the court at the sentencing of one of the teens, Laura Cannon would later say, "I thought Ray and I would be together for fifty years. I only got four months…I will never know what our children would have looked like…The only way I can hear my husband's voice is to listen to an answering machine tape."

W illiam Bratton and Rudy Giuliani had flown to the funeral for Officer Ray Cannon in separate helicopters. Bratton afterward happened to board his chopper first, and it was revving for takeoff when the mayor arrived from the church for his return flight. A cop mindful of safety asked the mayoral entourage to stay back while Bratton's craft lifted off. Giuliani stood there, holding down his comb-over against the prop wash as an aide shouted over the noise.

"Should the police commissioner really take off before the mayor?"

All the fine sentiments about nobility and sacrifice fell away. The mayor imagined he had suffered a deliberate slight. His people made it known that from then on the mayor's helicopter would always take off *first*.

Five days later, Giuliani was further incensed by a story in the *New York Daily News* about the NYPD's plan to further knock down crime. Patrice O'Shaughnessy, the *Daily News* reporter who had interviewed Bratton during his first week and written the "I'll Stop the Fear" article, decided to follow up with a piece on Bratton's first year, and she asked about the war on drugs. The result was a December 11 front-page photo of Bratton and a headline that Jack instantly knew signaled the demise of the very plan it announced:

BRATTON'S JUGGERNAUT.

Below that were subheads accompanied by NYPD emblems:

COPS PREPARED TO INVADE QUEENS IN '95 DRUG-WAR OFFENSIVE

COMMISH'S '94: YEAR OF SUCCESS & SYMBOLISM

The *Daily News* reported that murder was down 19 percent in 1994. There had also been eight hundred fewer shootings, eleven thousand fewer robberies, and fourteen thousand fewer car thefts.

"This is the biggest reduction in crime the city has ever seen," Jack Maple was quoted saying. "I don't have a police cemetery, a police hospital, where we're hiding all the crime victims. It's not just numbers, we're talking about lives."

Jack felt sure he would have been allowed to go ahead with the drug offensive and save many more lives if the front-page picture had been of the mayor and the headline had read GIULIANI'S JUGGERNAUT. Jack's instant analysis that "it's over" was confirmed when Giuliani told the press that he would never approve such a limited plan.

"Going back to the Ford and Nixon administrations, I've worked on drug strategies," the mayor told reporters. "So I demand more of a drug strategy maybe than would ordinarily be the case. The real achievement here is not for it just to be a law enforcement measure."

Jack returned to the subway on December 21, when he was notified that a firebomb had exploded on a number 4 subway train in downtown Manhattan. The evidence strongly suggested that the device had exploded prematurely, burning the legs of its maker, an unemployed computer technician named Edward Leary, who was planning to extort money from the city with a series of bombings. Leary had been taken to New York Cornell Medical Center to be treated for his leg burns and was emphatically protesting his innocence when Jack arrived from the scene. Jack did not even break stride as he delivered a line that was pure cave cop.

"Liar, liar, pants on fire," Jack told him.

On New Year's Eve, Jack was back in Times Square. Nine years had passed since he welcomed in 1986 by wrestling with a crook in horse manure while wolf packs chanted "snatch gold!" Where he had once stood in the Playboy sweater, he now wore his Burberry trench coat. But as he dispensed with figurative horseshit in the NYPD, he continued to apply what he had learned in the Transit Police. The resulting drop in homicides during 1994 translated into 405 more people alive to begin a new year in which it seemed things might actually get better.

The descending ball had been aptly refurbished with rhinestones and strobe lights. Jack's rosy prediction about Times Square did not seem so laughable as the post-performance cast and crew of *Beauty and the Beast* celebrated the start of 1995 along with some out-of-towners who happened to also be in a restaurant with windows looking out on the street. They kept on after the crowds outside dispersed. A group of two dozen weary cops trooped past the plate glass, and one of the partiers inside waved to them. A cop replied in kind and smiled. Another partier began clapping, and in the next moment, everyone inside gave the cops a standing ovation.

The final gun victim of 1994 had been a twenty-nine-year-old Bronx man shot in the chest by a pair of masked gunmen who raided his apartment at eleven thirty p.m. in search of money and jewelry and drugs but fled with nothing. The same man became the first murder victim of 1995 when the doctors pronounced him dead at 12:25 a.m.

The operations desk notified Jack after he had continued on with Miller and Bratton from Times Square to Elaine's. Giuliani knew that Bratton often went with them there, and their merry clique seemed to stoke the mayor's jealousy and resentment. Giuliani's staff had begun to mutter "stay out of Elaine's" to Bratton's staff as if it were one word.

In January, Bratton decided to elevate John Timoney to first deputy commissioner and Louis Anemone to chief of department. The promotions were to be announced at City Hall, and Bratton took them into the mayor's office beforehand. Timoney thanked the mayor privately and did so again afterward. But during the press conference, he expressed his gratitude only to Bratton.

Timoney was subsequently summoned back to City Hall. Bratton came with him, and they were led to a basement conference room that was half-jokingly known as "Rudy's star chamber." Peter Powers there informed Timoney that he had failed to thank the mayor for the appointment. Timoney pointed out that he had done so twice.

"Not in front of the TV cameras," Powers said.

"What are you, nuts?" Timoney exclaimed.

Giuliani had come to blame Miller for depriving him of what was his due by engineering media attention for Bratton. The grievance appeared to turn more personal when Giuliani strode around a corner in City Hall in time to see a female aide jump up and playfully throw her legs around Miller's waist. The mayor was said to have a romantic interest in her.

On February 10, 1995, Giuliani ordered Miller's staff in the NYPD Office for Public Information to be cut in half. All those who remained were to be replaced with cops chosen by City Hall.

At a command staff meeting in police headquarters, Bratton and Timoney and Jack were speaking of resigning en masse when Miller rose from the table and excused himself. A few minutes later, somebody called for them to turn on the TV. They watched the live coverage as Miller announced that he was resigning the job of his dreams after only a year and a month.

"The information we put out here is not information you're supposed to control," Miller said. "It's not the mayor's information. It's the public's information."

He added, "I'm loyal to the police commissioner and loyal to the mayor, but there were loyal Nazis, too."

Miller's eyes were welling. He was quitting to preempt the others at the command staff meeting from feeling obliged to do the same. Bratton and Jack resolved to stick it out.

CHAPTER 11

Rudy Giuliani and William Bratton did agree that the time had come for the Transit Police to merge with the NYPD. Cave cops held a kind of wake at Kennedy's Bar on West 57th Street near District 1.

"Where are they going to get thirty-five thousand transit shoulder patches?" Jack Maple joked.

Jack was by then living three blocks away, in a twenty-story white brick building at 220 Central Park South, a residential address that would have been beyond his imagining when he walked past there with muzzle flash burns two decades before. The city's real estate titans offered high-ranking officials reasonable rents, and Jack's status as a deputy police commissioner enabled him to move with Brigid into a rent-stabilized studio on the eleventh floor.

The windows overlooked Central Park, and Jack gazed down to see a man dig a hole just on the other side of the perimeter wall. The man proceeded to have vigorous sex with the dirt.

"*Hey, you!*" Jack shouted from on high. "*Stop fucking my park!*"

The man looked over his shoulder as if the Almighty himself was calling down. He quickly rose, pulled up his trousers, and fled.

In October 1995, Pope John Paul II visited New York and said Mass for more than 150,000 people in what Jack had come to call his park. Jack and other police higher-ups had individual pictures taken with the pontiff, which they hung in their respective offices. Jack afterward decided to have a bit of fun by getting a cop who was known to be literate in Latin to add a supposed papal message on his photo. One of the chiefs did not fail to notice the inscription.

"The pope wrote on your picture?" the chief asked.

"Yeah, he didn't write on yours?" Jack replied.

The chief subsequently sought out the same Latin-literate cop and asked him to slip into Jack's office when it was unoccupied and translate what the pope had written on the picture. The cop reported back that the inscription said, "To Jack Maple, I am so glad we met. You are my kind of guy. Please come visit me at the Vatican any time."

The chief told the cop not to say anything to Jack, which of course the cop immediately did. Jack subsequently stopped by the chief's office.

"Where's your picture of you and the pope?" Jack asked.

"Fuck you, Maple," the chief replied.

Bratton had a larger apartment just down the block from Jack's, at the corner where Central Park South meets Columbus Circle. The circle is toward the upper end of the Macy's Thanksgiving Day Parade route, and both Jack and Bratton were there to watch as the balloons and marching bands proceeded downtown. The sky was slightly overcast and the temperature was a touch cooler than average for the date, but the winds of the early morning had eased and it all seemed a glory to two guys born in civil service bassinets.

"Don't blink, or it'll be over," Jack told Bratton.

CHAPTER 12

The mission continued, and crime declined to where the city's murder rate was the lowest in a quarter century.

"I have never seen anything as extraordinary as this, and I have been in government for 40 years," Queens District Attorney Richard Brown was quoted saying. "People were throwing their hands up, and now when I go to community meetings there is a sense and a feeling of pride that things are getting better."

John Yohe heard from some of his old comrades in Brooklyn North that maybe there was something to CompStat and the rest after all.

"They'd figured this was just another bullshit department thing like everything else," Yohe would recall.

But they were starting to wonder.

"They were seeing some changes," Yohe said. "They felt they were actually making a difference, having some impact."

And Yohe was quick to say who he thought was driving this apparent miracle.

"If there was no Jack Maple, it never would have happened," Yohe later said. "He had that passion and that drive and that quirkiness that all came together and that's what made it work."

On his part, Jack was quick to credit the cops who proved they really were New York's Finest. He felt that Bratton had set exactly the right tone early on with the battlefield promotion of Arlene Beckles for courage under fire. Jack now suggested that Bratton promote the cop he considered the finest of the Finest for courage after fire.

CHAPTER 13

Five days before Christmas 1995, Steven McDonald steered himself into the auditorium headquarters for one of the promotion ceremonies that always seem particularly nice in the holiday season. Patti Ann and Conor were present, as was the rest of Steven's family, including Thomas. Steven was presented with detective shield 104, once carried by his maternal grandfather, Smiling Jim Conway.

The son who had not yet been born when his father was shot went up to the wheelchair and leaned forward. Steven was able to lower his head slightly so eight-year-old Conor could kiss him.

"[Steven] exemplified everything the NYPD strives to be," Bratton later said. "He was a role model for all of us."

Bratton understood that Steven was particularly important at a time when the police were aggressively addressing crime not just in rich neighborhoods but also in poor ones.

"[Cops] have a difficult job to do, and they need to always remember that they have a responsibility to do it the right way. That was Steven's message: The job is too important to behave inappropriately. If he could find it in his heart to forgive the awful transgression that happened to him in his life, police officers should be able to treat people like human beings no matter what circumstances they find themselves in, no matter what they are facing."

CHAPTER 14

O n New Year's Eve, Jack was with Brigid just down Central Park South at Bratton's apartment for dinner. Miller was there, and they all then caught the subway at Columbus Circle down to Times Square. Two elderly women on the train were saying how much safer the city felt even on this traditionally tumultuous night.

Rudy Giuliani was accorded the honor of pushing a button to trigger a green laser that set the famous ball descending for the start of 1996. Some five hundred thousand people joined in the countdown, a crowd that Giuliani pronounced "the largest ever in the history of Times Square."

"Times Square is back and is the center of the world again," Giuliani said.

The Times Square event resulted in only seventeen minor arrests for disorderly conduct, befitting a city where CompStat had aided another big drop in crime, for a two-year decline of 39 percent in murder and a 27 percent drop in felonies. The first murder of the year was at dawn, but was not reported until January 3, when a forty-nine-year-old woman was found dead in her apartment as the result of a stray bullet, likely from celebratory gunfire at four a.m. on New Year's Day.

The crime numbers in New York came to the attention of *Time* magazine, and Bratton sat for an interview. He also posed for a photograph under the Brooklyn Bridge. What would become the cover shot for the January 15, 1996, issue showed Bratton with the collar of his trench coat turned up and a radio car in the background, its roof lights flashing.

Where the *Time* cover six years before had declared "the rotting of the Big Apple," this one announced: WE'RE FINALLY WINNING THE WAR ON CRIME. HERE'S WHY.

The mayor certainly noticed that the cover photo was of William

Bratton and not of him. But Giuliani's response was unexpectedly muted, perhaps because he was occupied by a major blizzard that struck the city the day before the magazine hit the newsstands. He was given a chance to take center stage, and he oversaw the city's response from police headquarters, in the same room used for CompStat. He seemed to delight in giving full meaning to the name "Command and Control Center."

"The mayor awoke at 4:15 a.m. to monitor the cleanup," the *New York Daily News* reported. "He was on the road much of the day in his Suburban code-named Eagle One with time out for the televised briefings he led from Police Headquarters, which coincided with the morning, evening and nighttime newscasts."

The *Daily News* further reported that Eagle One had stopped to assist two sisters who were shoveling out their driveway in Queens.

"How are you managing?" Giuliani asked. "Has the Sanitation Department been diligent?"

The mayor then borrowed a shovel and began digging with them.

"Actually, he did a very nice job," one of the sisters said afterward.

The scene was captured by a TV news crew.

"Good footage," a mayoral aide was quoted saying off-camera.

At the regular weekly City Hall meeting with Bratton four days later, the mayor made only one terse comment about the *Time* magazine cover.

"Nice trench coat."

Then, the mayor and his people learned that Bratton had a six-figure contract to write an autobiography.

"What I'm concerned about is that it follows the ethical and legal guidelines that are set for this," Giuliani told the *New York Times*, raising the possibility that it might not.

In the meantime, City Hall began insisting on approving promotions and transfers that were traditionally at the discretion of the police commissioner. Chief Timoney submitted a list of fifteen transfers in preparation for a limited version of what was to have been Operation Juggernaut, minus the name and initially targeting Brooklyn North, not Queens. The transfers were stalled, and Timoney's repeated calls went unanswered. He finally got a mayoral aide on the phone and was told to come to City Hall for a chat. Timoney went over the list, and the aide nixed the first three names, asking if one commander had ever said anything positive about the mayor that was publicly reported.

Word of troubles between Giuliani and Bratton reached the *New York Times*.

"The grousing, almost always behind the scenes, has forced both Mr. Giuliani and Mr. Bratton to explain and defend their relationship once again, which they did on Friday with an air of increasing frustration," the *Times* reported on March 10, 1996. "It even prompted the Mayor to accuse 'people in the Police Department' of trying to foment a showdown with his most prominent appointee."

City Hall began saying that there was also an ethical issue with a personal trip Bratton had taken with two wealthy businessmen. Mayoral aides spoke darkly on background about examining plane logs and travel records. Giuliani began calling Bratton to check on rumors that Giuliani himself had almost certainly started.

"It was death by a thousand cuts," Bratton later wrote in the book at issue. "Ethics investigations, constant headlines, meddling micromanagement, leaks, delays, disrespect."

Jack urged Bratton just to laugh it off. Jack had angered bosses through his whole career, but he always prevailed because he had been in the right, as he felt certain Bratton was now.

"It's fun to be investigated!" Jack told him.

Meanwhile, Jack kept pushing his crew to implement his plans. Jack continued to dispatch Vertel Martin, now a lieutenant, and other Transit Police ringers to wherever he felt the NYPD still needed to be shown how police work should be done.

One big difference from the Transit Police days was that Jack was not out there with them. He was orbiting between headquarters and Elaine's and his apartment on Central Park South, with occasional visits to a decreasing number of homicide scenes. He seemed to Vertel to have become a little too taken with himself.

"He started to think he was *all that*," Vertel later said. "He's sending us out to get the bad guys. Meanwhile, he's sitting there drinking espresso and acting like a big shot."

Jack kept in his office a stack of boating magazines such as once provided him with an escape in ECAB. He was flipping through glossy pictures of yachts as Vertel began telling him about the latest Maple mission. She reached a limit.

"Yo, motherfucker, are you even listening to me?" she asked. "Are you that big that I'm talking about putting my people in harm's way and you're reading a fucking boating magazine?"

Vertel told him that she wanted to transfer to the one place outside his office where she would be safe from those in the department who had come to hate her during the many times she had been dispatched to teach them by example.

"I want to go to IAB," she said.

What had been the Internal Affairs Division (IAD) in both the transit and city police was now the Internal Affairs Bureau (IAB).

"Okay, I'll have you there tomorrow," he replied.

The next day, Vertel headed as directed to a particular location.

"The next thing I know I'm reporting to the top floor of a Catholic school in Brooklyn," she would recall.

She wondered as she entered if she had been given the wrong address. But it proved to be one of IAB's hideaway bases. She strode on in and introduced herself.

"I'm like, 'I'm Lieutenant Martin from Deputy Commissioner Maple's office,'" she remembered.

She was assumed to be there to rat on the rats.

"They think I'm there to spy on them," she recalled. "I was treated as such until I had to make my name."

She spent the first days just observing how the unit operated.

"I realize no police work is going on at all, just paperwork," she said.

She was eventually given a squad of a half dozen investigators. She figured she embodied everything they did not want in a supervisor.

"Female, Black, gay," she later said. "All the checkboxes."

She also understood that they had come to IAB only because it was a necessary stop on a career path.

"Everybody's mindset was 'I'm going to do my time, do as little as possible so I don't have to sully up my reputation by locking up cops, and get out of here,'" she later said.

That was about to change.

"I go, 'Look men and ladies, it's time for us to do some police work here,'" she recalled. "'We're all going out together, and I'm going to show you how it's done.'"

A few smirked. Others just stared.

"They're all looking at me like I have two heads," she would remember.

One of the cases involved a drug dealer who was said to have information about a dirty cop. Vertel led the team on a visit to the dealer's residence and began by checking everybody present for outstanding warrants.

"Nine out of ten," Vertel recalled. "Everybody had a damn warrant. I said, 'Okay, we're locking everybody up.' The team goes, 'We don't do that.' I'm like, 'What do you mean we can't do that? They got warrants. We're locking them up.'"

She caused a stir back at the base.

"They were like, 'Martin's team went out there and had the nerve to lock criminals up,'" she later said.

Between the leverage imparted by the arrests and the subsequent interrogations, the team got the information it needed. She kept pressing and began to see a change in her team.

"They started appreciating doing the real police work," she later said. "Not to mention the overtime."

She discovered that catching crooked cops was harder than just catching crooks.

"You're dealing with a person who knows the system and has a lot more to lose," Vertel later said.

She learned that one IAB investigator had been working for two years on a case involving a Brooklyn detective sergeant who was said by an informant to be running six numbers spots for the Lucchese crime family.

"We can't solve the case," one of the bosses told her. "He's too smart."

"Where does he live?" Vertel asked.

The answer was an address on Long Island.

"Get me a helicopter," Vertel said.

Aerial photographs showed the detective sergeant had multiple acres on the water with houses not only for him but also for his mother and sister, who were said to assist him with managing the spots. Vertel applied for a wiretap warrant, but the judge said she had not exhausted all other possible remedies, as required by law.

The judge asked Vertel if she was familiar with *California v. Greenwood*. She understood he was referring to a 1988 Supreme Court case allowing the warrantless search of garbage bags outside the curtilage, or immediate surroundings, of a home.

"Trash," she told the judge.

Her squad spent the next three weeks surreptitiously inspecting the refuse the detective sergeant and his family set out.

"Everything was there," Vertel said. "DNA on [gambling] slips."

In the interrogation, Vertel started out with the detective sergeant as if she were afraid not to be pleasant. He reacted to her as she expected.

"This little colored girl," she would recall.

She quietly told him that he faced RICO charges, which meant his considerable assets, along with those of his mother and sister, were subject to forfeiture whether or not he confessed. She then became more emphatic.

"I said 'If you don't cooperate, I'm locking everybody up and I'm taking all their shit!'" she recalled. "Guess what: He confessed right away."

Vertel proceeded on to other cases, a number of which involved officers who had started out as lone crooks, then joined up with those of their ilk in self-protective groups.

"Cop gangs," she said. "These guys were rogue, dirty, worse than the criminals that you would lock up in the street."

O ne day in mid-January 1996, Thomas McDonald arrived at the Street Crime Unit's base to start another tour and saw a figure who looked like a biker.

"Hey, Tom McDonald, what's up, bro?"

"What's up?" Thomas replied tentatively.

"Bro, it's Kevin Gillespie!"

"Holy shit! What's up, man?"

A former housing cop, Gillespie was now assigned to street crime and was starting his three-month trial period. He finished it on March 14, becoming an official member of the unit.

That night, the various teams started out in the Times Square area and were supposed to meet at the meal break for pizza. But one thing led to another, and the time came for them to disperse across the city in search of illegal guns.

"Everybody starts fanning out," Thomas would recall.

Thomas and his partner were in the 28th Precinct when they heard Gillespie's team announce on the radio from the 46th Precinct in the Bronx that they had spotted a BMW taken in a carjacking a short time before.

"We think we got that car, we're following it."

Thomas and his partner headed toward the Bronx.

Then they heard on the radio, "We're in pursuit."

Then, "Shots fired! Shots fired! Shots fired!"

Thomas sped to the scene and learned that Gillespie had been approaching the BMW when gunfire suddenly erupted from inside. Gillespie had been fatally wounded in the shoulder above his bulletproof vest.

The primary gunman, Angel Diaz, had been paroled five months before, his twelve-and-a-half- to twenty-five-year sentence as a recidivist armed robber having been reduced to three to seven years on appeal because the gun had not been recovered and proven operable. Diaz had since armed himself with a pair of 9mm pistols that he fired at Gillespie and then at two off-duty cops as he fled. Diaz was shot four times, but survived.

Two other suspects were still at large. And, one day from the anniversary of Sean McDonald's death, Thomas again stood in the Bronx with a group of fellow cops as a boss told them to go after cop killers.

"Go out and find these guys!"

Gillespie's wife, Patty, was notified at their Long Island home. She left their two children, seven-year-old Daniel and four-year-old Bobby, with a neighbor.

"Kevin got hurt," she told the neighbor. "I have to go."

She called home from the hospital.

"Kevin is no longer with us," she said.

At the Street Crime Unit base, an entry was made in the command log:

On 3/14/96 at approximately 21:49 Hrs., PO Kevin Gillespie, shield 4503 of the Street Crime Unit was killed in the line of duty following an exchange of gunfire with armed suspects within the confines of the 46th Precinct. May God have mercy on his soul and watch over his family.

Three days later, a heartsick Thomas escorted Steven past the cheering crowds at the St. Patrick's Day Parade. Thomas spoke of the fallen friend who would have otherwise been with them.

"He was a sweetheart," Thomas said. "I'm marching for him. I always march with my brother, and I'm marching for Kevin. I'm going to the wake after this."

The wake was followed by the funeral on the morning after St. Patrick's Day. Gillespie's two sons wore kid-sized police hats. The priest read aloud a letter the older boy had written to his father.

"I'm sorry that you died. I love you. You are good. You are like God to me."

One of Gillespie's partners, Officer Gary Lemite, delivered a eulogy and said that Gillespie always "did the right thing" as a cop and as a father. Lemite added, "I would like the Bronx DA to do the right thing as well."

Lemite meant seek the death penalty for the young man charged with firing the fatal shot. Steven was there, of course, and a reporter sought his opinion. Steven was still a cop who had forgiven his teen assailant. But he was also a cop who had since seen the impact on Patti Ann and on police widows.

"I am against the death penalty," Steven said. "But I think the killers of Officer Gillespie should be punished and suffer for as long as Mrs. Gillespie suffers."

When the coffin was carried from the church, Steven and Thomas and thousands of other cops listened to a pair of trumpeters play taps and watched five NYPD helicopters fly over low in the missing man formation. Giuliani and Bratton then headed for their own helicopters, which waited to fly them to a police academy graduation later that day. Giuliani took off first, but Bratton made the mistake of giving a lift to Lou Matarazzo, current president of the PBA.

"What is he doing giving a ride to an *enemy*?" a City Hall aide was heard to mutter.

Relations between Giuliani and the PBA had become tense over financial issues. Overtime had all but dried up, and the very cops who were out winning the war by risking all were in many instances taking home less than sanitation workers. Gillespie had died while supporting his family on $35,000 a year.

The day after the funeral, on what would have been Gillespie's thirty-fourth birthday, the Street Crime Unit went back to work. They met for dinner and went out and made seven gun collars, bringing the total since the first of the year to 255, each of which brought the risk of suffering Gillespie's fate.

"We make a difference," Gillespie's partner, Trish Heckman, said.

The weekend after Kevin Gillespie's funeral, William Bratton went home to Boston to see his parents and ponder his next move. He figured that Rudy Giuliani's people would be unrelenting in their effort to force him out by whatever pretext might work. The commissioner returned with his mind made up. Late that Monday afternoon, he informed some of his top people that he intended to resign the following morning.

On Monday night, Bratton was dining with Jack Maple and John Miller at an Italian restaurant on West 72nd Street when he was notified that an off-duty cop had been shot in a housing project on the Lower East Side. Jack went to the scene. Bratton headed for Bellevue Hospital. He stood with the mayor as doctors treated Sergeant Adam Alvarez.

Bratton and Giuliani spoke to the wounded sergeant's family and then to the press. Bratton told reporters that Alvarez had been riding an elevator up to his sister's apartment with a gift when two men boarded and demanded money. One of the men had been armed with a silver pistol, the other with a bottle. Alvarez had resisted and drawn his own gun. He fired one shot, but missed. The robbers shot him in the lower abdomen and struck him over the head with the bottle as he tried to handcuff one of them.

"He's being operated on right now, but the surgeons...feel that he will be okay," Bratton said.

"Hopefully, this will have a happy ending," Giuliani said.

Bratton apparently gave the mayor no notice of his imminent departure until the following morning. Word leaked to the media about the same time, and a press mob was waiting as Bratton walked from police headquarters to City Hall. He was wearing a blue double-breasted suit, blue shirt, and a yellow tie. He was smiling.

"It's going to be an interesting day," he said. "And the sun is shining."

The accent was still Boston, but Bratton was now a major New York figure, nearly as widely recognized as Steven. The press mob stayed with him as he went up the steps into City Hall. He strode on to the mayor's office. The door shut, and the two men stood alone in a moment of truth in which the truth would not be spoken.

After about half an hour they emerged. Both men were smiling as they went in to the press conference. The mayor stepped to the podium first, as was only fitting.

After the official announcement of Bratton's resignation, there was speculation in the press that Giuliani might name either Jack or John Timoney as the new police commissioner. Giuliani had already decided on Howard Safir, who had been serving as fire commissioner.

"A lightweight," an indignant Timoney remarked before departing the NYPD in a fury.

Howard Safir had previously been a drug agent and a US marshal and had once taken LSD guru Timothy Leary into custody. Safir would tell people that he was inspired to go into law enforcement by an uncle who, as an NYPD detective, arrested bank robber Willie "That's Where the Money Is" Sutton. The *Daily News* chose not to report the uncle's remark when he was told of the appointment: "Howie? Howie's a jerk."

On Friday, March 29, Safir attended a regularly scheduled CompStat meeting over which Jack and Anemone presided. Giuliani and Safir had asked Jack to continue on in his present position, and he was leaning toward staying. He could thereby make good on his vow to cut violent crime in half.

But Bratton's then wife, Cheryl Fiandaca, sent a message to Jack that her husband was hurt that his beloved "Jackster" had not followed him out the door. Bratton would later say that Fiandaca had been acting without his knowledge.

"She guilted him," Bratton said.

Early that Monday afternoon, on an April Fool's Day exactly eleven years after that April Fool's Day when the decoy squad first set out, Jack informed Safir in person that he was all but sure he would be leaving. He afterward sat in his office, undid his bow tie and sighed.

At 3:15 p.m., he reknotted his tie and spoke to Bratton. He then put in a call to Safir.

At 4:11 p.m., Safir called back. Jack officially resigned from a position he still could not quite believe he ever held.

"We had a good run," he said.

Jack then donned his double-breasted suit jacket and homburg hat. A photo in the *Daily News* showed him striding from police headquarters in his two-tone shoes.

JACK HITS THE ROAD, the headline read.

PART
V

The April 20, 1998, session of CompStat was about to commence. The mayor of the City of New York was personally switching the wooden nameplates on the table at police headquarters so that he, and not the vice president of the United States, would be seated at the center.

The NYPD was continuing to employ CompStat, as Jack Maple had predicted they necessarily would when he followed William Bratton out the door two years before. The result had surpassed his 1994 promise to cut violent crime in half in four years. Murder was down by two-thirds, on the way to the lowest rate since 1964.

After Vice President Al Gore learned of the remarkable results, he had his office contact the NYPD to say he wished to see the crime-fighting marvel in action. He hoped to present the department with a Hammer Award for "reinventing government."

Word of Gore's plans reached Rudy Giuliani when he was in New Mexico giving a speech to local Republicans about New York's miracle crime decline. Giuliani told the gathering that the crime stats showed this was how a president should address the problem, but he insisted he had given no thought to running for national office.

The mayor is said to have gone into a tizzy about Gore, perhaps because he feared his fellow Republicans might not cotton to him basking with the man most likely to be the next Democratic presidential candidate. His chief mayoral spokesperson, Cristyne Lategano, insisted her boss had no desire for the Hammer Award. She said he in fact felt it was "not an appropriate award."

"The mayor deserves better, the police department deserves better, and the police commissioner deserves better," she added.

In any event, Giuliani ordered the meeting canceled. Howard Safir is said to have lobbied for it to go ahead, minus the unwelcome award. Giuliani relented, under certain strictures, ostensibly to prevent Gore from turning the meeting into a "political photo op."

On the day of the visit, Gore arrived at police headquarters only to be consigned to wait in a side room. Giuliani is said to have forbidden Safir from receiving Gore in his office. Safir was also told not to give Gore any mementos, including the NYPD jacket that was ready for presentation.

Meanwhile, Giuliani stormed into the Command and Control Center. The original seating had been arranged so Gore would be between Giuliani and Safir. The idea was that the police commissioner would be best able to explain the CompStat meeting that the vice president had come to observe. Giuliani personally switched the name plates.

Just after the appointed hour, ten a.m., Gore was escorted into the room. He liked to know in advance exactly where he was headed, and his staff had briefed him on the location of his assigned seat. He hesitated for a moment behind the seat that Giuliani had appropriated, then took the one to which the mayor had relegated him.

Giuliani barred all press and prohibited even official pictures of the event. Deputy Mayor Randy Mastro sought to eject Gore's official photographer, even after the man pledged not to snap so much as a single frame.

Gore was all graciousness as he praised Giuliani for his great victory over crime and proposed that New York be a model for America. The cops in attendance noted that Gore proved to have done a lot of homework for a guy who was just looking for a political photo op. His questions were knowledgeable and probing, though he kept having to lean over to use the microphone installed at the seat the mayor had claimed.

At one seemingly unremarkable moment during the CompStat session, Gore had asked Safir a question. Sergeant John Yohe was at his usual spot, sitting behind a computer, concentrating on the technical aspects of the session and did not immediately realize that Safir had, in turn, asked him a question.

"Safir says something, I'm not even listening to him," Yohe would recall. "It sounded like the grownups on *Peanuts*. I don't know what he's saying. He said this thing and two hundred people turned around to look at me."

Yohe realized he had to say something. He rose and did his best to answer a question about CompStat he had not even really heard and then sat back down. Safir seems to have felt that Yohe was correcting him or otherwise making it look like the commissioner did not fully understand CompStat, which he in fact did not.

The next day, Yohe got a call from Anemone.

"I got good news and bad news," Anemone said.

"Great, chief. What's the good news?" Yohe asked.

"The good news is it's a beautiful day outside," Anemone said.

The bad news was that this was the last day at CompStat for the street nerd who had put in untold hours improvising and scrounging with no funds and outdated software. Safir had ordered Yohe transferred to Queens forthwith.

"Right then and there, I was banished," Yohe later said.

Anemone had Yohe stop into his office before he departed.

"Just keep your mouth shut," Anemone advised him. "These guys are animals."

Yohe took along a souvenir he would later put on his desk in civilian life. The wooden seating sign reads AL GORE, VICE PRESIDENT.

M ayor Rudolph Giuliani continued to claim credit for saving the city. His outsized sense of himself was parodied by the cops in a Bronx precinct who substituted the usual official photos on the wall of the police commissioner, the chief of department, the chief of patrol, the borough commander, and the precinct commander with five photos of Giuliani.

And there was an abiding irony: Giuliani did not appear to understand what was causing the murder rate to fall. He seemed to imagine that the salvation of New York had begun with his declaration of zero tolerance for "quality of life" violations and a crackdown on his bugaboo, the odious squeegee men.

In truth, the squeegee men had mostly been vanquished in the final weeks of the Dinkins and Kelly administration. Giuliani approached policing with the anger of an exile, his family having departed a "changing" Hawthorne Street in Brooklyn for Long Island when he was nine years old. He never revisited his early childhood home during his time as mayor.

Giuliani announced a crackdown on jaywalking, though he himself paid little heed to "don't walk" signals. He also announced a crackdown on speeding and became apoplectic when a newspaper columnist reported the mayor's vehicle had passed a loaded school bus on the right in the Battery Tunnel at thirty miles per hour above the limit. He accused the columnist of lying, even though there was incontrovertible E-ZPass toll evidence.

"If this can happen, this is no longer America," Giuliani declared.

The perception of the zero tolerance mayor and of the NYPD in the Black community had seemed confirmed when a Haitian immigrant named Abner Louima claimed that a cop had yelled "It's Giuliani time" while sodomizing him with a broken broomstick in a Brooklyn station house on August 9, 1997. Louima later retracted the claim, which he had apparently made to rouse public support when he feared he might not be believed. The medical evidence of his injuries was still enough for Police Officer Justin Volpe to plead guilty in federal court to the assault.

Volpe told the judge that somebody had hit him during a melee outside a nightclub and he had mistakenly believed Louima was the assailant. Volpe admitted that he had struck Louima as he sat handcuffed in the back of the police car. Volpe said he had subsequently taken Louima into the bathroom at the 70th Precinct station house and jammed the broken broomstick in his rectum.

"I was in shock at the time, Your Honor," Volpe said. "I was mad at the time."

Volpe reported that after the attack, "I told [Louima], 'If you tell anybody about this, I'll find you and I'll kill you.'"

Volpe further acknowledged, "While I was in the bathroom, there was another police officer in the bathroom with me. That police officer saw what was going on, did nothing to stop it. It was understood from the circumstances that that police officer would do nothing to stop me or report it to anyone."

Volpe had been counting on the bond between police officers even when he was doing something that betrayed every decent member of the department and left an indelible scar on the entire NYPD. He was sentenced to thirty years in prison, but that did not keep the actions of this one demented cop from further affirming the negative view many people in minority neighborhoods had of police officers in general.

CHAPTER 3

Meanwhile, Howard Safir sought to prove himself a smart commissioner, a leader with his own big ideas, not just somebody carrying on what Jack Maple started.

"The Rodney Dangerfield of law enforcement," William Bratton had called his successor.

Safir noted that the Street Crime Unit continued to be remarkably effective. He decided to build on its success by quadrupling its size from around seventy (sixty cops on the street, ten or so command and administrative staff).

The commander of the Street Crime Unit, Captain Richard Savage, warned that the sudden influx would necessarily make the unit less selective and tightly knit while tasked with the same dangerous mission of aggressively getting guns off the street wherever crime was highest.

Savage further noted that there would be more SCU newcomers than could be teamed up with an experienced member to tutor them and confirm they had the necessary smarts, temperament, and motivation.

"One of the problems is that they don't know each other anymore," Savage told a reporter. "They've lost that intimacy of training and coordination."

Savage was ignored and retired in protest. He left a warning that Safir was inviting disaster in his desperation to get the respect he felt he was due.

Some cops took to calling Safir Fredo, after the feckless son in the *Godfather* saga, who at one point exclaims, "I'm smart, too!"

The heedless buildup of the Street Crime Unit went ahead, and the Safir regime claimed success, suggesting that the expansion was a major factor in the further reduction of crime. The unit reported a 50 percent increase in the number of people stopped and searched that year, from eighteen thousand to twenty-seven thousand.

"There's an esprit de corps that the street crime unit engenders among its troops," Safir said. "I wish I could bottle their enthusiasm and make everyone take a drink of it."

But the number of arrests declined. Only one in five stop-and-frisks resulted in a collar, an indication that the cops were less skilled, less experienced, and less supervised. The street crime veterans who would not be surprised by the eventual result included Thomas McDonald, who had left the unit the summer after Gillespie's death, before the Safir surge.

Thomas had not expected to be assigned to the Auto Crime Unit, as he knew nothing about cars and did not even own one. He arrived to discover that Sean McDonald's brother, Andrew, was already there. Auto Crime proved to be the only unit whose members were still automatically awarded a detective shield after eighteen months. Thomas figured that Chief Timoney had decided, before his own departure, to take care of the brothers of Steven McDonald and Sean McDonald. Timoney may have also considered that Auto Crime was a less dangerous assignment. He surely did not want even to think of what the loss of a second son would do to either family.

Thomas and Andrew had begun working as partners. They got a reminder of how wild even Auto Crime could become when they were in Harlem, working plainclothes in an unmarked car. They heard a report over the citywide radio of a carjacking on the Upper East Side.

"We look and here comes the car," Thomas would remember.

The driver gave them what Thomas later called "the fish eye" and did a good job of appearing not to have noticed that he had been spotted.

"He did a perfect parallel parking job," Thomas later said. "Real cool, real smooth."

The man stepped out and began casually ambling away in what Thomas later described as a "punk rock motorcycle jacket." Andrew stepped out and grabbed him.

The man then executed what Thomas would call "this real smooth jailhouse move."

"He does this spin move and comes right out of his jacket and this guy starts running like a fucking deer," Thomas would recall. "It's a thing real crooks practice. In a flash, Andy's left holding the guy's leather jacket."

Andrew gave chase on foot, and Thomas set off after him in the car but hit traffic. The suspect tried unsuccessfully to commandeer two other cars and then a post office truck. Thomas ran up and broke the truck's driver's side window and tried to stop the guy from pulling away.

The truck lurched ahead, and Thomas fell back, banging his head. Thomas hopped back up, and he, Andrew, and an off-duty cop all ended up struggling with the suspect in the truck. The off-duty cop had drawn his off-duty revolver, which flew out of his hand and landed in the suspect's lap. More cops arrived.

"Now, it's the blue octopus," Thomas recalled. "There's a million cops on him."

The suspect then let out a cry.

"He starts saying, 'I got AIDS! I got AIDS!'" Thomas remembered. "Everybody let go. He started running again."

The suspect was quickly recaptured and finally handcuffed. He said he had hijacked the car in order to come to Harlem and buy clothes and a gun in preparation for sticking up a drug deal in Washington Heights.

The suspect came from a family of thieves but had been the straight one and was said to have attended an Ivy League college on a scholarship, graduating cum laude. A brother had then come out of prison and introduced him to crack.

On the way down to Central Booking, Andrew drove while Thomas sat in the back with the suspect, who proved to possess a kind of split personality, one moment jabbering street criminal doggerel about how he would throw somebody off the top tier when he got to Rikers Island, and the next moment offering a discourse about the role of the Treaty of Versailles in the rise of fascism and the outbreak of World War II.

"Andy was looking at me in the rearview mirror, 'WTF?'" Thomas recalled.

The suspect refused to take an AIDS test and the court declined to order one, so Thomas and Andrew and the other cops worried that they had been exposed. Thomas ended up having to undergo a decidedly unpleasant course of antiviral drugs.

All that had happened in what was a supposedly low-risk assignment.

Thomas was left with all the more reason to join the many cops who felt that Safir's sudden expansion of the high-risk Street Crime Unit was a dangerous mistake.

"He fucked it all up," Thomas said simply. "It doesn't work like that. It's got to be hand-picked guys."

CHAPTER 4

On February 4, 1999, a jittery team of newbie Street Crime cops—who some would later suggest were not exactly the best of the best—approached an unarmed twenty-three-year-old street peddler named Amadou Diallo as he went up his stoop into his building's vestibule in the Bronx. Sean Carroll thought Diallo was pulling a weapon.

"Gun!" Carroll called out.

Carroll fired a shot, and another cop reared back in surprise, losing his footing and falling backward from the steps. His comrades imagined this cop had been shot, and they all began firing, a total of forty-one bullets in all. The unarmed Diallo was hit nineteen times.

Over the days that followed, the Reverend Al Sharpton organized daily acts of peaceful civil disobedience blocking the entrance to police headquarters. As many as two hundred protesters were arrested at a time for disorderly conduct and generally released after an hour. They included some of the city's most prominent Black leaders, including former Mayor David Dinkins. A woman who said she was representing the actress Susan Sarandon called the office of Deputy Police Commissioner Edward Norris, successor to Jack Maple.

"Ms. Sarandon plans to be arrested tomorrow, but she has a luncheon appointment and wonders if she can be arrested first," the woman told Norris.

Norris got off the phone and gave orders for Sarandon to be arrested last.

The four cops involved in Diallo's death were indicted for murder, and the PBA held a demonstration the day of a pretrial hearing at the Bronx courthouse where Larry Davis had been acquitted a decade before.

"It's a tragedy, not a crime!" they chanted.

Steven McDonald spoke, his words amplified by a microphone from a sound truck emblazoned with the words cop shot. The vehicle was ordinarily used to cruise neighborhoods where a cop had been shot, offering a reward for information leading to the arrest of the shooter.

Steven paused periodically as the ventilator delivered the air that enabled him to speak and had kept him alive thirteen years since the split second that changed everything.

"I feel a lot in common with the men who were put in a difficult situation that night," he said. "They had to make a difficult choice. Tragically, it turned out to be the wrong one."

One newspaper reported that after Steven McDonald spoke, the accused officers "leaned across a barricade to shake his hand." But of course he could not shake anybody's hand.

Steven was able to travel in his van to the courthouse in upstate Albany after the cops secured a change in venue because they felt they could not get a fair trial in the Bronx. The judge barred Steven from the courtroom on the grounds that his presence could sway the jury. He was not there during the closing arguments, when defense attorney John Patten picked up a black wallet from the table in front of the jury and held it between his thumb and extended fingers so its edge faced them.

"Ladies and gentlemen, this is Amadou Diallo's wallet," Patten said.

Patten set the wallet back down and took up a small black gun from the table.

"This is a .25 automatic," he said.

Patten extended his pointing finger along the barrel, and the top of the gun did not look very different from the edge of the wallet.

"This was mistaken for that," Patten said.

This particular gun had been modified into a harmless starter's pistol, but it made a convincing enough clunk as it rejoined the wallet on the table. Patten reminded the jury what his client, Sean Carroll, had cried out that night just before the shooting began.

"Gun!"

Patten then evoked the memory of Kevin Gillespie.

"There's an officer who waited until he saw the gun, and now he's dead," Patten said. "He never saw another thing...Gillespie waited, and now he's dead."

Patten spoke of his client in the immediate aftermath of the shooting.

"The moment he discovered this was a wallet, he held Mr. Diallo's hand, he stroked his face and said, 'Don't die,'" Patten told the jury.

All four cops were found not guilty. Carroll retired, and two became firefighters. The fourth, Kenneth Boss, remained in the police department, staging a long and eventually successful legal battle to regain authorization to carry a firearm. Diallo's mother, Kadiatou, worried aloud that Boss "might do it again." She retained such grace as to praise him after he was credited with saving two stranded boaters.

"I'm at peace, and I don't want him to be followed by this the rest of his life," she told the *New York Daily News*. "He's the one who stubbornly believed he wanted to be a police officer... that he has something to offer, to help people. And that is good. And that is what I want."

She went on, "For the rest of his life, whatever else [Boss] does, he'll be remembered as one of the officers involved with Amadou. I don't want to add to what he went through. I pray for healing."

She then spoke of the cop very much as Steven had years before when forgiving the teen who shot him.

"I wish for him to move on in a constructive way, to do good, and that is what he is doing."

CHAPTER 5

J ack Maple followed the Diallo case from his second home, a boat at the end of Long Island. He suggested that considerably fewer than forty-one shots may have been fired at Diallo if the cops had been trained to first take cover when they believe they are under fire. They would thereby have been able to reduce the threat while evaluating whether it was real or imagined and how best to respond. He countered the usual station house advice that a cop's first duty is to get home safe to his or her family.

"The first job of any police officer is to make sure *everybody* gets home safely," Jack said.

There remained the question of why Diallo had been stopped in the first place. And that led to the question of how many other people were being stopped and what percentage of them were minority and in which precincts. Cops are supposed to fill out a Unified Form 250 whenever they stop and frisk someone, detailing the time and place and justification. The Civilian Complaint Review Board estimated that cops had been doing so less than half the time. But that still left 175,000 UF250s between 1988 and the first quarter of 1999 for the New York State attorney general to examine. The result was a compilation of statistics: Black people were 25.6 percent of the city's population but 50 percent of those stopped, whereas white people were 43.4 percent of the population but only 12.9 percent of those stopped. The ratio of stops-to-arrests for Black people was 9.5 times to one. For white people, the ratio was 7.9 times to one.

In the first significant and manifest change in CompStat since Jack's departure, the department began including UF250s along with the felony numbers. The UF250s stats were used primarily to measure police behavior, not crime. And the use of them encouraged a more fundamental change, as the people now running CompStat proved to not fully understand its genesis and basic principles.

Numbers became everything. Cops were judged by their "activity," meaning arrests and summons as well as stop-and-frisks. And that led to de facto quotas. Precinct-level supervisors perpetually dreaded the next Comp-Stat. Individual cops sought to placate their immediate bosses. Cops felt that they were not so much fighting crime as making numbers, that they had gone from "shoveling shit against the tide" to simply shoveling shit.

"It was turned into a disciplinary tool," Thomas McDonald said of CompStat. "Guys were like, okay, 'Hey, grandma, come over here, put down your grocery bags and put your hands on the wall.'"

Jack had intended CompStat to be a tool for managing crime, not cops. The essential CompStat statistic for him was a reduction in the number of victims, not an increase in arrests.

And, as he repeatedly said, there had to be a sense of fairness.

But, the policing fundamentals of CompStat were still at work. Crime continued to decline. And those now running the NYPD were able to imagine they were also smart, too.

CHAPTER 6

Homicides had fallen to 903 a year in 1999 when Steven McDonald addressed a roll call of cops in the Central Park Precinct, the last place he had been assigned and where he still had a locker.

"He told rookies and veterans alike to always think about officer safety," Jimmy O'Neill, then the precinct commander and later to become police commissioner, would recall. "And to always treat everyone they encountered on patrol with the same level of respect and kindness they'd afford their own, closest friends."

Steven was essentially telling them to patrol with the same spirit of fairness with which Jack had begun the transformation of New York. Only Steven was not seeking to impose these principles with a computer display at headquarters that held commanders accountable for addressing each dot wherever it appeared. He was summoning them from the core of the individual cops who now stood before him where he himself had once stood. His words had added power in this station house where the contents of his locker were just as he had left them thirteen years before.

O'Neill was listening as both a precinct commander who made regular trips to CompStat and a cop who had come to the job as a calling.

"That's what had such an impact on me: Steven was saying that putting your life on the line for strangers is not an easy vocation, but he knew the men and women of the NYPD could—and would—make a difference in people's lives," O'Neill would remember.

O'Neill would add, "In fact, Steven's was a life that underscores why most people decide to become police officers: Cops want to make a difference. Cops want to do good. Cops want to lead lives of significance. And Steven did that every single day of his life."

The significance became all the more manifest as the number of homicides in the city dropped to 673 the following year. Jack saw it as a measure of saved lives; 1,222 fewer killings in 2000 than in the year CompStat was implemented. The Safir regime saw it as just one measure of performance, the others including the number of arrests.

On March 16, 2000, an undercover police officer approached a twenty-six-year-old off-duty security guard named Patrick Dorismond as he stood outside a Manhattan bar, trying to get a yellow taxi home to Brooklyn, not always an easy proposition for a Black man living in the city.

The undercover officer told Dorismond that he was looking to buy some marijuana. Dorismond angrily rebuffed him, apparently taking offense that this stranger would presume just by looking at him that he would know such a thing.

A dispute ensued, and the undercover officer's partner intervened with a drawn gun. The unarmed Dorismond fell fatally wounded, the third unarmed Black man to be killed by New York cops since Amadou Diallo thirteen months before.

Rudy Giuliani sought to defend the cop by disparaging the dead man, depicting him as a violent thug with a significant criminal past. Giuliani authorized Howard Safir to release Dorismond's juvenile record, which showed an arrest for robbery and assault.

"People have the right to know the background and record of a person involved in a criminal situation," Giuliani told reporters. "He's no altar boy."

Giuliani failed to mention that the juvenile arrest resulted from Dorismond punching another youngster in the nose in a dispute over a quarter and that the charges were dropped before the case even went before a judge. Nor did Giuliani mention that Dorismond's arrests as an adult for assault and weapon possession had been reduced to disorderly conduct.

In fact, Dorismond had never been convicted of a crime. And he actually had been an altar boy, at Holy Cross Church in Brooklyn.

"Jesus said, 'He who is without sin, let him cast the first stone,'" the priest there said as he prepared for Dorismond's funeral. "Patrick's dead, and they're still throwing stones at him."

At the wake, Dorismond's mother, Marie, stood by the coffin, an anguished Haitian immigrant who worked as a nurse at Kings County Hospital and had named her son after a favorite Catholic priest.

"My son is not a criminal!" she now cried out.

A houngan, or voodoo priest, stepped up.

"I put a curse on the manhood of Rudolph Giuliani and Howard Safir," he declared.

Of course, only coincidence was at work when Giuliani and Howard Safir were diagnosed with prostate cancer within six weeks of each other. The men were apparently unaware of the curse but were struck by the coincidence.

"You couldn't write this script," Safir said.

"This is a very strange and ironic thing," Giuliani said. "We're both dealing with the same thing at the same time."

CHAPTER 8

The New York City Charter limits elected officials to serving two four-year terms, and Rudy Giuliani was in the third year of his second in 2000. He was seeking to capitalize on his crimefighter image as he prepared to run for the US Senate seat being vacated by Daniel Moynihan, who was retiring.

As much as he talked about crime and as many times as he had rushed to the bedside of wounded cops, Giuliani now spoke little about illegal guns. He clearly did not want to alienate conservative voters outside the city whose support helped put him as many as nine points ahead in the early statewide polls.

But Giuliani's early lead in the polls began to slip as his smearing of Dorismond and general self-righteousness was accompanied by an increasingly messy personal life. He did not help himself with conservatives when he announced his separation from his wife at a press conference without first bothering to tell her. He subsequently arranged for news photographers to take pictures of him dining with his mistress, Judith Nathan, and then walking her home. He was continuing on to the mayor's residence when he chanced to spy a couple necking on a bench in a church courtyard.

"That's disgusting," he said to an aide.

The houngan's curse could not be blamed as Giuliani fell as many as ten points behind the presumed Democratic candidate Hillary Clinton. But the cancer diagnosis he announced to the press on April 27 added to his reasons for dropping out. He officially did so on May 19.

That meant the upstate conservatives were no longer an immediate concern. And Giuliani again became the guy whose name had appeared on the cover page of "Police Strategy No. 1: Getting Guns off the Streets of New York" at the start of the city's transformation six years before. He suddenly seemed to remember the introduction, which said, "With 90% of the illegal guns in New York flowing into the city from other states, this is clearly a problem that transcends any one city's boundaries. Federal legislation and federal enforcement action are imperative."

In June, Giuliani announced that the city was filing a lawsuit against two dozen gun makers for "deliberately manufacturing many more firearms than can be bought for legitimate purpose" and "deliberately undermining New York City's gun control laws by flooding markets with looser gun laws with firearms that the manufacturers know are destined to be illegally resold in New York City."

"This is an industry that is profiting from the suffering of innocent people," he declared. "What's worse, its profits rest on a number of illegal and immoral practices."

More guns, Giuliani said, meant more death.

"The single biggest connection between violent crime and an increase in violent crime is the presence of guns in your society," he said. "The more guns you take out of society, the more you are going to reduce murder. The less guns you take out of society, the more it is going to go up."

For reasons that apparently extended beyond voodoo and his diagnosis, Safir resigned three months later. He was replaced by Bernard Kerik, a former NYPD detective and New Jersey jail warden who had been Giuliani's driver during his 1993 campaign. Kerik had subsequently served as Giuliani's corrections commissioner.

Now, in August 2000, Kerik was the new police commissioner. He was widely viewed as even less qualified than Safir. He indicated his self-appraisal when he had busts made of himself. But, like Safir, Kerik was careful never to upstage his boss.

Back in William Bratton's first days as police commissioner, Giuliani had ceded center stage by declining to host a press conference at City Hall featuring piles of recovered illegal guns. He now did exactly that with a display of firearms that had been recovered by the NYPD and would soon be melted down into either manhole covers or coat hangers. He who had fretted about being photographed with a gun six years before now completed the photo op by reaching for the flashiest weapon in the pile, a pearl-handled revolver.

CompStat kept making the city safer, and thousands of New Yorkers were moving about unaware that they might have been murder victims were it not for a former transit cop who was now in a fight against advanced colon cancer.

Jack Maple was proving as unique a cancer patient as he had been a cave cop. Laughter erupted from the room where he was being examined at Memorial Sloan Kettering Hospital. A trio of nurses emerged red faced and laughing.

"Your friend just told us he'd feel better if we were naked, too," one of them informed a Maple pal.

Jack continued to work as a consultant, having helped Newark and New Orleans and Birmingham and other cities actually address crime. He was also a consultant with a TV show that he inspired, *The District*. Craig T. Nelson played the Jack Maple character and struck the actual Jack as behaving a little too grandly on and off the set. Jack took an opportunity to bring Nelson down a peg as they were walking across a studio parking lot in Los Angeles. A recent blast of chemo caused Jack to faint, and people came running over.

"Craig pushed me," Jack said as he lay on his back. "I'm dying of cancer and I said something he didn't like and he pushed me."

"Jack! Don't tell them that!" Nelson said.

"Craig, don't make it worse by lying," Jack said. "I'm dying of cancer and you pushed me down."

Jack's buddies would have laughed harder if the latest hospital tests had not confirmed that he was, in fact, dying.

"I'm really going to miss this place," Jack told a friend.

"What place?" the friend asked.

"Earth," Jack said.

Jack's great earthly reward remained the rent-stabilized studio apartment overlooking Central Park. He spent his last moments there on the morning of August 4, 2001, in the company of his NYPD lieutenant now wife, Brigid, and a longtime friend. He took a final breath and grimaced and then he was gone. He was forty-eight.

Brigid turned up the air-conditioning and told the friend that she did not want to notify anybody. They sat for six hours as the sounds of the city rose from the street below.

"Do you think we're going to get in trouble?" Brigid finally asked.

"I don't know, Brigid," the friend said. "You're the police lieutenant."

Brigid told the friend to make a call. The police and an undertaker responded. Two very nice young men from the Frank E. Campbell Funeral Chapel wheeled Jack's remains onto Central Park South.

Jack was waked at Campbell's, where everybody from Judy Garland to the Notorious B.I.G. had been mourned. Vertel Martin was heartbroken and later sat with a glass of Chablis by the skating rink at Rockefeller Center, which was closed for the summer. She spilled some on the floor, a street gesture of respect to a fallen comrade.

On August 8, 2001, Jack was accorded a full inspector's funeral at St. Patrick's Cathedral, complete with pipe band and honor guard. Giuliani delivered a eulogy, for once giving full credit where it was due, perhaps in part because by doing so, he was taking it away from Bratton, who was in attendance. Giuliani said that Jack had risen from a transit cop to become "nothing less than a nationally, internationally, recognized icon."

"The cop who cleaned up New York," Giuliani said. "He was a revolutionary who wore bow ties, double-breasted suit, what do you call those shoes he wore?"

John Miller spoke and cited some essential Maple math, by which there were 7,937 people who otherwise would have been murdered.

"St. Patrick's holds three thousand people," Miller said to the standing-room-only crowd. "You could fill this cathedral to capacity twice and still need room for another 1,937 people who are out there walking around alive because of Jack Maple."

Miller added, "He changed how we walk down the street and whether we decide to stay out late; whether or not we ride the subway or go to a certain neighborhood."

The honor guard carried Jack's coffin back onto Fifth Avenue and folded the NYPD flag that had been covering it. The flag was ceremoniously presented to Brigid O'Connor. A pair of trumpeters played taps. Three helicopters flew overhead.

Jack's mortal remains were then slow-marched downtown and across West 42nd Street. A friend who often strode the Deuce with him in the bad old days knew exactly what he would have said about it being closed off at rush hour for him to pass along it one last time.

"How delicious!"

Some of Jack's old crew had been speaking of raising funds to have a statue erected of him to stand with those of military chaplain Father Francis Duffy of the Fighting 69th and the showman-composer-lyricist George M. Cohan. But the bad old days were on their way to being forgotten. And most of the people on the street who were forced to pause while his hearse passed would not likely have understood the significance even if they had been told it was somebody named Jack Maple.

Giuliani was the name that the public most associated with the decline in crime. He was also a stridently divisive figure whose rantings about zero tolerance had made him an intolerant zero. He took religious exception to a painting of the Virgin Mary in the Brooklyn Museum he had never seen and announced the formation of a "decency task force." He then marched with Judith Nathan past the museum in the West Indian Day Parade on September 3, oblivious to the jeering crowds that associated him with the torture of Abner Louima and the deaths of Amadou Diallo and Patrick Dorismond.

On September 10, 2001, a month and a day after Jack's funeral, Giuliani was barely noticed by passersby as he emerged with an entourage from City Hall. Nary a person shouted "Rudy!" or bothered to snap his picture. The mayor was a tiresome figure whose time seemed to have passed.

T he following morning, two hijacked airplanes flew into the Twin Towers of the World Trade Center. Rudy Giuliani was unable to use his command post, having installed it on the twenty-third floor of a forty-seven-story building adjacent to the Twin Towers at the World Trade Center. Never mind that New York already had a command post at NYPD headquarters. He had established the world's only command bunker in the air in close proximity to what a 1993 bombing had established as a bull's-eye for terrorists. And he had shrugged off numerous warnings that the location was unwise.

"Seven World Trade Center is a poor choice for the site of a crucial command center for the top leadership of the City of New York," concluded a 1998 memo issued by an NYPD study group.

Burning debris ignited diesel fuel tanks that had been installed in the bunker's ceiling to power its generator. The blaze would rage for seven hours before the building collapsed.

His command post out of action, Giuliani had gone instead to a firehouse twenty blocks uptown, where he and his entourage now had to break in. Nobody had stayed behind when the firefighters of Engine 24, Ladder 5 responded to the Twin Towers. Eleven of them were killed as Giuliani sought to take command from the safety of their quarters.

A survivor from Ladder 5, Firefighter Chris Waugh, was among a group of first responders who bore Mychal Judge's body from the burning ruins. Father Mychal had raced to the stricken towers from his friary in a white fire helmet and a turnout coat with FDNY CHAPLAIN stenciled on the back. A photograph of Waugh and the others carrying Mychal's body out from the burning ruins would be described as "the modern *Pietà*."

Mychal's remains were transported to the medical examiner's office, where he was logged in as DM0001, officially recorded as the first fatality of Disaster Manhattan, as 9/11 was termed. Steven was notified at home by a friend in the NYPD. Conor was fourteen at the time and would remember a rare time when he saw his father crying:

"Tears pouring down his face," Conor would recall.

When Steven arrived in his van, a morgue attendant led him in his wheelchair to a refrigerated room. The attendant pointed to one of five bagged bodies.

"Here's Mychal Judge's remains," the attendant said.

Detective Tom Nerney, a friend of both Steven's and Mychal's, also arrived. Nerney insisted that he be the one to fingerprint Judge. He was also in tears as he gently rolled the tips in the ink and then pressed them to the card.

Steven departed having lost a spiritual mentor—they had been as close as any two cops in a radio car, truly *anam cara*, friends of the soul, or soul mates.

Later, Steven learned that the dead also included Fire Marshal Ronald Bucca, the Flying Fireman, who had appeared at his bedside in Bellevue. Bucca had refused to take a tax-free disability pension, instead pushing himself through months of agonizing physical therapy until he could resume full duty. He was the only firefighter on September 11 to climb all the way to the fire on the seventy-eighth floor of the South Tower. Bucca must have placed his turnout coat protectively around several civilians when it collapsed, for it was later found still wrapped around them.

"We always talked about getting together," Steven said. "And then he was gone."

Steven might have also lost a brother. Thomas had finished eighteen months in Auto Crime and become a detective just like Steven. But after Thomas was assigned to the 115th Precinct Squad in Queens, he discovered that detective work was not for him due to the endless DD5 reports and not enough time in the street. He decided that what he really wanted was the Emergency Service Unit.

The hitch was that traditionally detectives who wanted to join ESU had to give up their shield. Thomas made a rare request to Steven to use his influence as an NYPD icon. Steven asked Thomas to research if there had ever been any exceptions to the ESU shield rule. Thomas reported back that there was one, Detective Joseph Viggiano, a notable alumnus of the 75th Precinct.

Steven telephoned Patrick Kelleher, who had just gone from chief of detectives to first deputy commissioner.

"No," Kelleher said.

"No disrespect, sir, but there is a guy there right now," Steven said, citing the Viggiano exception.

"I'll call you right back," Kelleher said.

Minutes later, the phone rang.

"Your brother can keep his shield," Kelleher told Steven before immediately hanging up.

That was in May 2000. Thomas underwent training and joined Joe Viggiano on Truck 2 in Upper Manhattan that November. His immediate supervisor was Sergeant Mike Curtin, who pushed his E-men to be self-reliant and inventive in the face of the sudden challenges.

"Best boss I ever had as a cop," Thomas later said.

Thomas was working with Viggiano when what they at first took to be an unmarked police car pulled up alongside them. The driver's side window came down, and Thomas saw that FDNY Chaplain Mychal Judge was at the wheel of what proved to be a fire department car.

"Thomas! Thank God you're here!" Judge exclaimed.

"Father Mike! What are you doing?" Thomas asked.

"I got to go to a ceremony," Judge explained. "I'm lost."

"Ceremony for who?" Thomas asked.

Judge named a firehouse in the South Bronx.

"Can you help me, please?" Judge asked.

Thomas and Viggiano would have helped Judge no matter what, but there was the added incentive of a little mischief. ESU had a long standing rivalry with the FDNY, even though a number of the cops had family members who were firefighters, Viggiano's brother among them.

"We'll take you," Thomas said. "Follow us."

Thomas and Viggiano had their lights and siren going when they escorted Judge up to the firehouse, thereby dramatizing for the firefighters that a couple of cops were delivering them their fire chaplain. Judge later reported the FDNY reaction.

"Thomas, they were going to kill me," Judge said. "Why didn't you tell me?"

"You're welcome, Father," Thomas said.

The various ESU trucks, or units, rotated in two members at a time into the elite A-Team, based in Fort Totten in Queens. They there received special training and worked with the full-time A-Team members.

At the start of September 2001, Curtin hoped to add one extra and send three Truck 2 cops. He himself was due for the next rotation and tried to include Thomas, along with a cop named Bobby Yaeger, in the next rotation. But an inspector intervened, citing the two-at-a-time rule.

"Mike was disappointed, let's put it that way," Thomas later said. "Mike was going to go. But he said, 'No, you and Bobby go, do the work, get the experience.'"

Thomas and Yaeger started on Monday, September 10. New rotations overlapped with the previous one by a week, so they could receive training before actually working with the A-Team.

After a four p.m. to midnight shift, Thomas was awakened at home that Tuesday morning by a commotion downstairs. He rose to see everybody in front of the television, watching the burning South Tower of the World Trade Center. They told him it had just been struck by an airplane.

"It's on the TV, and as I'm watching, here comes the second plane," Thomas recalled. "I'm like, 'Oh, shit, I got to go to work.'"

The phone began ringing. Yaeger was calling from his own home fifteen minutes away.

"You ready?" he asked Thomas.

"Yeah, I'll be right there," Thomas said.

Thomas roared up to Yaeger's house in his Mustang. They sped on, with the traffic all coming out of the city as they headed in. They then came up over a hill on the Grand Central Parkway at the edge of Queens.

"It's a sea of brake lights," Thomas would recall.

Thomas went up on the shoulder, as others did the same, waving police placards to a state trooper who stood at the edge of the road.

"It's all cops," Thomas said.

Thomas reached Fort Totten and parked his Mustang by the entrance just as Lieutenant John McArdle pulled up in an ESU vehicle. Thomas and Yaeger hopped in and they were on the Bruckner Expressway headed to Truck 2 when they saw the South Tower collapse in the distance.

At Truck 2, they met up with the corrections department equivalent of ESU. They all continued in a convoy toward the World Trade Center and had just reached City Hall Park when the North Tower collapsed.

"All the papers, thousands of papers coming down, and all the dust, it was everywhere," Thomas would recall.

Thomas would later learn that those who died in the second collapse included Curtin and Viggiano. Among the still living was a lone figure.

"Joe McCormack came wandering around the corner by himself," Thomas would remember.

McCormack's father, also named Joe, had been an ESU cop in Truck 2 decades before. The elder McCormack had been assigned to the back door of a Bronx house where a mental outpatient had barricaded himself with a shotgun on September 29, 1983. A hostage negotiator was seeking a peaceful conclusion to the standoff when the man suddenly emerged with the shotgun.

"Don't hurt me...I just want to talk to you," a witness heard one of the cops say.

The man fired and the blast ricocheted off a tree, fatally wounding forty-year-old McCormack in the side, where his bulletproof vest offered no protection. He left three children, the eldest thirteen-year-old Joe.

On this other September day, eighteen years later, his son, now thirty-one, had been with members of ESU Truck 4 and Truck 10 at the entrance of the North Tower. Sergeant John Coughlin then told McCormack, "I need you to go back to the truck. We need a rope harness."

McCormack managed to dash two blocks and back without being hit by falling debris. He returned to discover Coughlin had already led the others inside. He was about to follow when rumbling from above signaled that the tower was beginning to come down. He somehow survived and seemed shell-shocked when Thomas saw him appear.

"It looked like his eyes were bleeding, but it was tears coming through the dust," Thomas would recall.

The comrades who had arrived at the entrance with McCormack had been killed. They included Coughlin and Police Officer Stephen Driscoll, who had been in Street Crime with Thomas. Also, Police Officer Brian McDonnell, whose name was widely misheard as "McDonald" as word of the dead spread. Thomas discovered this when he encountered a surviving sergeant.

"He said, 'I thought you were dead,'" Thomas would remember. "All the guys said that because of Brian McDonnell."

Thomas would later be asked how long he had taken part in the effort to recover the dead. His answer applied to everybody in ESU.

"From the beginning to the end."

That meant eight months and nineteen days.

Vertel Martin had responded to Ground Zero from her IAB base, arriving minutes after the second tower fell. Jimmy Nuciforo was also there, as was Billy Carter. Somebody called out that they saw a gun in the debris and moved to pick it up. It was still in the gun belt of a dead cop, George Howard of the Port Authority Police.

In the aftermath, the Maple-ettes were sure that if Jack had survived and become police commissioner, he would have viewed the attack as a murder case with nearly three thousand victims. The official cause of death for each of those killed at the World Trade Center was listed as "homicide," but the NYPD decided against including them in the annual count. The official tally for murders in 2001 was not 3,472, but 649, a drop of twenty-six from the year before.

Vertel Martin was continuing to assist with the recovery effort when she received a radio message to report immediately to the Police Academy. She there met with Chief Charles Campisi, the longtime head of IAB.

"Vertel, we need somebody to run the 9/11 missing persons task force," he said, by her recollection. "Will you do this job for us?"

"Yes, chief," she replied. "But I'm not going to do it with these idiots. You want the job done, you got to let me pick my people."

He did not object to her description of IAB investigators.

"You pick whoever you want," he said. "You get an expense account, equipment, whatever you need."

Vertel later learned why she had been chosen and why Campisi so quickly agreed to her conditions.

"Nobody else wanted it," she said.

The magnitude of the task was indicated by the line that stretched around the block at the 69th Regiment (the "Fighting 69") Armory on Lexington Avenue as people entered the cavernous drill hall with toothbrushes and hairbrushes and other DNA samples of missing loved ones. More than four thousand people filed reports on the first day. Many more reports came via phone calls and letters. Flyers went up all over lower Manhattan with photos of the missing.

Vertel and her squad worked sixteen-hour shifts, seven days a week for month after month on thousands of reports. Some proved to be for people dead long before 9/11. An overwhelming number of the missing had almost certainly been in one of the towers, though only a scant few intact remains were recovered, and clearly a good many never would be.

Momentary relief in the crushing grimness would come whenever an investigator determined that one of the missing was in fact alive. The victory would be signaled by the ringing of a bell that Vertel put up when her unit moved into its headquarters on Hudson Street at the edge of Ground Zero. The *ding* of what became known as "the found bell" kept the squad going.

"It gave you hope," Vertel later said.

The city's spirit was on display for the whole country five weeks later, with the Concert for New York at Madison Square Garden, where Steven and so many other police officers had graduated. The stars of the night were not the movie actors or big names in music, but the first responders. Firefighter Mike Moran, brother of fallen FDNY Chief John Moran, got roars of approval when he called out, "Osama Bin Laden, you can kiss my royal Irish ass."

Harrison Ford, who had once ridden with Kevin Gillespie, stepped onto the stage with Police Officer Michael Gerbasi, who had nearly lost an arm while rescuing people from the Twin Towers. The world seemed to have been shocked into the right priorities as the crowd appeared barely to notice the actor but went wild over the cop. The Who performed to rousing applause. The band members then applauded the cops and firefighters, among them a devoted Who fan, Steven McDonald.

"We could never follow what you do," lead singer Roger Daltrey told them from the stage.

Senator Hillary Clinton was greeted with boos that were edited out and replaced with cheers in the DVD. Rudy Giuliani received actual cheers, more restrained than those for the true stars of the night, such as Mike Moran, but genuine nonetheless. The man whose time seemed to have passed on September 10 was on his way to being known as "America's mayor."

In the aftermath of 9/11, Giuliani had consciously modeled himself on the way Father Mychal Judge ministered to the grieving loved ones after TWA Flight 800 went down off Long Island in 1996.

"In many ways, it was a prelude to the World Trade Center," Giuliani later said.

Giuliani sought to channel Mychal's particular kind of strength through love and compassion, summoning what was best in people to face horrific loss. Giuliani did not rail against the hijackers. He instead extolled and honored first responders such as Police Officer Moira Smith, who had been one of the first cops to respond to the World Trade Center, and was last seen urging people toward an exit in the South Tower. A trader with Eurobrokers later described her as "intense, but calm," her blue eyes steady, her voice ever even.

"Don't look, keep moving," she said again and again.

People kept moving when they otherwise would have frozen in terror. She was credited with saving literally hundreds of lives. A famous photo shows her leading a bleeding executive to safety. She then returned to the tower and was killed when it collapsed. Her gun belt was later recovered from the ruins, along with her dented shield, number 10467.

Fallen officers are traditionally awarded posthumous Medals of Honor a year after their death, but Giuliani wanted to be the one to perform the honor, and he would have been out of office by then.

"I think it's appropriate that Mayor Giuliani give them their medals since they gave their heroic sacrifice during this administration," Police Commissioner Bernard Kerik was quoted saying.

On December 4, Giuliani presided over a medal ceremony at Carnegie Hall for Smith and the twenty-two other members of the NYPD who perished on 9/11. Her two-year-old daughter, Patricia, crossed the stage in a red velvet dress and shiny black party shoes, her tiny right hand in her father's white-gloved left.

Her father was Police Officer James Smith, and he was wearing his dress uniform as he led her to where Giuliani stood waiting to posthumously award her mother the Medal of Honor. Another child might have cried or fled or clutched her father's leg, but Patricia inherited more of her mother than her Irish eyes and nose.

As the whole packed hall resounded with a standing ovation, Patricia strode with her father toward center stage. Three or four steps into it her left index finger went to her lips, but she kept walking and her eyes stayed steady under her light brown bangs.

She stopped when her father stopped, and Giuliani bent over to place the emerald-green ribbon around her neck. She looked impossibly small as the eight-pointed gold star hung just above her knees.

Her father saluted, and the mayor joined the applause. Patricia's eyes went to the audience, her index finger still at her mouth. She continued with her father to the far end of the stage.

As they went down the steps to rejoin the audience, her father swept her up in his big left arm. He carried her up the side aisle as the next family stepped up to receive a posthumous Medal of Honor.

Patricia lay her head on her father's shoulder as he crossed the back of the hall and went down the far aisle to the row of seats marked for them. The posthumous awards continued, with children and siblings and parents showing that grace and courage are family traits. The family of ESU Police Officer Joe Viggiano had also lost his brother, Firefighter John Viggiano.

When the last medal was bestowed, the lights dimmed and Lee Greenwood sang "God Bless the U.S.A." The faces of the twenty-three officers who died at the World Trade Center flashed on a screen, and suddenly there was Patricia's mother.

Moira Smith gazed from the screen with the flags of her country and her city in the background, her eyes bright, her mouth forever on the verge of a smile.

"God Bless Them. God Bless the NYPD," the closing message read.

Then the lights came up, and all the great musicians who have played Carnegie Hall could not match the sound of those cops singing "God Bless America" after they had lost so many of their own.

CHAPTER 12

The limits of Rudy Giuliani's resurgent political stature in the city were made clear when he suggested that he was so vital to New York's recovery that the mayoral election should be postponed. This reminder of his authoritarian tendencies triggered an overwhelmingly negative reaction. The election went ahead, but Giuliani retained enough influence among voters that his endorsement was decisive in billionaire Mike Bloomberg's victory over liberal Mark Green. Other big factors were Green's ability to annoy even people in total agreement with him and Bloomberg's spending of $68,968,185 on his campaign.

In his final days in office, Giuliani renamed the Manhattan Detention Complex, also known as the Tombs. It now officially became the Bernard B. Kerik Complex after Giuliani's onetime corrections commissioner and then police commissioner, who would be departing with him. The new name would be removed in 2006 when Kerik was on his way to pleading guilty to eight felony charges—among them tax fraud and lying to White House officials—and serving a four-year term as federal inmate 84888-054. Many cops considered that his greatest sin was in the immediate wake of 9/11, when he appropriated for himself and his mistress an apartment at the edge of Ground Zero meant to be a resting place for recovery workers. He remains the only convict to have had a New York jail named after him.

Vertel Martin continued her work with the missing persons task force until February 2002, when she got a call from headquarters. She was informed that she was now eligible to retire and therefore could no longer receive overtime. She had been working for five months at her mental and physical limits in an increasingly dispiriting and exhausting mission. And the department's primary concern was that she might make overtime that could translate into a higher pension.

"That showed me they didn't give a fuck about the good job I was doing," she later said. "Not to mention most of those motherfuckers were making overtime and doing nothing."

She reached an instant decision.

"I go, 'Okay, you tell them I will be filing my papers at headquarters in about thirty minutes,'" she would remember.

She hung up and made an announcement to her squad.

"I'm retiring in thirty minutes. You're beautiful. I hope you get somebody you can work with."

A short time later, she strode into headquarters. She left with RETIRED stamped on her ID card. Her squad presented her with the found bell. She pronounced it her most prized possession.

On the Sunday before the first anniversary of 9/11, Steven McDonald led the Walk of Remembrance, which began at Father Mychal's friary and retraced his steps to the World Trade Center that morning. The procession paused at each fire and police station that Mychal had passed, the participants praying as if at the Stations of the Cross for the first responders lost from each command.

"Through this pilgrimage, I want people to remember Father Mike's example of faith in God and service to people," Steven told a reporter.

A reminder of the dangers first responders continued to face came with the murder of two undercover detectives on March 3, 2003. Detective Rodney "Jay" Andrews of the Firearms Investigation Unit (FIU) had already made two solo undercover gun buys before going off duty that day. He was playing basketball with his sons—ages eleven and twelve—when he got a call asking him to come in to serve as a partner in a third.

Detective James "Haitian Sensation" Nemorin had made one buy of a .357 Magnum revolver from gang members in Shaolin, as they called Staten Island. But the New York State penal code classified the illegal sale of anything less than ten handguns a class E felony, on par with possession of a stolen credit card or a cloned cellphone, carrying a penalty ranging from probation to a maximum of four years. The sale of just a single crumb of crack was a class B felony, carrying a penalty of five to twenty-five years.

Had the law treated a gun sale as seriously as the sale of a crack vial, Nemorin could have simply arrested the seller on the first buy and used the threat of heavy time to flip him. They then could have used their informant to snare the supplier and other gun dealers.

Without such leverage, the FIU cops would have to make a second buy to double the seller's liability with the threat of two consecutive sentences. Nemorin had arranged to purchase a TEC-9 assault pistol from the same Shaolin crew that night. He had an uneasy feeling that the seller might either suspect he was a cop or be planning a rip-off. He decided he could use a partner, in particular Andrews, a thirty-four-year-old former Navy SEAL who was fast and strong enough to have been a professional baseball prospect had he not chosen to become a cop.

Nemorin, age thirty-six, was at the wheel when he and Andrews headed for Shaolin in a Nissan Maxima. They there picked up twenty-four-year-old

Ronell Wilson and seventeen-year-old Jessie Jacobus for the second buy. Wilson objected to Andrews's presence and worried aloud he might be a cop. The transmitter disguised as a beeper on Nemorin's belt recorded his response.

"He's my brother-in-law. He's cool," Nemorin said. "You deal with me before. What you talking about the police for? ... You know my brother-in-law live with me so he wants to come with me ... What is the big deal? Everybody's leery. Listen, I'm leery, I'm leery, too. I don't want to get caught up."

"It's mad hot, man," Wilson said. "It's mandatory, we got to search you."

"Get outta here," Nemorin replied. "Do you know how long I been doin' business?"

"That's not the fact of it," Wilson said.

"I do business internationally man," Nemorin said. "I'm from Haiti, bro."

"Yo, are you refusing to pat down or what?" Wilson asked.

Andrews spoke, trying to smooth things.

"Hold up, hold up, son," Andrews said. "I know you dealing with my brother-in-law."

"I'm dealin' with a lot of shit," Wilson said. "I'm the n—r in charge."

"There's nothing to worry about," Nemorin said at one point. "Look, we're not going to deal in front of him, okay? I'm coming. I could step out and we do the deal outside."

Wilson directed Nemorin to make a quick series of turns and the backup team lost sight of the car. The voices continued to come via the transmitter, along with hip-hop music.

"That's it, that's it," Nemorin said. "All right? All right?"

Twenty seconds later, the backup team lost the transmitter's signal and heard only static. Jacobus would subsequently testify that Wilson suddenly drew a .357 Magnum and shot Andrews in the head. Wilson then put the gun to the back of Nemorin's head.

"Where's the shit at?" Wilson asked, according to Jacobus's account.

"Don't shoot! I got a family! I got a family! Don't shoot!" pleaded Nemorin, who had a wife and three kids, ages seven years, five years, and twenty months.

Wilson fired. He and Jacobus pulled the two mortally wounded cops from the car and left them lying in the street. The interior and windows were spattered with blood as they drove to a nearby parking lot.

"Why did you do that?" Jacobus asked by his own account.

"I don't give a fuck about anybody," Wilson replied.

They searched the car for the cash, but the twelve marked $100 bills of buy money were still in Nemorin's jacket pocket when the backup team found their two comrades. Sergeant Richard Abbate went up to Andrews first.

"I saw that he had one eye closed and one eye opened," Abbate later testified. "He had sustained a wound to his head. I then approached Detective Nemorin. There was a long line of blood coming from his head."

Paramedics were there in minutes. A pair of ambulances rushed the two detectives to St. Vincent's Hospital on Staten Island. Mayor Bloomberg arrived with his new (and returning) police commissioner, Raymond Kelly. It fell to them to inform the detectives' wives that their husbands were dead. Andrews's wife, MaryAnn, was also a cop, working the street in the 90th Precinct of Brooklyn. Nemorin's wife, Rose, posed the hardest question Bloomberg had encountered since he first ran for mayor.

"What do I tell my children?"

Three dozen soldiers in desert camouflage joined the hundreds of police officers in dress blues outside Our Lady of Refuge Church in Brooklyn on the morning of Nemorin's funeral, a reminder that the nation was poised for a war to disarm Saddam Hussein as the city prepared to bury the first of two detectives killed while trying to get another gun off the streets. A gentle breeze rippled the Stars and Stripes as the pipe band's color guard started up Ocean Avenue, the muffled drums beginning a ritual performed at funeral after funeral following 9/11 and now at another. A hearse followed with Nemorin's coffin. The black limousine behind it stopped, and Nemorin's family stepped out into sun-splashed darkness. His two young sons stood in white shirts and ties, watching the pallbearers shoulder their father's flag-draped coffin.

"Detail, ten hut!" a voice called out.

The fallen detective's wife joined the white-gloved salute by placing her right hand over her heart. Rose and James Nemorin had been married in the very church in 1995. She spoke to the coffin as she had to the groom, a soft endearment in Creole.

"*Ti chou*," she said. "Little darling."

A lone bagpiper began playing "Amazing Grace." An honor guard went up the steps bearing the flag-draped coffin of the man who had come to New

York from Haiti when he was twenty-one with the hope of someday joining the NYPD.

"*Wap kite nou! Wap kite nou!*" a grief-stricken woman cried, also in the language of Haiti. "You're leaving us! You're leaving us!"

The service was conducted in Creole, French, and English. Bloomberg was among the speakers.

"We owe James and the valiant men and women who carry on the twilight struggle to stop the flow of firearms into the streets more than we could ever express," he said. "Some of those officers are here in this church today. For their own safety, I can't salute each one of them."

He meant the cops who continued to work undercover. They had arrived and would depart by a side door.

"And, sadly, I can't even say that all 8 million people in this city appreciate their dedication and bravery. But I can tell you that the vast majority of the 8 million people who live here do give their everlasting thanks."

Nemorin's father, Aubriant, who had flown in from Haiti, directed his words to the coffin.

"Your mother told me to tell you, 'May the sorrow be light upon you; may the peace of God be with you. Thank you, my son. Goodbye. Goodbye.'"

A fellow cop recounted waiting with Nemorin for an earlier gun buy. Nemorin's cellphone had rung. One of his sons was calling. He told the boy he was at work.

"Yeah, I'm out catching bad guys," Nemorin had said.

Nemorin had laughed.

"No, you can't talk to them!"

Andrews's funeral was held the next day at the Elim International Fellowship Church in another part of Brooklyn. The ritual was performed again, including eulogies by the mayor and the police commissioner.

"Jay loved his job and was passionately devoted to the work he was doing. He saved many, many lives," Kelly said.

Jay's widow, Detective MaryAnn Andrews, spoke with her older son standing beside her at the pulpit.

Her voice quavered as she recalled a wise and wonderful man who more than anything else had been a father.

"He loved his boys," she said. "May he rest in peace."

318 • Michael Daly

Detective Adam Frasse, a former partner and close friend, was next. He recalled being in the squad room, fretting that a case was unraveling. Andrews would be studying a *Baseball Digest*, his earphones blasting Led Zeppelin.

"He'd turn to us and say, 'Don't worry, we'll handle this,' " Frasse recounted.

Frasse remembered Andrews once saying of his comrades, "See these guys here? Not only would I go to war with them, I'd go to war for them."

Frasse then reported that his wife was scheduled to have their second child in just three days.

"If it's a boy, he will proudly be named Jay Andrew Frasse," Frasse announced.

Boy or girl, Frasse pledged to teach the child about Andrews's courage and integrity and decency.

"And that we should all strive to be like him every day of our lives," Frasse said.

Frasse's wife had come to the funeral and she emerged with him from the church, his white-gloved hand in hers. She fell in behind him in the long formation of cops.

"I didn't quite know what to do," Kara would later say.

White gloves all around her rose in salute as the coffin was borne back to the hearse. The service had taken longer than anticipated, and the ten helicopters assembled for the flyover had been circling over Prospect Park, causing people to fret that there had been a new terrorist attack. The honor guard folded the flag that had covered the coffin while twin trumpeters played "America the Beautiful." A police captain presented the flag to the Andrews family.

The pipe band then led the way down the street, the drummers again striking up the mournful beat the city had so often heard. A voice called out an order, and Kara Frasse stepped right face while nine months pregnant. The baby would be a boy, named Jay.

Mayor Bloomberg was left with an up-close lesson in the scourge of illegal guns. Giuliani's lawsuit against the gun manufacturers had been largely forgotten in the immediate aftermath of 9/11. Bloomberg now made it a priority.

Chapter 14

The NYPD under Mike Bloomberg and Raymond Kelly continued to rely on the mechanics of CompStat. Murder fell to a quarter of what it had been during Kelly's previous tenure—to 587 in 2002, though up slightly to 597 the following year.

So what if nobody seemed to fully grasp the founding principles of CompStat and the department was becoming only more focused on personnel management rather than fighting crime? Who cares if cops were complaining that they were increasingly ruled by numbers of arrests and summonses?

To his credit, Kelly did pay particular attention to Steven McDonald, whom he viewed as the soul of the NYPD. Two days before Christmas 2003, Steven arrived in dress uniform at police headquarters for a promotion ceremony. He expected to be elevated to second grade from third, but when the moment came, Kelly announced that he would now become Detective First Grade Steven McDonald.

"Tremendous courage in overcoming adversity," Kelly said in explaining the surprise elevation to a rank held by only one hundred cops in the NYPD.

Steven was back in his dress uniform for the funeral of two detectives who were killed in Brooklyn on the eve of the third anniversary of 9/11. Detectives Robert Parker and Patrick Rafferty had responded to a woman who asked them to protect her from her abusive twenty-eight-year-old son. The son had grabbed Parker's gun and fatally shot both detectives.

Bloomberg's street education continued when he visited the Brooklyn station house where the detectives worked. He ran into a familiar figure.

"MaryAnn, what are you doing here?" Bloomberg asked.

"I work here," replied Detective MaryAnn Andrews, widow of Detective Rodney Andrews.

MaryAnn Andrews had remained a working cop, and she had transferred to Detective Borough Brooklyn South, where she had made one thing immediately apparent:

"She doesn't want people to feel sorry for her," a longtime detective would recall. "She came to work and she did her job. It had to be hard on that woman. Most people would lay down and not do anything."

The day after Thanksgiving 2005, Bloomberg was in the emergency room at Kings County Hospital in Brooklyn, watching detectives examine a bulletproof vest. One of them squeezed with his fingertips the seam of the left arm hole where Police Officer Dillon Stewart had been struck and fatally wounded by one of five shots suddenly fired at him while he was making a car stop. Blood had seeped in and now oozed back to the surface.

At the funeral, Bloomberg rose and touched Stewart's coffin before taking the pulpit to deliver a eulogy. The mayor spoke of Stewart not just as a hero cop but also as a hero dad who went from patrolling the streets throughout the night to working on his family's house during the day. He addressed Stewart's widow, Leslyn, directly.

"Every board he cut and every nail he drove was a measure of his devotion to you, Leslyn, and to the secure and happy life he was determined to create with you and your two little girls," Bloomberg said.

Stewart's daughters were five and six. Kelly spoke next.

"It is hard to say exactly what motivated Dillon Stewart, at the age of thirty, to make a remarkable choice," he began. "A choice to leave a stable career as a financial accountant to serve the public as a New York City police officer. It was simply his nature to want to help others...And so Dillon answered the call."

On July 14, 2007, Bloomberg and Kelly were back in the emergency room at Kings County Hospital Center as the trauma team fought to save twenty-three-year-old Police Officer Russel Timoshenko. He had been shot twice in the face while making a car stop opposite the Little Red Riding Hood preschool, four blocks from the Brooklyn hospital. His partner, Herman Yan, was shot in the arm.

Surveillance video showed three suspects fleeing into an alley, where three guns were recovered, a .45 automatic, a 9mm automatic, and a TEC-9.

One of the suspects was arrested the next day. The other two managed to flee to Pennsylvania, where they hid out in a wooded area for three days before they were captured by the New York/New Jersey Regional US Marshals Fugitive Task Force, a team of detectives and US marshals that now included Sonny Archer. Sonny had encountered a bear among the trees. The bear fled.

Timoshenko held on for another two days. The doctors then said the twenty-three-year-old's final moments were near, and all 150 officers in the 71st Precinct filed past his bed. Yan was present at the end, his arm in a cast.

"A lot of crying," Kelly later noted.

Steven brought Conor to the wake. Conor had graduated from a Jesuit high school on Long Island and had taken the police test but was now at Boston College. Many people assumed he would go on to Wall Street or a big law firm. He had in the meantime volunteered to help in New Orleans following Hurricane Katrina.

The line at the wake took him up to the coffin and Timoshenko's mother.

"Take care of your father," Tatyana Timoshenko said to him, her tone as intimate as if she and Conor were kin.

Conor said he would. He knew as almost nobody else imagined that his father's existence was a continual trial so agonizing as to make forgiveness a perpetual effort.

"Why don't you go to church?" Steven had asked Conor at another time.

"I don't have to," Conor had said. "You're Jesus Christ."

"Don't say that. I am not Jesus Christ."

"You've been in that chair a lot longer than He was on the cross."

Here at the wake with Timoshenko's mother, Conor understood that his father had come to symbolize the way of the true cop. Conor had the sudden sense that this was where he would find significance, that this was his destiny, to be among cops, to become one of them.

"That's when I knew," he later said.

His entire life, Conor had needed only to look at his father to be reminded of what can happen to a police officer. But he had also seen the good a cop can inspire, and not just what a cop can lose but also what a cop and his family can receive. Conor felt not so much cheated as blessed and indebted.

"I felt there was a lot more expected of me because of what my family was given," Conor said.

He was crystalline clear about the example set by his father.

"Character. Integrity. Honesty. Courage."

The sense of destiny that came over Conor at Timoshenko's wake stayed with him as he went on to graduate from Boston College and spent ten months in Denver working at a shelter for runaway teens. He in the meantime took the police test.

Conor and Steven were visiting Father Mychal's grave in a Franciscan burial ground in New Jersey when Conor's cellphone rang. He answered it to learn that he had been accepted into the next class at the NYPD academy.

In the spring of 2010 Conor took the oath and became one of 1,250 cops in training.

"My life changed before I was even born," he said. "When my dad got shot in '86, there was a lot of love that the city gave my family. I just felt compelled to do this…I want to do my best to protect and serve the people that helped give my family a second life."

He received considerable press attention, reporters noting that Conor was being sworn in twenty-four years almost to the day of when his father was shot.

"I know everyone says I'm Steven McDonald's son, but I'm my own individual person," he was quoted saying. "I have my dues to pay, and not one bit do I feel that I am owed anything. I feel I owe a lot."

One of Steven's drivers, Andras "Andy" Cserenyi, was later quoted saying, "To see the heritage, from great-grandfather to grandfather to Steven, and now Conor, no words can be said."

Steven himself said afterward, "I was very proud of him that he did that and prouder still he decided to take on this challenge to protect New York City. It's not a job that anybody can do; you find that out right away."

Steven said of all good cops, "You're there because you love helping other people and sharing what's special about yourself."

That seemed particularly true about Conor, who appeared to possess innately the empathy that his father had demonstrated so dramatically.

"He has a sympathetic heart toward the difficulties of life," Steven now said of the grown Conor. "He can better understand the Shavod Joneses of the world."

Patti Ann voiced her approval of Conor's choice, emphasizing that he had not been nudged into joining.

"I admire him and I'm proud of him," she said. "It was completely his decision."

Patti Ann nonetheless harbored the fears that anybody would assume she had.

"Obviously, I'm concerned for his safety. I'd be lying if I said I didn't feel that way."

As graduation neared, the cadets were issued their shields and service weapons. Barry Driscoll received shield 17842, once that of his father Police Officer Stephen Driscoll, who had been in street crime with Thomas McDonald and had been killed on 9/11. Conor received shield 15978, which Raymond Kelly had once worn. The gesture on Kelly's part seemed only fitting, as Conor had become in some sense the son of the department itself.

At the December 27, 2010, graduation ceremony, both Kelly and Bloomberg made prominent mention of Steven.

"An outstanding advocate and spokesman for his fellow officers," Kelly said in his remarks. "Thank you, Steven McDonald."

Bloomberg also spoke.

"Steven McDonald is a legend in the NYPD for the bravery he showed," the mayor said.

Kelly and Bloomberg also both cited the decline in crime during their tenure, though they did not mention that murder was up slightly from 471 in 2009 to 536 as the city came to the end of 2010. That was still 1,165 murders fewer than two decades before.

Kelly noted that the new graduates spoke forty-eight languages and came from fifty-three foreign countries. But however more diverse the NYPD had become, its essence was unchanged and on full display as Conor stood beside Steven after the ceremony.

"To walk in his footsteps, it's an honor," Conor said. "I just want to help people. That's what I want to do."

Conor said this despite being acutely aware that his father had been left unable to walk at all. Steven beamed from his wheelchair and took a breath with the help of the ventilator.

"It's a happy moment," Steven then said. "I don't want my son to be hurt. I just want them to get out on the street and do their job."

Steven predicted, "The best days are ahead of us, because of Conor and his classmates."

As was the practice with academy classes that graduate in December, the city's newest cops were assigned to Times Square on New Year's Eve. The days had long since passed when robbery crews chanted "Snatch gold! Snatch gold!" as the ball dropped. The prediction that had once earned Jack only derision had come true. The Crossroads of the World was again a place for families and tourists.

One new concern had begun on 9/11. Cops were reminded to look out for anything that might portend a terrorist attack. Conor was among those who welcomed in the New Year wearing a radiation detector as a precaution against a dirty bomb.

"Any time large numbers of people come together, we put in our counterterrorism overlay," Kelly said.

The big moment passed without incident.

But Mike Bloomberg had not forgotten his many trips to emergency rooms after a cop was shot in the city. He remained New York's most passionate and persistent voice against illegal guns.

Bloomberg's predecessor had also rushed to the bedside of many shot cops and grew up in the very neighborhood where Russel Timoshenko was fatally wounded. Rudy Giuliani seemed to forget all that when he was running for president in 2007 and again needed conservative voters.

At the very time of the Timoshenko shooting, Giuliani had been down in Georgia, saying that he thought gun laws were pretty much adequate. He acted as if he had nothing to do with the city's ongoing lawsuit against the gun manufacturers.

In September, two months after Timoshenko was shot to death by men armed with three illegal guns, Giuliani addressed a National Rifle Association gathering in an effort to secure its endorsement.

As he began his speech, Giuliani's cellphone rang. He paused to speak to his wife, Judi Nathan, who was about to board a plane.

"Hello, dear, I'm talking to the members of the NRA, right now, would you like to say hello?" Giuliani said with a laugh. "Have a safe trip...Talk to you later, dear...I love you."

Various talking heads afterward debated whether he should have taken the call. Nobody seemed much bothered that he was addressing the front organization for the very gun industry he once denounced as criminal and immoral.

On January 24, 2011, a month after Conor McDonald graduated and placed himself in harm's way, Bloomberg held a City Hall press conference that featured Steven and thirty-three other people affected by gun violence. Steven was the first to speak.

"Good morning, I'm New York City Police Detective Steven McDonald, and I was shot in the line of duty in 1986...Every day in America, thirty-four Americans are killed by guns. Here are thirty-four Americans to tell their stories, thirty-four lives changed by guns."

The thirty-three others included Diana Rodriguez of the Bronx. Her eighteen-year-old daughter, Samantha, had been killed by a stray bullet on Mother's Day 2006.

"It has to stop," she said.

There was also Lynette Alameddine, whose twenty-year-old son, Ross, had been killed during the mass shooting at Virginia Tech in 2007.

"I hold a lock of his hair in my locket, and that's all I have left," she said.

And there was Tatyana Timoshenko, who had first met Bloomberg in the emergency room on the night her police officer son was fatally wounded.

"He was just twenty-three years old," she noted.

Steven's son was now twenty-four and out in the street in uniform on this cold winter's day.

At the event's end, Steven departed in his motorized wheelchair. Steven spoke to two fellow cops who stood nearby as he prepared to set off in his van.

"Be safe everybody," he said.

CHAPTER 15

Later in 2011, Raymond Kelly too often found himself at press conferences announcing the arrest of multiple officers. The more benign case involved sixteen cops in the Bronx charged with fixing traffic tickets as a courtesy to relatives and friends of other cops, an age-old practice that had already been ended by a new computer system. A far more serious case involved eight former and present cops charged with smuggling guns and bootleg cigarettes.

An especially disturbing case involved a cop who was alleged to have falsely arrested a young Black man and was recorded afterward saying that he had "fried another n—r." There was also a narcotics detective who had been planting drugs on a suspect. The judge in the case had spoken of a pervasive "cowboy culture" in the unit.

Yet if there continued to be a handful of bad cops, there were tens of thousands of good ones, such as the rookie now wearing shield 15798.

Conor continued to live at home for a time, and on a typical morning Steven called out into the predawn stillness from his wheelchair. A father's tenderness wafted on the breath generated by his ventilator.

"Boy-o!"

Steven had, as always, awakened to make double sure his son was up in time for work.

"Dad, I'm getting ready!" Conor replied, having, as always, set his alarm.

Conor put on the new Coldplay album to get himself going, finished dressing, and quickly checked the latest sports and news on his computer. He then headed out into the early-morning darkness to begin another tour.

"Hey, Dad, I love you!" Conor called out.

"Be safe," Steven said. "Think smart. Think tactics."

Patti Ann was also awake. She watched her son depart once again to risk what had happened to her husband when she was pregnant with Conor.

"Call me when you get there," she told him.

Conor climbed into his car and drove through the city to the Midtown South station house.

Upon arriving, Conor donned his uniform, Kelly's old shield gleaming on his chest.

In the course of an earlier tour Conor had descended into the subway as some teens were horsing around. He was puzzled why they suddenly stopped.

"Then I realized I'm wearing my uniform," Conor later said.

There also had been a day when Conor and his partner cornered a suspect in a gunpoint robbery, New York still far from crime-free.

But on this particular day, he was dispatched to do crowd control at the filming of the new Batman movie *The Dark Knight Rises* downtown, close to the Occupy Wall Street protest.

Others assigned to the film detail included a veteran detective, maybe fifteen years older than Conor and with that many years on the job. The detective told him not to be discouraged by negative stories about cops in the news.

"Don't get down on the job," the detective said. "It's a good job. You know you work with good guys. They talk about their families. You know if you're in a bad spot they have your back."

Conor had already decided that only a small minority of cops were less than they should be. He found the rest to be dedicated and ever ready to race into direst danger for the sake of complete strangers.

"The 99.9 percent," Conor said.

He was keenly aware he was just a rookie, only beginning to learn what it is to be a cop.

"You don't really understand the job until you're on the job," he said. "Liberal or conservative, you finally get on the street, and you realize it's a whole different world... You see what society doesn't want to see."

He was learning that idealism was something a cop had to work at, just as his father had to work at forgiveness.

"I want to serve and help people," he said. "Some people don't want to be helped."

The tour ended without event, and Conor returned to the station house after sundown. He changed back into jeans and a red hoodie, looking as young as he was as he drove past night spots filled with other young people.

"Passing these bars on a Saturday night," he said. "It's tough for a twenty-four-year-old."

He could not even think of going out

"I got to wake up again at five a.m."

He drove on.

"You just keep telling yourself you're doing a good thing…doing God's work."

He did not forget the risks.

"Putting your life on the line is not an easy vocation."

A reminder of that awaited him upon his return home.

"So, how'd it go today?" Steven asked.

"I saw Batman," Conor replied.

During dinner, there was talk of Steven's maternal grandfather, the Bronx detective who had been shot while capturing a trio of gunmen. There was also talk of Conor's encounter on another day with the suspect in a gunpoint rape.

"My heart's pounding," Conor recalled.

"Conor's not going to avoid trouble," Steven noted. "You just have to trust that he was listening when they told him how to handle those situations."

Steven voiced unshakable faith in his son's fellow cops.

"Extraordinary people," Steven said. "He's going to be with the right people to handle these very dangerous situations."

Steven knew from his own experience that even the best of training and backup is no guarantee. He and Patti Ann could only do what other families do when a cop is on the street.

"Like everybody else, you just have to block it out until you see them again," Steven said.

Conor rose from the table and headed upstairs to catch some sleep. He had to be up again for another early tour.

"Dad," he called out. "Five o'clock."

Along with a second cop, the McDonald household had come to include an elected official.

In 2006, Patti Ann had decided for run for mayor of their suburban town of Malverne. The incumbent had shrugged off the candidacy of the woman who had been known for twenty years as Steven's "stoic wife" and "the picture of devotion."

"I like Patti Ann," Anthony Panzarella said. "She's a lovely lady. But I don't think she can do what I can do."

Patti Ann noted that she had served as a trustee on the village board for nine years, since assuming the seat her father had held prior to his death.

"I can do the job," Patti said.

She won in what was termed an upset.

"What she's been through with me the past twenty-one years," Steven said. "She's the most selfless person I've ever met."

The NYPD pipes and drums played at the swearing-in ceremony at Malverne Village Hall. Mayor Patti Ann McDonald stood with Conor on one side and her mother, Sheila Norris, on the other. The eighty people in attendance gave a standing ovation as she walked down the aisle to hug and kiss Steven.

The congratulatory calls included one from US Representative Carolyn McCarthy. She had been a nurse when her husband, Dennis, was among the six killed by a crazed gunman aboard a commuter train on Long Island in December 1993. Her son, Kevin, was one of the nineteen wounded. She successfully ran for Congress three years later to do something about guns.

"Did you ever think you'd be where you are today, and the path your life has taken?" McCarthy asked Patti Ann.

CHAPTER 16

In August 2011, the former members of Jack Maple's crew gathered at North Shore Hospital on Long Island, where Sonny Archer had been admitted in critical condition after suffering a torn aorta in a car accident while pursuing a fugitive. He succumbed to his injuries on August 21. He was forty-eight, the same age as his mentor, Jack, when he died.

The funeral was at St. Athanasius Church in Brooklyn. Vertel Martin was asked to deliver a eulogy. She is not one to temper what she has to say. She preceded her remarks with a recommendation.

"All the clergy might want to put their fingers in their ears because I am about to speak some truth," she advised.

She essentially said in more colorful terms what Jack might have said: Archer was a giant in every sense who did not tolerate small-minded bullies or heartless victimizers.

After Archer's coffin was carried from the church, Brigid stood outside and said that Jack must have needed backup on high.

"Sonny's the one he would want," she said.

At the Regional US Marshals Fugitive Task Force, Archer's comrades left his personal effects exactly as he had left them, with his bulletproof vest hanging over the chair and a plaque on his desk.

WE WORK FOR GOD, it said.

As Jack had predicted, Archer and the other cops had made New York into the safest big city in America. Jack had not foreseen that the drop in crime would trigger such a rise in real estate values that a developer bought the twenty-story building at 220 Central Park South as a teardown. Brigid fought to remain in the apartment that had been Jack's great reward, but she was finally forced to take a buyout along with the other tenants.

"I would have stayed there forever," Brigid said.

The new building was a forty-one-story glass tower expected to rake in more than $1 billion in profits. The penthouse would go for $240 million, a record. A mid-tower triplex went for $200 million.

"It has a very nice terrace," the lead architect noted.

CHAPTER 17

The real estate boom extended to the outer boroughs, and the New York of *The Bronx Is Burning* became the city of "Brooklyn is booming." A new wave of immigrants and hipsters from beyond the Hudson settled in neighborhoods on the far side of the Brooklyn Bridge that the cops had made safer. But the root causes of crime remained, and the cops had to continue addressing it.

On the night of January 31, 2012, Officer Kevin Brennan and two other members of Brooklyn North Anti-Crime were setting out from the 90th Precinct station house in hipster Williamsburg when they heard a radio report of shots fired at a housing project. The cops pulled up to the scene and saw a young man hop over a short iron fence and begin running. Brennan was in the passenger seat as the cop at the wheel drove just on the other side of the fence, parallel to the fleeing young man.

"I observed a black firearm in his right hand, and he was pointing it at me," Brennan subsequently testified in Brooklyn Supreme Court.

Brennan would recall the cop at the wheel yelling for him to fire.

"Shoot him, Kev, shoot him!"

Even in the heat of a chase and in the face of mortal danger, Brennan realized the shouts and the squealing of tires were sure to have brought people to the windows of the housing project building. He did not fire.

"If I shot at him and I missed, I didn't want to shoot an innocent person," Brennan would later explain.

The young man ran on into the building. Brennan figured he would either go up the stairs or out the back. Brennan guessed the latter.

"I just took a chance," Brennan would later say.

Brennan circled around the back to see the young man bolt out the rear door and sprint across a basketball court toward the back of the next building.

"It was the same man, same clothing, same gun," Brennan would recall. Brennan radioed to his partners.

"He's coming out the back, he's coming out the back!"

The recording of the transmission also picked up Brennan shouting to the young man.

"Police! Don't move! Get down on the ground!"

The young man just kept running. Brennan listened for the sound a gun makes when it is tossed away and hits the pavement—what is known as a "Brooklyn bounce."

"It makes a clinking noise," he would note.

No clinking noise came as the young man dashed on into the next building and up a rear stairway. Brennan was right behind him and saw the young man lose his footing as he reached the top step.

"I figured it was kind of my best chance," Brennan would recall. "I put my head down to do like a football tackle."

He heard a gunshot as the young man shot him in the back of the head from five inches away. He would later be asked what he felt.

"I don't really know how to describe it," Brennan said. "I remember my body like shaking."

He fell on top of the young man. He was losing consciousness when he heard his assailant say something.

"Fuck you! Die!"

Brennan only thought of his baby daughter, Maeve. He regained consciousness as his fellow cops were carrying him from the building.

"My daughter turns six weeks old tomorrow, I don't want to die," he kept saying.

He could barely see as he was placed in the back of an ambulance.

"I was conscious for most of the ride," he would recall.

Brennan was soon at Bellevue, where it was determined that the slug had not penetrated his skull. Raymond Kelly arrived and watched in amazement as a doctor reached into the wound with tweezers to extract it.

"The bullet was removed from the back of my head," Brennan later reported, then adding to be more precise: "Most of the bullet."

Several bullet fragments remained, but Brennan survived with some loss of vision in his left eye and some damage to his upper spinal cord. He could have just settled back with a disability pension, but in the way of Mary Buckley and others, he pushed himself through grueling physical therapy and was able by force of will to return to duty. He was subsequently promoted to sergeant.

His assailant had been arrested, and as the case came to trial, Brennan and his partner returned to the scene of the shooting with prosecutors. He ended up joining his partner in arresting two suspects in a home invasion robbery and taking a loaded 9mm pistol off one of them.

"It was like old times again," Brennan said.

At the trial, Brennan watched from the stand as the prosecution played surveillance camera footage from the night he so nearly died. The accused gunman, twenty-three-year-old Luis Ortiz, watched blank-faced from the defendant's table, his left leg jiggling. The prosecution showed Brennan a still photo.

"It's the defendant shooting me," Brennan said.

His wife, Janet Brennan, watched from the second row of the spectator benches in the twenty-first-floor courtroom. She was there through the whole three-week trial. She had to listen to the defense attorney, John Burke, argue during the final summations that her husband and his fellow cops had concocted a case against his client.

"A script," Burke said.

On this same day, 781 new cops graduated in a ceremony in the new Barclays Center, a cavernous arena built on a patch of Brooklyn that had been the scene of at least three killings in the bad old days.

"With safety and security, everything is possible," Mayor Bloomberg told the graduates. "Without it, nothing is."

Raymond Kelly also spoke, noting that the graduates represented forty-nine countries and spoke more than forty languages but shared a common mission.

"You want to make a difference," he said. "Day by day, officer by officer, action by action."

Kelly noted that the graduates included the daughter of NYPD Lieutenant Frederico Narvaez, who was shot to death sixteen years before in Brooklyn while coming to the aid of a woman who had rushed up to his car and pleaded for protection from an armed stalker. Police Officer Katrina

Narvaez, who was nine years old at the time, had later said that one of her fondest memories was of her father taking her to Coney Island and buying her a baby dolphin stuffed toy at the aquarium that she then lost on the Cyclone roller coaster. He of course bought her a new one, which she still treasured. She was now wearing an equally prized memento on the chest of her dress uniform.

"His shield," Kelly noted.

Among the other graduates was twenty-one-year-old Police Officer Samantha Raffo, who posed with her family for a post-graduation photo. She looked impossibly young. Her dress uniform had not stopped a female relative from giving her a kiss on the cheek.

"Oh, lipstick!" Raffo said.

She wiped away the lipstick and stood sparkly-eyed in the city she was now sworn to protect.

"They say it's much safer," she said.

She described with two words how she felt: "Very excited."

The new cops were on their second day when the jury began its deliberations in the case against Luis Ortiz for shooting Brennan. The jurors reached a guilty verdict in three hours.

CHAPTER 18

Instead of a saved city's gratitude, the cops got what they took to be arrest and summons quotas, no matter what fine distinctions the bosses sought to make.

The stop-and-frisks continued to be recorded on a UF250. A supervisor would be heard telling his cops, "I want 250s!" whether or not they happened to encounter anybody suspicious enough to justify being frisked. The cops would comply, only for the supervisor to demand the same number or more the next time. A cop who came in with fewer was liable to be told his activity was slipping and instructed to go out and get more.

Otherwise, the bosses might demand to know why the total number of 250s was down. One sergeant became so desperate that he stopped to "interview" passersby, taking enough info to complete the forms.

And the increasing reliance on numbers was accompanied by a decreasing reliance on true leadership. The official message to cops was "Do your job," but it really was "Keep your numbers up."

The supposition was that more "activity" meant less crime. And nobody can rightly deny that one result of these thousands upon thousands upon thousands of frisks was to make people more cautious about carrying illegal guns. Even so, much the same result may have been achieved if cops had simply been trusted to follow their instincts while staying within the bounds of reason and the law.

As it was, the unrelenting pressure to keep up their "activity," particularly in the higher-crime areas, resulted in so many frisks that the department was accused of the wholesale violation of civil rights.

Where a young Jack Maple would have waited until he saw a telltale bulge or a furtive motion that suggested someone was likely carrying a gun, cops were too often making stops based on youth and race. And what ensued was too often not just stop-and-frisk, but stop-and-frisk-and-go-in-your-pocket-and-maybe-your-underwear-and-maybe-even-your-socks. Cops too often failed to stop with a simple pat-down for a weapon and continued to search for a small bag of pot or some other excuse to make a collar. Most of the time they did not find even that. But they did leave one more bit of resentment.

The NYPD made 4.4 million such stops between 2004 and 2012, with the annual total rising from 314,000 to 646,000, only 6 percent of them resulting in an arrest, only another 6 percent in a summons, and 88 percent in nothing at all. The vast majority of those stopped were minorities, and in August 2013, Manhattan Federal Judge Shira A. Scheindlin ruled that the tactics amounted to "indirect racial profiling" and were therefore unconstitutional.

For her part, Scheindlin contended that the city's "highest officials" have "turned a blind eye" as the cops in the street pursued the tactic "in a racially discriminatory manner."

"In their zeal to defend a policy that they believe to be effective, they have willfully ignored overwhelming proof that the policy of targeting 'right people' is racially discriminatory and therefore violates the United States Constitution," the judge wrote.

She spoke of the "human toll of unconstitutional stops," which she called "a demeaning and humiliating experience."

"No one should live in fear of being stopped whenever he leaves his home to go about the activities of daily life," she wrote.

The New York City Council was already considering whether to install an inspector general for the NYPD. Scheindlin now appointed an attorney named Peter Zimroth to ensure that the NYPD adopted tactics that did not violate the law even as they sought to enforce it. Zimroth was raised in Brooklyn and attended Abraham Lincoln High School, whose alumni include two police officers who were shot to death in the line of duty. He went on to become a prosecutor and served for a time as the corporation counsel, the city's top lawyer. He also had an extremely brief but fateful career as a movie extra, meeting and marrying the actress Estelle Parsons, who won an Academy Award for Best Supporting Actress for her portrayal of Blanche in *Bonnie and Clyde*.

As corporation counsel, Zimroth voiced the view that sometimes a lawsuit can be a learning experience leading to better ways to govern. That was certainly not the view of Mike Bloomberg. The mayor went so far as to suggest that the combination of a stop-and-frisk monitor and the NYPD inspector general could lead a cop to hesitate for a fatal instant.

"*You* go to the family and explain to the wife or the husband that he's not coming home that night," Bloomberg said with the emotion of someone who has been to many emergency rooms in such circumstances.

Bloomberg and Raymond Kelly continued to insist that the stop-and-frisks were conducted within the guidelines established by the US Supreme Court. They maintained that there is a legitimate reason why the great majority of stops were in minority neighborhoods.

"Because that's where the crime is," Kelly said after Scheindlin's decision was released.

He and Bloomberg noted that if the murder rate had continued at where it was eleven years before, 7,363 New Yorkers who were presently alive would be dead, the overwhelming majority of them young men of color.

"The New York City Police Department saves lives, and it trains its officers to act within the law," Kelly declared.

Bloomberg said, "This is a very dangerous decision made by a judge who I think just does not understand how policing works."

Bloomberg contended that the city had not received a "fair trial." He suggested that the judge had made up her mind from the start.

"This decision only confirms that," he added.

He pointed to the declining number of gun arrests despite an unending influx of guns as added proof that the stop-and-frisk strategy is working.

"They're leaving their guns at home," Bloomberg said.

Bloomberg's contention seemed to be supported by the charge sheets posted outside criminal court in Manhattan and in Brooklyn on the day Scheindlin handed down her ruling. Just two gun arrests were listed among more than one hundred cases. A case in Brooklyn involved a man named Meredith Lamron who was charged with attempting to steal a cellphone while pistol-whipping the victim so badly his face was shattered.

"Eye socket, jaw, nose," the prosecutor said. "He had several teeth knocked out."

Lamron was arrested soon after the attack and identified by four eyewitnesses.

He insisted it was all just a case of mistaken identity.

"He stated he was waiting for a bus when police apprehended him," his lawyer told the court.

Lamron had a problem beyond the witnesses who had followed him after the attack and reported seeing him ditch a bloodstained outer shirt.

"He had blood on his sneakers, tank top, and pants," the prosecutor noted.

The police had approached him after receiving a detailed description. And the blood along with the multiple identifications indisputably constituted probable cause for stopping him, so nobody was suggesting the cops had acted unconstitutionally.

But Lamron was only stopped after the attack.

One immediate question was whether the crime might have been prevented if Lamron had been stopped and frisked beforehand. A larger question was whether there would necessarily be many more crimes as bad or even worse if the New York cops greatly reduced such stops.

Those who answered quickly and emphatically in the affirmative failed to consider the example long set by Jack and other astute street cops.

As a transit cop out making collars, Jack had proven that you can catch people carrying guns without stopping seemingly everybody who fits certain demographics, that the art to it is in choosing who to stop.

And, as the creator of CompStat, he had warned that there had to be fairness for the strategies to achieve their ultimate goal of making New York the city it should be.

Bloomberg would later apologize as a presidential candidate in 2020 for the stop-and-frisk excesses. In the meantime, he promised that the city would contest the judge's ruling.

"You're not going to see any change in tactics overnight," Bloomberg said. "I wouldn't want to be responsible for a lot of people dying."

He all but came out and said that the blood would be on Scheindlin's hands if her decision held and the city's murder rate rose from its current record low of less than one a day. The rate previously was six a day.

Bloomberg voiced a position he would continue to hold through a third term made possible when a compliant city council voted to extend the previous limit of two.

"People also have a right to walk down the street without being killed or mugged," he said.

E ven though minority neighborhoods benefited most from the crime reduction, many residents continued to view the police as adversaries. And that feeling was joined by a larger, more pervasive sense that if New York had become the safest big city in America, it had hardly become the fairest.

One ironic measure of how much the NYPD had reduced fear of crime was that liberal progressive Bill de Blasio became the favorite to succeed Mike Bloomberg while running what many saw as an anti-cop campaign.

De Blasio upended the mayoral race with a remarkably effective ad featuring his mixed-race son, Dante, then fifteen. Dante happened to be attending Brooklyn Tech, the same high school Jack attended before departing to become a Transit Police trainee. The thirty-second campaign ad begins with Dante sitting in his family's kitchen, saying "my dad," his father, is the only one with the courage to break with "the Bloomberg years." He says his father would also tax the rich to fund education and build affordable housing.

"And he's the only one who will end a stop-and-frisk era that unfairly targets people of color," Dante adds.

Dante came across as exactly himself, an immensely likable teenager, with an audacious afro that was an homage to Jimi Hendrix and a voice that was notably confident but not in the least strident. He had no love for the camera. He was clearly there because he loved his dad.

And it was just as clear that he was a kid who felt loved.

The brief cut to the candidate and his African American wife, Chirlane McCray, in the kitchen was really more a shot of Dante's mom and dad.

Dante then reappeared as the happy result of their union.

Here was the opposite of scandal.

Here was what the future looked like.

Here is what true New York looked like.

If you loved the city, you had to love this kid.

The last scene is of Dante walking down a city street in an unzipped Brooklyn hoodie with his dad at his side. Dante promises in a voice-over that Bill de Blasio would represent every New Yorker, no matter where they live or what they look like.

"And I'd say that even if he weren't my dad," Dante says.

When he won, de Blasio faced the question of how to make New York a fairer city without making it less safe. Friends and advisors urged him to consider bringing back Bill Bratton for a second tenure as NYPD commissioner. This group included Chief Dean Esserman of the New Haven, Connecticut, police. The son of a Manhattan society physician, Esserman had married a homicide detective whose mother was a Santeria priestess, leading to jokes that the joined clans were headed by two doctors: one medical, the other witch. Esserman always wanted to be a cop, an ambition that had stayed with him as he went to Dartmouth and became an attorney. He did manage to become counsel to the Transit Police when Jack Maple and William Bratton were there. He then surprised everybody by getting a job as assistant chief in New Haven, and then he rose to chief, achieving notable success there in both reducing crime and strengthening ties with the community. He had been friendly with de Blasio since their sons attended preschool together.

Esserman had stayed close to Bratton, who had gone on from the NYPD to become chief of police in Los Angeles, where he not only reduced crime but also improved relationships between the police and the people. Bratton managed to receive accolades from community leaders even as he was expanding stop-and-frisk, targeted specifically to address the gang problem. He would compare the strategy to chemotherapy: lifesaving if administered properly and in the right dose, deadly if not.

But Los Angeles was not New York, and in 2009 Bratton had resigned to return as a private citizen to the city he had come to love. His time as NYPD commissioner remained an interrupted childhood dream, and he now got a chance to resume it.

De Blasio announced the Bratton appointment at a press conference at a former Catholic school in Brooklyn that had been converted into a community court geared toward alternatives to incarceration for nonviolent crimes.

The mayor began his remarks by noting the presence of various state and city officials, along with a particular individual.

"I want to especially acknowledge and thank a true New York hero," de Blasio said. "If there's anyone in this room who deserves that moniker, if there's anyone in this room who has earned our respect and appreciation, it is Detective Steven McDonald. Thank you, detective."

Bratton was holding the children's book that had set him on the path to New York and that had now brought him back here.

"I'm just really glad that some other kid didn't take out that book," de Blasio said.

De Blasio then jokingly imagined aloud a news item: "Bill de Blasio named a library book today as police commissioner."

The mayor-elect turned serious when asked how the appointment jibed with his call for the curtailment of stop-and-frisk.

"Bill Bratton knows that when it comes to stop-and-frisk, it has to be used with respect and it has to be used properly," de Blasio said.

When Bratton spoke, he also mentioned one other cop in particular.

"And I'd like to acknowledge him, and I think the police officers in this room will remember him with great fondness. And that's the late great Jack Maple."

With Jack present in spirit and Steven present in the flesh, Bratton pledged to combine the lessons of his first tenure in New York with those of his time in Los Angeles and apply them to the needs of the present—keeping crime down while building trust in the community, for the sake of the cops as well as the people.

"That can happen and it will happen in New York City," he said. "That is my commitment to this mayor. I love this profession, and I love this city."

Now sixty-six, Bratton held up the book he first saw when he was nine in Boston. He placed particular emphasis on the pronoun when he spoke the title aloud.

"*YOUR Police.*"

PART
VI

Williaim Bratton understood that the renewed challenge was for kids in every neighborhood in New York to feel that a police officer really was their friend and protector. He was starting anew with an understanding of what was at the core of the city's greatness, what made it New York. He demonstrated that while making a kind of subway homecoming, touring the underground, a commissioner again.

As Bratton rode downtown in early 2014 during the first weeks of his second tenure, he looked at a pole in the car's aisle and waxed poetic. He spoke of how countless hands of every race and kind grab such poles when the trains are crowded: manicured and grimy, dainty and tough, one atop the other. He said that this is what he would present to someone as a symbol of New York in old times and new.

"It's the center pole," he said. "Every day five and a half million people hang on it."

He added, "And by and large they get along."

The train rumbled past the local stop at West 81st Street, by the Museum of Natural History. Bratton shares Jack's love for the small details that make a magnificent city, and he admired aloud the tiles on the station's wall that represent various animals and sea creatures. His gaze went to the people who comprised the latest collection at the center pole and he was clearly thrilled just to be living in New York, much less to be its police commissioner once again.

Bratton's attention then shifted to the window of the door at the end of the subway car.

With a patrol cop's eyes, Bratton spied a man striding up and down the aisle of the next car in a manner that was sure to intimidate the other passengers as the train rumbled downtown. Bratton said nothing as he stepped off the train at the next station. Along with him came his plainclothes security detail.

Bratton entered the next car, where the man he had spied and an inebriated companion were shouting and generally putting the rest of their fellow riders on edge. The troublemaking two did not seem to recognize the commissioner, but they apparently knew cops when they saw them. They quieted and sat down.

"Where are you headed?" Bratton asked.

The two sat silent. A burly man who was well over six feet tall rose from his seat beside a female companion. He clearly could have done battle with the rowdy ones if he had been so inclined, but he just as clearly was glad to be spared the necessity.

"Thank you," the man told Bratton.

The troublemakers got off the train. Bratton and his companions followed to make sure the two did not cause a ruckus on the platform. The cops had recently begun cracking down on subway panhandlers, so naturally Bratton had no sooner resumed riding uptown than one appeared. The man began what must have been his usual spiel.

"My name is Anthony. I just got out of prison..."

The man stopped upon noticing the two detectives from Bratton's detail.

"I'm going to shut up," the man then said. "I didn't see all the officers. I apologize."

Bratton and his companions got off at West 125th Street. He spoke briefly with a cop in a small booth at the end of a platform who had the mind-numbing duty of keeping an eye on the dark tunnels beyond via video monitors.

"A pleasure meeting you," Bratton told the cop, seeming to mean it.

Bratton encountered two other uniformed cops by a bank of MetroCard machines.

"We get a lot of swipers," one of the cops reported.

Swipers were the new token suckers, who would jam turnstile slots with paper in times before the system went electronic. The crooks would then employ their mouths to suck out the tokens people had deposited. One police solution had been to spray a little Mace on the slot, which made for some seriously scrunch-faced token suckers.

More modern crooks jammed up the MetroCard dispensers so people were unable to purchase or replenish one. The crook would then produce a MetroCard of his own and offer to swipe the would-be traveler through—for a premium price.

The two cops told Bratton that they engaged in an endless cat-and-mouse game with the swipers, alternately keeping an eye on the machines and trying to surprise them in the act of selling swipes.

"We know them, and they know us," one of the cops said.

Bratton continued up to the surface and crossed Harlem's main thoroughfare to the station at St. Nicholas Avenue. Bratton saw a woman jogging along the far side of the street.

"Alone at ten thirty at night," he remarked.

He saw her as the personification of the new New York.

"The change..." he said.

His voice carried no hint that he felt he—or even he and Jack—deserved credit for the transformation. He had always shared Jack's belief that ultimately the credit should go to the cops who actually made it happen. The cops on Bratton's security detail included Sergeant Kevin Brennan, the one who had withheld fire for fear of hitting innocents and had somehow survived being shot in the head.

Bratton's appreciation for what New York's Finest had accomplished and the price they were willing to pay was again manifested in the way he greeted two other uniformed officers when he returned to the subway. He chatted with them for a few minutes and teased one for wearing a hat that looked a size too large.

"I lost some weight," the cop said.

"A pleasure to meet you," Bratton said, as genuinely as before.

When Bratton descended to the trains, a man was pacing the platform edge, ranting in Spanish. A detective in the detail who had once been slashed on the arm by a maniac approached the man and spoke quietly to him in Spanish.

"The police have high authority, but not as high as God!" the man announced.

"You're right," the detective said.

The man did not seem to expect such an affirmation, and he appeared to be suddenly drained of his fury. He stood silent as the detective and his partner joined the Bratton tour on an express train.

After switching to a local train, Bratton and his companions got off at the Broadway-Lafayette station and took a passageway to the Bleecker Street stop. He waited on the downtown local platform as an express roared by. He watched the subway cars flash past.

"That's in every movie ever made about New York," he said in quiet delight, beholding again the real thing.

He gazed down at the local track bed and saw something sleek and fat scurry under a rail.

"Still the best-fed rats in New York," he said. "Some things never change."

Two stops on a local took him to the City Hall station near police headquarters. He returned to the street with his companions around midnight. He gazed at the Woolworth Building and the Freedom Tower just beyond, remarking on how one of the city's oldest skyscrapers stood with its newest.

He looked from the towers to his phone and got an unneeded reminder that even America's safest big city still had its dangers. There had been a shooting at West 135th Street and St. Nicholas Avenue, ten blocks uptown from where he had watched the lone woman jog past as a symbol of the new New York.

"Right near where we were," he noted.

A gusting wind added to the bite of the thirteen-degree temperature just after midnight on February 26, 2014, when Bratton attended the twenty-fifth annual memorial for Police Officer Eddie Byrne on the street where the twenty-two-year-old was assassinated while sitting in a patrol car outside the home of a witness.

"To say again that his short, young life meant something, that Eddie Byrne counted," Bratton told the assemblage. "He mattered. Just like every one of you count. Like every one of you matter every time you put on that uniform... You matter because you are the guardians at the gate. Like Eddie Byrne, whose life and death still has meaning."

The young cop's assassination had been one of 1,896 murders that year, an average of more than five a day. Bratton could now report that the city had just gone ten days without a single homicide.

"The beginning of that safer New York started right here on this corner twenty-six years ago," Bratton said. "In Eddie Byrne's honor, I'll make sure it continues."

A lieutenant who had been keenly feeling the bone-chilling cold looked over to see a familiar figure sitting immobile as the cops began to applaud.

"There's Steven McDonald," the lieutenant remarked aloud.

The sight of Steven was a reminder of the applause he had received at Byrne's funeral nearly three decades before. He had attended each and every Byrne memorial since then, in all weather and circumstances. And in the course of each year he had been a constant that helped carry the NYPD through its trials and controversies.

Whatever leaders happened to occupy police headquarters or City Hall, there had always been Steven McDonald.

"Even as things transform, they need stability," his driver and forehead-rubbing friend Jon Williams later said. "And Steven McDonald was that stability, no matter who the commissioners were, no matter who the chiefs were. Whether the mayor was Dinkins or Giuliani or Koch, the city always loved Steven."

Williams summed it up.

"He was bigger than politics."

The safer New York may well have started with the outrage over Byrne's murder, but it had been made possible by a unique combination of spirit such as Steven's and strategies devised by the genius cop whom Bratton now sought to memorialize.

On September 23, 2014, Bratton presided at the dedication of the Jack Maple CompStat Center in police headquarters. A plaque bearing Jack's likeness in bronze was installed by the entrance. His homburg hat, his bow tie, and a derringer he carried were displayed inside glass cases.

"Welcome everybody to the room that Jack built, the Jack Maple Comp-Stat Center," Bratton told the crowd.

Two of Jack's comrades from his Transit Police days had come with a polished wood urn containing his ashes. Bratton called them over for a picture in front of the portrait.

"Let's have one with the real Jack," Bratton said.

CHAPTER 2

In the first week of December 2014, Police Officer Conor McDonald was assigned to be on hand at a march protesting the failure of a Staten Island grand jury to indict the cop who was videotaped applying a choke hold to a gentle giant named Eric Garner in his final moments.

Garner had helped support his wife and six kids via the decades-old tradition of selling untaxed cigarettes, either in packs or as singles called "loosies," in a pocket park on Bay Street in Staten Island. The loosie business had gotten a big boost after Bloomberg hiked cigarette taxes along with his 2003 ban on smoking in bars and restaurants. The state had added its own taxes, and a pack was going for $11. Garner would travel to Virginia to buy packs for $8, then sell them for $9. He sold loosies for 50¢, translating to $10 a pack, or a $2 profit for him.

Another legacy of Bloomberg was 311, which the public could call for less urgent services than 911 emergencies. At least one landlord and perhaps a shopkeeper or two made a number of 311 calls about people selling loosies and maybe pot on Bay Street. One seller was supposed to be named Eric.

Such small-time hustling was a threat to civil society as viewed by the broken windows theory, to which Bratton still subscribed, having brought back Bob Wasserman and George Kelling on a consultant contract paid for by the New York Police Foundation. The 311 calls came to the attention of Chief of Department Phil Banks, who dispatched a sergeant from his office to surveil Bay Street. The local precinct received a memo. Garner was arrested twice.

On July 17, 2014, Garner was out on $1,000 bail and back to selling loosies when he was approached by two plainclothes cops who had been dispatched by a police lieutenant who had chanced to drive past Bay Street on the way to the precinct. Police had made a total of ninety-seven arrests and issued one hundred summonses on that very spot. A witness with a cellphone camera made a video of this latest arrest.

"We can do this the easy way or the hard way," one of the cops can be heard saying.

"For what, what did I do?" Garner asked.

"For selling cigarettes," the cop answered.

"I'm minding my business, officer, I'm minding my business," Garner said. "Please just leave me alone. Please."

One of the cops, Police Officer Daniel Pantaleo, reached to take Garner's wrist in preparation for cuffing him.

"Don't touch me. Please, do not touch me. Every time you see me, you want to mess with me," Garner said. "It stops today."

Garner moved his arm away, a mild response in keeping with a man not known for violence. Pantaleo sought to bring the hulking Garner down by yoking him around the neck, a violation of a departmental prohibition against choke holds.

What may have saved Pantaleo from indictment is that a close examination of the video shows he had released his choke hold on Garner just before the forty-three-year-old father of six began crying out that he could not breathe. The cop was by then shifting around to press the prone Garner's head into the pavement.

"I can't breathe! I can't breathe!" Garner kept crying out.

A sergeant who was on the scene called out: "*Let up*, you got him already."

Pantaleo glanced up but kept pressing down.

The medical examiner would rule Garner's death a homicide resulting from "compression of the neck [choke hold], compression of chest, and prone positioning during physical restraint by police." The personal effects vouchered after his death included his own cellphone, on which he had a photo of his son, Eric Jr., that he had been proudly showing people earlier in the day. Eric Jr. had just received a basketball scholarship to Essex County College.

What Garner had not mentioned and what would receive no public attention was that Eric Jr. had been coached and mentored by an NYPD detective, Wendell Stradford of the Cold Case Squad, a Jack Maple protégé and close friend of Sonny Archer. What the whole city would remember were words that Conor McDonald saw in December emblazoned on signs and chanted by demonstrators after a grand jury failed to indict the cop who had put Garner in a choke hold.

"I can't breathe! I can't breathe!"

CHAPTER 3

During the protest march, Conor McDonald was posted at the corner of Broadway and Waverly Place along with Detective Larry DePrimo, who had become an internet sensation after he chanced upon a shoeless panhandler in Times Square on a bitterly cold night in 2012. DePrimo had asked the man his shoe size and headed for a Skechers store two blocks away. A tourist took a cellphone video of the cop presenting the panhandler with a brand-new, $100 pair of all-weather boots, along with thermal socks.

"The officer expected NOTHING in return and did not know I was watching," the tourist wrote on her Facebook page when she posted the soon-to-go-viral video.

DePrimo now stood with Conor, who had joined the NYPD with a simple sentiment: "I wanted to help people." But the protesters just saw a couple of cops. The protesters hurled insults and made obscene gestures.

"How do you spell murder?...NYPD!" they chanted. "How do you spell racist?...NYPD!"

The march was led by the families of Sean Bell and Ramarley Graham, young Black men who had been unarmed when they were shot to death by New York City police officers. Demonstrators held photos of Michael Brown, a young Black man who reportedly had been unarmed when he was shot to death by a cop in Ferguson, Missouri. Some eyewitnesses said Brown had been killed after he raised his hands, and the protesters' chants of "I can't breathe!" were joined by "Hands up! Don't shoot!" Other chants involved questions and responses.

"Whose streets?"

"Our streets!"

"What do we want?"

"Dead cops!"

"When do we want them?"

"Now!"

Sergeant Andy McInnis, whose brother, Michael, had been one of Steven's first drivers, was also there. He offered an observation about the protesters who snarled at him.

"They all have really nice teeth," he said. "They must have really good orthodontists. My kids' teeth are a mess."

A number of other cops at the protest were from the NYPD legal bureau, which was headed by Deputy Commissioner Larry Byrne, brother of the murdered Eddie Byrne. The legal division cops were there to ensure that the law was observed and that everyone's rights were respected.

"They're refs," a police official later explained.

Those cops included Lieutenants Philip Chan and Patrick Sullivan. They were present when a number of protesters continued onto the Brooklyn Bridge on Saturday evening. Bottles and other debris came down upon the cops on the roadway from the pedestrian walkway above.

Up on the walkway, Chan observed a man lifting a forty-five-pound wire trash basket with the apparent intent of pitching it over the railing onto the roadway below. Chan ordered the man to put it down, and the ensuing criminal complaint would say that the man complied.

Chan still felt that a line had been crossed, and he went to arrest the man. The man pulled his arm away rather than be handcuffed. At least one of those ubiquitous cellphone cameras began filming.

"Record it! Record it!" a woman protester can be heard shouting.

But this time what the video recorded was not police violence but violence against the police.

Other protesters can be seen moving in to "de-arrest" the man. Somebody yanks Chan and elbows him, and he is momentarily distracted from trying to apprehend his assailant.

Sullivan has by then moved in to help and he seeks to complete the arrest of the first man. Chan joins him. The struggle continues, and Chan is punched, suffering a broken nose. Both cops are pummeled. Sullivan ends up sprawled on the walkway as a male protester begins kicking him.

The would-be trash basket thrower finally manages to break free with the help of the others, slipping out of his coat. But he loses his backpack in the process, and it stays with the cops as he flees down the walkway toward Brooklyn.

"We're left holding the bag," a police official later said.

The police inspected the backpack and found two brand-new hammers. They also found a City University of New York ID for Eric Linsker, as well as a passport in the same name and house keys and some pot.

"Which proves he is as dumb as a bag of hammers," the official said.

At three forty-five a.m. the next day, police arrested twenty-nine-year-old Eric Linsker for assault at his apartment in the Crown Heights section of Brooklyn, where murder was down more than 89 percent, rape by more than 73 percent, robbery by more than 86 percent. Linsker is white and from Millwood in suburban Westchester County, where Black people comprise around 1 percent of the population. He had gone on to Harvard and the famed writer's program at the University of Iowa. He was now a CUNY professor and had won awards for his poetry. One reads: "Fuck the police / To rise as you / Disappear below current / Interpretations of observations / Fuck the police."

He pled guilty to a reduced charge.

CHAPTER 4

The great majority of the protesters had been peaceful as they continued across the Brooklyn Bridge from Manhattan into the 84th Precinct. The uniformed cops there included Police Officer Rafael Ramos, who had been nicknamed Pote while growing up in East New York, one of Brooklyn's most dangerous neighborhoods.

Tu eres como chuleria en pote goes the Puerto Rican expression that gave rise to his moniker: "You are like goodness in a jar."

Pote's goodness had steered him clear of the Sex Boys, the Crazy Homicides, the Sons of Nuns, and the other gangs of East New York. And it had led him in his teenage years to declare his ambition to become a cop.

"I want to make a difference," he had told his friend Israel Marrero. "I'm tired of the stuff that's going on in our neighborhood."

The NYPD remained his ultimate goal as he went to work as a carrier for Airborne Express/DHL and then as a school safety officer. He happened to be assigned to the Police Officer Rocco Laurie Intermediate School on Staten Island, which is named after a murdered cop.

By the front desk where Marrero would sit was a huge reproduction of NYPD shield 11019. That was the one worn by Officer Rocco Laurie, who, along with his partner, Officer Gregory Foster, were assassinated by Black militants on the Lower East Side in 1972.

"[Ramos] would be sitting and looking at it every day," the school's principal, Peter Mecallari, would remember.

But Ramos seemed only more determined to become a police officer. His combination of unshakable goodness and true street wisdom already made him the perfect school safety officer.

"He had a way about him," Mecallari recalled. "The kids adored him... He never screamed at them. He handled every situation calmly."

Ramos would help set the tone of the day when he greeted the arriving students outside the school. And he could keep order inside just by being there.

"He'd walk through the halls, and he'd expect the same kind of respect he's given to them," Mecallari later said. "He was very quiet, not loud, not pushy."

When there were disputes between students, Mecallari would leave one party with Ramos while he went to investigate.

"The kids didn't mind staying with him at all," Mecallari said. "He'd talk to them, calm them down if they were upset."

The students would tell Ramos what they would not tell Mecallari or the teachers.

"Usually, he would get things out of them we weren't able to," Mecallari would recall.

Ramos was a fervent Mets fan, and he would often talk to the students about sports. He would talk to Mecallari and the staff about what was of paramount importance to him: his two sons.

"Always about his family, always about his boys," Mecallari later said. "He was very proud of them. He wanted the best in life for them."

Ramos still lived in Brooklyn, and he would drop his older son at the private Staten Island Academy on his way to work. He remained as hopeful as ever that he would be able to join the NYPD, whatever the danger.

"He always wanted to be one. He wanted to give back to the community," Mecallari said.

Mecallari remembered telling Ramos, "You *are* giving back to the community."

Ramos just missed being called for one police academy class. A subsequent one was canceled. But the long awaited big day finally came in 2012.

"He was ecstatic," Mecallari recalled.

The school's big loss was the city's big gain. Ramos was thirty-eight—more than fifteen years older than many recruits. He made it through the academy, and he was living his dream in the 84th Precinct.

Officer Rafael Ramos was just another uniform to the protesters who trooped across the Brooklyn Bridge chanting about racist killer cops and continued on to apartments in neighborhoods made safe by the police. Ramos just kept being what many considered him as—an all-but-perfect cop. He hoped also to be a chaplain through his local church, and he had just reached the end of his formal training. His duties for the NYPD required him to miss his ordination on December 20.

Ramos's regular partner was late that day, and Police Officer Wenjian Liu volunteered to fill in. Liu's usual assignment was on the same pedestrian walkway of the Brooklyn Bridge that the protesters had used earlier in the month. He was now detailed with Ramos to the 79th Precinct, in the vicinity of a Bedford-Stuyvesant housing project where there had been a spike in violence, despite the NYPD's continued efforts. Their presence was in keeping with Jack's principle of rapid deployment.

In the midafternoon, Ramos and Liu were parked on Tompkins Avenue on a meal break. Liu was nearing the twentieth anniversary of his arrival in America, having landed from China on Christmas Eve 1994, at the age of twelve. His father had labored in a garment factory when the family first arrived, and Liu would come by after school to help him finish the work. Liu had studied accounting in college, but he had decided to become a cop after the attack on the World Trade Center. He wanted to repay the country that had given him and his family such opportunity.

"Right after 9/11, he put his full energy into becoming a police officer," his father would recall.

During his seven years as a cop, Liu had telephoned his father at the end of every tour.

"He called me every day before he finished work, to assure me that he is safe, and to tell me 'Dad, I'm coming home today. You can stop worrying now,'" his father would later say.

Liu confided to a friend that he was well aware of the risks that came with the shield.

"I know that being a cop is dangerous, but I must do it," a friend would remember him once saying. "If I don't do it and you don't do it, then who is going to do it?"

Liu had gotten married just three months before to a woman named Pei Xia Chen, known as Sanny, who had also been raised in China. They hoped to start a family right away.

Ramos had seen his older son continue on to Bowdoin College. His younger son was in a private school in Brooklyn.

As the two cops sat in their radio car, twenty-eight-year-old Isma-aiyl Brinsley was drawing ever closer, near the end of a 2.3-mile trek across Brooklyn holding a clamshell-shaped white Styrofoam food container in front of him.

"As if he didn't want to tilt it," an investigator who viewed surveillance video snippets along Brinsley's route would later say.

Brinsley had arrived in New York on a midmorning bus from Baltimore, where he had begun the day by shooting his girlfriend. He had left behind his cellphone, which contained video footage of him at an anti-police demonstration in Union Square in Manhattan. He instead took his girlfriend's phone and used it during the ride northward to post a message on Instagram, along with photos of the silver Taurus semiautomatic pistol he had used to shoot her. He now had other plans:

I'm Putting Wings on Pigs Today. They take 1 of Ours...Let's Take 2 of Theirs #ShootThe Police #RIPErivGardner [sic] #RIPMike-Brown This May Be My Final Post...I'm Putting Pigs In A Blanket.

Security cam video shows that Brinsley proceeded from the bus station to the subway and a southbound Q train. A surveillance camera at the Atlantic Terminal Mall in downtown Brooklyn clearly shows him not long afterward, carrying the food container in his left hand while holding his girlfriend's cellphone to his ear with his right. Detectives would later find the phone stashed under the covering of a radiator inside a mall vestibule. The detectives would trace his steps from there by interviewing hundreds of people and studying video after video after video along the possible routes.

"Bodegas, private residences, apartment buildings, you name it," an investigator later said. "Hit or miss. Then we start getting some hits."

After a hit, they would adjust the search to the most likely route. Some of the video was crystal clear, but in other footage the figures were just fuzzy shadows in black and white. And the cameras on the busier streets would show hundreds of people going past.

"It's literally a game of *Where's Waldo?*" the investigator said.

The detectives would be helped by Brinsley's distinctive jacket, olive green cloth with brown leather arms and a round patch with a red arrowhead on the breast. They would spot him in thirty videos altogether, walking neither fast nor slow with his food container.

Along the way, Brinsley turned into a drugstore, but it is not clear whether he bought anything. He stopped at one point to ask someone directions to a particular housing development. He seemed to get a little turned around on the way but managed to reach what might have been expected to be his destination. But he just walked around the periphery of the development and proceeded on.

During his trek, Brinsley twice passed within a block of a police station house, and he almost certainly saw cops along the way. But he kept going, from the Atlantic Terminal to Myrtle Avenue, east along there, then briefly up to Park Avenue, then back to Myrtle. He had posted a video of himself more than a year before praying at the Al-Taqwa mosque, but that is on Fulton Street, away from his route on December 20. He continued to hold that food container as if it contained food, giving no indication of being capable of doing what he was about to do.

"That kind of is what's most disturbing about this," the investigator later said. "It would almost be less disturbing if he was showing some kind of sign he was a homicidal maniac."

He appears only normal, even in video footage from the final two minutes. Myrtle Avenue had taken him to Tompkins Avenue, and he stopped to speak to two men who would later tell police that he inquired about their gang affiliation, asking if they were "blue or red." They said they were neither. He urged them to check out his Instagram account. He then told them to watch what he did next.

Yet another video shows Brinsley standing by the parked radio car and catches the sound of gunshots. He then fled into a nearby subway station, where he committed suicide with the silver Taurus pistol. He left the food container beside the radio car. There was not a trace of food inside. Brinsley had used it to carry the gun, likely figuring that if he were stopped and frisked, the police would not think to check it.

CHAPTER 6

The voices of the first cops who responded to a report of shots fired crackled over a scanner carried by a twenty-seven-year-old medic named Baron Johnson as he stood in a deli a few blocks away.

"Officer down, ten-thirteen! Officer down, ten-thirteen!"

Johnson dashed across the street to the base of the Bedford-Stuyvesant Volunteer Ambulance Corps and called to his partner, twenty-three-year-old Tantania Alexander.

"We gotta go, we have an officer down!" Johnson would recall shouting.

Alexander was drained from an unsuccessful effort earlier in her shift to save someone who had gone into cardiac arrest. But she immediately roused herself.

In its earliest days, in 1988, the BSVAC had been a volunteer ambulance corps that could not afford an ambulance. Its members had initially responded to calls by dashing through the streets with their equipment.

"Everybody laughed except one person," a charter member would recall. "The person we helped."

They now had a proper ambulance emblazoned with SAVE A LIFE RESCUE SQUAD. A third medic, Pedro Adorno, was out front, and he hopped in with Johnson and Alexander. They were racing toward the corner of Tompkins and Myrtle Avenues with Johnson at the wheel when another call came over the radio.

"Dispatch, there's two officers shot and put a rush on the bus!"

Traffic up ahead on Myrtle backed up, and Johnson began weaving in and out, swerving around cars, blaring the siren. He saw numerous police cars at the corner. An officer was waving frantically for the ambulance to pull onto Tompkins Place.

Johnson did as bidden. They hopped out, the first and only ambulance on the scene. He saw two badly wounded uniformed officers in the front of a radio car.

"Where are they shot?" Johnson asked. "Who's wounded the worst?"

"They're both shot in the head and neither of them are breathing," a frantic officer replied.

Alexander and Adorno hurried over to Liu on the passenger's side. Johnson approached the driver's side. He pressed his fingertips to Ramos's neck to check for a carotid pulse.

"He's not breathing and he has no pulse!" Johnson called out.

"Get him out of the car!" other officers shouted. "Get him out of the car!"

The officers helped Johnson ease Ramos to the street. The cop lay open-eyed with a grievous head wound as Johnson again checked for a pulse.

"There was still no pulse, not even the smallest bit," Johnson would remember.

Johnson began administering CPR. He noticed the officer was wearing a wedding band. He kept on, all the more determined.

"It was really bad, chances were really minimal," Johnson would remember. "We were still going to give it our all. I said, 'If there's going to be a miracle, I'm not going to miss it.'"

Johnson kept doing everything he could, gazing down at those eyes that gazed right back at him with a seemingly stunned expression.

"It looked like he was caught off guard," Johnson would recall.

Johnson stayed at it.

"I prayed and I prayed as I pushed," Johnson would remember. "I kept telling him 'Talk to me,' saying to him, 'Move if you can hear me. Try to blink your eyes. Just do something!'"

Johnson heard officers around him screaming to their comrade.

"Please, Ramos, don't die! Don't die!"

Johnson himself kept calling to Ramos.

"Can you hear me? Move. Say something if you can hear me!"

The other two medics, Alexander and Adorno, were doing what they could to save Officer Liu on the passenger side. Alexander saw he was not breathing. She checked for a carotid pulse.

"Nothing," she would remember.

Other cops helped her and Adorno get Liu from the car. She was administering CPR when an FDNY ambulance arrived, and those paramedics took over.

Alexander and Adorno joined Johnson in working on Ramos; thirty presses on his chest, then two squeezes of the air-giving Ambu bag, then thirty more presses and two more squeezes. Ramos was still showing no signs of life when they got him on a backboard and into the BSVAC ambulance.

Johnson again took the wheel and sped off.

"Time is not on our side," Johnson later said.

Alexander, Adorno, and a cop got in the back. Alexander let the cop take over the CPR.

"Ramos! Ramos! Ramos!" the cop kept saying.

Ramos did not answer. Alexander was busy applying dressings to the wounds.

"Head, chest, and thigh," she recalls.

At Woodhull Hospital, the Bed-Stuy ambulance crew kept at it as they wheeled Ramos into the emergency room. They followed the doctor's instructions to cut away his clothes and they stood ready to assist however they might be able as the trauma team set to work.

After what seemed a desperate eternity, a doctor shook his head.

"We pretty much knew what that meant," Johnson would later note.

Ramos and Liu were pronounced dead. Johnson was in tears. Alexander was taking it even harder.

"We started doing this because we want to save lives," Johnson later said. "You do everything that you're trained to do. You're told that if you do these things, you can help save somebody's life."

Johnson and his comrades then returned to their ambulance, ready for the next call.

CHAPTER 7

Liu's wife, Sanny, arrived. She was informed that her husband of three months was dead. She sat in mute shock beside the body of her soul mate, who had dimples and always seemed to be smiling, who needed only to look at her for her to know what he was thinking, who always made sure she had a scarf when it was windy and an umbrella when it rained, and who was so excited about starting a family.

"I couldn't even talk for I don't know how long," she would remember.

She could still feel his presence. She was not ready to believe he was just gone.

"I feel connection with his spirit," she would remember. "He wants a baby."

She decided she had to do something.

She rose and went up to somebody from NYPD Employee Relations, the liaison with the families. She asked a question.

"Is it possible to collect his sperm?" she asked. "So in the future one day my husband can have a child?"

The Employee Relations representative made a call and informed her that it could be attempted, but they would not know until a doctor at Cornell Medical Center in Manhattan conducted a test to see if the sperm was still active. She signed a consent form.

As always, cops had converged on the hospital as word of the shooting spread. More than a hundred stood in a line outside and saluted as two NYPD ambulances bore the bodies off to the medical examiner's office. Only a few people knew that one of the ambulances would make a discreet stop at a medical facility before proceeding on to the morgue.

A doctor reported the test results within a couple of hours.

"They said, 'It's good news, it's active,' then they store it," Sanny would remember. "It give me hope."

She had another question when she spoke to the doctor.

"I said, 'Is it possible I start right away?'" she would remember. "They said, 'No, you have to wait.'"

The usual waiting period is six months to a year. The standard hospital protocol reads: "At the time of a man's sudden death, intense bereavement may cause a woman to attempt to 'hold on' to her deceased partner by requesting sperm retrieval. Denial, a normal process of self-deception that is part of the grief process following a tragic loss, may initially drive the wife to request the procedure. A pregnancy may be planned as an act of love or memorial in the face of death. Sperm preservation could provide the false impression that the man will live on through his retrieved sperm and its fertility potential."

Sanny summed it up as "To see if I am mentally stable."

In the meantime a cellphone video that a cop had made in the emergency room was texted to Conor and thousands of other fellow officers.

"It took like two minutes," Conor later said.

The video showed the cops who had crowded into the hallway turning their backs on de Blasio as he arrived and made his way through them on the way to seeing the families. Many cops remained of the opinion that de Blasio had only been in a position to run for mayor because they had made the city safe enough for him to win on an anti-cop ticket. They also felt he had essentially turned the streets over to anti-cop demonstrators and had been slow to react to chants about wanting "Dead cops!...Now!"

The current PBA president, Pat Lynch, went so far as to suggest de Blasio bore some responsibility for the deaths of Ramos and Liu.

"That blood on the hands starts on the steps of City Hall in the office of the mayor," Lynch said. "When these funerals are over, those responsible will be called on the carpet and held accountable."

The younger of the Ramos sons, thirteen-year-old Jaden, understood that his father and Liu had been killed not for who they were but because of what they were.

"It's horrible that someone gets shot dead just for being a police officer," he posted on Facebook after learning his father had been killed. "I will always love you and never forget you."

Sanny does not think she slept that first night, but she would vividly remember having what might have been a kind of waking dream in which her husband appeared.

"My husband, the night he died, he came into my dream," she would recall. "He wear a white gown. I heard a baby crying. He said, 'It's a baby. Yes, it's a girl. Come take it.' I didn't see his face, but I knew it was him."

On Christmas Eve, the twentieth anniversary of Liu's arrival in America, the bodies of the two murdered officers awaited their funerals. Ramos's was held two days after Christmas at Christ Tabernacle Church in Queens. Vice President Biden and then governor Andrew Cuomo spoke, their images appearing on Jumbotrons that enabled the twenty-five thousand cops outside to see and hear the service. A good number of the cops turned their backs when Mayor de Blasio appeared on the screens.

"Our hearts are aching today," de Blasio said. "We feel it physically. We feel it deeply. New York City has lost a hero—a remarkable man because of the depths of his commitment to all around him."

De Blasio was hunched over, though that may have only been because of his considerable height in relation to the lectern. But his voice was definitely muted. He extended condolences to a larger family.

"The family of the NYPD that is hurting so deeply right now, men and women feeling this loss so personally, so deeply."

De Blasio likely could not have said anything that would have made things better, but at least he did not make them worse. Steven hoped that seeing the two dead officers and their wives at the hospital might have shocked the new mayor into better understanding the enormity of what cops face. Conor further hoped that the spontaneous back turning in the corridor alerted de Blasio to the distance between himself and those who risked everything every day.

Steven and Conor then fell in with the formation outside as the honor guard carried the coffin from the church. Joanne Jaffe, now a three-star chief, placed a white-gloved hand on the shoulder of each of Ramos's sons. She then hugged the older boy and the left side of his face pressed against her shield. Her hands cradled his head just as she had cradled the lone surviving baby's head at the Palm Sunday massacre three decades before in the same crime-plagued neighborhood where Rafael Ramos—then just ten—had earned the nickname Pote for his goodness.

The funeral for Officer Wenjian Liu was delayed while relatives traveled from China and the family determined an auspicious date on the Chinese calendar and a feng shui expert selected a gravesite at Cypress Hills Cemetery. The city proceeded to the end of 2014 and the arrival of 2015 with its annual rites in Times Square.

As the big moment neared, Lieutenant Jamiel Altaheri of the Transit Bureau stood by a subway entrance exactly where Lieutenant Jack Maple of the Transit Police had stood on another New Year's Eve a quarter century before.

Altaheri had been raised in the Yemeni community in downtown Brooklyn and moved to the traditionally Italian neighborhood of Bensonhurst after he became a cop and got married. His next-door neighbor seemed to have trouble placing him ethnically at first.

"He didn't know what I was," Altaheri later said.

But Altaheri's wife covers her head with a hijab.

"He sees me, he's cool," Altaheri remembered. "He sees my wife..."

Altaheri went over to introduce himself and held out his hand, as he would upon moving next door to anyone.

"He smacks my hand away," Altaheri recounted.

Sometime later, Altaheri noticed that he had not been seeing his neighbor come and go. He inquired at the neighbor's house if everything was all right and got a "What's it to you?"

Altaheri asked around and learned that the neighbor was in the hospital. Altaheri made further inquiries to find out which one and went to visit him.

"He was in shock," Altaheri recalled. "He started tearing up. He said, 'I'm not tearing up for you, I'm tearing up for myself. I feel like such a piece of shit.'"

Altaheri later reported, "From then on, we were the best of friends."

Altaheri subsequently moved to the Bronx, where his ten-year-old daughter, Nadine, was called a "terrorist" by some of the kids at school. He recalled, "She asked me, 'How is it people call me a terrorist and you're a police officer?'"

Altaheri and his wife went to the school and made efforts to raise awareness about bullying and bigotry. Word reached City Hall, and Altaheri and his daughter were specially invited to the mayor's State of the City Address. They led the gathering in the Pledge of Allegiance.

And now Altaheri stood like Jack Maple by the subway entrance on New Year's Eve, ready to acknowledge that he was supposed to be underground but also ready to say he was on a break. He proved to be all the more like Jack or any other good cop when he saw a man and a woman behind a barricade in obvious distress.

"Is everything okay?" Altaheri asked.

The man was Roger Higgenbottom. He had terminal cancer, and one thing he had done after being diagnosed was marry his wife, Diana. Another top item on his bucket list was to see the famous ball drop in Times Square on New Year's Eve. They had traveled from their home in Wisconsin and planned to take position hours ahead of time, but he had been overcome by the effects of his most recent chemo and the pain from a tumor.

With the clock ticking toward midnight, Roger had summoned all the strength he could muster to rise from his hotel bed. He and Diana had made their way to Times Square only to find themselves cordoned off in a packed pedestrian area where they would not be able to see the ball.

Altaheri escorted the couple past the police barricade. The Higgenbottoms arrived just below the ball at 11:57 p.m. They could not have asked to be in a better place on earth as they joined the countdown and cheered in 2015 three minutes later.

Altaheri would later send NYPD hats and shirts to the couple's home in Wisconsin. A photo would show a smiling Roger wearing his NYPD gear in a hospital bed. He would die soon after, eighty-four days into the New Year, having told his wife that his fondest memory was of the time Altaheri had appeared as if an angel and brought them in to see the ball drop. Altaheri would subsequently be promoted to captain, at thirty-three the youngest in the department. He would spot a familiar face during the ceremony at police headquarters. Diana had come to surprise and congratulate him as a way of saying thanks.

Altaheri would recount the story at a gathering of Muslim cops on Eid, the breaking of the fast during Ramadan. He would offer a fundamental of policing, corollary to what drove CompStat.

"See yourself in other people's shoes," he would tell them.

He saw being a cop as an opportunity to recognize, defend, and practice that good.

"Every day on this job is a blessing," he would say.

CHAPTER 9

In the meantime, the end of 2014 and the beginning of a new year saw Lieutenant Tony Giorgio of the NYPD Ceremonial Unit meet with the Liu family. Giorgio, whose mother attended Juilliard and started out as a rock drummer before becoming a cop, had organized every line-of-duty funeral for twenty years. He now consulted with the Liu family so he could incorporate the ways of the Finest with those of their Chinese heritage.

Rather than at a house of worship, the January 3, 2015, send-off was held at an Italian funeral parlor that had adapted as the Brooklyn neighborhood of Dyker Heights became increasingly Asian. The ceremony began with a small, private ritual conducted by Buddhist monks. Mourners were unfettered by Western stoicism and openly expressed their grief while burning joss paper, most of it in the form of "ghost money" bearing the likeness of the Jade Emperor in denominations of up to $1 billion drawn on the Bank of Heaven and Hell, to be spent in the afterlife. There were no eulogies.

Then came a second, departmental ceremony, which did include speakers, among them Wenjian's widow, Sanny Liu. She called her husband a loving, devoted soul mate. The few cops present who knew about the stop on the way to the medical examiner's office took special note when she said Liu would live on in her and his family.

"You are an amazing man," Sanny then said directly to her husband.

Mayor de Blasio, Police Commissioner Kelly, and Wenjian's father also spoke. Everyone joined the formation outside while Liu's relatives made three final bows to the coffin. The lid was closed, and the coffin was covered with an NYPD flag. Incense was lit that symbolized Liu's spirit and would be kept burning all the way to the cemetery. Sanny held a stick of it along with a framed portrait of her husband in uniform and followed as the NYPD honor guard bore the coffin out to the street.

Sanny handed the incense and the framed portrait to a relative as the same ritual that had been performed for Ramos came to the moment the widow is presented with the folded flag and given a white-gloved salute. One difference was that Sanny herself was wearing white gloves in keeping with her own tradition. She clasped her gloved hands before her as she clutched the flag with the base of the triangle nestled in the crook of each arm, the point just below her trembling chin.

Sanny was again holding the framed photo and incense as she and the relatives made their way to limousines marked FAMILY in Chinese and English. The pungent smoke wafted in the air along with the slow drumming of the pipe band. She would remember the wintry weather and the overwhelming turnout.

"Very cold," she later said. "So many people."

She was struck by the sight of one particular figure in a wheelchair, breathing with a ventilator.

"He was in uniform," she would recall of Steven. "I said 'Oh my God.'"

Sanny saw Steven again five months later, at the funeral for twenty-five-year-old Police Officer Brian Moore, who had been one of Conor's good buddies at the police academy. Moore had been working plainclothes and was at the wheel of an unmarked car when he and his partner, Erik Jansen, spotted a man adjusting something in his waistband on a residential street in Queens. Moore pulled over and called to the man, showing his shield.

"Police, man," Moore said. "You holding something? You got something on you?"

The man turned toward the car, pulling a gun.

"Yeah, I got something," he said.

The man fired three times. Two bullets hit the car. A third hit Moore in the cheek. His funeral was held in the same Long Island church as the funeral for young Eddie Byrne. Steven proceeded along the long line of cops waiting to salute the coffin when it arrived, just as he had twenty-seven years before. He received no applause this time, for he was now a sight so familiar as to have become part of tradition and ritual.

Conor was with Steven when he spoke with Sanny.

"He introduced his son to me," Sanny would recall.

Sanny felt an immediate bond with Steven. She understood when she spoke to him that he was somebody held dear by what she had come to call "my new blue family."

CHAPTER 10

The 822 newest members of the Finest family included Jack Maple's son, Brendan, now twenty-five and in his last two months at the academy. He had triggered a small panic at headquarters when he put in for a shield number that did not match his father's old shield number in the records.

The panic passed when they discovered that he had requested his mother's shield.

Elizabeth was there on July 3, 2015, when Brendan graduated at Madison Square Garden, a black band of mourning on his and everyone else's shield in memory of Moore. Brendan's face reddened at the mention of his name during Bratton's remarks to the gathering. A reporter spoke to Brendan afterward.

"It's definitely some big shoes to fill," he said of his father while wearing his mother's shield. "Right now, I just want to be myself and go from there."

Rookies with significant NYPD connections, or "hooks," can generally get themselves assigned to choice precincts in Manhattan. But Brendan was a Maple in more than name, and he made his choice by searching online for the place with the highest crime rate.

On his third day at the 75th Precinct, Brendan was summoned by his commanding officer.

"Maple. I didn't know who the fuck you were," the commanding officer said. "Look at this text I got."

Brendan saw that somebody had inquired, "Did Jack Maple's son really report for duty at the 75?"

The precinct was the subject of a 2014 documentary, *The Seven Five*, centering on a corrupt cop named Michael Dowd, who was arrested in 1992. The film suggests that Dowd and a handful of his fellow officers went bad because of a bad neighborhood. He was in truth a sociopath who started out bad and teamed up with a few others to form a cop gang.

Brendan witnessed another truth of the 75th Precinct and of the adjoining 73rd and 67th precincts.

"It was about seven a.m., and a call came over the radio for an infant that wasn't breathing, turning blue," he would recall. "I was the second car on scene."

One of the cops from the first car sprang into action.

"The cop grabbed the kid and mom, tossed them in the back seat and flew to Brookdale [Hospital], on the way there calling over the radio to shut down Linden Blvd. Every cop car in the seven-five, seven-three, six-seven shut down the intersections about 1.5 miles of Linden. Some cops leapfrogging from one intersection to another."

He added, "It was just something really cool to witness how they did all that so fast."

Brendan was never more Jack Maple's son than at a moment when he was off duty and strolling with his fiancée, Ashley Gardner, through Times Square on the way from seeing the Broadway show *Wicked*. Times Square had indeed become a realm such as his father prophesized, though there was one corner that was a kind of a nature preserve from the bad old days. The spot was two blocks below the Deuce and a half block east from the parole offices where his father had once based a detective squad and, on occasion, wandered around nude save for a raincoat. A few lower-than-low-level dope peddlers occasionally ranged from there, one happened to approach Brendan and Ashley, the son looking remarkably like the father at that age and therefore not at all like a typical cop.

"Coke, coke," the peddler said.

"What else you got?" Brendan asked.

"Heroin," the peddler said.

"Let me see what I got," Brendan said.

Brendan reached in his pants pocket and produced his shield.

"Oh, look what I got!" Brendan exclaimed.

Brendan was unaware that his father had done exactly this at almost this same spot more than a quarter century before, when he himself was a rookie. Jack had subsequently been able to achieve the same effect with just a steady look as he said, "I am not who you think I am," and then, "I am who you think I am now." Brendan would almost certainly develop the same ability, though he would have considerably less need for it as he moved through a city transformed.

At work, Brendan began using a new NYPD smartphone that was a bit like having the Jackster in his pocket. The Phone of the Future gave cops timelier intelligence than Jack could have imagined: any other 911 calls regarding that address and what type of calls they were; everybody residing there with a criminal record; the name and photo of any who were wanted; any residents known to be emotionally disturbed; surveillance video, both real time and when the complaint was made; reports from a citywide matrix of sensors called ShotSpotter that recognizes and pinpoints gunfire; and alerts from a network of license plate readers, which allow cops to see where a car is, where it has been, and when exactly it was there.

Brendan found the phone particularly useful when he was assigned to Brooklyn North Warrant Squad.

"Use it all the time in warrants, seeing people's patterns coming and going over bridges to help determine when they may be coming or going," he reported.

The Phone of the Future also enabled him to access NYPD incident reports. He put that to use after they swooped down on a location to grab several suspects and discovered one of them was not there.

"We had no other addresses associated with him until I got out the phone and looked at prior domestic reports and saw he had an on/off girlfriend that lived nearby," he recalled. "We went there. Sure enough, he was in there, hiding in a bar cart."

A fourth generation of the McDonald family became a detective in January 2016. Conor had gone from patrol in the Midtown South Precinct to the warrant squad in Queens, where his paternal grandfather had worked. Conor put in for and received detective shield 97, which had belonged to Brian Mulheren.

"He saved my dad's life," Conor now said as he stood wearing the shield of the Night Mayor who had ordered Steven moved from the hospital that had given up on him to one that managed to keep him alive.

On July 12, 2016, Steven marked the thirtieth anniversary of when he was shot and very nearly killed by making a video at his home to be posted online. He began with an expression of gratitude stretching back to the first day at the hospital and including the 10,950 days since then.

"I want to say thank you for the support and the help you have given me all these years," he said. "Thirty years is a long time. I never thought I'd be around that long."

He went on, "I'm very proud to be part of the New York City Police Department and to be a friend, I'd like to believe, to all of you."

He continued, "Today is my thirtieth anniversary of the shooting, and in four days it will be my thirty-second anniversary in the New York City Police Department, and it has been so special to me, and I can pass it on to my son. My wife, Patti Ann, has been a great support to us both. You all have a place in my heart that can never be taken by anyone else. Thank you."

Steven and Patti Ann then returned to the edge of the wooded patch in Central Park at what had been the fateful hour. They afterward rode past throngs of people in the new New York who were out enjoying a summer afternoon with little or no thought of crime.

"Look!" Steven said. "Look!"

Back at home during the three decades since the shooting, Patti Ann sometimes stepped into Steven's room when he was sleeping, his extended arms held in place by bedsheets.

"Almost like the cross," Patti Ann would remember.

Like Conor sometimes did, she would see Christ in Steven.

"He would almost look like that," Patti Ann later said. "I loved going in and he'd be sleeping and his face was so at peace."

O n the Sunday before the fifteenth anniversary of 9/11, Steven led the Walk of Remembrance, as he had every year since the first one. The procession was preceded as always by a Mass at the Church of St. Francis in Manhattan, this time on the same day Mother Teresa was canonized in Rome.

"For the first time, we pray to St. Teresa of Calcutta," FDNY Chaplain Chris Keenan said from the altar.

To many on the walk, Steven was a living saint. The procession then again proceeded along Mychal Judge's route from the friary to Ground Zero. The First Station of the Cross was to be said at the fire station for Ladder 12, but the company proved to be out on a run involving a man stuck in an elevator. And rather than wait for the Bravest to return, the new plan was to meet the firefighters farther down Seventh Avenue whenever their job was done.

As it happened, Ladder 12 was able to extricate the man quickly and swing around to meet the procession just as it reached a stretch of Christopher Street that had been renamed Stonewall Place. The block had recently been designated the Stonewall National Monument. It includes a pocket park and the Stonewall Inn, scene of the 1969 riot that sparked the gay rights movement.

In the immediate aftermath of 9/11, Steven had been surprised by revelations that Mychal was gay. Steven had long since come to accept Mychal's sexuality and to embrace the whole of him. Even the staunchest Catholics among the cops and firemen on the walk seemed just as accepting.

The procession continued downtown, the participants that year including the newly appointed police commissioner, Jimmy O'Neill. Bratton had stepped down to take a job with Teneo, a self-described "global CEO advisory" firm with connections to Bill and Hillary Clinton. Bratton had recommended O'Neill to become his successor at the NYPD.

Cynics would say that O'Neill's first lucky break came when he happened to be the head of the Transit Police video unit when Bratton first came to New York. That put O'Neill in a position to make a series of videos featuring the new chief, who was not adverse to being in front of a camera. A second lucky break came when O'Neill happened to be commanding officer of the Central Park Precinct at the time Bratton wished to propose to his future wife, Rikki Klieman, on the carousel. O'Neill was able to open the carousel in the middle of winter, earning him the enduring gratitude of the newlyweds.

But O'Neill was also street-smart and steady. As chief of department he had demonstrated both willingness and flexibility when it came to establishing better relations with city residents. He was also essentially decent. He was particularly devoted to his octogenarian mother, though he did get so busy in his first couple days as commissioner that he failed to call her.

"It's okay, I'm not dead," she texted him.

O'Neill's decency and his love of cops was further evidenced by his admiration for Steven. And O'Neill had such a humble air during the 9/11 walk that you would not have imagined he was the new police commissioner if you did not already know it.

Conor had been studying for the sergeant's exam, and he was promoted at the end of September, seventeen days after the memorial walk. Steven was of course there in uniform at the ceremony, although he was unable to join the others in rising and saluting when the color guard came in or to applaud when it was Conor's turn to step onto the stage.

As the entire command staff and the other promotees and their families and comrades watched, Conor strode up to Steven and bowed to kiss him on the forehead. Steven could feel it as keenly as he felt Conor's first stirrings inside a pregnant Patti Ann.

"I have to salute him now," Steven said.

On Christmas of 2016, Steven and the rest of the McDonald clan gathered at the home where they had grown up. His sister Theresa had bought her parents' place and had added a big deck, where she now set up a heated tent for the occasion. The music included Steven's favorite album, *Quadrophenia* by The Who from 1973, when he was sixteen and would dance, dance, dance. He now could only tip his head from side to side with the beat, but he was not ready to stop when the heat gave out. His siblings sought to keep him warm by covering him with more and more blankets. Only his eyes were showing as he rocked on.

In the first week of the new year, Steven spoke at a high school and swung by the Soleman shoe stand in Penn Station. He picked up a pair of brown dress shoes his driver Andy Cserenyi had dropped off the day before. They were gleaming on his feet as he headed off to a dinner hosted by the Long Island chapter of Legatus, a Catholic business leaders organization.

Patti Ann had undergone a medical test that left her worried enough to stay home and await the doctor's call. She received the results soon after Steven departed and called while he was en route. She said all was well.

"Everyone, Patti Ann's okay!" Steven exclaimed.

Steven's speech at the dinner was about love and forgiveness, which made it much like many others he had given. But Cserenyi, Patti Ann's mother, and others who were present felt this one was particularly special for reasons they could not immediately explain.

"The speech was amazing, very positive," Cserenyi would later say. "The evening felt different. There was a calm in the room."

Patti Ann's mother would later tell her that she noticed something different about Steven.

"She said he had an aura around him," Patti Ann would report.

Patti Ann ate Chinese food at home with Conor, who slept over that night. Conor headed off to work the next morning, and Steven later called him.

"Dad!" Conor said.

"Are you okay?" Steven asked.

"Yeah, I'm fine, Dad," Conor said. "I love you!"

Steven urged him to put any free time he had into preparing for the lieutenant's test.

"You studying?" Steven asked.

"Yes, Dad, I'm studying," Conor assured him.

Steven was still in bed as he discussed with Patti Ann his plans for the day.

"I'm going to stay in bed today because I'm not going to be able to eat anything because tomorrow is bowel program," he said, by her recollection. "I don't want anything to go wrong tomorrow so I can go to the Botanical Garden."

They had arranged to go the following evening to Bar Car Night at the annual holiday train show at the New York Botanical Garden in the Bronx. The festive event features an after-dark viewing of model trains running past more than 175 illuminated miniature replicas of New York landmarks.

But they had nothing scheduled on this day. Patti Ann went off to another part of the house as Steven remained in bed. He was under the care of one of the nurses who assisted him around the clock.

"Then, the next thing I know..." Patti Ann later said.

The nurse began to shout frantically, and Patti Ann dashed into the room. Steven was blue, and he was unconscious. He was not breathing.

"How the hell did this happen?" Patti Ann demanded.

The nurse had no immediate answer.

"Did you call 911?" Patti Ann asked.

"No," the nurse said.

Patti Ann telephoned the Malverne cops directly.

"He's gone, he's gone, he's not here," Patti Ann now screamed.

The police arrived moments later.

"Do something!" Patti Ann called out.

She was unable just to stand there.

"I couldn't stay in the room," she would remember. "I couldn't believe it was happening."

She went downstairs and called her mother.

"Get over here, Steven's gone!" Patti Ann told her.

She also called Cserenyi.

"Steven's gone!" she cried, then hung up.

Cserenyi called her back, and she told him what had happened. He arrived there before the ambulance departed. He drove Patti Ann to Franklin General Hospital.

Cserenyi was in the room as the doctors fought to revive Steven. They asked for Steven's ventilator settings, and Cserenyi knew the numbers by heart.

Steven was stabilized but still unconscious when he was transferred to North Shore University Hospital. The doctors there were as pessimistic as the ones at Bellevue had been three decades before. But this time it seemed they might be right.

Conor arrived with his fiancée, Katie Sullivan, and asked a number of others in the room to join them in forming a circle of love and faith around his father. Conor announced to Steven who was there.

"Dad..." he said.

Conor then led the circle in prayer, his voice strong with life and devotion and belief such as had shone from his father's eyes. Those eyes were now closed, but there was still the hope that Steven could hear and maybe feel in the area above where the bullets had cut off all sensation. There remained a chance he could register a touch on his cheek. His crown was covered with a white knit hospital cap, but his forehead was bare and invited a kiss such as Conor had given him at the promotion and so many other times.

On Steven's chest lay a copy of the Prayer of St. Francis, along with the text of Mychal Judge's last homily, delivered on 9/10 at a Bronx firehouse. Conor read aloud words that apply equally to the NYPD as to the FDNY and to all those who stand ever ready to sacrifice their lives for the sake of others.

"That's the way it is. Good days. And bad days. Up days. Down days. Sad days. Happy days. But never a boring day on this job. You do what God has called you to do. You show up. You put one foot in front of another. You

382 • MICHAEL DALY

get on the rig and you go out and you do the job—which is a mystery. And a surprise. You have no idea when you get on that rig. No matter how big the call. No matter how small. You have no idea what God is calling you to. But he needs you. He needs me. He needs all of us."

On through Friday and then Saturday and Sunday into Monday, Conor formed a succession of circles at Steven's bedside. A number of the people who held one of Steven's hands remarked on their surprising warmth. The mayor appeared and joined in the prayer, knowing and actually seeming to feel the words. Some of those present saw this as evidence that Steven shared Mychal Judge's ability to summon what was best in people.

Cardinal Timothy Dolan entered and noted the many religious figurines people had brought.

"There are more statues in here than at St. Patrick's Cathedral," he joked.

Steven's father, David, was outside the room, recalling aloud the days after they learned that the shooting had left his son paralyzed. David said he would lie in bed at night and try to remain completely immobile and imagine what Steven must be enduring. His body rebelled after only a few minutes.

"I couldn't do it," David remembered.

As morning turned to afternoon, David remained in the hallway and looked at all the cops who continued to come to the hospital to offer their support. They were ready to do anything at all, if anything at all could have been done.

"It's still the only job," David said.

The final hours were approaching when Sanny Liu appeared. She gave no hint that she had gone ahead with an attempt to have her fallen husband's baby.

"It's not easy for me to do this procedure," she later allowed.

But Dr. Pak Chung and his associates at Weill Cornell Medical Center had helped her through it with the experience and expertise gained from assisting more than four thousand successful conceptions. One of them now involved a murdered police officer.

"They give me a lot of comfort," she would report. "They help me overcome the fear."

The first attempt had been successful.

"Just one shot," she would later say. "No kidding."

Chung had spoken the words she most wanted to hear: "Congratulations, you're pregnant."

Chung also said that she should stay at home and avoid being around groups of people for the first three months. She was only two months pregnant when she heard that Steven was in the hospital.

"You know what, I have to be there," she said. "I have to see him."

Conor took Sanny into Steven's room. She held Steven's hand with one of her own and with the other completed the latest circle, which included Conor and Katie and Patti Ann, who was at the foot of the bed in a Rangers sweatshirt. Sanny listened as Conor led them in the Prayer of St. Francis and the Holy Rosary.

"I was so nervous," Sanny would recall. "I didn't know the prayer yet. I didn't know what to say."

But she did not need to know the words to feel a bond as she stood there in her first trimester of pregnancy, just as Patti Ann had been with Conor when she stood by Steven's bedside in 1986 and nobody thought he would survive the night. Steven had kept on, decades beyond what was thought to be possible for someone on a ventilator, becoming his own miracle, for which more than one doctor had said there was no medical explanation. Conor was now grown and himself a cop, but he and Sanny's unborn child were somehow siblings, just as she and Patti Ann were sisters of a kind, just as they were all kin in that big blue family.

Others who came in to bid Steven a final farewell included his former driver Jon Williams, now retired. Williams felt there were too many people present for something so private as a final forehead rub and a call of *Steve-o!* But Jon-nie! understood why everybody was there.

"Steven McDonald was an angel that actually walked among us," Williams said. "You had to have been in his midst."

Also waiting outside the door was another of Steven's former drivers, Thomas Spillane. He entered with his eight-month-old son, Thomas James, in a stroller. Patty Ann instantly brightened on seeing little TJ. The baby was clutching a small toy giraffe and had eyes alight with life at its newest and purest.

"Oh, look..." Patti Ann said.

Little TJ was one of the last in line. Conor emerged from the room and returned the shields that the former drivers had left on Steven's chest. Then it was time for Patti Ann and Conor and Katie and Thomas to have some private final moments.

This time, his adoring younger brother Thomas did not say *Steven, don't die*. He knew that Steven had suffered enough.

A doctor turned off the ventilator. The end came as peacefully as this champion of peace deserved.

At 1:09 p.m. on January 10, 2017, Steven was pronounced dead. A team of cops came in and lovingly wrapped him in an NYPD flag. They placed him on a gurney and wheeled him to an elevator. A crowd of uniformed cops was waiting outside the hospital and saluted as Steven was lifted into the back of an NYPD ambulance. A police helicopter hovered protectively overhead.

The wake was held Wednesday and Thursday at St. Agnes parish hall in Rockville Centre on Long Island. Thousands attended, the line wrapping around the block on both nights and mourners still waiting long after the posted hours. They stepped up to see Steven wearing his dress uniform in an open dark wood casket. He had lost all the uncommon warmth he had in the hospital.

"He's so cold," his sister Dolores said upon touching him.

His lifesaving nurse Nina Justiniano arrived and stood by the coffin with Conor, who had saved his father's life before he was born. She had not seen Conor since he was an infant, and now here he was, fully grown, in uniform with a nameplate reading MCDONALD.

"I was stunned," she later said. "He looked so much like Steven. I see Patti Ann in him, but I saw Steven."

CHAPTER 14

Nina Justiniano returned to the funeral home the following morning in her nurse's uniform, complete with the cap that signified her as a graduate of Brooklyn Jewish, the black band marking her as an RN. She boarded one of the seven buses chartered along with a dozen vans for friends and family. She rode with cops she had come to know during the months at Bellevue. Other cops and nurses who had tended to Steven over the ensuing decades were also aboard.

Dozens of police motorcycles led the way for the silver hearse, followed by limousines with the immediate family and the vans and buses. Nina peered out the window and saw cops saluting from highway overpasses. Firefighters suspended giant American flags from pairs of upraised tower ladders.

"I can't tell you how that made me feel," Nina later said.

When the procession reached St. Patrick's Cathedral, Nina witnessed an NYPD funeral for her first time. The solemn ceremony was all too familiar to the thousands of cops who stood at attention and saluted in the street. A lone piper among the Emerald Society's band played "Amazing Grace." An honor guard carried Steven's flag-draped coffin up the front steps.

The cops then filed inside and filled the cathedral. The coffin stood before the altar, the NYPD flag having been replaced by a white pall for its time in the cathedral. Conor sat with Patti Ann and Katie at the front, to the right. Conor was sixteen days from his thirtieth birthday. Steven had turned thirty on the day he marked his son's baptism by forgiving Shavod Jones.

As on any day, the same gospel was being read at every Catholic Church in the world. The passage just happened to be Mark 2:1–12, in which Jesus forgives and heals a paralyzed man.

Monsignor Seamus O'Boyle, who is Patti Ann's cousin and presided at her wedding back in 1985, rose to give the homily. He noted that Steven would not have called the Gospel reading a coincidence.

"There were no coincidences, but God-incidences," O'Boyle quoted Steven saying.

O'Boyle observed that it was coming up on Martin Luther King Jr. Day and that Steven was a great admirer of the civil rights leader.

"Martin Luther King famously said hate cannot drive out hate; only love can," O'Boyle noted.

Police Commissioner Jimmy O'Neill, who had started as a cave cop with Jack Maple, also spoke. He said he first met Steven in 1999, while commanding the Central Park Precinct. That was when Steven had addressed the roll call.

"What we can learn from Steven's life is this: The cycle of violence that plagues so many lives today can be overcome only by breaking down the walls that separate people. The best tools for doing this—Steven taught us—are love, respect, and forgiveness."

Conor rose to speak, giving his mother a hug and pausing to kiss the coffin.

"I never thought this day would come," he then began. "My father was the real Superman."

He said there had been many hardships since the shooting, but his father had continued on with unflagging purpose.

"Despite being in a wheelchair and dependent on a ventilator," Conor said. "There were many ups and downs, lots of tears shed, but more hope shared. He was the greatest man I could have asked for to be my father."

Conor told the assemblage that forgiveness had not been just a onetime pronouncement in a dictated letter. It had been an ongoing effort that began anew each time Steven awoke.

"When many of us would have let anger fester in our hearts, my father forgave the young man who shot him every single day," Conor said. "He made it his mission to have all of us realize that love must win."

Conor said that his father had been proud to serve as a Navy corpsman with the Marines, but the high point had come when he joined the NYPD in 1984.

"Doing the greatest job in the greatest city," Conor said.

His father's life had seemed complete with the most important element of all.

"My mother, Patti Ann."

The assemblage rose for a standing ovation that lasted a full minute, sounding like holy rain. Conor reported something his father had told him about the moments after he was shot.

"His thoughts were all about mom," Conor said. "He knew he had to fight to see her again and fight he did."

And she had joined him in the long fight that followed.

"My parents created the most phenomenal life out of such darkness," Conor said.

The son of the cop who had once declared himself the luckiest man on earth made a declaration of his own.

"What a lucky son," he said.

Conor now read aloud the Prayer of St. Francis with much the same voice as he had in the hospital. And everyone who could hear him could almost have been at Steven's bedside.

"God bless America, the city of New York, and our saint—my dad—the legend, Steven McDonald," Conor ended by saying.

The ritual Steven had so often witnessed continued, only it was his coffin that was carried into the street and saluted by cops in formation. It was his widow who was solemnly presented with the folded flag.

A *New York Daily News* photographer took a picture of Patti Ann bending down over the bare wood coffin.

GOD'S COP, the front page would read.

Nine police helicopters flew overhead in formation. The NYPD pipes and drums struck up "Irish Soldier Boy" as they led the procession down Fifth Avenue. The temperature had dropped, the day turning chilly as if the city itself were feeling the loss of Steven's warmth.

And on the cathedral steps, distinct in her nurse's white amid the police dress blue stood Nina Justiniano.

"He was the love of my life, although we fought like dogs," she said.

After the bus ride to the burial at the Cemetery of the Holy Rood on Long Island, Nina attended the gathering at the parish hall adjoining St. Agnes Cathedral in Rockville Centre. She then returned to Harlem, where she still owned the brownstone that she had purchased and kept with Steven's mouthed encouragement: "Go for it."

Nina had gone ahead with her plan to seal the building and keep up with the payments on the $29,999 mortgage and pay the taxes. She had come in regularly from her home in Queens to maintain the yard. Her grandson, Myles, was no sooner big enough to hold a rake than he was put to work on the leaves.

In the meantime, Nina had proceeded from Bellevue to work in the burn unit at New York Hospital, maybe the toughest nursing duty in the city. She also worked in the ICU, and a doctor came in one day saying he had a patient who did not want to go to the hospital.

"So, we'll take the hospital to him," the doctor said.

Nina volunteered, and the doctor gave her an address on Fifth Avenue. When she arrived the doorman directed her to an elevator that opened into what she would learn was the apartment of Bill Paley, builder of the CBS empire.

Nobody was there to greet her, and she paused for a few moments beside a favorite of his art collection, Pablo Picasso's *Boy Leading a Horse*, then valued at more than $100 million.

"I don't see anybody," she recalled.

She finally ventured into the sprawling apartment in search of her patient.

"I can't find the man's room," she remembers. "I ended up in the kitchen."

She finally came upon the master bedroom, and the hospital had indeed been brought to Paley; it was at least as well equipped and staffed as the ICU unit. Paley lay unconscious, hooked up to tubes and machines that were keeping him alive despite kidney failure compounded by other ailments. Two other nurses were already in attendance.

"Mr. Paley doesn't like Black people, and if he was in his right mind, you wouldn't be here," one of the nurses told Nina.

"Aren't we happy and glad that he's not in his right mind?" Nina replied.

Nina had no way of knowing if there was any truth to it. Paley was not generally considered to be a racist, and among those who visited him was Franklin Thomas, a Black former businessman and onetime NYPD deputy commissioner for legal affairs who later became president of the Ford Foundation. In reality, it might have been the nurse who did not like Black people.

Nina got a sense of what Paley did favor after she noticed a framed photograph of a nurse wearing a cap that did not signify a school she recognized. She sought to solve the mystery when one of Paley's daughters came in.

"That's his wife," the daughter said, by Nina's recollection.

"Oh, your mother was a nurse," Nina said.

"No, daddy loved nurses," the daughter replied.

Nina saw that along with the Picasso, Paley had a painting by Pierre-Auguste Renoir.

"I got the chance to look at them up close," she later reported. "Breathtaking."

At lunchtime, she was served fish and got a sense of how Paley had been living.

"I don't know what sea that fish came out of," she later said. "It was the best I ever tasted in my life."

But for all that, and even though she never saw Paley at a sentient moment, she was left with the impression that he shared a quality with other wealthy people she had cared for amid splendor.

"He wasn't happy," she said.

For her part, Nina kept to her conscious decision to be happy, locking away a host of affronts of which the nurse's comment about Paley and Black people was only the latest. She had more to lock away after some private nursing customers who expected her to be Italian because of her last name didn't even try to hide their displeasure when they discovered she was Black.

390 • Michael Daly

But she was still of resolute good cheer as she began working two jobs, as a school nurse in Harlem and as an instructor at a nursing program in midtown Manhattan.

Her nursing students there were of seemingly every ethnicity, including three sects of Muslims.

"The only race in my class is the human race," she announced.

She ended one session by going over questions for an upcoming Certified Nursing Assistant exam.

"A male resident eighty-six years old, how often is his hair washed?" Nina asked. "Once a week? Daily? Three times week? As often as he chooses?"

"As often as he chooses," a student called out.

"Thank you, because you give personal service," Nina said. "Now you're thinking like a nurse."

She ended the class in rousing tones.

"All right, nurses, read that book," she said. "Remember, no TV. Make sure your mind is in the book."

She added "Stay safe" as she watched them file out.

"Those are my fledgling nurses," she said. "They're coming forward. We need fresh blood."

Nina was unaware of the strategies that Jack Maple began implementing in 1994, but she did note that her old Harlem neighborhood became markedly safer over the ensuing years. She continued to set her hopes on someday moving into her brownstone.

"That was my dream," she said.

She figured the time may have come when she went to the station house near her brownstone. The commander of the 32nd Precinct welcomed her as one of their own when she said she had been Steven McDonald's nurse.

"[The commander] told me, 'I cleared your block,'" Nina recalled. "I said, 'Good, I'm going to come now, fix up that building and move in.'"

Her husband had died and Nina sold her house in Queens in 2016. She figured on putting the proceeds and her savings into the brownstone.

In the meantime, Nina, her daughter, and the family dog shared a one-bedroom apartment in the same building where she was raised. She was again across the street from the church where Garelik had promised more than a quarter century before to provide better police protection. She slept in the living room.

"We living in a small place, small rent, because we going to move into this house," she said when she checked on the brownstone. "You know you make sacrifices. I am going to be on the sofa until the other place gets fixed."

Her brownstone had been landmarked back in 1981 when the block was a war zone. The city Landmarks Preservation Commission had now begun hitting her with fines and threatening legal action if she did not undertake certain repairs. She still needed to secure a loan to cover the full cost of the new roof and other renovations needed to make it habitable. She went ahead and lined up an architect, an engineer, and a contractor. The next step would be a host of permits.

She was admittedly nowhere near as proficient as the rapacious real estate developers who had begun parlaying the newly safe streets into big bucks. She was herself inundated with would-be buyers. Somebody was caught trying to steal her deed and the deeds of the other buildings on the block.

"They want it, and they are not getting it," she said of all the offers.

She posted a sign on the shuttered front door reading:

NO TRESPASSING

PRIVATE PROPERTY

NOT FOR SALE

KEEP OUT

VIOLATORS WILL BE PROSECUTED

While the nonprofit Landmarks Conservancy had begun naming such illustrious New Yorkers as former NYPD Commissioner Raymond Kelly and Elaine Kaufman "living landmarks," its governmental affiliate, the Landmarks Commission, had named Nina a defendant in New York State Supreme Court. The 2015 suit's stated intent was "to seek civil penalties and to compel defendant to repair an historic building designated as an individual landmark."

The fines kept mounting, and Nina continued her efforts to reduce them to where she could make the repairs. Her interim lodgings periodically became more crowded when her grandson Myles was home from Bates College, where he was captain of the lacrosse team.

"Myles is on the sofa with grandma," Nina reported.

She had schooled him on what to do if he was pulled over by the police when traveling between New York and the campus in Maine.

"Be respectful with cops," she counseled. "Don't move. They will kill you because they fear you. Don't flinch when they come near you. Answer, 'Yes sir, no sir.'"

Nina remained entangled in complications involving the loan and permits and unresolved fines. The suit was in its second year and still unresolved when she learned from a news report that Steven had died.

Just as she had in 1986, Nina set her troubles aside to be with Steven, now for one last time.

CHAPTER 16

S even months after Steven's funeral, on July 25, 2017, cops converged at New York Presbyterian Hospital. They came just as they had the night Sean McDonald was killed, just as they had at so many other hospitals for so many other shot cops, among them Steven McDonald, Edward Byrne, Chris Hoban, Michael Buczek, Keith Levine, Ray Cannon, Kevin Gillespie, Dillon Stewart, Russel Timoshenko, Rafael Ramos, Wenjian Liu, and Brian Moore.

Only this time there was joy, not grief.

Sanny Liu had gone to the maternity unit and at 4:35 a.m. had given birth to a six pound, thirteen ounce baby girl. She said she was not surprised by the gender because that's what her husband had told her to expect when he appeared in her twilight dream the night he was murdered. The celestial white he wore in her vision had inspired the name her mother-in-law, Xiu Yan Li, now revealed to a reporter: "Her name is Angelina. Like an angel, like my son's an angel."

The family released a photo of Sanny holding her newborn angel. Angelina was wearing a dark blue knit cap that had a familiar emblem and four gold letters: NYPD.

Sanny was home with seven-month-old Angelina on January 10, 2018, when Patti Ann McDonald arrived with Conor in his NYPD uniform at the Central Park Precinct station house. They were there for the unveiling of a memorial plaque on the first anniversary of Steven's death.

Conor spoke, then introduced "my amazing, powerful mother." He stepped away from the podium and she took his place. She turned back to Conor, and for just that moment you could see how hard it all was for her even as she made it look otherwise.

"Don't go away," she said to Conor.

He remained behind her as she described how hard everything had been for Steven even though he made it look otherwise.

"Steven made life confined to a wheelchair and a respirator look extremely easy," she said. "He never showed the pain he suffered each and every day while going through daily medical procedures that were excruciating. He never complained about the pain that would wake him up on a constant basis. At times Conor and I would question all the pain and suffering we watched Steven endure. Was it worth it? Did it have any meaning?"

She said that at such moments Steven would read aloud the letter addressed "Dear Officer McDonald" he had received along with a hand-knitted sweater for Conor five years after the shooting. It had been written by an unnamed cyclist who had been in the park that same afternoon, hoping to do three or four laps.

Patti Ann now read it aloud as he had.

I started to feel a very strong premonition, the feeling that something was going to happen to me...But I had so looked forward to this training time alone and I refused to let it bother me. By the time I reached the farthest north part of the park, I was in a total state of dread. I knew something was wrong. I just didn't know what...

The cyclist had started downtown, having only started one lap.

Police cars were screaming past me. I had never seen so many. But now I knew that whatever it was I had been feeling was just answered for me by those cars.

When I returned home and later heard the news reports on the radio I realized what it was in the park that Saturday. You see, I always felt after that time that you somehow protected me. I don't know how. I don't know why, but I felt that you personally had kept me safe.

Every stitch with which I knitted this sweater for your little boy was knitted with love and deep thanks.

Love, A Friend

Patti then said, "The sacrifice that Steven gave has been given by so many of his brothers and sisters in blue."

She noted that a number of line of duty families were in attendance.

"You understand what I mean," she said. "Steven would want you to know that this letter affirms that their sacrifice and his have not been in vain. Their sacrifice has made this city one of the safest cities in the world."

She turned to Conor, who was still there, in that same blue uniform.

"I just wanted to say I was so blessed that I was pregnant with Conor when this happened," she said.

She embraced him.

"I love you, Conor."

Cardinal Timothy Dolan gave the benediction. He later told Patti Ann and Conor that a remarkable number of people had been approaching him about officially taking up the cause for sainthood for Steven.

"That would mean you're a relic," Dolan told Conor.

The Church did begin the initial steps in the long process toward a possible St. Steven. The family was advised not to throw out anything, including the boxes and boxes of letters he received from people who had been touched by his message of forgiveness.

In the meantime, a Long Island youngster put down "Steven" when a priest asked him to write down the saint he had chosen for his confirmation name. The priest informed him that it was spelled "Stephen" by all the saints.

"Not mine," the youngster said.

"Who's your saint?"

"Steven McDonald."

The priest paused.

"You're right," he then said.

Steven was already recognized as a secular saint. The many monuments in Central Park came to include a marker near the site of the shooting, unveiled on the thirty-second anniversary of that July afternoon.

Just before this July 12, 2018, unveiling ceremony, Jimmy Secreto—a sergeant that fateful day and now a three-star chief—took Conor up a small grassy hill to a patch of woods. Secreto stopped at a clearing that few people would just chance upon.

"This is where it happened," Secreto said.

The two emerged from the trees and descended to the unveiling ceremony. Conor addressed the gathering.

"You think of all the possibilities of what could have happened on this day thirty-two years ago, and it seems very senseless what happened, why it happened," he said. "We all have a chance to make this world a better place, and that's what my father taught me...I truly believe that if a man who was shot by a fifteen-year-old kid—when he did nothing but just try to talk to him—can live a life of love and compassion, I think we all can do that."

Conor closed with something Steven said every single day.

"Love is the way."

At the appointed moment, a uniformed officer pulled a black cloth away from the marker. This plaque was set into an unhewn piece of schist, a remarkably strong stone in a 450-million-year-old geological formation running down the island of Manhattan—the literal bedrock that supports skyscrapers further downtown and the skyline that for many people is synonymous with New York.

But those are just buildings.

DETECTIVE STEVEN D. MCDONALD

Born out of tragedy July 12, 1986, came a life of service and forgiveness. Steven became a messenger of hope and goodwill to the community and the City that he loved.

FIDELIS AD MORTEM

3.1.1957–1.10.2017

EPILOGUE

At the start of 2020, the NYPD had achieved what Deputy Commissioner John Miller called "police nirvana."

"Arrests going down, summonses going down, complaints against police officers going down, stops going down, use of force going down and crime going down at the same time," Miller later said. "Everything was perfect."

Back when Miller started with Jack Maple and William Bratton, murders in New York were approaching two thousand a year. The annual toll was now around three hundred.

And Miller saw no reason to expect anything but continued success as he stayed on through Bratton's second tenure and Jimmy O'Neill's time, and now the arrival of someone who intuitively understood the importance and the limitations of numbers.

Dermot Shea had worked his way up in the ranks to become the new commissioner in December 2019. He had the aspect of somebody who did their homework as a kid and actually liked math without being exactly a nerd. Shea possessed Maple's ability to rattle off statistics, though in doing so he struck people as more of a grind than a nut. Both men had the same overarching priority.

"I don't want to hear about your numbers. I want to hear if your enforcement is geared toward reducing the number of crime victims in your area," Shea said again and again.

Shea's mantra—what mattered was the number of victims—was also the underlying principle of the four basic strategies that Jack scribbled on a napkin at Elaine's a quarter century before.

Maple's son, Brendan, was doing his part in the Brooklyn North Warrants Squad, now as a detective. He married Ashley Gardner, who had been with him when he encountered the drug dealer after seeing *Wicked*.

Conor McDonald was a sergeant in the chief of department's office, responding to major incidents, his name rising on the lieutenants list thanks to studying at Steven's urging. Conor married Katie Sullivan and danced at their August 2018 wedding with joyful energy familiar to anybody who knew Steven before the shooting.

"I have the moves," Conor later said.

The fathers had led the way, and the sons were carrying on, along with the other good cops. New York seemed more than ever to be on its way to becoming the Emerald City.

On March 1, 2020, a thirty-nine-year-old health care worker in Manhattan became the city's first confirmed case of COVID-19. The number of infections reached one thousand on March 17, when Patti Ann was scheduled to be the first woman to signal the start of the St. Patrick's Day Parade.

The virus threat prompted New York's governor and New York City's mayor to officially cancel the event, but both quietly gave their blessing for a group of less than fifty marchers so as not to interrupt a 258-year tradition.

Just after dawn, two dozen soldiers and parade officials assembled in the rain outside the armory of the 69th Infantry Regiment, where thousands had lined up with DNA samples of missing loved ones in the days after 9/11. The fabled Fighting 69th—in which Smiling Jim Conway served—traditionally leads the parade, and the soldiers first conducted a ritual regimental toast, shared via Skype by comrades deployed overseas.

Patti Ann was there, having received a phone call asking if she wanted to be among the few to help a parade older than the US Constitution keep a perfect record.

"I said, 'Are you kidding?'" she would recall. "Steven would have been there in a heartbeat."

Just before seven a.m., Patti stood ready, her green-gloved hand holding a white police whistle borrowed from a sergeant. An officer of the Fighting 69th gave her a countdown.

"Three, two, one…"

She raised the whistle to her lips and gave it a good, loud trill, breaking one tradition while signaling the continuation of another. She was joined by Conor in marching uptown in the rain, both smiling. The NYPD Emerald

Society's color guard was present, as were a dozen soldiers and a bagpiper. Everybody maintained the recommended social distance, and there were some 245,950 fewer than the usual number of participants. But they were *there*. They drew cheers from construction workers and a scattering of others who were still out and about in a vacant city made spooky by the viral threat.

After Patti Ann came down with COVID-19, more than one person wondered if she caught it from that whistle. Conor subsequently got sick, as did John Miller around the same time. Miller ended up in the ICU, but recovered. The McDonalds did as well.

But thirty-eight cops were not so lucky. Nearly 20 percent of the thirty-four thousand uniformed members of the NYPD were out sick by the first week of April.

Ambulance sirens filled the city night and day as the first great surge of COVID-19 killed 18,679 New Yorkers, on the way toward a pandemic total of more than thirty thousand. Refrigerator trucks were parked outside hospitals and filled with bodies. Funeral homes and crematoriums were overwhelmed.

For a time, COVID-19 was an all-eclipsing public safety concern. The citizenry did not feel much more secure because overall crime was down by 28 percent that month as compared to the previous April, led by double-digit declines in robberies and grand larceny. Shootings declined by nearly 10 percent, though murder rose nearly 30 percent, perhaps because of the tensions of a citywide lockdown. There had been sixty-two killings as opposed to fifty-six the same month in 2019. The virus killed as many as 1,169 in a single day in New York.

Crime in general continued to decline in May, though murder again rose, as did shootings. The good news was that the number of cops out sick was returning to the usual 3 percent. There was reason to hope that the spike in violence would also subside along with the virus, and New York would essentially resume its course to police nirvana.

Then, just after eight p.m. Central Daylight Time on May 25, a clerk at a corner grocery store 1,200 miles away in Minneapolis called 911 to report a man passing a counterfeit bill. A dispatcher sent squad car 320, then car 330 as backup.

As George Floyd was arrested, he appeared to have an attack of claustrophobia when the officers sought to place him in the back of car 320. The cops laid him down in the street. Police Officer Derek Chauvin from car 330 pressed his knee on Floyd's neck.

Video shows that Chauvin just kept pressing as Floyd repeatedly said he couldn't breathe and begged the cop to stop. Chauvin remained impassive as Floyd called out to his dead mother in the realm beyond.

"Mama!…Mama!"

Floyd fell silent. Video would show that Chauvin finally raised his knee from a lifeless Floyd after nine minutes and twenty-nine seconds. The time was initially reported as eight minutes and forty-six seconds, and that was used as the duration for "die-in" protests in cities across America, including New York.

The NYPD could have talked all it wanted about crime stats and lives saved. The number that mattered to the protesters was 8:46 out of Minneapolis.

As with the anti-cop protests in New York six years before, many of the demonstrators appeared to be young white people who had come from other parts of the country. A number of the out-of-towners detained while protesting racism resided in areas where people of color were being pushed out by rising rents that accompanied a drop in crime.

"Whose streets? Our streets!" protesters again chanted.

And, as in 2014, Conor McDonald was among the cops called racist murderers. He also was among the nearly three hundred who were injured, suffering a concussion while making an arrest when the protests turned violent. There was widespread looting in downtown Manhattan.

Conor was not one of the cops videoed using more force than appeared necessary. Indelible video was taken during a protest near the Barclays Center in Brooklyn as twenty-four-year-old Police Officer Vincent D'Andraia strode down the street beside Deputy Inspector Craig Edelman. A twenty-year-old artist named Dounya Zayer was among the protesters who were in the street. She was videoing D'Andraia as he advanced.

"You guys get out of the street," D'Andraia commanded.

"Why?" Zayer asked.

The image went blank as Zayer's phone was knocked from her hand. Another phone videoed brawny D'Andraia shoving petite Zayer with such force that she flew backward, landing by the curb and striking her head.

"Stupid fucking bitch," somebody, apparently D'Andraia, was recorded saying.

D'Andraia seemed not to care whether or not he had injured Zayer. Neither D'Andraia nor the inspector beside him broke stride as Zayer lay stunned. She slowly rose and held her hand to the back of her head as the two cops continued down the street, for that instant seeming as disturbingly indifferent as Chauvin had been for those long minutes. The Brooklyn district attorney's office charged D'Andraia with assault. He would plead not guilty.

Along with the demonstrations in the streets, the faraway killing of Floyd triggered intense individual reactions across New York.

The three seconds when Floyd called out to his dead mother cut as deep in Nina Justiniano as her feelings for her own departed mother and her continuing grief as the mother of her own lost Jason. With that and the rest of the video, Nina experienced a sudden rupturing of her racial hurt locker, where she had stored a lifetime of injury in order to keep going.

"It's like opening up wounds that I thought I had just buried away," she said. "I lived my whole life trying to get through it, trying to not let it bother me."

Injuries decades old came rushing back. She suddenly had difficulty with things she had just learned to live with.

"At this age, sixty-eight years old, I'm hurt," she said.

She was sure that what she felt was shared by all of America's persons of color, that racial hurt lockers were bursting open from Minneapolis to New York and beyond.

"We served this country. We helped build this country," Nina said. "I tell you we love America, we loved you, but you don't love us back. We loved you consistently for four hundred years and we forgave you for four hundred years, but you hate us. Where does all this hate come from?"

Nina had learned enough about hate to have told Steven in the hospital that it would poison him. Even as he managed to forgive the teen who shot him, she had been forgiving a lifetime of hurt that was part of four centuries of injury to an entire race.

One challenge for her after Floyd's killing was not to join others in seeing all cops as Chauvin, not to view the police as she had before Steven.

"I had one police officer that changed me, and Steven was that police officer," she said.

As the holder of New York State Registered Professional Nurse license 31 7938-1, as a repeated witness to both police brutality and police nobility, and as the recipient of a string of pearls along with a courtesy card from the PBA, Nina took the position that cops should be held to the same standards as people of her calling.

"All I want from the police is for them to be treated like the professionals they need to be," she said.

Due to the pandemic, the public school where Nina worked as a nurse was closed, along with the nursing program where she taught. She was assigned to a "regional enlightenment center" in Harlem, which provided child care for the children of first responders and health care workers. The arrival of the vaccines in New York meant she also began working twelve-hour shifts on the weekend, giving shots. She proved able to get eleven doses out of a Moderna vial that supposedly only held ten.

"You just have to know what you're doing," she said.

Her grandson Myles had graduated and taken a job with a Boston financial firm. She held on to the hope that the day would come when he would see his grandmother ensconced in her brownstone. She paid a lawyer $18,000 she could not afford to seek a reduction in the mounting fines she would never be able to pay.

"I have faith. I really believe things are going to work out for me in the end," she said. "One bathroom and a roof, and we're going in."

She remained set on her goal even as shootings spiked in the streets surrounding her dream home. Violence rose across the city, likely due to the continuing effects of the pandemic and the George Floyd killing. Protesters who declared an area around City Hall an "Autonomous Zone" on June 24 retained a passionate belief that the police were a big part of the problem, not the solution.

NO COPS read a spray-painted sign at the perimeter.

And on multiple placards was a mantra born of Floyd's death.

"Defund the police!"

As in a park five blocks downtown during the Occupy Wall Street protests of 2011, the occupiers in City Hall Park camped out on cardboard under tarps. Somebody produced a jumbo TV screen and hooked it up to a power supply feeding an elevator between a subway station Jack had patrolled as a cave cop and a stretch of pavement he had often walked as a deputy commissioner on the way to police headquarters. A video feed enabled the protesters to watch as demands to defund the police reached the city council's budget deliberations.

Back when Jack was dying of cancer, he may have been the only person in New York who enjoyed watching the city council proceedings on public access cable. He said he liked it because it was additional proof that much of human existence is as screwed up as the Transit Police of his youth before it got a load of him.

"The whole world is transit," he sometimes observed.

He would have seen that conclusion further affirmed had he been able to watch the council address the police budget.

The other party in the process was de Blasio, who seemed to have partly recovered his senses after his brief presidential run the year before. The man who became mayor with a brilliant campaign ad featuring his son had sought the presidency with an ad showing how little he knew about New York and his standing in it.

"The good thing about New Yorkers is they look the same whether they're really pissed off at you or they like you," he says in the ad.

The dislike for him did not stop at the city limits and he dropped his candidacy for president. He remained a mayor who sought to retain his credentials as a progressive while also seeking to associate himself with the success of the cops.

That complicated his position on defunding the police. And it was all playing out while the pandemic seemed to be defunding the whole city, inflicting a $9 billon loss in revenue. A senior official with inside knowledge of the situation says that de Blasio faced a problem of "political math and actual math" if he wanted to get a budget passed.

"The mayor's job was to make it look like a billion dollars [in cuts] without it being a billion dollars," the official later said.

De Blasio ended up working out a deal with the city council in which the school safety division would be moved from the NYPD to the Department of Education—on paper a $450 million cut in the police budget. An upcoming police academy class was canceled. There was at least talk of a $350 million cut in overtime made more difficult by the manpower demands of the protests but eased by the pandemic-related cancelation of such big events as New Year's Eve in Times Square and the Thanksgiving Day Parade.

"We think it's the right thing to do," de Blasio said of the deal. "It will take work. It will take effort, and we're going to be reforming that work in the meantime."

Many of the protesters who watched the June 30 budget proceedings on the outdoor big screen TV seemed to consider the supposed $1 billion cut a sham.

"Some people are never happy," de Blasio shrugged.

Protesters continued to occupy City Hall Park. De Blasio gave the police permission to clear it on July 21, after nearly a month. The cops moved in before dawn the next day. The official tally was one arrest and no injuries.

"It was less and less about protest," de Blasio said afterward. "More and more it became an area where homeless were gathering."

Commissioner Shea called it "another step towards getting back to normalcy here in New York."

But shootings continued to rise. Guns remained the big problem, and somebody who did not check the arrest numbers might have assumed cops were not making as many firearms collars. After all, the inherent danger of making a gun arrest was compounded by the possibility of getting involved in a controversial shooting. And between bail reform and a curtailment of arraignments because of the pandemic, the arrest would often be just an inconvenience for the suspect. Add to all that the dispiriting effects of the protests and word of a new database allowing the public to view any and all misconduct allegations against each officer. And there was talk that cops would no longer enjoy immunity from being personally sued for actions in the course of their duties. Also, the department had bowed to pressure from City Hall and disbanded anti-crime, the plainclothes units such as Steven was working with when he was shot. Anti-crime was said to make too many stops while seeking to get guns off the street.

The stats showed that New York cops had actually made 29 percent more gun arrests in 2020 than in the previous year, up to 4,243 from 3,299.

In early December 2020, Brendan Maple received a tip that a man named

Chad he was seeking on a warrant was dealing drugs out of a white van at Fulton Street and Albany Avenue in Brooklyn. A seventy-year-old woman had been shot in the face as she rode in a bus at the same intersection the month before.

Brendan found the white van and Chad. Brendan recovered a revolver under the steering wheel and arrested Chad for gun possession.

The next morning, Brendan saw Chad standing on the very same corner, unmistakable in the same red pants and black coat he had been wearing the day before. Brendan pulled over.

"Chad, they let you out?" Brendan asked.

"Were they not supposed to?" Chad replied.

Brendan and Conor and the rest of the NYPD were on alert in April of 2021, when the jury in the George Floyd trial began its deliberations in Minneapolis. Derek Chauvin was found guilty on all counts: unintentional second-degree murder, third-degree murder, and second-degree manslaughter.

"Justice has been served…" Commissioner Shea tweeted.

Shea still faced the question of how to restore police nirvana in New York. Violent crime kept rising in the streets and in the subways despite the continued use of CompStat enhanced with algorithms to predict when and where crime was most likely to occur as well as the small number of criminals most likely to commit it. This "predictive policing" and "precision policing" had been combined with community policing that included a webpage where a citizen could punch in their address and call up the names and emails of cops assigned to their particular radio car sector. But there were ever more shootings and a growing apprehension that the city was unraveling back into the bad old days.

It seemed that fear was being further affirmed just before five p.m. on May 9, when a report went over the police radio of shots fired at West 45th Street and Broadway in Times Square. Police Officer Alyssa Vogel heard the call when she was nine blocks away in the Midtown North station house, grabbing a bite to eat and talking on FaceTime with her mother. Her mother was caring for Vogel's seven-month-old son, Christopher.

In the next moment, Vogel and her partner, Police Officer Liam Moyles, dashed out to their squad car and were at the scene in no more than a minute.

Two fellow officers were tending to a forty-three-year-old woman from New Jersey who had been shot in the leg. One of the officers pointed down the block.

"I think there's a baby down there," he said.

Vogel's body camera recorded her reacting as a new mother as well as a cop.

"A *baby*?"

Vogel raced down West 45th Street and saw four-year-old Skye Martinez from Brooklyn on the sidewalk. Skye had been waiting with her parents outside a toy store when one of Times Square's remaining street hustlers got into a dispute with his brother and began firing, missing his target but hitting her and two other innocent bystanders. She was remarkably calm as she now lay with a bullet hole in her left thigh, the blood bright red on her tan pants.

A fellow cop had borrowed a belt to use as a makeshift tourniquet, but Vega had an actual one on her gun belt. Vogel applied it, knowing it was extremely painful but also necessary. Skye momentarily lost her composure and cried out.

"It's going to be okay," Vogel told her. "It's going to be okay."

Vogel ran her hands over Skye to ensure she had no other wounds. Vogel then scooped the child up in her arms.

"Like she was my own kid," Vogel later said.

An onlooker made a very different cop video that would go viral, this of twenty-eight-year-old Vogel dashing down the street with the wounded Skye. Vogel initially set out for her radio car but came to an ambulance first.

Skye's mother was right behind and joined Vogel and Skye in the back of the ambulance, along with the wounded New Jersey woman whom the other cops had been aiding.

The girl had regained her calm and lost it only when she was suddenly surrounded by a pediatric trauma team at Bellevue Hospital. The doctors said Skye might have suffered a broken femur, but she would be fine. So would the New Jersey woman and a twenty-three-year-old tourist from Rhode Island who was struck in the foot. The alleged gunman would later be arrested in Florida.

The day after the shooting was Mother's Day, Vogel's first as a mom.

She attended a family gathering at her brother's home. Her brother, John McCormick, is a cop with the 13th Precinct detective squad. Their father, also named John, retired as a detective with Brooklyn North Narcotics. Her husband, Mauritius Vogel, is a cop with Manhattan Special Victims. She had been a schoolteacher until she took the police test with him on a whim.

She would now be receiving a battlefield promotion to detective in recognition of the run with the wounded child.

At headquarters, Alyssa Vogel met Conor McDonald. She left him with the impression that she felt she had only done what any willing cop would have done.

"A regular human being," Conor noted.

As she prepared to report to Midtown North for the first time wearing detective shield 3891, Vogel said what she would have said anyway about working there.

"I love it!"

To hear her excitement was to hope there may be good new days ahead for the whole city.

But the question remained how New York would emerge from the traumas of 2020, whether spirit such as Steven McDonald's and smarts such as Jack Maple's could save it again.

On the night of July 10 in the year of the pandemic and protests, Steven visited Conor in his sleep for the very first time.

"I had a dream of Dad last night," Conor told a friend the next day. "Could not see him. He was a bright light. I knew it was him somehow. He was at the foot of my bed.

"No words were spoken. However, this light kept emanating and I could understand him—somehow.

"His message was simple. Stop complaining. Get over myself and all my worries, and keep with the mission. Pretty much, how he always kept ramming into my head that I could do better, and stop making excuses. He told me it was far from over."

ACKNOWLEDGMENTS

This book would not have been possible were it not for my editor, Sean Desmond.

I am most thankful for the time I was lucky enough to spend with Jack Maple and Steven McDonald before we lost them. I am deeply indebted to their families.

On Jack's side, they include Brendan Maple, Elizabeth Sheridan, Jacqueline Maple, Anna Marie Maple, and Brigid O'Connor, who rightly wishes we had never called that undertaker.

On Steven's side they include Patti Ann McDonald, Conor McDonald, and Thomas McDonald, along with Katie Sullivan McDonald and the rest of that remarkable clan. Also Murphy.

Among the medical people, I thank Nina Justiniano and Baron Johnson and the BSVAC.

And then there are Mother Transit's favorite sons and daughters, including Vertel Martin, Jimmy Nuciforo, Wayne Richardson, Bill Courtney, Billy Carter, Wendell Stradford, Wayne Richardson, Moe Doran, Jeff Aiello, Joe Quirke, Carol Sciannameo, Bobby Nardi, Patrick Lanigan, Mike Sapraicone, George Kalergios, Paddy Fennell, Jerry Lyons, Jawann Olajide-Stuckey, Dean Esserman, Matty Stanish, Mike O'Connor, and of course the late great Sonny Archer.

On the NYPD side, they include Sanny Liu, Andrew McDonald, John Miller, Robert Dalia, Dave Martelli, Andy McInnis, Jimmy Secreto, Joanne Jaffe, Brian Mulheren, John Yohe, Eugene Whyte, Mary Buckley, Fiona Buckley, Jamiel Alteheri, Jimmy O'Neill, Andy Cserenyi, Dermot Shea, Alyssa Vogel, James Byrne, Scott Schillinger, Jon Williams, Christopher Pizzo, Daniel Noonan, Keith McLaughlin, Tony Giorgio, Malcolm Reiman,

Tom Ridges, Kevin McCarthy, Bill Clark, Kara Frasse, and the late great Adam Frasse.

On the writerly side, thanks to Douglas Daly, Ed Kosner, Richard Babcock, Mark Jacobson, Richard Price, Chris Mitchell, Tracy Connor, Flip Brophy, John Avlon, Noah Schatchman, and Rachel Kambury.

Those who supplied other support include Tom Tobin, Anne Desmond, Sealy and Tim Gilles, Fred Siegel, Jan Rosenberg, Deirdre and Chris Holleman, Denise Spillane, Vina Drennan, the Bucca family, and James Hamilton.

INDEX

Abbate, Richard, 316
Abraham Lincoln High School, Brooklyn, 337
Adorno, Pedro, 361–62
Alameddine, Lynette, 325
Alexander, Tantania, 361–63
Altaheri, Jamiel, 367–69
Altaheri, Nadine, 368
Alvarez, Adam, 274
Alvarez, Eddie, 99
Andrews, MaryAnn, 316, 317, 319–20
Andrews, Rodney "Jay," 314–18, 319
Anemone, Louis, 225, 228, 229, 240–41, 244, 245, 259, 275, 281
Archer, Fermin "Sonny," 186–87, 207–8, 232–34, 237, 246, 321, 330, 351

Baker, Josephine, 152–53, 189
Bamonte, Anthony, 196
Barclays Center, Brooklyn, 334, 400
Battle, Samuel, 38
Battle, Stoney, 157, 158
Beckles, Arlene, 218–19, 263
Bedford-Stuyvesant Volunteer Ambulance Corps, 361
Bell, Sean, 352
Bellevue Hospital, 61, 63, 131, 274, 333, 385, 388, 406
    Chapel of Our Lady Helper of the Sick, 71
    McDonald at, 1–2, 24, 25, 31–32, 34, 35, 45, 48, 50–52, 55–58, 66–68, 71, 74, 104, 303, 281
    nursing school of, 37, 41
    Stuckey taken to, 209–11
    Thanksgiving at, 63
Biden, Joe, 366
Bilodeau, Robert, 169
Bishop Loughlin High School, Brooklyn, 100–101, 117, 221
Bloomberg, Michael, 312, 316–20, 323, 334, 340
    court's stop-and-frisk ruling and, 337–39

illegal gun problem and, 318, 324, 325
311 calls and, 350
Bonaventura, Charles, 29
Borelli, Joe, 225, 226–27, 234, 246
Boss, Kenneth, 290
Boston Police Department, 118, 201–3, 212, 225
Bouza, Anthony, 140–41, 142, 146
Bratton, William, 3, 118, 201–4, 207, 230, 231, 257, 259, 265, 341
    career in Boston Police Department, 118, 201–3, 212, 225
    crime reduction and, 220–21, 263
    fatal shooting of Ray Cannon and, 254
    fatal shooting of Sean McDonald and, 241, 242
    Giuliani and, 257, 260, 265–67, 273, 274–75
    as LAPD head, 341
    Maple's crime-fighting plan and, 204, 205–6
    Maple's crime stats and, 225
    meetings with Giuliani and Maple, 244–46, 252
    as NYPD head, 3, 118, 215, 217, 240, 241, 244–46, 257–66, 274–75, 341–42, 377, 397
    as NY Transit Police head, 3, 203–7, 212
    subway tour by, 345–49
    Turnaround, 221
Brennan, Janet, 334
Brennan, Kevin, 332–34, 347
Brinsley, Ismaaiyl, 358–60
Broadhead, He-Allah, 171–72
broken windows theory, 200, 203, 205–6, 227, 350
"Brooklyn bounce," 333
Brooklyn Eagle, 121, 122, 188, 244
Brooklyn Jewish Hospital School of Nursing, 41–43
Brown, H. Rap, 28–29, 52
Brown, Lee, 97, 102, 107, 227

Brown, Michael, and Ferguson protests, 352
Brown, Richard, 263
Bucca, Ronald, 57, 303
Buckley, Mary Ellen Nugent, 61–64, 74,
    80–86, 211, 334
  daughter Fiona, 63–64, 74
  daughter Fiona's letter to defense lawyers, 83
Buczek, Michael, 80, 393
Buggy, Richard, 168–69
Burke, John, 334
Burke, Tommy, 203
Burt-Beck, Carol, 99
Butters Bar, Rockville Centre, Long Island,
    7, 12
Byrne, Edward, 79, 348–49, 353, 371, 393
Byrne, Larry, 353

Cafarella, Michael, 253–54
Campisi, Charles, 308
Cannon, Laura, 254, 256
Cannon, Ray, 253–54, 255, 393
Cannon, Raymond, Sr., 254–55
Capellupo, Frank, 242
Cardillo, Phillip, 96
Carlisle, Belinda, 20, 21
Carrera, Vinnie, 166
Carroll, Sean, 288, 289
Carter, Billy, 175, 307
Caruso, Phil, 81
Cassiola, Peter, 123, 124
Castellano, Paul, 180
Central Park
  "airline pilot" incident, 13, 16
  drug dealing and, 13, 16–17
  letter from a cyclist to Steven McDonald,
    394
  McDonald on foot patrol in, 13, 14, 17, 51
  McDonald shot in, 21–22, 395
  McDonald on patrol in wheelchair, 92
  NYPD assignments to, 13
Central Park Five, 93, 194
Central Park Jogger, 92–93, 193–94
Cephas, Herman, 190
Chan, Philip, 353–54
Chauvin, Derek, 400, 405
Chung, Pak, 382–83
Clark, Walter "Call Me Bill," 73–74
Clinton, Bill, 378
Clinton, Hillary, 297, 309, 378
Club Paradise (film), 20
Collins, Gail, 81
CompStat, 222–30, 231, 235, 275, 279, 280,
    299

enhanced, predictive and precision
    policing, 405
  Jack Maple CompStat Center, 349
  misuse of, 290–91
  UF250s added to, 291
Convent Avenue Baptist Church, Harlem, 88
Conway, James "Smiling Jim," 8–9, 13, 264
cop gangs, 270, 372–73
Costello, Frank, 180
Coughlin, John, 306
Courage under Fire (film), 85
Courtney, Billy, 187–88, 209, 222
Craig Hospital rehabilitation facility, 74–75
Cserenyi, Andras "Andy," 322, 379, 381
Cuomo, Andrew, 366
Cuomo, Mario, 107
Curley, Bob, 113
Curtin, Mike, 304, 306

Dalia, Robert "Bobby," 26, 27–34, 52, 92
  driving Patti Ann McDonald, 25, 31–34,
    51, 67, 102
  Medal of Valor incident, 27–28
Daltrey, Roger, 309
D'Andraia, Vincent, 400–401
Darby, Regina, 87
Davis, Larry, 61–63, 64, 74, 80–84, 288
de Blasio, Bill, 340, 341
  anti-cop campaign, 340
  anti-police violence and, 353–54, 365
  Bratton appointed NYPD head, 341–42
  cops turning their backs on, 365, 366
  "defund the police" movement and, 403–4
  funeral for Liu, 370
  funeral for Ramos, 366
  mayoral race ad, 340–41, 403
  presidential ambitions, 403
de Blasio, Dante, 340–41
Deeken, Chaplain Julian, 55
DePrimo, Larry, 352
Devine, William, 30
Diallo, Amadou, 288–90, 291, 295
Diaz, Angel, 271–72
Dinkins, David, 93–94, 97, 107, 116, 282,
    288
  Safe Streets, Safe City plan, 98, 108
District, The (TV show), 299
Dolan, Cardinal Timothy, 382, 395
Donnie Brasco (film), 196
Doran, Richie, 170
Dorismond, Marie, 296
Dorismond, Patrick, 295–96, 301
Dove, John, 208

Dowd, Michael, 372–73
Driscoll, Barry, 323
Driscoll, Stephen, 306, 323
Dunne, Joe, 226–30

Early Case Assessment Bureau (ECAB), 137–38, 144
Eastern District High School, Brooklyn, 186–87
East New York, Brooklyn, 355
Edelman, Craig, 400
Elaine's, Manhattan, 196–99, 218, 220, 221, 259
Emerald Society Pipes and Drums, 76, 166–67, 241, 385, 386, 398–99
Esserman, Dean, 341
Eubanks, Julie, 170–71
Evans, Carl, 47

Fiandaca, Cheryl, 275
Floyd, George, 399–400, 401, 405
Ford, Harrison, 309
Foster, Gregory, 355
Foster, Josephine Delamane, 121
Francis, Jeanette, 35, 50
Francis of Assisi, St. 93
    Prayer of, 56, 57, 59, 93, 381, 383, 386
Frasse, Adam and Kara, 318
French Connection, The (film), 134
Fried, Gregory, 68, 70, 239

Gardner, Ashley, 373, 397
Garelik, Sanford, 39, 129, 143, 146, 165, 390–91
Garner, Eric, 350–55, 357
Gerbasi, Michael, 309
Gillespie, Kevin, 113, 115, 271–73, 289, 309, 393
    wife Patty and children, 272
Gilligan, Thomas, 38
Giorgio, Tony, 370
Giuliani, Harold, 117
Giuliani, Rudolph, 94, 116–18, 215, 220, 221, 231, 236, 240, 274, 301, 312
    blizzard of 1996 and, 266
    Bratton's resignation, 275
    Cannon shooting and, 254
    claims credit for saving the city, 279–80, 282
    Dorismond shooting and, 295–96, 297
    getting guns off the street and, 297–98, 318
    Gore and the Hammer Award, 279–80

    kills Operation Juggernaut, 258, 266–67
    lawsuit against gun makers, 298, 318, 324
    Maple eulogy by, 300
    meetings with Bratton and Maple, 246, 252–53
    names Safir commissioner, 275
    9/11 terror attacks and, 302, 309–10
    outsized ego, 257, 259, 265–66, 273, 280, 282, 298
    PBA and, 273
    political ambitions, 297, 324–25
    renames the Tombs after Kerik, 312
    Silver Gun Bandits and, 243–44
    TPD merger with NYPD, 261
    voodoo curse, prostate cancer and, 296, 297
Goetz, Bernhard, 84
Gore, Al, 279–80
Gotti, John, 180
Graham, Ramarley, 352
Green, Mark, 312

Harlem Hospital School of Nursing, 37, 41
Harris, Sharron, 46, 87–88
Hartjen, Fred, 8–9
Hawkins, Yusef, 94
Heckman, Trish, 273
Higgenbottom, Roger and Diana, 368, 369
Hoban, Chris, 80, 393
Holiday, Billie, 39
Horn, Jerry, 61
Howard, Al, 38
Howard, George, 307
Hunt, Gary, 27
Hunt, James, 253–54, 255

Irish Lesbian and Gay Organization (ILGO), 107

Jack Maple CompStat Center, 349
Jacobus, Jessie, 315–16
Jaffe, Joanne, 96–97, 114, 366
Jansen, Erik, 371
Jeter, Darryl, 165–66
Johnson, Baron, 361–63
Johnson, Jimmy, 32–33, 102–3
Johnson, Peter, 92
Johnston, Robert, 13, 211
Jones, Leonora, 88–89, 90, 91, 102
Jones, Shavod "Buddha," 46–47, 51, 59, 65, 101, 106, 113, 238, 248–49
    McDonald and, 87–91, 102
    McDonald's forgiveness of, 70, 71–74, 385, 386

Jordan, Joe, 203
Judge, Father Mychal, 55–58, 63, 92–93, 250, 304–5, 309, 313, 377, 381, 382
  death on 9/11, 302–3
Justiniano, Nina, 3, 35–45, 51–54, 63, 65, 129, 388–92
  COVID-19 and, 402
  crib death of child, 35, 40–41, 45
  death of Steven McDonald and, 384, 385, 386, 388, 392
  Harlem brownstone and, 45, 59–60, 388, 390–92
  nursing profession and, 37, 40, 41–45
  PBA curtesy card for, 52, 402
  racial injustice and, 39–40, 43, 44, 389, 401–2
  saving Steven McDonald, 1–2, 48, 49–50, 55, 59, 66
Justiniano, Wilfredo, 45, 52–53

Kahn, E. J., III, *Steven McDonald Story, The* (Kahn), 88, 91–92
Kalowitz, Rita, 169
Kaufman, Elaine, 197
Kelleher, Patrick, 304
Kelling, George, 200, 201, 203, 227
Kelly, Raymond, 107–8, 316, 317, 319, 320, 323, 324, 325, 334, 338
Kerik, Bernard, 298, 310, 312
King, Father John, 167
King, Martin Luther, Jr., 38–39, 386
King, Peter, 20, 21
Klieman, Rikki, 378
Koch, Ed, 11, 31–32, 73, 76, 94, 96
Kowsky, Monsignor John, 49, 55, 58, 70
Kunstler, William, 29, 81, 83

LaGuardia, Fiorello, 38
Lamron, Meredith, 338–39
Lategano, Cristyne, 279
Laurie, Rocco, 355
Lawrence, Leroy, 190–91
Leary, Edward, 258
Leary, Timothy, 275
Lemite, Gary, 272–73
Lennon, Janet, 226
Levine, Keith, 393
Lindsay, John, 96, 126
Linsker, Eric, 354
Liu, Sanny, 358, 364–66, 370–71, 382–83, 393
Liu, Wenjian, 357–58, 362–64, 367, 370, 393

Louima, Abner, 282–83, 301
Lozada, Irma, 152, 182, 185, 165–67
Lynch, Pat, 365
Lyons, Jerry, 176

"Mad About You" (song), 20, 21
Maginnis, Peter, 79
Malverne, Long Island, 14, 19, 329
Maple, Anna Marie, 125, 126
Maple, Brendan, 196, 371–74, 397, 404–5
Maple, Isabel, 124
Maple, Jack, 3, 121–52, 162, 164, 166–81, 186–207, 211–12, 267–68, 299, 336, 342, 367, 368, 403
  abusive drunk story, 135
  accountability demanded by, 244–46
  antics by, 261–62, 299
  arrests by, 128, 133–37, 139, 143–44, 191–92
  assigned to the TPF, 152
  beauty salon shooting and, 219
  being right in what he did, 135–36
  boat bought by, *Quaalude*, 144, 145, 146, 148, 150, 216
  Bratton and crime-fighting plan, 203–6
  as Bratton's chief of operations, Boston, 212
  brief times as a "house mouse," 133
  "broken calls theory" of, 206
  Central Park South apartment, 261, 262, 330
  colon cancer and death, 299–301
  commanding officer, RORSF, 186–88, 201, 205, 207
  comment on the Diallo case, 291
  CompStat and, 222–30, 235, 244–46, 263, 275, 339
  confrontation with district attorney, 192
  creates Charts of the Future, 187–92, 200, 244
  creates cold case squad, 123
  crime reduction and, 212, 246–47, 257–58, 263, 265, 299, 300, 390
  crime stopping as an avocation, 138
  "crookology" and, 174
  daughter, Jacqueline, 148
  debt and, 149, 151, 162
  decoy squad and, 169–78
  as detective supervisor, 179
  diet of, 147
  in District 1, Manhattan, flurry of arrests, 137–38
  in District 12, the Bronx, 136

in District 20, Queens, back in uniform, 134036
in District 34, Coney Island, 162, 164
The District and, 299
drug bust gone wrong and, 130–31, 166
early poverty and odd jobs, 124–26
at Elaine's, 197–99, 218, 220, 221, 259, 267
fatal shooting of Sean McDonald and, 240
favorite movie, 227
as fearless about speaking the truth, 143
FIST unit, 206–7, 212
geek team, 222–23, 224, 244
getting guns off the street and, 236, 241, 247
Giuliani's jealousy and, 260
the homeless in Grand Central Terminal and, 132–33
iconic dress of, 3, 118, 147, 150, 158, 179, 276
Internal Affairs following, 134
Jack Maple CompStat Center, 349
as the "Jackster," 221, 245, 253, 275, 374
lesson in caution, killing of deranged man, 129
lessons for rookies by, 152
Lozada and, 152, 165
marriage to Karen Brunetz, 127, 151, 162
Martin and, 152–53, 161
mayoral meetings and, 246, 252–53
meeting with Bouza, "hang on to them suits" line, 146
murders of his grandparents and, 2, 3, 121–24, 246–47
at Narcotics, 231–32
number of arrests, 145
as NYPD deputy commissioner, 3, 215–37
NYPD office, 226
O'Connor romance, marriage, 197–98, 261, 300
Operation Juggernaut, 252–53, 257–58
opposition to beatings, 128–29
overtime controversy, 133, 135, 140, 143, 144
piracy arrest by, 145
in plainclothes, 130, 139, 143, 150
plainclothes task force, 165
at the Plaza, 147–48, 150–51, 159–60
police-involved shootings and, 217, 219–20
principles for reducing crime by, 220, 357, 397
Priority Yellow campaign and, 144, 169
processing arrests at the ECAB, 137–38, 144

promotions for his squad and, 179, 181
promotions, 145, 146, 152, 186
prostitute murders and, 235–36
pursuit of participants in sexual assault, 194–95
reputation of, 134, 146–47, 162
resignation of, 275–76, 279
Richardson and, 157, 161
shooting of suspect and muzzle flash burns, 131, 132
Sheridan romance, marriage, 162, 164, 169, 179, 196
son Brendan, 196, 371–74, 397, 404–5
spotting concealed weapons, 139–40, 152, 339
subway bombing and, 258
Times Square and, 133–34, 161–62, 373–74
transformative strategy of, 122
in TPD, 3, 127–52, 162, 164, 166–81, 186–207, 339
watch caper, 157–59, 161, 169
weapons seizure by, 161
White Glove Squad created by, 159–60, 161, 166
wife's panties incident, 129, 146
written statements and, 138–39, 146, 159, 169, 174, 178
Maple, Karen Brunetz, 127, 148, 151, 162
Marrero, Israel, 355
Martel, Vertel, 222
Martelli, Dave "Diamond Dave," 51, 88, 104, 248–50
Martin, Vertel, 152–57, 181–85, 189, 232–33, 313
eulogy for Archer, 330
FIST unit and, 206
joins the IAB, 268–70, 308
Maple and, 152–53, 158, 159, 161, 176–77, 267–68, 300
9/11 missing persons task force, 308–9, 312–13
9/11 terror attacks and, 307, 308
Mastro, Randy, 280
Matarazzo, Lou, 273
Matias, Reyes, 193-94, 92–93
MBTA Police, 203
McAllister, John, 23
McArdle, John, 305
McCarren, Thomas, 63
McCarthy, Carolyn, 329
McCormack, Joe, 306
McCormick, Francis, 122, 123–24

McCormick, Isabel, 121–23

McCormick, John, 407

McCray, Chirlane, 340

McDonald, Andrew, 111–12, 238, 239, 240, 242, 284–86

McDonald, Anita Conway, 2, 8, 10, 24, 35, 50, 53–54, 112, 113

McDonald, Clare, 7, 24

McDonald, Conor, 68, 70, 75, 106, 250–51, 321, 371, 381, 383, 385, 398, 400
  becomes a detective, 375
  birth of, 67–68
  christening of, 71–72
  cops turning their backs on de Blasio and, 365
  COVID-19 and, 399
  dream of his father, 407
  father's death and funeral, 380–87
  father's memorial plaque unveiling and, 393–96
  funeral for Ramos and, 366
  godparents, 71
  joins the NYPD, 321–28, 407
  posted at Garner protest, 350, 352–53, 400
  promoted to sergeant, 378
  resemblance to his father, 251, 384
  St. Patrick's Day Parade (2020) and, 398–99

McDonald, David, 8–9, 17–18, 24, 112, 382

McDonald, Dolores, 384

McDonald, Janet, 238, 240, 241, 242

McDonald, John, 111–12, 239, 242

McDonald, Patti Ann Norris, 2, 7, 10, 14, 19, 20, 63, 65, 66, 80, 327, 375–76, 379, 399
  first wedding anniversary, 58
  husband's will to live and, 2, 3, 58–59
  loyalty and support of Steven, 67, 90
  as mayor, Malverne, 329
  notified of Steven's shooting, 24–25
  Officer Dalia and, 25, 31–34, 51, 67, 102
  sister Julie, 20, 71
  son, Conor and, 251, 393–96
  son, Conor's birth, christening, 67–68, 71–72
  son, Conor's decision to join the NYPD, 323
  Steven as paralyzed and, 26, 49–50, 65
  Steven's commitment to forgiveness and, 250
  Steven's death and funeral, 380–87
  Steven's injuries and, 25–26, 58
  Steven's memorial plaque unveiling, 393–96

St. Patrick's Day Parade (2020) and, 398–99

McDonald, Sean, 111–12, 241
  fatal shooting of, 238–39, 271–72, 393

McDonald, Steven, 1–2, 7–11, 180, 211
  ability to speak, 70, 76
  address to brother's police academy class, 112
  in anti-crime unit, 18–19, 20–21
  baby of, and will to live, 2, 58–59, 67
  bicycle thieves and, 1, 18–19, 21–22
  Bishop Loughlin High School visit, 100–101
  brother Thomas's request to keep shield, 303–4
  Central Park patrol and, 13, 14, 17
  character and personality, 7, 10, 12–13, 50, 52, 398
  Christmas (2016), 379
  Christmas Mass (1986), 65–66
  collar of robbery suspect, 17–18
  daily mantra of, 396
  death of, 380–84
  death penalty and, 273
  de Blasio and, 366
  declaration at baby's baptism, 3, 71–72, 73
  depression, anger, and despair, 50, 57, 59, 70
  detective shield 104 presented to, 264
  example set by, 322, 323
  faith of, 66, 101
  Father Mychal and, 55–56, 58–59, 63, 92–93, 303, 313, 377, 381
  first arrest, lesson learned, 11
  first wedding anniversary, 58
  forgiveness and, 93, 264, 273, 342
  at the funerals for fallen officers, 79, 80, 241–42, 349, 366, 371
  as a hero, icon, saint, 3–4, 74, 377, 395–96
  hospitalization, rehabilitation, 1–2, 24–26, 53–54, 74–76
  injured firefighter Bucca and, 57
  injuries, severed spine, 1, 23, 26, 34, 35, 48, 49–50, 65
  joins the NYPD, 7–8, 10–11, 386
  letter from a cyclist, 394
  memorial plaque unveiling, 393–96
  9/11 terror attacks and, 309
  nurse Justiniano and, 1–2, 49–50, 53–55, 59, 66
  NYPD demonstration at David trial and, 83–84
  NYPD support for, 51

O'Neill and, 378
pain and indignities of condition, 54–55, 58, 69, 100–101, 249, 321, 394
preaching with his presence, 93
precinct visits by, 105
pride in the NYPD and, 104
promotion to Detective First Grade, 319
as role model, 264
shooter of, Shavod Jones, and, 46–47, 51, 87–92, 102
shooter Shavod Jones's death and, 248–49, 250
shooter Shavon Jones forgiven by, 70–74, 101, 242, 385, 386
shooting of, 1, 22–23, 393
son Conor born, 67–68
son Conor joins the NYPD, 323–24, 326–28
son Conor promoted to sergeant, 378
son Conor visits, 68, 70
as the soul of the NYPD, 319, 342
speaking about love and forgiveness, 102, 105
speaking at Central Park Precinct, 293
speaking at City Hall press conference, 325
speaking on the Diallo shooting, 288–89
speaking to Legatus, 379
speaking to students, 94–95 100, 104, 249, 379
St. Patrick's Day Parade and, 74, 79–80, 106–7, 272
as symbol of the risks faced by officers, 81
as symbol of world's suffering, 66
thirtieth anniversary of shooting, 375
at trial of shooter Larry Davis, 80–81
Underground disco, arrest at, 12
van and remodeled home donated to, 75
visit to comatose Central Park jogger, 92–93
wake and funeral, 384, 385–87
Walk of Remembrance led by, 313, 377
wedding of, 14
Williams and, 102–6
McDonald, Theresa, 379
McDonald, Thomas, 17, 20, 24, 71, 74, 109–10, 112, 240, 241, 291
in Auto Crime Unit, 285–87
death of his brother and, 384
in ESU, 303–7
ESU shield rule and, 303–4
fatal shooting of Gillespie and, 271–73
joins the NYPD, 109, 110, 111–15

9/11 terror attacks and, 303, 305–7
parole of brother's shooter and, 248
partners with Andrew McDonald, 285
in Street Crime Unit, 114, 238, 241, 246, 247, 271, 285
McDonnell, Brian, 306–7
McInnis, Andy, 353
McInnis, Michael, 353
Mecallari, Peter, 355, 356
Meehan, James, 146, 162, 164
Melting Pot, The (Zangwill), 94
MetroCard swipers, 346–47
Metropolitan Hospital, 23, 74, 92, 248
Michaux, Lewis, 39–40
Miller, John, 180, 196–98, 220, 221, 246, 274
eulogy for Maple, 300–301
Giuliani's jealousy and, 259
on "police nirvana," 397
resignation of, 260
Silver Gun Bandits and, 243–44
Minetta, Ralph, 28–29
Miranda, Javier, 241
"misdemeanor homicide," 178, 218
Moore, Brian, 371, 372, 393
Moran, John, 309
Moran, Mike, 309
Morello, Joseph, 132
Morgan, Cyril, 130–31, 166
Moyles, Liam, 405–6
Moynihan, Daniel, 297
Mulheren, Brian, 24, 32, 55, 63, 65, 67, 375
Murphy, Kevin, 253–54, 255

Naked City, The (film), 4
Narvaez, Frederico, 334–35
Narvaez, Katrina, 334–35
Nathan, Judith, 301, 324
National Memorial African Bookstore, 39–40
Nelson, Craig T., 299
Nemorin, Aubriant, 317
Nemorin, James "Haitian Sensation," 314–18
Nemorin, Rose, 316
Nerney, Tom, 303
New York City
bankruptcy threat and cop layoffs, 9–10
car radio thefts, 196
chain snatches in the subway, 143–44
Christmas tree lighting at Rockefeller Center, 215, 253
City Hall Park occupation (2020), 402–3, 404

New York City (*cont.*)
counterterrorism in, 324
COVID-19 in, 398, 399
crime and crack cocaine epidemic, 180–81
crime reduction in, 253, 257, 263, 265, 279, 291, 324, 330, 348–49, 397
crime spike, shootings (2020–21), 402, 404, 405
Crown Heights riot, 107
Dinkins-Giuliani mayoral race, 116–18
Dinkins-Koch mayoral race, 93–94
final gun victim of 1994, 259
Greenwich Village, 194
Harlem brownstone auction, 45
Harlem riots, 38
homicide rate, increase in, 2, 29, 84
homicides in 1990, 97–98
homicides in 1991, 98
homicides in 1998, 279
homicides in 1999, 293
homicides in 2000, 294
homicides in 2001, 307
homicides in 2002 and 2003, 319
homicides in 2010, 323
homicides in 2014, 348
homicides in 2017, 4
homicides in, 2020, 397
jewelry store smash-and-grabs, 157–58, 168
killing of Brian Watkins, tourist, 1990, 97–98
Macy's Thanksgiving Day Parade, 262
McDonald's shooting in Central Park, 1
mentally ill on streets of, 85
Mets win the World Series, 57–58
MTA, 203
as murder capital, 227
murder of Yusef Hawkins, 94
murders New Year's Day (1986), 177
New Year's Eve (1996), 265
New Year's Eve (2002), 324
New Year's Eve (2014), 367, 368
New Year's Eve wolf packs, 175–77
9/11 terror attacks, 302–7
Palm Sunday massacre, 96–97
Phone of the Future and, 374
Pope John Paul II visit, 261
population of, 4
racial discrimination in, 340
racial tensions, 45
real estate boom, 330–31, 332
rioting and anti-police violence (2020), 399–401

as safest big city in America, 330, 347
Silver Gun Bandits (1994), 243–44
Stonewall National Monument, 377
St. Patrick's Day Parade, 74, 79–80, 106–7, 272, 398–99
street crime, 39, 45, 108, 112, 121, 168
subway bombing, 258
Thomas Jefferson High School shootings, 98–99
Times Square, 128, 133, 134, 150, 151, 161–62, 165, 169, 170, 176, 194, 324, 373
Times Square shooting of child (2021), 405–6
Underground disco, murders at, 12
West 42nd Street (the Deuce), 134, 161, 176, 187, 301, 373
white flight, 46, 117
wolf pack robberies, 168, 175–77, 194, 212
World's Fair of 1964, 125
See also Bloomberg, Michael; de Blasio, Bill; Dinkins, David; Giuliani, Rudolph; Koch, Ed; Lindsay, John
New York *Daily News*
column by Gail Collins, 81
headline: FORD TO CITY: DROP DEAD, 10
headline: ONLY 15 YEARS OLD, HE'S CHARGED AS THE KID WHO SHOT A COP, 47
headline: SON A JOY TO BEHOLD, 68
Maple cleaning up 42nd Street, 161
New York Daily News
Giuliani and blizzard of 1996, 266
Giuliani's anger and, 257
headline: GOD'S COP, 386
headline: JACK HITS THE ROAD, 276
headline: TOP COP TARGETS ILLEGAL WEAPONS, 236
headline: TOP COP WILLIAM BRATTON: I'LL END THE FEAR, 221
on Safir's appointment, 275
New York Post
headline: DAVE DO SOMETHING! 98
headline: JOURNEY OF HOPE, 74
New York Presbyterian Hospital, 393
New York Times
Giuliani's tension with Bratton, 266, 267
headline: GIULIANI OFFERS PLAN TO CURB GUNS, 236
McDonald at trial of Larry Davis, 80–81
Nietert, Kenney, 47
9/11 terror attacks, 302–11
Concert for New York and, 309
ESU officers responding, 305–7

fallen officers and, 306–7, 310, 323
missing persons task force, 308–9
number killed, 307
recovering the dead, 307
Walk of Remembrance, 313, 377
Nixon, Richard M., 126
Norris, Edward, 288
Nuciforo, Jimmy, 176–77, 189, 194–95, 232–34, 237, 246, 307
NYPD (New York Police Department)
anti-police violence, 353–54
arrest and summons quotas, 336
attacks on and murders of officers, 61–64, 79, 80, 116, 207, 238–39, 253–54, 271–74, 314–18, 319–21, 332–34, 355, 371, 393, 395
bad cops in, 325
being ruled by the numbers, 319
Brown as second Black commissioner, 97, 107, 227
Cardillo killed in Harlem mosque, 96
collars, credited to first in pursuit, 12
community relations, 345–49
CompStat, 222–31, 235, 275, 279, 280, 290–91
corrupt cops indicted, 81
counterterrorism and, 324
COVID-19 and, 399
CUPI, 122, 128
death of Eric Garner and, 350–55, 357
"defund the police" movement and, 402–4
derision toward "cave cops," 146
Diallo shooting uproar, 288–90
distrust of, Harlem, 37–39
diversity in, 104, 323
Employee Relations, 32, 102
as the Finest, 4
first Black police officer, 38
forgiving a cop killer unacceptable, 73–74, 80
gun arrests (2020), 404
"highway therapy," 136
hiring new cops (1992–93), 111
Internal Affairs Bureau (IAB), 268–70, 308
killings of unarmed Black men and, 295, 352
layoffs and bitterness, 9–10, 11, 15
Lindsay hiring new cops and hiring freeze, 126
Louima scandal, 282–83
Maple and crime stats, 222–25

Maple as deputy commissioner, 3, 215–37
Maple's Charts of the Future and, 244
Maple's office, 226
McDonald as icon, 3–4, 319, 342
morale killers and apathy in, 15–16
motivations to become a police officer, 293
9/11 terror attacks, 302–11
officers lost on 9/11, 310, 323
overtime and earnings, 30, 273
Palm Sunday massacre, 96–97
prohibition on choke holds, 351
recruits (1984), 10
reduced murder rate, lowest (2017), 4
response by related to victim's identity, 193
retired shields, 11
rioting and anti-police violence (2020), 399–401
risks faced by, 4, 8, 73, 79, 81, 169, 207, 239, 253–54, 314, 319–21, 332–34, 348, 366, 371
robberies (1982), 29–30
rookies graduating (2012), 334–35
rookies with "hooks," 372
shortcomings, 215–16
the "61s," 18, 21
stop-and-frisk policy, 336–38, 342
St. Patrick's Day Parade and, 74, 79–80, 106–7, 272, 398–99
.38 revolvers replaced by 9mm, 207
"three-quarters" disability pension, 211
TPD merger with, 261
Unified Form 250, 291, 336
Walk of Remembrance, 313, 377
Ward as first Black commissioner, 11, 96–97
"What's the count?," 200
See also Bratton, William; Maple, Jack; McDonald, Steven; specific commissioners and officers
NYPD units, squads, and special operations
anti-crime units disbanded (2020), 404
Auto Crime Unit, 285
Brooklyn North Anti-Crime, 332
Brooklyn North Warrant Squad, 374
Career Criminal Squad, 231
Ceremonial Unit, 370
Cold Case Squad, 351
Emergency Service Unit (ESU), 61, 303–7
Firearms Investigation Unit (FIU), 314
Firearms Task Force, 236
Highway Unit 3, 26, 30, 31, 33
Narcotics, 215, 216, 231–32, 246–47

NYPD units, squads, and special operations (*cont.*)
Neighborhood Stabilization Units (NSUs), 11–12
Operation Enforcement, 200
Street Crime Unit, 114, 122, 168–69, 246–47, 271, 273, 284–85, 288, 323
Street Crime Unit, number of gun collars, 273
Street Narcotics Enforcement Unit (SNEU), 14, 16, 21
NYPD precincts
5th Precinct, 228
13th Precinct, 407
20th Precinct, 27
23th Precinct, 22, 27, 29, 113
25th Precinct, 16, 17, 32, 51, 293
32nd Precinct, 390
46th Precinct, 271
67th Precinct, 373
71st Precinct, 321
73th Precinct, 373
75th Precinct, 98, 114–15, 177, 229, 232–33, 236, 303, 372
77th Precinct, 81, 237
79th Precinct, 102, 246–47, 357
84th Precinct, 356
90th Precinct, 332
NYPD Blue (TV show), 74

O'Boyle, Monsignor Seamus, 385–86
O'Connor, Brigid, 197–98, 261, 300, 301, 330–31
O'Connor, Cardinal John, 32, 66, 88
O'Connor, Mike "Iron Mike," 203–4
O'Dwyer, Bill, 129
O'Dwyer, Paul, 129
O'Hara, Maureen, 66, 67, 73
O'Neill, Jimmy, 293, 377, 378, 386, 397
Ortiz, Luis, 334, 335

Paley, Bill, 388–89
Palm Sunday massacre, 96–97
Panic in Needle Park, The (film), 27
Pantaleo, Daniel, 351
Parish, Owen Ray, 36–37
Parker, Robert, 319
Parsons, Estelle, 337
Patten, John, 289–90
PBA (Patrolmen's Benevolent Association), 9, 52, 81, 273, 288, 402
pamphlet by, "Welcome to Fear City," 9
remodeling of Steven McDonald's home, 75

Pellechia, Ronnie, 170
Peninsula Hospital, Rockaway, Queens, 43
Powell, James, 38
Powers, Peter, 221, 259

Quiet Man, The (film), 10, 14, 66, 67, 68
Quirke, Joe, 174

Rafferty, Patrick, 319
Raffo, Samantha, 335
Ramos, Jaden, 365
Ramos, Rafael, 355–58, 362–63, 366, 393
Randall's Island, 114
Ransohoff, Dr. Joseph, 34
Rapp, Robert, 129
Razor's Edge, The (film), 10, 14
Regional US Marshals Fugitive Task Force, 321, 330
Reid, Bobby, 11
Reiman, Malcolm, 80
Richardson, Wayne, 157–58, 161, 173, 181
Robberstad, Denis, 23
Rodriguez, Diana, 325
Rodriguez, Rodolfo, 241
Rodriguez, Samantha, 325
Romano, Phil, 38–39
Roosevelt, Theodore, 94
Ross, Mark, 174
Ryan, Nancy, 92–93

Safir, Howard, 275, 276, 284–85, 294, 298
Compstat and, 279–80, 281
expands Street Crime Unit, 287
voodoo curse, prostate cancer and, 296
St. Blaise's Day, 70
St. Clare's Hospital, 131
St. Francis Friends of the Poor, 85
St. Joseph's School for the Deaf, 123
St. Patrick's Cathedral, 385–86
St. Vincent's Hospital, 41, 44
Sarandon, Susan, 288
Savage, Richard, 114, 284
Scheindlin, Shira A., 337, 338
Schlaefer, Rev. Joseph, 255
Sciannameo, Carol, 169–70, 176
Secreto, Jimmy, 14–15, 21, 395
Seedman, Albert, 96
Seven Five, The (documentary), 372–73
Shafeeq, Abulawali, 208, 211
Sharpton, Al, 288
Shea, Dermot, 397, 405
Sheridan, Elizabeth, 162–64, 169, 170–73, 177, 179, 196, 372

Smith, Ernest, 171–72
Smith, James, 310–11
Smith, Joe, 102
Smith, Moira, 309–11
Smith, Rennie, 158–59
Spillane, Thomas, 383
Stanford, Wendell, 351
Steven McDonald Story, The (Kahn), 88, 91–92
Stevenson, Willie Dean, 36
Stewart, Dillon, 320, 393
Stewart, Leslyn, 320
Stuckey, Jawann Olajide-, 208–12
Sullivan, Katie, 381, 383, 385, 398
Sullivan, Patrick, 353–54
Sutton, Willie, 275

Teresa of Calcutta, St., 377
Thomas, Franklin, 389
Time magazine
    "The Rotting of the Big Apple," 98, 265
    "We're Finally Winning the War on
        Crime. Here's Why," 265
Timoney, John, 225, 231, 259, 260, 266–67,
    275, 285
Timoshenko, Russel, 320–21, 324, 393
Timoshenko, Tatyana, 321, 325
TPD (Transit Police Department), 3, 118, 127
    arrest powers of, 133, 134
    bad reputation of subways, 133
    bag snatches and, 190
    Bratton as chief, 3, 203–7, 212
    Central Robbery squad, 207
    decoy squad to combat wolf packs, 168–78
    District 1, 128, 137, 152
    District 4 (Union Station), 179–80
    District 12, 136
    District 20, 134, 136
    District 33, 181, 184
    FIST, 206–7
    Garelik as chief, 129, 165
    Maple at, 3, 127–81, 186–207
    Maple's Charts of the Future, 187–92, 200
    Meehan as chief, 146, 162, 164
    merger with NYPD, 261
    one-man patrols, 128
    Operation Enforcement, 200
    point system for promotions, 179, 180
    pursuit of participants in sexual assault,
        194–95

Rapp as chief, 129
RORSF, 186–88, 201, 205, 207, 244
"the Room," 128
scandal, false arrests, 180
shooting of fourteen-year old, 132
Tactical Patrol Force (TPF), 152, 154
.38 revolvers replaced by 9mm, 207
Times Square and closed circuit TV
    system, 165
wounding of Officer Stuckey, 208–11
See also Maple, Jack; *specific officers*
Trinity (Uris), 10, 67
Tso, Yee Bong, 175
Turnaround (Bratton), 221
Tyler, Harold, 117

Union Square Park, 12, 13
Uris, Leon, *Trinity*, 10, 67

Vassall, William, 37
Viggiano, John, Jr., 311
Viggiano, Joseph, 303, 304, 311
Vogel, Alyssa, 405–7
Vogel, Mauritius, 407
Volpe, Justin, 283

Wagner, Eddie, 47
Wallander, Arthur, 122
Ward, Benjamin, 11, 96–97
Wasserman, Bob, 202, 203, 225, 226, 227
Waters, James, 177
Waugh, Chris, 302
Wayne, John, 66, 67
White, Ernest, 47
Whyte, Eugene, 222, 228, 235–36
Williams, Jon, 102, 103–6, 249, 349, 383
Williams, Sarah Cronin, 107
Williamsburg, Brooklyn, 196, 332
Williamson, John, 116
Wilson, James Q., 200
Wilson, Ronell, 315–16

Yaeger, Bobby, 305
Yan, Herman, 320
Yohe, John, 222–23, 244, 263, 280–81

Zangwill, Israel, *The Melting Pot*, 94
Zayer, Dounya, 400
Zimroth, Peter, 337–38

ABOUT THE AUTHOR

Michael Daly is a special correspondent with the *Daily Beast*. He was previously a columnist with the *New York Daily News* and a staff writer with *New York Magazine*. He was a finalist for the Pulitzer Prize for commentary in 2002 and has received numerous awards.